EDUCATION UNDER PENALTY

WILLIAM CARDINAL ALLEN

EDUCATION UNDER PENALTY

ENGLISH CATHOLIC EDUCATION FROM THE REFORMATION TO THE FALL OF JAMES II 1547–1689

A. C. F. BEALES

READER IN EDUCATION IN THE UNIVERSITY OF LONDON, KING'S COLLEGE

UNIVERSITY OF LONDON
THE ATHLONE PRESS
1963

Published by
THE ATHLONE PRESS
UNIVERSITY OF LONDON
at 2 Gower Street, London WC2
Distributed by Constable & Co Ltd
12 Orange Street, London WC2

Canada
Oxford University Press
Toronto

U.S.A.
Oxford University Press Inc
New York

Printed in Great Britain by
WILLIAM CLOWES AND SONS LIMITED
LONDON AND BECCLES

To the memory of

WILLIAM

CARDINAL ALLEN

PREFACE

THE history of Catholic education in this country since the Reformation, even in outline, has yet to be written. Much work has been done on the period since Emancipation in 1829. Something has been done from time to time, too, on the eighteenth century; and by now several university theses exist (unpublished) on the struggle for 'education under penalty' in particular parts of the country between the Elizabethan religious settlement of 1558–9 and the first relaxing of the penal laws some 220 years later. Some of the story can never now be known at all, for during the penal centuries Catholic archives were not only frequently lost but (for reasons of safety) sometimes destroyed. But even so, there is still much to be done, especially in the archives of the Anglican bishops, and in 'regional' studies all over the country, before the definitive kind of work that Hastings Rashdall did for the medieval universities, or Professor David Knowles for the monasteries, can be attempted.

Nevertheless, it is known to be a record of heroism, sanctity and (as the penal laws gradually impoverished the old Catholic families, and put a premium on apostasy) of dogged determination. Furthermore, as a story its shape can already be discerned, albeit the inside of the shape is in places hardly less an explorer's blank than was Antarctica before the Fuchs-Hillary crossing.

The English Reformation was in fact a cataclysm for Catholic education, within one generation. The educational 'system', of parish schools and grammar schools and the two universities, still complete when Henry VIII dissolved the monasteries, was totally lost to Catholicism twenty years later, when Elizabeth I required of all teachers the oaths of supremacy and conformity. Thenceforward any deviation, Catholic or Puritan, was illegal. Thenceforward there were two spiritual resistance-movements, from Catholics, and from Puritans, determined in conscience to keep alive, somehow, the faith of their children. Penalties against them were stepped up whenever the European political situation made them more than usually a potential danger: as the Catholics found at the time of the Armada, the Gunpowder Plot, the Titus Oates plot, the Jacobite invasions and the Gordon Riots. In the intervals the penal laws were operated less

1*

resolutely, partly because of complaisant lords lieutenant and justices of the peace; and the religious minorities were able not only to plan but even to establish a policy for educational survival, firm enough to remain constant throughout the whole of the penal years. Educationally, neither resistance-movement was finally emancipated till the Act of 1871 which removed the last 'religious tests' from the older universities.

The Puritan picture can be seen today fairly clearly. Their strategy was to use private tutors, and to train up itinerant preachers on home soil. Their devoted labours met a rich reward for a fleeting twenty years in the seventeenth century, when during the Civil War and the Interregnum they planned a national system of schooling which, had the Stuart Restoration not swept it aside, might have given the country some of its salient nineteenth-century educational reforms all that much earlier.

The potential Catholic contribution to English education, by contrast, was largely lost, by exile abroad. Cardinal William Allen and the Jesuit Fr. Robert Persons are beyond doubt the founders of modern Catholic education in this country today, just as Cardinal Pole, during the Marian interlude, was the founder (at Trent) of the modern seminary system. But their foundations were laid abroad, upon the *diaspora* of Catholic dons from Oxford and Cambridge and Catholic schoolmasters from the grammar schools. And the edifices they built stayed abroad, for over two centuries, in the English colleges and schools, historic centres in which the humanities, and the advanced studies for the priesthood, were kept alive. It is from these centres that ordained clergy, having left England as boys to secure a Catholic formation proscribed on home soil, returned as missionaries and (so many of them) as martyrs. And it is these centres, transferred to England during the French Revolution two centuries later when the home climate had mellowed, that are England's Catholic public schools and the seminaries of today. The Venerable English College and the colleges in the Peninsula stayed on, but by 1800 the upper levels of Catholic education, lay and clerical, were firmly established, at home in England, to continue a tradition which, for all their long outlawry, had always been aggressively English.

That end of the picture, the exile end, is no longer obscure. It is the other end, the home end, that is still shadowy. We still do not yet know how Catholic education was kept alive at home for families not wealthy enough to send their sons and daughters to the schools and colleges abroad: i.e. for the bulk of the dwindling Catholic population. The dwindling explains why in the eighteenth century the penal laws fell gradually into desuetude. The minority became too small to matter. It was legally death at sight for a seminary priest to be found in the country; and the penalty for keeping a Catholic school had been as high as imprisonment for life; but, crises apart, and especially in the Catholic north, it was possible throughout the seventeenth as well as the eighteenth century to establish schools in which all the pupils could secure a basic religious and secular education, and those going on to the colleges abroad (the few) could do so with their groundwork behind them.

What is surprising about these clandestine schools at home, quite apart from the tremendous fillip they received during the three short years of James II, is their number and, in a few cases, a history going back to the Restoration and even earlier. As piecemeal research and 'regional' studies reveal it, this hitherto unsketched part of the picture takes on a fascination.

Qualitatively, one should have expected it all to happen. Universally, and historically, the Church saves the faith by saving the priesthood and the school. In our particular case the seminaries abroad guaranteed a supply of priests; the English provinces of the religious orders had been reconstituted within a generation of 1600; the Catholic landed aristocracy never burked its responsibility to neighbour and neighbourhood; and all the time, at the very lowest, there was that desperate cohesiveness that all minorities under pressure infallibly develop. But quantitatively the attested creation of Catholic schools at home, before Emancipation, is much more than could have been guessed.

This book is concerned with a self-contained part of the story, from the onset of State control in early Tudor times till the collapse of all hope of speedy recovery on the fall of the Catholic King James II. It is uneven, from the need to reserve relatively as much space as possible for those parts of it which are new to the literature of the problem. These are in particular: Catholic schooling in England itself under the penal laws, the educational (as against the religious and political) side of the colleges in exile, the part played by recusant education in the constitutional and parliamentary history of the country, and the false dawn under James II.

My deep thanks to archivists and librarians, and for the generous help of scholars past and present at work on affairs of the English recusants, are implicit in the footnotes and the bibliography. And they, no less than I, are much beholden to those who have gone before. Anyone at all who labours in recusant history has long had a trail ahead of him, in the bibliographical pioneering of Joseph Gillow and George Oliver in the nineteenth century, Bishop Challoner and John Kirk in the eighteenth. These men, though their voluminous researches can now be supplemented and here and there corrected from manuscript sources they did not enjoy, are the founders of a whole range of historical study, in which all who climb must mount on their shoulders.

But one's abiding thankfulness, on finishing any academic inquiry into English Catholic penal times, is that, when the temptation to destroy documents must have been so great, the clergy and scholars who led the anxious movement to preserve the faith for the future somehow contrived to bequeath to us the magnificent collections of contemporary archives on which, one day, the full story can be built.

In this book there is no systematic treatment of the feminine side of English Catholic education, which has a special study devoted to it, Dr. W. J. Battersby's *Educational Work of the English Religious Orders of Women* (see p. 19 note, below).

My *Biographical Catalogue of Catholic Schoolmasters at Work in England from 1558 to 1700, with an Index of Places* (Catholic Record Society, *Recusant History*, vol. vii, No. 6, 1964) contains full references, which are accordingly omitted from the notes where individual schoolmasters are mentioned in this book.

A.C.F.B.

King's College, London
October 1962

CONTENTS

PLATES

PART ONE

THE SIXTEENTH CENTURY

I

INTRODUCTORY: CATHOLIC EDUCATION AND THE COUNTER-REFORMATION

WHEN Dr. William Allen, Principal of St. Mary's Hall at Oxford, departed quietly from the realm in 1561 to organize the work of keeping alive the training of Catholic clergy and laity no longer possible at home under a new queen's Acts of Supremacy and Uniformity, the light was going out on an English educational tradition that had begun with Augustine's school at Canterbury a thousand years earlier.

For the next two centuries and more, until the French Revolution, the very notion of a Catholic education in the British Isles was alien and proscribed. The grammar schools and the universities were re-peopled with orthodox dons and teachers loyal to the new Anglican Establishment. Catholic dons and teachers conformed, or resigned, or were dismissed, or went into exile abroad, or sought the best of both worlds by conforming outwardly while continuing to teach from the standpoint of their faith. Catholic families were split asunder, on the fateful issue of whether to attend the Anglican parish churches and send their children to the Anglican grammar schools pending a change of wind, or hold fast to the faith of their fathers by doggedly refusing any compromise whatever.

When it became clear, at the opening of a new century two generations later, that the new order in England had come to stay, the waiting attitude, that had looked hopefully for a Catholic revival, changed to one of dogged holding-out. And this meant two things, each of them a key to understanding the tangled story of this 'education under penalty'. It meant that the tide of scholarship and teaching power that followed William Allen across the Channel, denuding the universities and the schools, into the English seminaries and colleges and schools his initiative created as far afield as Rome and Spain, itself became permanent and a tradition; while (secondly) a continuous battle was fought at home, by the Catholic minority, heartened by the clergy sent to minister to them from the same exiled seminaries, to bring up their children as conscience required, and to feed the colleges abroad at the same time.

Only once during the two centuries of the penal laws did it seem that their reward, for tenacity and sacrifice and devotion, was about to be reaped: at the accession of the Catholic King James II in 1685. But within three years all was lost, through the total inability of this last of the Stuart kings to sense how very deeply a horror of 'popery and wooden shoes' ate at the vitals of ordinary Englishmen. The supreme irony of the entire story lies in the fact that, when James was departing from Whitehall as William's Dutch guards marched in, boatloads of dons and scholars from the English College at Douay were on the way 'home', to take up the positions in Oxford and Cambridge, and the schools, that their fathers' grandfathers' kinsmen had relinquished. It had been a false dawn. Another century yet had still to pass.

Such is the shape of the problem that this book attempts to clarify. In one sense it is an aspect of an ever-present problem, the relations between Church and State in education. As such, it begins at a point in time when Catholic education in England is being outlawed, and the Tudor State is consolidating a paternal form of government tempered by parliamentary institutions; and it ends with the destruction, four generations later, of what might have been the beginning of Cardinal Newman's 'Second Spring'.

The foreground throughout—the struggle of the English Catholics in exile to maintain their seminaries and colleges and to supply the Catholics at home with clergy and sacraments, and of those at home to educate their own children and to recruit to the exiled colleges—is inevitably tinged with politics. The background throughout is religious: the unvarying Catholic teaching on education, whereby the purpose of man's life on earth is the service of God and his neighbour, and the fundamental purpose of education is to help him to do so the better. Catholic schooling may seem to differ little if at all, at any one time, from its contemporary partners in externals. But its aim and purpose are none the less rooted in theological assertions, in terms of a theory of education.

How far that theory was ever explicit in practice, until conditions in modern states, religiously diverse, obliged it to try to become so, has never been established. Nor is it crucial for the present study, which is concerned with a precise historical transaction. But Catholic educational theory, as formulated more than once in the centuries before the Renaissance, is one determinant of what our English episode was all about. And there are two others: the new educational practice expressly devised by the Jesuits to meet the challenge of the Protestant Reformation, and the wholesale reform of education set on foot by the Council of Trent.

These three elements are the stuff of English Catholic 'education under penalty'. Cardinal William Allen personifies the first of them, education as a person-to-person relationship modelled on the person of Christ. The English Jesuit, Robert Persons, typifies the second, the practical formation of character as a militant 'soldier of Christ'. And the third, the Tridentine educational reforms, were the work of no one more than the Englishman Reginald Cardinal Pole. We have to look at each in turn.

I. THE MEDIEVAL THEORY: ST. THOMAS AQUINAS

Though the earliest famous Christian treatise on the teacher is St. Augustine's *De Magistro*,[1] the most profound comes from the thirteenth century, as part of the *Summa Theologica* of St. Thomas Aquinas, a cameo set in the section *De Veritate* of the *Quaestiones Disputatae*. It formulates the relationship between pupil and teacher. Explicitly, or by implication, it offers us major pedagogical discoveries which, having forgotten the Scholastics, the modern world has made again independently since. It offers us likewise a refutation of some outworn habits not even yet universally abandoned from our classrooms.

St. Thomas's *De Magistro* rests on a notion fundamentally developmental and evolutionary: the Aristotelian principle that all change is a passing from being potentially something to being actually that something. It rests also on the Aristotelian synthesis of what any development into something also necessarily involves: the four 'causes' that explain the process. There must be a material cause, answering the question out-of what; a formal cause, explaining the determining principle (form) whereby we recognize the result as a statue and not a tombstone; an efficient cause, answering the question as to what effected the change; and a final cause, the purpose or end or *finis* in terms of which the change came to pass.

[1] English text, ed. J. M. Colleran, *Ancient Christian Writers*, vol. 9, pp. 115–86 (London, 1950).

The argument rests further on a vital distinction between the 'passive' intellect of the animal and the 'active' intellect of the human person. The animal intellect can *be led*; it can *be* trained. The human intellect, in addition to this power, which is passive, has the power of leading itself, of building on its training. Just as a person's own physical nature heals itself when ill, aided by an external agent called a doctor, so a person's own intellectual nature can educate itself, aided by an external agent called a teacher. The doctor is only a short cut to health. The teacher is only a short cut (by the method of 'instruction') to education—which the child could indeed acquire for himself, independently, by the more roundabout method of discovery.

The teacher, then, is only an 'external proximate agent'. What does the work of educating—the 'efficient cause' in the process—is the *intellectus agens* of the learner. The potentialities were all there at the start; the child is born with them; education is the actualization of those potentialities. And in so far as the process involves a change, from being only 'in potency' towards education to being (in varying degrees as between different people) actually educated, it is a process that can be defined in precise terms: self-development into an integrated character under the influence of an ideal.

Here in advance, embalmed in the thirteenth century, is a vindication of the activity-methods of intellectual education canvassed by John Dewey in our own day: though Dewey's philosophy, enshrined in his dogged insistence that 'there is only development', lacks a final cause and even a formal cause and is to that extent defective. Here too, in the *De Magistro*, is a vindication of the teaching-method of Pestalozzi and of Froebel. On the other hand, here is a condemnation in principle of the totally 'didactic' lesson, which tends to treat the child as if he were not in 'active potentiality' towards knowledge but merely in the 'passive potentiality' of the animal.

This is not the place to put Thomist education into its historical setting.[1] But neither must concentration on the mechanics of the educative process mislead us into supposing that education is above all 'intellectualist'. For while the child is the efficient cause in his own education, he is also one pole of a sacred relationship between persons,

[1] See M. H. Mayer, *The Philosophy of Teaching of St. Thomas Aquinas* (Milwaukee: Bruce, 1929), which contains the text of the *De Magistro* in English. Cf. also T. Corbishley, S.J., 'St. Thomas and Educational Theory', in *Dublin Review*, No. 424, Jan. 1945; G. J. Shannon, 'Aquinas and the Teacher's Art', in *Clergy Review*, London, June 1949; and a University of London M.A. Thesis (1955) by Miss M. Murphy (Sister M. St. Thomas, H.C.J.).

between teacher and pupil. It is the unanimous claim of every kind of Christian, Catholics and others alike, that the basis of this relationship, moreover, must be love, and a love approximating more to the *agape* of divine love than to the *eros* of human love. 'Eros recognizes value in its object and therefore loves the object; Agape loves, and thereby *creates* value in the object.'[1] In a Christian school the person-to-person relationship is sanctified, by the divine redemption in which all share. So deeply is this a part of all Christian teaching, and so closely is it bound up with the responsibility of the parents, in conscience, for the upbringing and education of their children, that it goes far to explain why the last Parliament of Elizabeth and the Parliaments of James I, faced (as we shall see) with Bills that would take Catholic children from their parents by force and educate them as Protestants, never in the end passed them.

We still lack a study that will bring out the full bearing of the *De Magistro* in historical detail, at both these levels, of intellectual training and personal dedication. It remains an isolated treatise. There is no means of knowing how far it influenced the actual teaching-methods of the later medieval schools, if at all, or the early post-Tridentine seminaries. There is a natural presumption that the Renaissance scholars, Cardinal Jacopo Sadoleto and Cardinal Silvio Antoniano, were indebted to the *De Magistro*; but none at all that the generation of Comenius and Locke, or Rousseau and Condorcet, or Froebel and Pestalozzi, or the later educational psychologists, each of whom was to stress some particular truth that had been part of the *corpus* of Aquinas' teaching, had studied his treatise. It comes into its own in the modern world with Rosmini, and in the Encyclical *Divini Illius Magistri* of Pope Pius XI in 1929, which puts it into a sociological setting by proclaiming the solemn partnership between parent, teacher, Church and State which is the central assertion of the Catholic attitude to educational administration today, and was also a cue for the Catholic educational 'resistance movement' which endured in England from the Elizabethan settlement to the Emancipation Act of 1829.

2. THE RENAISSANCE PRACTICE: THE JESUITS

In view of the debt which Catholic education throughout the world owes to the Jesuit schools of the Counter-Reformation, it is tantalizing

[1] On this see M. C. D'Arcy, *The Mind and Heart of Love* (London, 1954), and a useful article, 'Teaching and Education', by J. J. Figueroa, in *British Journal of Educational Studies*, iv. 24–31 (1955).

that the direct influence of Aquinas on the educational theory and practice of the Jesuits has apparently never been thoroughly investigated. The *De Magistro* of St. Thomas and the *Ratio Studiorum* of the Jesuits are really the two parts of one whole. Aquinas provides the philosophical theory, embedded in his massive treatise on theology and piety; Loyola provides the professional application of that theory, to the classroom and the community life of the student, dedicated to the formation of character in practical piety and faith. To both men, as indeed to all Catholic educational writers in all the centuries, anything less than that organic unity of formation in precept and practice would be a mockery of education itself. And if the essential religiosity of Catholic education does not immediately strike a reader who takes the *De Magistro* and the *Ratio* as 'texts', that is because examination apart from context, apart from the spirit they were written to serve, must necessarily reveal them stripped of what most makes them worthwhile. It was not for nothing that the *Ratio* took fifty-nine years of experience to perfect, and that everything that was not positive, or applicable to all places, was excluded from it; nor that it has remained acclaimed, by those who detest no less than those who revere what it stood for, as the most thorough educational treatise the world has yet seen.

The Jesuit schools arose involuntarily, from the need for a Counter-Reformation. St. Ignatius Loyola himself was not an 'educated' man. In the years following the assembling of his nucleus of hand-picked apostles in Paris in 1534, and following the inauguration of the Society of Jesus by Pope Paul III six years later, he envisaged the education of only Jesuit postulants, and at the great centres of learning rather than by any special educational foundations. But his hand was forced, by dint of students flocking to him; by the interruption of his postulants' studies at Paris and Louvain under persecution, wherefore he had to make special provision for their preliminary education within the Society; by the need to furnish some *proof* of their efficiency, as anti-Jesuit attacks grew in volume; and through non-Jesuits seeking to share the manifest excellence of what went on in the early colleges.[1]

The Jesuits were not in point of time the first of the teaching orders. St. Angela Merici had founded the Ursulines as early as 1535, for the

[1] There is a survey of early Jesuit foundations, by Alban Goodier, in *The Month* (London, 1906), cviii. 585ff. The rapid expansion of the movement can be gauged from the following figures of colleges: 100 by 1555, 372 by 1615, 728 at the suppression in 1773.

express purpose of teaching. This was an altogether revolutionary event, for it meant an order of nuns unenclosed. The Ursulines were soon, in fact, obliged to become enclosed, and thereby fetter their educational work for a long time to come. They were the first milestone.[1] The Jesuits were the second, with their roving worldwide commission.

Nor was their object to train scholars, but rather, as the General (Aquaviva) said of them in the year of the Armada, 'to carry the students on at least as far as "mediocrity" in learning, so that they may go forth into their respective vocations, ecclesiastics to their ministry, lay students to their own work in life, qualified in some degree with a sufficiency of literary culture'.

The striking contrast between the schooling enshrined in those words and that of the world at large in later centuries lies in that the Jesuit basis was not psychological or sociological but philosophical and religious. The schooling was not 'child-centred'; the centre was the Christian ideal. The teacher, though outwardly seeming at times to 'follow' the child, was there expressly to control and direct. The child's 'natural development' was deliberately restrained, in the interests of training and character-formation. The goal was not so much self-expression as self-control and self-formation. This is a vital point, and it lies at the heart of what St. Thomas had said in the *De Magistro*. The emotions had to be harnessed to the will, and the will trained by reason and the spiritual life. We shall find all this dominating the course of study in the famous school which Dr. Robert Persons was to establish in the Low Countries at St. Omer in 1593, the Stonyhurst of today.

It became explicit in the *Spiritual Exercises* of St. Ignatius, which the Pope authorized for publication in 1548, a more profound study than the later *Ratio Studiorum*, gathering together every problem in the formation of a Christian. The process, it insists, is one of self-education through self-activity. To that extent the teacher's function is passive, and for the same reason the pace of schooling must be determined by the learner's age, capacity, previous education and position in life. In modern educational jargon, the core of the Ignatian theory was 'the implanting of systematically-arranged value-complexes of the highest order under the most favourable conditions'.[2] And yet we must not

[1] See the history of the Ursulines by Bernard O'Reilly (1880); and the study of Angela de Merici by M. Reidy (1962).

[2] J. Lindworsky, S.J., *Training of the Will* (Milwaukee, 1929), 206.

forget that this manual of spiritual exercises was not a rule of thumb for use in a system of utter obedience (though this also is fundamental, and the Jesuit system would otherwise not be itself), but a manual for the directors of spiritual Retreats.

In the formal *Constitutions* of the Society of Jesus, promulgated in 1556 just a year after Loyola's death, there is little on the school curriculum. For the Jesuit colleges took over the curriculum of the Renaissance grammar schools prevailing in each country. In general, the course of studies was to comprise 'the humane letters, the different tongues, and logic, natural and moral philosophy, metaphysics, theology both scholastic and positive, and sacred science'. What the *Constitutions* did above all, in the seventeen chapters on 'Studies', each in the form of a text with explanations, was to re-consecrate everything *ad majorem Dei gloriam*. It is here that we find the all too little known precepts as to the choice of men for admission into the Society, the renunciation of all profit and remuneration (to this day the Pope makes no Jesuit a bishop without the concurrence of the Father General), the scrupulous provision for individual differences among the scholars, and the erecting of courses of study according to age, attainment and temperament.

In the upper reaches, of philosophy and theology, the textbooks most in use were those of Aristotle and Aquinas. A scrutiny of the lower part of the curriculum reveals it as that of the grammar schools: i.e. it was not 'elementary'—a point which renders inherently improbable the legendary maxim attributed to the Jesuits, 'Give me a child till the age of 7. . . .' Certainly when *parvuli* of this kind arrived from England to be schooled by the Jesuits at St. Omer, they were placed elsewhere *ad interim*.

The *Ratio Studiorum* itself, as a manual for schoolmasters, took fifteen years to distil: from 1584, when Claudius Aquaviva set up a committee of six to prepare it, till its publication in 1599 after exhaustive examination in the light of practice since 1540 all over Europe. It stands to the *Constitutions* as administrative regulations stand to statute law. That is why it cannot be properly understood apart from the *Constitutions* and the *Spiritual Exercises*. In form it is a handbook of rules, a manual of methodology.

Von Ranke was to say of it, as such, that six months of Jesuit schooling was worth two years of any other. Its universal effect throughout Europe, and that of the Jesuit colleges harnessed to it, can be measured by the gibe levelled against the French anti-clericals of the eighteenth century, that there was hardly a man sufficiently educated to battle against the Society but had been educated in its schools. For all the 'Papistry' of the Jesuits, the English Protestant schoolmaster Charles Hoole was recommending their 1590 Latin Grammar, *Jacobi Pontari Progymnasmata Latinitatis*, in mid-seventeenth century,[1] and as we shall see later, the English Puritan John Dury, protégé of Comenius and author of *The Reformed School* (1650), regarded the Jesuit colleges he had seen at work in Europe as models.

In sum, the *Exercises* and the *Constitutions* and the *Ratio* were an integral whole. Formation in terms of them made every Jesuit at once a religious, a schoolmaster and a missionary.[2]

3. THE COUNCIL OF TRENT AND EDUCATIONAL REFORM

But while there had long been a body of Catholic theorizing about education, and while there was now at work a high-powered Jesuit machine of men and texts and methods to accommodate that theory to the new religious conditions of the Reformation and reclaim the Protestant world, the educational practice of the Catholic Church at large, whose shortcomings had done much to make the Reformation possible, itself needed radical overhaul. There must be reform from within, by the Church's central authority. This was the urgent cue for the educational decrees of the Council of Trent, which opened in 1545 and closed eighteen years later at the very moment Elizabeth's oath of supremacy was being clapped on all schoolmasters.

Oddly enough, though education was traditionally and exclusively the work of the Church, the development of canon law on it had so far been very slight. Until as late as 1179 the regulation of the schools had been almost invariably by individual bishops, locally. Moreover, the decree of 1179, by the third Lateran Council, that there should be in every cathedral church a beneficed master 'to teach gratis the clerics of the church and also poor students', cannot be said to have operated everywhere; the successive re-enactments of it (as at Lateran IV in

[1] Cf. Foster Watson, *English Grammar Schools to 1660* (1908), 316 and note.

[2] There are English editions of the *Spiritual Exercises*, by W. H. Longridge (London, 1919) and T. H. Moore (New York, 1949). The *Ratio* was revised in 1832, 1853 and 1883. No English edition of it until 1933, in E. A. Fitzpatrick, *St. Ignatius and the Ratio Studiorum* (New York, 1933). The complete source-book for the documents is G. Pachtler, *Ratio Studiorum et Institutiones Scholasticae Societatis Jesu* (Berlin, 1887–94: 4 vols.).

1216) hint as much. By the time of the Reformation, indeed, the canon law of education had contrived to regulate very little beyond cathedral schools, free tuition and theological orthodoxy.

Until Trent 'invented' the modern ecclesiastical seminary, no 'educated' priest was a seminarian. Nor, for the most part, was he a university man. But every parish priest was in theory a schoolmaster. The religious education they gave in England in pre-Tudor times had centred on the *Pater Noster*, the Creed and the Ten Commandments. How well the substance was understood—how far the clergy were Latinist or the laity literate—is still an open question.

The whole field of clerical education in England just prior to the Reformation is still virtually unworked. It is well known that complaints on the score of defective education were numerous during the monastic visitations of 1517 and onwards. Thomas Starkey's contemporary *Dialogue between Pole and Lupset* worked out a systematic reform of teaching, from the two universities downwards. In 1531 the bishops themselves realized the need for a 'nucleus of trained men' in every religious house, and tried to meet it by prescribing a teaching of grammar 'sufficienter eruditus ad informandum religiosos in grammatica et aliis primitivis scientiis'. But what fraction of the 10,000–12,000 clergy in the land had had any sort of university training, or what proportion of the others had had any sort of priestly *formation* in the generations prior to the Tridentine seminaries, has yet to be explored by historians.[1]

For the masses, Henry VIII issued in 1538 an injunction that children should be taught their Christianity in English, and that, since the ultimate responsibility was parental, the clergy should teach the parents. There had been hitherto only primers and lay service-books. Catechisms were not used in schools before the Reformation. It fell to Henry VIII, once he had assumed the royal supremacy, to introduce the King's Primer (1547) and Cranmer his own catechism a year later. Nor was the Bible to be an instrument of general education in England

[1] On this unworked field see A. F. Leach, *English Schools at the Reformation* (1897), 106; J. W. Adamson, *The Illiterate Anglo-Saxon* (1946); J. W. Thompson, *The Literacy of the Laity in the Middle Ages* (California, 1939); G. G. Coulton, *Medieval Panorama* (1938), chs. 12, 31, 32; J. H. Miner, 'Schools and Literacy in Later Medieval England', in *Br. J. of Educational Studies*, xi (1962). See also William Allen's strictures in 1577, in T. F. Knox, *Letters and Memorials of William Cardinal Allen* (1882), 32. The whole problem has been posed, with some challenging evidence, in Philip Hughes, *The Reformation in England*, i. 50–1, 83–5, 104–5 (1950), ii. 82–3, 92, 138 (1953). For a neglected root of medieval clerical education see L. E. Boyle, O.P., *The Constitution* Cum ex eo *of Boniface VIII*, in *Medieval Studies*, xxiv, 263–302 (Toronto 1962).

till after the Elizabethan settlement, nor a school subject as such till the Anglican Canons of 1604.[1]

There had long been, then, a substantial element of hit-and-miss in education both clerical and lay throughout the Church; and reform was in the air long before Pope Paul III (Alexander Farnese) set up his Commission of Cardinals in 1537. Among these Tridentine Commissioners was Reginald Pole. Their meeting coincided in time with the arrival in Rome of Ignatius Loyola.

Their work at Trent, so far as it concerns pedagogy, was confined to the first year (fifth session) and the last, seventeen years later (twenty-third to twenty-fifth sessions). That the first matters to be regulated were those touching the effective teaching of scripture is significant historically because it stabilized religious education in the schools of Catholic countries long before the government in England was able to do so for purposes of Anglican uniformity.

Trent decreed that in those churches where there was a prebendary for lectures in theology, the bishop was to 'compel' him to 'expound and interpret' the Scriptures, personally or by competent proxy. In churches where the revenue was slight, and the clergy and laity few, 'let them at least have a master', to be chosen by the bishop with the advice of the chapter, to teach grammar *gratis* 'to *clerics and other poor scholars*, that so they may afterwards, with God's blessing, pass on the said study of sacred Scripture'. Similar lectureships in Scripture were to be established in the monasteries and convents of the regulars; and also in 'public colleges' established by the piety of princes and governments, provided the appointments should be approved by the bishop.

Legislation over the whole field—the secular clergy, the regulars of the religious orders, and the laity—filled the closing year.

The decree on the clergy (chapter eighteen) is expressly entitled 'Method of Establishing Seminaries for Clerics, and of Educating the Same Therein'. It is the basis of ecclesiastical education in diocesan seminaries today. Every diocese was directed to provide a seminary for the priestly formation of those of its youths who should be forthcoming. On entry they must be at least twelve years of age, and show

[1] See the early English Text Society edition (1901) of Archbishop Thoresby's *Lay Folks' Catechism* of 1357. The Catechism ultimately enjoined on all the Tudor schools (Dean Howell's) was based on the Edward VI *Shorter Catechism* of 1552. Cranmer's Injunction of 1547 introducing the English Bible into grammar schools is in W. H. Frere, *History of the English Church* (1910), i. 150–1. Mary substituted for it Bonner's Book of Homilies (Cardwell, *Documentary Annals*, 1839, i. 112–14). Her addition of the *Ave Maria* to the prayers to be learnt by heart in school was repealed in 1559.

evidence of vocation. They would take the tonsure and wear the habit. Preference would be given to the poor, but the rich were not to be excluded as such. The seminary would be governed by the bishop, through two canons of his cathedral chapter. The course of studies should comprise 'grammar, church music and the other liberal arts', and particularly Scripture. The seminary would be maintained by a tax on every benefice in the diocese. Where dioceses were too poor, their provincial synod might set up a joint seminary for several. All *scholastici* must be doctors or licentiates in theology or canon law, and professorships were to be conferred only on those who 'can discharge the office personally'. The bishop would prescribe the studies, and he might 'compel' qualified theologians and others to teach in his seminary.

So comprehensive and thorough is all this, even to the safeguarding of academic qualifications and the prohibition of absenteeism or pluralism; and at the same time so obvious is it, that scholars may wonder all the more how the medieval priesthood had been adequately educated and formed without some real system of the kind.

At the same time, these decrees taken alone raised a ticklish problem: the regulars in the orders. For over three hundred years, higher education had been very largely the contribution of the Dominicans and Franciscans in the universities. As regulars, they were responsible to their own provincials and not to diocesan bishops. This autonomy had bedevilled their early days in Oxford, and was more than once fought out in the streets. It is that very autonomy that was to provoke so much bitter hostility to the Jesuits among the Catholic secular clergy in Tudor and Stuart England, and complicate the early struggles of the colleges in exile. Trent met the issue realistically. In chapter four of session twenty-five it was decreed that no regular was to serve 'any prelate, prince or university' without permission from his own superior. If he were sent to a university for the sake of his own studies, he was to 'dwell in convents [monasteries] only', on pain of being proceeded against by (sublime touch) the bishop.

The religious education, finally, of the adult laity deserves notice. Trent laid down (chapter four of session twenty-four) that every bishop must explain to his people the efficacy and use of the sacraments, through a vernacular Catechism expounded to the people by every priest. The clergy were also to explain the Mass, during Mass, in the vernacular, on all festivals.

This is the origin of modern catechetical instruction in Catholic education. Its result in England was immediate—the first post-Reformation Catholic catechism in English, in 1567, by Lawrence Vaux, Warden of Manchester Collegiate Church till he went into exile following William Allen. His version of the catechism, published in Louvain primarily for his own scholars, had a long vogue in England.[1]

Action on all the decrees followed quickly enough, under the impetus of St. Charles Borromeo, Archbishop of Milan, who at once ordered seminaries to be started in every diocese of the Roman State. The Rome Seminary itself was founded in April 1564, less than a year after the Council closed, and entrusted to the Jesuits. The fact that by the time William Allen opened the English College at Douay there were others already in existence beside the Roman (Milan, Portugal 1565 and Germany) disposes in advance of a mistaken claim made in the eighteenth century that the English at Douay were the first in the field of Tridentine seminaries.[2]

One question must be left for consideration later: how far Reginald Cardinal Pole, prominent at Trent, was in fact the instigator of the decrees prescribing seminaries, and therefore of modern Catholic clerical education.[3]

And one irony must be anticipated: something that Trent could hardly have foreseen. In the year the Council ended, Queen Elizabeth ordered that the oaths of allegiance and supremacy, corner-stones of the religious settlement at her accession, be imposed on all schoolmasters, thereby rendering a Catholic education in England illegal. At once there began an exodus of Catholics, many of them laity, and not all

[1] There were six editions before 1600; and one as late as 1885 edited for the Chetham Society by Thomas Law. As to the Catholic Bible in English, there was none till the end of the century; Doway New Testament 1582, Old Testament 1610. The other major Catholic catechisms used in England before the restoration of the Hierarchy in 1850 were: 1554 *Summa Doctrinae Christianae*, of Bishop Peter Canisius; 1649 Doway Catechism, by Henry Turbeville; 1688 the Doway 'Abstract', published London, for younger boys; 1697 the 'Abstract' by Mairesse; 1772 Bishop Challoner's 'Abridgement', published St. Omer; and his English 'Catechism of Christian Doctrine', 1836 and 1859 revisions.

[2] For the historical settings of the Tridentine decrees, see H. J. Schroeder (ed.) *Disciplinary Decrees of the General Councils* (Herder, 1937). For narrative of the Council, see the work of Sebastian Merkle (Herder, 1901). For the *Acta*, the edition by Stephen Ehses (Herder, 1914). For the decrees, J. Waterworth, *Canons and Decrees of the Council of Trent* (London, 1848 and 1881). The first study of them in English was that of A. T. Drane, in *Christian Schools and Scholars* (London, 1867), vol. ii. ch. 12. The claim, echoed by P. Guilday in *English Catholic Refugees* (1914), 65–6, is in the Seventh Douay Diary (Catholic Record Society, xxviii (1928), 328).

[3] *See* p. 24 below.

wanting to be priests. Now, the Tridentine system, of seminaries for the clergy and collegiate education for the Jesuits, and of convent education for nuns, had not been devised for laity. Thus, with the English grammar schools no longer available for the more resolute of the Catholics, and with a movement of lay exiles beginning that was to become at times a *diaspora*, the Tridentine system was about to be called upon to adapt itself, and devise a policy of schools for the laity, not only those in exile but those at home in a land from which the Catholic teachers of the traditional past would soon be estranged.

For the moment at least, the new papal university just set up, in Flanders at Douay in 1562, was attracting to itself as dons the first companies of exiles from Oxford and Cambridge fellowships. Names later famous in the annals of the dispersal crop up as early as that: Richard Smith of Merton, Owen Lewis of New College. The foremost of them all, William Allen, from what is today Oriel, was destined within five years from then to be the founder of the entire educational movement of the English exiles.

II

THE ROYAL SUPREMACY BEFORE ELIZABETH I

1. HENRY VIII AND EDWARD VI

To appreciate the situation facing the Catholic schools in England when the oaths were extended to schoolmasters in 1563 and the destruction of the old system began, the accession of Queen Elizabeth I is not the best starting point. For royal intervention in the education of the country became logical and likely from the moment that her father threw off spiritual allegiance to Rome and asserted the royal supremacy, thirty years earlier.

Legally, the policy of State control of education pursued after the Elizabethan religious settlement began with the Act of Supremacy in 1534. Practically, it began the following year, with royal injunctions whereby members of the two universities were to take oaths renouncing papal allegiance, and canon law was abolished from the curriculum.[1] The increase of royal control under Edward VI after 1547, and under Elizabeth after 1558, was but a development within a theory of the supremacy already operative; and the reaction to Catholicism under Mary was not constitutional, but a change of direction only.

What made the intervention so relatively easy was that the functioning of schools and universities depended on the licence to teach, the *licentia docendi*. This licence was given by the bishop of the diocese in which the master qualified. It had long served as the normal means of securing religious orthodoxy in the schools. In times of heresy, moreover, it had been a powerful ecclesiastical weapon—as after the Act of 1400 against teachers of Lollardy. With the bishops now subordinate to the Crown after 1534, control by licence automatically passed to the sovereign. And it operated on schools, universities, printing. It was destined to endure till the nineteenth century, though obsolete in part much earlier.

[1] Cf. C. E. Mallet, *Hist. Univ. Oxford* (1924), ii. 62–4; J. B. Mullinger, *Hist. Univ. Cambr.* (1873), ii. 35; M. H. Curtis, *Oxford and Cambridge in Transition* (1959), 51.

The auguries had been clear even before the Act of Supremacy itself. The first exodus of Catholic scholars, priests and religious and university men emigrating to Ireland, Scotland, Paris, Salamanca, Bologna, Padua and Louvain, occurred soon after 1530.[1] The dissolution of the monastic houses in 1536–9 reacted on the universities by damming up the supply of poor scholars, blocking endowments and plundering popish books; though in the field of lay education the loss caused by the dissolution was less than formerly supposed, since the monasteries had long ceased, most of them, to teach any but interns.

Henry's work for education, destructive and constructive alike, has been exaggerated. On the constructive side, there were indeed refoundations and improvements of schools, and there were new creations. But the Crown was not itself paying for educational advance. Money had been raised through the dissolution. More was intended by the Chantries Act of 1547. The refoundations at Canterbury and Durham and elsewhere bear witness that it was not the intention of this first Chantries Act to impair educational facilities. The Act itself implied that as others were already despoiling the chantries the king would nationalize the plunder and use it to finance his foreign wars and the schools. The 'calamity' that A. F. Leach deplored lies in the second Chantries Act, after Henry's death.[2]

This destructive side of the king's work has also been overstressed. The case against it in the works of Leach, that the suppressions of chantry and guild schools were wholesale; that refoundations were confined to grammar schools only, not including 'elementary' schools; that the reprieve-warrant, 'continuatur schola quousque', was frequently not followed up; and that the net devastation was colossal, is today a reopened question.[3]

Whatever the verdict, the legacy of Henry VIII was of course the result of a religious and political rather than an educational policy. This is clear from the preamble to the first Act, which arraigns the papal and superstitious uses to which the various kinds of institution had been put, and from the fact that the lay chantries of the guilds were exempted.[4] The schools that remained, after the inquest, continued as *religious* instruments, Catholic or Protestant according to the

[1] See *American Catholic Hist. Review*, xl. 2 (1929).

[2] Cf. A. F. Leach, *English Schools at the Reformation* (1897); *Educational Charters* (1911); *Schools of Medieval England* (1915).

[3] See articles in *Br. J. of Educational Studies*, by Joan Simon, iii and iv (1955), xii (1963) and W. N. Chaplin, xi (1963).

[4] Cf. Norman Wood, *The Reformation and English Education* (1931), 30, 34.

policy of the incoming monarch. The Reformation and Counter-Reformation, as affairs of State, meant that the schools were now a weapon as well as a fount of orthodoxy. For while the school was henceforth an instrument of the Established Church of England, the Established Church was to become more and more a department of State.

Under Henry VIII the test had been the oath of supremacy. It was an immense impartiality that sent to Smithfield, on 30 July 1540, three hurdles bearing two victims each, one Catholic, one Lutheran.[1] Under the two Protectors, Somerset and Northumberland, following Henry's death, the Crown became a Protestant and heretical Crown, and a Catholic education was accordingly outlawed on grounds both religious and constitutional. The roots of the Elizabethan legislation lie therefore in the six years of Edward VI.

Administratively, that short reign tried to fill gaps in the 'map' of education. Somerset ordered every cathedral without a free grammar school to found one, and to give the master a house and the usher a room. But there was more than routine in the scrutinies carried out. The visitation of the universities shows—from the Protector's letter of September 1548—that the intention was 'to bring about the adoption of a uniform reformed Church service', and to root out papist personnel.[2] It is no coincidence that in the same year there was founded on the Continent the first of the English Catholic exiled schools. Elizabeth Woodford, of the Canonesses of St. Augustine, opened St. Ursula's School for girls in Louvain.[3]

Theologically, it is the Protectorate of Northumberland that marks the first attempt at a policy of religious uniformity in education, at all levels, throughout the country. In the schools, this centred on the Catechism, which was authorized for use in 1553 along with the Forty-Two Articles of Religion. In the universities we have at the same time a landmark of equal significance, in the sending of Commissioners in 1553 to impose the Articles on all proceeding to degrees, thereby establishing a doctrinal religious test. It has been said of this episode that 'when, under Mary, the opposite party regained the ascendancy, they took example . . . by the illiberality of their antagonists, and imposed a like subscription in favour of Catholic doctrine'.[4]

[1] Joseph Gillow, *Bibl. Dict. of English Catholics* (1886), ii. 254.

[2] N. Wood, 111–12. Similarly, the regius chairs in divinity founded in 1546 (Martin Bucer at Cambridge, Peter Martyr at Oxford).

[3] The whole of the feminine side of the problem is dealt with in W. J. Battersby, *Educational Work of the English Religious Orders of Women*, not yet published.

[4] Mullinger, ii. 145–6.

The framework of royal supremacy over education is thus clearly to be seen already before the Catholic Queen Mary arrived to repeal it. Its keynote was orthodoxy and conformity. Its instruments were university visitation and episcopal injunction. It already had, too, a positive side—the prescription of the Catechism in schools. As yet, there had been little resistance and no systematic dismissal of schoolmasters, though a few long-sighted Catholics had already left the country.

2. QUEEN MARY TUDOR

When Mary Tudor rode in state through London in the summer of 1553, a fortnight after her accession, an address of welcome was delivered by a London schoolboy who had won the honour in open competition—Edmund Campion, of Christ's Hospital, then recently founded in Newgate Street.[1] By the time Cardinal Pole arrived from Rome as papal legate fifteen months later, it was clear that the re-Catholicizing policy of the new queen was bent on utilizing the whole of the educational system.

Religious orders exiled during the Protectorate began to return immediately—the Franciscan Observants to Greenwich, the Dominicans to Smithfield.[2] Individual teachers returned in their wake, beginning with the Rev. Sir John Madde (Mudd), who had been exiled under Henry VIII and now came back to teach 'gentlemen's children and others' at Knaresborough.[3]

On a petition from the lower house of Convocation the queen issued instructions to 'examine all schoolmasters and teachers of children and, finding them suspect in any ways, to remove them and place Catholic men in their rooms'.[4] A 'Bill against seditious priests or teachers to be schoolmasters' was introduced into the Commons in the following year (5 December) by one Draycote.[5]

[1] The irony is that the future martyr also delivered the address of welcome on Elizabeth's visit to St. John's College, Oxford, in 1566.

[2] The others returning were: Bridgettines (Catherine Palmer), at Syon Abbey 1554; Carthusians (Dom Maurice Chauncy), at Sheen, May 1555; Benedictines (Abbot Feckenham) at Westminster Abbey; Carmelites, recalled from exile in Scotland; Dominican Nuns, at Langley, Herts. See P. Guilday, *English Catholic Refugees* (1914), 215, 285, 401, 57, 43, 347. They were all expelled again in June and July 1559, following the Elizabethan legislation.

[3] H. Foley, *Records of the English Province S.J.* (1875 f.), iii. 239.

[4] Cardwell, *Documentary Annals* (1839), i. 112.

[5] *Commons Journals*, i. 39.

It is not possible to assess the proportion of Protestant schoolmasters dismissed during the reign. But the trend may be gathered from the fact that, when the queen was married to Philip II of Spain in Winchester Cathedral in 1554, only one of the group of Wykehamist boys who wrote congratulatory verses ventured to mention religion.[1] The few documented cases of ejected masters do include three leading schools. John Fenn, of New College, whom we shall meet again, was appointed to the mastership of Bury St. Edmunds Free Grammar School in 1553; at Shrewsbury in 1556 the bailiffs were searching to find 'an honest and able person to serve the office of Head Schoolmaster of the Free School', in place of John Eyton, who had been there since 1551: and in the following year Preston Grammar School was put under Peter Carter, of St. John's College, Cambridge, who had just completed his M.A. degree.[2] At Reading School the headmaster, Joceline Palmer, became one of the Protestant martyrs. He had gone from his Coventry home to be educated at Magdalen, and had secured his post at Reading through Sir Francis Knollys. He was forced to resign in 1555, on account of a paper he wrote attacking the Privy Council for burning Bishop Hooper. In July he himself was burnt. The master who had been his predecessor, Thomas Thackham, returned to the school and ruled it till 1560.[3]

But it certainly does not do to assume that all the masters and ushers who left, and those who replaced them during Mary's five years, were Protestants and Catholics respectively. Statements such as that 'Reve or Ryve seems to have fled the Roman persecution under Mary; at all events he was succeeded [at Berkhamstead School] in 1555 by William Barker. . . .' are idle without evidence. Nor does it follow, without evidence, that the reason why no master could be got to stay at the Crypt Grammar School at Gloucester was that the neighbourhood was unfavourable to the new religious regime.[4]

Some schools lapsed through a device new to Tudor constitutional practice. Since 1548 it had been usual for schools 'reprieved' under the Chantry Act inquiries to receive their funds through the Court of Augmentations. This Court was abolished in the first year of Philip and Mary (1554). Some schools were able to continue none the less,

[1] A. F. Leach, *Winchester College* (1899), 282.

[2] G. W. Fisher, *Annals of Shrewsbury School* (1899), 4; Gillow, i. 412–13.

[3] *Vict. County Hist.*, Berks., 251–2.

[4] A. F. Leach, in *Victoria County History*, Hampshire, 11, 75, and Gloucestershire, ii. 346.

by reason of other endowments: for example, Cirencester, Newland, Cheltenham, Whalley.[1] But not all.

The actual increase of schools by new foundations, during Mary's reign of five years, seems to have comprised one grammar school each year established by the queen 'of her own bounty', and some fifteen in all by private individuals.[2] Clitheroe (1554) and Repton (1557) were new foundations, the latter by Sir John Port. Derby (1554), Banbury (1555) and Basingstoke (1557) were *re*-foundations. The last of these is particularly significant, since not only was the Holy Ghost School re-established at Basingstoke but its gild was restored as well —evidence of the queen's attempt 'to effect a restoration of the confiscated property of monasteries and chantries to pious uses'.[3] As early as October 1553, indeed, the Commons were discussing a Bill for giving lands to grammar schools among other deserving causes, and it was passed by 27 November.[4] Before the end of the same year, steps had begun for securing the Catholic orthodoxy of what went on inside the schools.

We are on clearer ground as regards the two universities. There was no immediate visitation, but both universities were notified in the very first summer (1553) that all the constitutional changes made since the death of Henry VIII were void. The Duke of Norfolk and Stephen Gardiner, lately in the Tower, were reinstated as High Steward and as Chancellor of the University of Cambridge—offices which Northumberland, in depriving them, had himself assumed. A change of heads took place in every Cambridge college except three (Gonville, Jesus and Magdalene), and those ejected included a future Archbishop of Canterbury (Matthew Parker), a future Protestant martyr (Nicholas Ridley) and the late king's tutor (Sir John Cheke).[5] Religious tests followed in 1555. Articles were drawn up asserting papal supremacy and the truths of the Catholic religion, and all proceeding to a degree in the universities were required to profess them. The heresies of Luther, Zwingli and the newly ejected Regius professors of divinity were condemned. Cardinal Pole, now Chancellor of both universities,

[1] *V.C.H.*, Glos., ii. 390, 416, 424; Lancs., ii. 604. And cf. Joan Simon, in *Br. J. Ed. Studies*, iv. 45.

[2] School Inquiry Commission *Report* (London, 1864), appdx. 49.

[3] For these schools see *V.C.H.*, Lancs., ii. 605; Derby, ii. 231, 216; Hants., ii. 372f; and C. W. Stokes, *Queen Mary's Grammar School, Clitheroe*, Chetham Soc. N.S. 92 (1934).

[4] *Commons Journals*, i. 29, 31.

[5] The displacements and appointments are listed in Mullinger, ii. 149 and note.

followed this up next year with visitations, to purge the university libraries of heretical books and to revise the statutes.

This overhauling of Oxford and Cambridge was Pole's first campaign, of three. It could touch but few of the total clergy of the country, since (as we have seen) relatively few clergy were university men. But what chiefly appalled the cardinal was the ignorance of the clergy at large, as both a concomitant cause of the Reformation and a 'natural breeding-ground of heresy'.

His second campaign accordingly was one to secure competent preachers and sound books. One of the major Acts of Mary's first Parliament had given the universities the right to license preachers. Prior to Pole's arrival the queen had reserved to herself the sole authority for issuing written licences. The channel now became a bishop's licence. Bishop Bonner in London recognized none but those issued by himself or Pole. As part of the same safeguards, foreign booksellers were expelled the country unless 'denizen or merchant known'. A list of forbidden books promulgated in 1555 included the Edwardian Prayer Book and the works of all the reformers. Before the queen's death in 1558 the repressive measures enacted on the score of preaching and books had reached their peak: anyone found in possession of any of the prohibited works exposed himself to the death penalty.[1]

None of this involved new machinery for control. It was but a matter of reversing the engines of the existing machinery, in an attempt to regain the *status quo ante* Henry VIII's Reformation Parliament of 1529–36, and to watch the running of the machine by the traditional method of visitation. Bonner in London, Gardiner in Winchester, Goldwell in St. Asaph and Pole in Canterbury carried out diocesan visitations. Bonner's articles for London are representative of them all. They stressed the need to purge out unsound schoolmasters, and to sustain the *Latin Grammar* of Lyly which Henry VIII had enjoined on all grammar schools as long ago as 1540.[2]

Much of this was foreshadowed in the cardinal's opening speech to his Canterbury provincial synod, in which he berated the ignorance of

[1] Mary's order on preaching is in Cardwell, i. 105; Pole's in Cardwell, i. 151; Bonner's in Frere, ii. 364; Mary's order on printing, in Strype, *Cranmer*, iii. 50–1.

[2] Bonner's text is in Frere, ii. 331–59; Goldwell's, in Wilkins, *Concilia*, iv. 145. Pole's Canterbury Visitation (carried out by Nicholas Harpsfield: articles in Frere, ii. 425) has been edited for Catholic Record Soc. by L. E. Whatmore (xlv and xlvi, 1950–1). Gardiner's visitation (Cardwell, ii. 322) is omitted from N. Wood's list in *Reformation and English Education*, 44.

the clergy.[1] That the domestic reforms and the visitations achieved very little is hardly surprising. There was so little time—only three years to go—before the death of both queen and cardinal. Elizabeth and her Archbishop Matthew Parker were to find in their turn the same problem of clerical ignorance beyond even the whole decades they were able to devote to it.

The really historic event is the promulgation of Pole's *Constitutions* for Canterbury. It is these *Constitutions* that enshrine his third and final attempt at educational reform and at the same time make him an architect of the decrees of Trent. These twelve *Constitutiones Legatinae* were issued from Westminster Abbey in February 1556, just over two years after he had formally received the country back into the Catholic Church.

The decree we are concerned with is the eleventh: *pro reformatione Angliae*. One part of it dealt with the universities, appointing Nicholas Ormanetti as Visitor and giving a priority to the restoration of the Divinity Schools at Oxford. Another part ordered that all schoolmasters should be examined and approved by the bishops, with a ban on teaching for three years as penalty for default. But the most important sections are those on the schools and clerical education.

For the future, the clergy were to be trained (as of old) in the Cathedral Schools—one school for each diocese. But there was much more here than a formal harking back. The detailed provisions laid down have all the ring of what Trent was to ordain for the whole Catholic Church seven years later. Boys of the age of eleven or twelve—preference to poor boys—ability to read and write necessary on entry—tonsure and habit—life in community under the dean and chapter—books approved by the bishop—down to the article's own summing up of its intentions as being in short a '*kind of seminary*'.

The influence of this decree upon what was afterwards done at Trent cannot be measured with precision. The presence of Pole at the earlier sessions of Trent, and the marked similarity between his provincial and Trent's global enactments, however, make it impossible to deny a connection or resist the presumption of *post hoc propter hoc*.[2]

Nor should the nature of the schools envisaged by the legate be

[1] W. Schenck, *Reginald Pole* (1950), 143, 147.

[2] *Pole's Constitutions* are in Wilkins, *Concilia*, iv. 126. The Latin text of *Decretum XI* is reprinted from Wilkins (iv. 135) in N. Wood, 42 note. It is summarized in A. T. Drane, i. 433ff. Its influence on Trent is asserted by Drane, and by J. G. Snead-Cox, *Cardinal Vaughan* (1912), ii. 35.

construed too narrowly. Though they have been regarded as purely seminaries for the clergy, and though such a view would explain the reference to 'children' priests later, in the Elizabethan injunctions of 1559, there is nothing to preclude the very natural assumption that the 'other boys' mentioned in Pole's decree were in fact lay boys, receiving their education in these seminaries for reasons of geographical or other convenience, and not destined for the priesthood unless 'for any reason they are wanted' (qui quocunque desiderabuntur). Indeed, that was to be precisely the situation at the first school for English Catholic boys in exile from Elizabeth when Robert Persons, S.J., established it in the Low Countries.[1] Thereafter the preliminary training together of scholastics and lay boys runs right through the history of English Catholic education during penal times, and even after the return home upon the outbreak of the French Revolution. St. Edmund's College, the seminary for the south of England, stemming from the English College at Douay, perpetuates it today. Only positive reasons would warrant our declining to discern that very duality in Pole's decree of 1556. Wherefore, on this count as well as the inherent probability that they served as a model for the decrees of Trent, and thus as model for Catholic ecclesiastical education since, Pole's *Constitutions* must rank as the most far-reaching educational achievement of the Marian Counter-Reformation.

But in one direction no less historic the cardinal stonewalled throughout: he declined to admit to England Jesuit teachers.

Ignatius Loyola, rejoicing at the return of England to the bosom of the Church, had begun as early as 1554 to receive 'young Englishmen in our Germanic College [in Flanders]', and was already conceiving a large college from which to fertilize all the heretic lands. In January 1555 he addressed a plea to Pole. But three years later the General of the Jesuits was told ruefully that Count Feria, who was on a special mission to England for Philip II, had 'three times had audience of Cardinal Pole on a project for having members of the Society come to England; but had not found in him the concurrence for which he had hoped'. With the exception of Thomas Lith, received into the Society of Jesus in Rome by Loyola himself in June 1555, the catalogue of English Jesuits was not to begin till 1561.[2]

[1] The school at Eu. See p. 65 below.

[2] P. Guilday, *English Catholic Refugees*, 123, and sources there cited. Documents in L. Deplace, *L'Angleterre et la Compagnie de Jésus*, 13–14, 16, 27. A list of the first Jesuit Englishmen is in Deplace, 77–9, beginning in 1561. See also J. H. Pollen, 'The First Jesuits in Great Britain', in *The Month*, 1909, 428–31.

The queen and the cardinal died in 1558 on the same day (17 November). If the five years of their reaction were too short for results to be assessed, at least the policy at work was emerging. There was no replacement of the chantry schools lost under the Act of 1547, nor any large-scale creation of grammar schools. But there was more in Pole's eleventh decree than just the cathedral schools of the past.[1]

Just as Mary's omission to restore the monastic properties does not lessen the reality of her religious aims, so the paucity of new schools is no valid argument, by itself, as to her intentions in education. The record is mixed. What integrates it is the royal determination—which she shares with her father before her and with her sister afterwards—to proclaim norms of orthodoxy and to enforce them. That was the Tudor character. The screw was turned most tightly where the resistance was heaviest: in Mary's reign not in the universities nor in the schools, but upon the printers and distributors of banned Protestant literature. That the queen and cardinal wished for the banishment of all schoolmasters who favoured the reformed doctrines is certain; but that they achieved this on more than a tiny scale, in those five years, has no attested evidence to support it. On the contrary, the fact that there were so few expulsions of Catholic schoolmasters in the first few years of Elizabeth's reign (as we shall see) indicates that their arrival or restoration under Mary had not been wholesale.

In the control of education the period of Mary and Pole means merely that the instruments taken from the Church by Henry VIII and the Protectors were restored to it: licence and visitation and sanctions. Nothing new—only developments within that framework—emerged. In human terms, at least one of these developments went to the limit: the death penalty for possessing these books. In what was to follow, the like would happen again only twice: the death penalty for any priest found in the country who had been ordained abroad (Elizabeth, 1585), and life-imprisonment for unlicensed schoolmastering (William III, 1700).

The twenty-five years since Henry's Act of Supremacy had been a ding-dong, the repression of Catholics by the Protectors giving place to a persecution of Protestants under Mary. Elizabeth was to seek a middle way. Unhappily it was to prove impossible to find, not only because Catholicism was a fundamental factor in the international politics of the day and therefore of the security of the realm; but because, when all parties, Anglican, Papist and Puritan, valued educa-

[1] Cf. N. Wood, 40 note.

tion from a deeply religious standpoint and claimed freedom in it as a matter of conscience, repression served only to deepen their (incompatible) religious foundations all round. Until the dawn of an age of true tolerance, a tolerance born of respect and not inhibited by fear, the several arenas in which the educational resistance movements would have to fight were long since predetermined: the printer, the university, the school, the schoolmaster and the parents.

III

THE DESTRUCTION OF THE CATHOLIC SYSTEM 1558-80

1. THE FIRST PENAL LAWS ON EDUCATION

So palpable is the ding-dong movement after Elizabeth's accession, 'settlement' replacing the Edwardian and Marian 'ascendancy', resistance rejecting settlement, sanctions threatening resistance, rebellion defying sanctions, persecution coercing both rebels and loyal, in a remorseless *crescendo* of cause and effect, that, until the length of this half-century reign had convinced everyone that the Anglican pattern in education had come to stay and had stabilized the relative positions of all the parties involved, contemporaries were dominated by its sheer chronology. Not till 1603, with State policy set, on the coming of a new Stuart dynasty, and the enduring Catholic resistance equally set, either in exile abroad or underground at home, did the sequence of events themselves cease to be the major determinant and allow a recognizable situation to emerge.

But we today can discern in the Elizabethan events two phases: grouping and waiting, followed by coercion and resistance. The line of division is the year 1580–1, the year of the Jesuit mission and of Parliament's first really persecuting Act.

The educational policy of the later Tudors was quite clearly determined by their religious policy. The declared need for religious uniformity in troublous times implied that there must be no freedom of thought on religion; and this in turn postulated that there should be no freedom of instruction in the schools. In an age of deep religiosity such a policy was of course bound to fail. Its extreme sanction—trial and execution for treason—found hundreds of staunch believers ready to defy the law in the name of a higher sanction still. It also drove so much of the educated class abroad that it impoverished the country.

The terms of reference for all that was to follow lie in the two major Acts of Parliament whereby the queen, in her first year 1558–9, sought a workable religious settlement. They were put through as soon as Parliament had made over to the new queen all that the Chantries Acts had granted to Edward VI and dissolved all the monastic houses that had returned under Mary.[1]

The Act of Supremacy (April) required from every person, before proceeding to a university degree, an oath renouncing all papal authority, acknowledging the royal supremacy, and subscribing to the Articles of the Church of England. Here there was a loophole, duly exploited by Catholics and Puritans even after it was removed in 1581 and 1588; that, as the oath was to be taken at the end of the course, it was still possible for the recusant to follow the university course itself if he could find a college and a tutor sufficiently lenient.

The Act of Uniformity (May) was more searching. It was aimed at two cardinal points of the Catholic religion: the unity of the Church, and the Mass. Its framers knew well that no Catholic subject could obey it with a clear conscience.[2] It is the operation of this Act that proves the subsequent persecution to have been religious and not political; for the law was an inroad on conscience, and many condemned priests and schoolmasters were offered their lives, at the very last moment, on the scaffold, if they would conform. From now on, faced with the oaths, a priest could refuse, and resign, and live as a layman; or apostatize, by accepting the new order; or compromise, by outward conformity; or refuse and be deprived, and go about saying Mass secretly and living on the charity of Catholics or by clandestine teaching.

But these were the only two penal statutes till 1563, and their operation was not at first severe. For a time, Catholic laity could still

[1] See above, p. 20. The dissolutions concerned Dartford, Sheen (Carthusians, who went to Bruges), Greenwich, St. Bartholomew's, Smithfield, Westminster and Syon (Brigettines, who went to Termonde). Cf. H. N. Birt, *Eliz. Relig. Settlement* (1907), 67, 71. A contemporary Memorandum (*Hist. MSS. Comm.*, Salisbury MS., i. 163) sets out the 'considerable' business to be done in this Parliament, including two purely educational items: that none below the rank of baron should keep a schoolmaster in his house, and that children of the nobility should be educated (at home in the universities, or abroad) from twelve till eighteen.

[2] The form of the oath is in N. Wood, 58 note. The main studies of the Penal Laws are: John Starkey's *Abstract* (1675); B.M.Add.MSS. 17,022; Anstey, *Guide to the Laws of England affecting Roman Catholics* (1842); R. R. Madden, *History of the Penal Laws enacted against Roman Catholics* (1847); Lilly-Wallis, *Manual of Law specially affecting Roman Catholics* (1893).

leave the country and retain their property (provided they did not go to Rome).[1]

In achieving the supremacy and uniformity in practice, the educational agencies of greatest weight were obviously the two universities. As power-houses of opinion they would be allies for the Crown if once secured. Cambridge had already contributed to the Reformation more than Oxford. Every Archbishop of Canterbury from Warham to Abbot (except Pole), and most of the Elizabethan bishops in their turn, were Cambridge men. Oxford's loss now, through expulsions and withdrawals, was accordingly the greater.

The visitation of Oxford was led by Sir William Cecil, that of Cambridge by Sir Thomas Parry. College by college was examined. Little evidence is forthcoming as to undergraduates (possibly because they had no emoluments worth seizing), but the ejection of heads of colleges and senior fellows was on a heavy scale.[2] Certainly the purge was sufficiently thorough for there to be no further *royal* visitation of either university during the reign. The queen appeared content to leave the religious discipline of the universities to the Ecclesiastical Commission, the vice-chancellors, the college heads and the bishops.

[1] A. O. Meyer, *England and the Catholic Church under Queen Elizabeth* (transl. J. R. McKee, 1916), 29–31.

[2] There is a summary of the findings, College by College, in Birt, ch. 7. As to scholars extruded:

The *Oxford* deprivations included Richard Marshall (Dean of Christ Church), Drs. Tresham and Richard Smith (Christ Church), Thomas Reynolds (Warden of Merton), Dr. Coveney (President of Magdalen), William Chedsey (President of Corpus), Dr. Wright (Master of Balliol), John Smith (Provost of Oriel), Hugh Hodgson (Provost of Queen's), Henry Henshaw (Rector of Lincoln), Thomas Slythurst (President of Trinity), Alexander Belsire (President of St. John's) and his successors William Eyre and William Stocke, William Marshall (Principal of St. Alban's Hall), James Dugdale (Master of University), Seth Holland (Warden of All Souls'). See Dom Bede Camm, in *The Month* (London, 1907), cx. 21.

At *Cambridge*, Thomas Peacock was displaced at Queens' College by William May, John Christopherson at Trinity by William Bill, Thomas Cosyn at St. Catherine's by Joseph May, William Taylor at Christ's by Edward Hawford, George Bullock at St. John's by James Pilkington, John Young at Pembroke by Edward Grindal, William Mowse at Trinity Hall by Henry Harvey, John Redman at Jesus by Edward Gascoigne. The Marian head of Corpus, Joseph Pory, stayed. See Mullinger, ii. 170f., 176f.

The list sent by Nicholas Sander to Cardinal Moroni in May 1561 gives Oxford's losses as six College Heads, five fellows who said the visitation was heretical and ten priests and six fellows from New College alone, together with the lay professor of Greek Literature (Dr. Etheridge) and many other laymen, of whom fourteen had gone overseas. Only ten of the Choir of 100 had made their (Anglican) Easter Communion. Sander's list for Cambridge gives four heads of Colleges and sixteen priests from Trinity (*Cath. Record Soc.* i. 3–4). Anthony à Wood's estimate was twenty-two from New College, Oxford, and five from Trinity (*Annals*, ii. 144–5).

Most of the evidence for the effect of the Acts on the universities comes from these individual episcopal visitations during the next decade. The Bishop of Winchester visited New College, Magdalen and Corpus, at Oxford, in 1561, and Merton in 1565. The Bishop of Ely visited St. John's, Cambridge, in 1565. King's College, Cambridge, had a visitation from the Bishop of London in 1565. Its Provost, Dr. Philip Baker, was reported to have much 'popish stuff'. On the first occasion the bishop admonished but did not dispossess him. On a second visitation he fled. Midway between these two visitations Corpus was searched for popish books, especially because students and tutors were known to ridicule their new Latin prayer book. When a descent on Exeter College, Oxford, in 1569 found nobody forthcoming to denounce the Catholics known to be there, the Visitors clapped the sub-rector (William Wyat) into gaol. The following year, the rector himself (John Neale) was expelled for refusing to attend the Anglican service in the college.

Resistance was recurrent, too, among the students. The Spanish ambassador reported home in May 1560 that 'Oxford students, and law students in London, have been taken in great numbers. They have also arrested those that came to my house on Easter Day to hear Mass.' Six Oxford students were sent to the Tower the following November for resisting the removal of a crucifix from the college chapel.[1]

The double pressure, visitation and expulsion, of course produced double result—impoverishment and emigration.

The impoverishment is well attested. Catholics were officially barred; the poor could not go up; the rich (as yet) were tempted to look more to trade as being lucrative. At Oxford in 1561 there were only eight degrees in arts, three in physics, one in law and none at all in theology, since Scholasticism was out of favour and nothing had yet been put in its place. The unattached (non-collegiate) student was disappearing likewise; there were only eighty-nine of him by 1562, and practically none by 1600.[2]

The emigration is academically saddening to watch: 'the very flower of the two universities . . . carried away, as it were by a storm, and scattered in foreign lands',[3] in a stream that was to continue well

[1] For the visitations, N. Wood, 118ff.; J. H. Pollen, *English Catholics in the Reign of Elizabeth* (1920), 252ff., and 65, 99 for citations from *Spanish Calendar*.

[2] Cf. Mullinger, *Cambridge*, ii. 200ff.; Mallet, *Oxford*, ii. 122.

[3] Nicholas Sander, *Rise and Growth of the Anglican Schism* (1585), ed. David Lewis (1877), 261.

into the next century, albeit remaining as English as if its exile had never occurred.

It is tempting to see parallels between the Catholic exile movement from England to the Continent and the migration of Continental Protestant exiles into England. But the differences were even greater. Considered as political currents, the English Catholic exiles were divided, as we shall see, and never united on the practical question of *how* the counter-attack should be effected: whereas the Continental Protestants were homogeneous in their determination to undermine their own home governments. From the standpoint of the economic historian, again, the English Catholic exiles were a cross-section of the population, where the Continental refugees coming to England were mostly artisans; the English workman stood to suffer from the influx, the French and Flemish and Spanish worker never. Thirdly, the scale of the movements did not tally; at most 3,000 Catholics escaped from England, but in their place there arrived as many as 150,000 Protestants from the mainland of Europe.[1]

The Catholic exiles retired across the Channel, the first of them in the autumn of 1559 immediately upon the two Acts, to a centre of learning famous since the early Renaissance, when it had known Luis Vives; warm to Englishmen through its association with the late Lord Chancellor Thomas More, whose execution for refusing the oath of supremacy had shocked all Europe twenty-four years before; and conveniently close to England should the new regime prove short-lived. This was Louvain. Two houses, called nostalgically Oxford and Cambridge, were opened. For the next few years Louvain was to be the centre of English Catholic university scholarship and apologetics.

Their leader at first was Nicholas Sander, of Winchester and New College, founder of the Louvain school of apologetics, author later of a primary source book, *The Rise and Progress of the Anglican Schism.* To Louvain Oxford lost its Regius professor of divinity (William Soane), its vice-chancellor (Francis Babington), its reader in Greek (John Bavant of St. John's), its proctor from Oriel (Richard Barrett) and dozens of college fellows, including over twenty from New College led by Owen Lewis. Cambridge lost Richard Hall of Pembroke, John Seton of St. John's, Thomas Bailey the Master of Clare Hall, George Bullock the Master of St. John's, Thomas Sedgwick the Regius professor of divinity and many more. These are all names of distinction in university history. They were but the first losses.

[1] Cf. the analysis in *American Cath. Hist. Review*, xl. 4 (1929).

To this nucleus came individual scholars constrained by any of a variety of academic reasons: some because in resigning their fellowships they were then debarred from their M.A. on grounds of recusancy (as Jasper Heywood of Merton); some from the frustration of having to fall back on tutoring in a private school (as James Fenn of Corpus Christi College, Oxford). And the trek continued almost until the French Revolution. The first English Catholic priest of modern times educated entirely in England was not born till 1771.[1]

While it is doubtful whether the total of these educational exiles at any time exceeded 3,000, their influence on English literature at large, quite apart from their contribution to the theological literature of apologetics, was considerable. Their educational campaign began as early as 1564, with the books of Richard Smith and Nicholas Sander, printed in Flanders and smuggled over to England. How far the reorganized press censorship in England and the injunctions of the Ecclesiastical Commission were ineffectual is shown not only by the Star Chamber decrees that tried to enforce them (1566, 1586), but by the need for eight royal proclamations on the subject of illicit books.[2] When in 1566 Parliament legislated against the Louvain writers, the result was only to add to their company. Sander himself put their total output from Louvain in these early years at 20,000 copies. Their historian puts the total for the whole reign at over 200 different works,[3] despite risks and costs (the Douay New Testament of 1582 cost over £3,000 in modern sterling). Perhaps their most subtle influence in England was that, being one side of a burning religious controversy, they impelled readers of the other side to read them also, and sometimes to be persuaded by them.

The religious settlement, then, had lamentable effects on the universities. By contrast, the treatment of schoolmasters, the mainstay

[1] James Simkiss. See F. C. Husenbeth, *Sedgley Park* (1856), 75. The major study of the effects of 1558–9 on the universities is that by C. M. J. F. Swan (1956). An excellent introduction is ch. 2 of A. C. Southern, *Elizabethan Recusant Prose, 1559–82* (1950). In addition to the first expulsions (p. 30, above), seven leading Oxford men who went to the German College in Rome are listed in *Stonyhurst MSS.*, Anglia IV, i. c. f. 211 (i.e. Greene's Collectanea C). A complete list of the English exiles who became Jesuits (sixty-two by 1599) is in Deplace, 77–9. Lists of Catholic fellows at Oxford under Elizabeth (totalling over 100) are also in *Ushaw Magazine*, Dec. 1910 and Mar. 1912, and in *Downside Review*, xxxii. 41–68 (1913).

[2] R. Steele, *Tudor and Stuart Proclamations* (1910); N. Wood, 237f.

[3] A. C. Southern, 31; and 45ff. for a study of the leading writers, Sander and six other Wykehamists: Thomas Dorman, Thomas Harding, John Martiall, Robert Pointz, John Rastell and Thomas Stapleton.

of the educational system at large, was lenient. The licence to teach was reimposed, but, for the first four years, without the oath. This may have been due to a fear lest, as the new Archbishop of Canterbury, Matthew Parker, was to find with his clergy,[1] wholesale expulsions should deplete the grammar schools before successors trained in Anglicanism could be produced.

Now, there *were* ejections of schoolmasters before the oath was made obligatory for them in 1563. The grounds for ejection lie in the royal injunctions of 1559, which laid down that 'no man shall take upon him to teach but such as shall be allowed by the Ordinary, and found meet as well for his learning and dexterity in teaching as for sober and honest conversation, and also for right understanding of God's true religion'.[2]

How many schoolmasters were ejected? Certainly many must have conformed, according to the waiting policy adopted by the Catholics until long after the excommunication; for the previous two reigns had been unforeseeably short, and this queen also might not endure. Many other schoolmasters no doubt disappeared discreetly. For the rest, when the Ecclesiastical Commissioners were given extended powers against Catholics in 1561, and the prison lists began to swell, it would be a fair inference that schoolmasters were amongst the public notabilities most easily identified and dealt with. But the evidence is not extensive.

There are, to begin with, three spectacular cases long well known: Eton, Winchester and Durham.

At Eton, the Catholic provost, Dr. Henry Cole, had been replaced in July 1559 by Dr. William Bull, upon whose death just two years later the queen was highly displeased to find that the fellows had elected to succeed him Dr. Bruerne. A visitation was therefore carried out forthwith by the Archbishop of Canterbury (Parker) and Bishop Horne of Winchester. It ordered the expulsion of three fellows and a chaplain, the resignation of Dr. Bruerne and the ultimate nomination of Dr. William Day by the commissioners from a short-list prepared

[1] In 1559 there were about 9,000 parishes (Creighton said 9,410, Strype 8,911), and about 7,500 clergy. The total deprivations were estimated by Dom Norbert Birt at 700 (*Eliz. Religious Settlement*, 124, 161–2, 191, 203). This figure has been challenged by other historians—see details in A. O. Meyer, 29 note. The lowest estimate is that of Camden, i.e. 181; the next lowest that of H. Gee, *Elizabethan Clergy* (1898), i.e. 200. Parker's complaint, to Grindal, in 1560, on the shortage of educated Protestant clergy, is in his *Correspondence*, p. 120.

[2] Frere, iii. 21; and quoted in N. Wood, 57.

by the fellows. This saved face all round, and allowed the Protestant reform of Eton to proceed.[1]

At Winchester the scholars themselves mutinied against the new religious services outright, in 1559. Troops were called in from Southampton, and the headmaster, Thomas Hyde, was arrested.

> When the headmaster was in prison, and the schismatical master called them to the schismatical sermons, they were so far from obeying that they kept away even from the public prayers, and shut themselves up in their dormitories. When he found fault with their disobedience, they asked if he wished to destroy the souls of innocents. Then when the master attempted force and called in the military commander from the nearest seaport, about twelve of the boys took to flight; the rest, influenced by the prevalent terror, went most unwillingly to the church.[2]

At Durham, the other case of open disturbance, the master William Thewles was likewise deprived and harassed.[3]

To these three, the papers of Nicholas Sander add nine more: Freeman of St. Paul's, who, when faced with expulsion, was told by his wife that 'ego pro utroque nostrum mendicabo'; Harris of Bristol Grammar School, formerly secretary to Sir Thomas More; Bennett of Salisbury; Sebastian 'qui organa pulsabat' in St. Paul's; John Fenn of Bury St. Edmunds, a Wykehamist and fellow of New College; William Good of Wells Cathedral Grammar School; Thomas Iveson of Durham; Thomas Plumtree of Lincoln and John Potts of Leicester.[4]

Only one of these nine, Thomas Iveson, was a veteran. He had been master of Giggleswick School as far back as the time of Henry VIII. Of Bennett and Sebastian nothing further can be gleaned for certain;

[1] The visitation is dealt with in Birt, 203ff., and in L. Cust, *Eton College* (1899), 35. The career of Dr. Henry Cole is obscure thereafter. He may well be the Dr. Henry Cole of Yeling (Ealing), Middx., in the Recusant Returns of 1577, given as 'doctor of law, littell or nothing worth' (*Cath. Record Soc.*, xxii. 47). On the other hand, his imprisonment after 1560 (see *D.N.B.*) may have lasted till his death, which occurred about 1580.

[2] Nicholas Sander, Report to Cardinal Moroni, 1561, in *Cath. Record Soc.* i. 45–6. The two visitations which the bishop carried out following the Winchester meeting (1562, 1571) are in Frere, iii. 131–3 and 327. Thomas Hyde had himself been educated at Winchester before going to New College. Sander reports him as still in prison in 1561 (*C.R.S.* i. 21, 44). He is listed as a priest at the English College, Douay, in 1568 (*C.R.S.* ix. 65). In 1580 he set out from Douay for the English mission, with four other priests (Worthington, Jonson, Hemsworth and Ostliff) (T. F. Knox, ed., *Second Douay Diary*, London (1878), 160). According to *D.N.B.* he died at Douay in 1597.

[3] N. Wood, 44f.

[4] The first four from Sander to Moroni, in *C.R.S.* i. 21, 44. The others from his *De Visibili Monarchia Ecclesiae* (1571), reprinted in Tierney-Dodd, *Church History* (1839), ii. appdx. 44, p. cccxvii f.; also in H. Gee, *Elizabethan Clergy*, 229, and in N. Wood, 271ff., whose study includes no others.

and of Plumtree only that he was martyred at Durham in January 1569. The others are all known to have gone abroad. They have well-attested careers in the later colleges in exile.[1]

From elsewhere in contemporary and later sources thirteen further schoolmasters emerge who were dispossessed before the key-year 1563. But they come from important schools: Shrewsbury, Winchester (the usher John Marshall), Blackburn (Lawrence Yates), Grange-over-Sands (Thomas Somers), Ripon (Edmund Browne), Preston (Peter Carter), Tideswell (Nicholas Garlick), Hampton (Richard Alcocke), Stratford-on-Avon (John Cottam), Brentwood (John Greenwood), Wolverhampton (Madox), Chichester (Robert Owing) and Thomas Cotham from 'a grammar school in London'.

Though these 25 men are the only ones that can be documented, they are assuredly not the whole story of pre-1563 deprivations. 'The same may be understood', said Sander laconically, 'of many others.' None the less, the treatment of the schools in those first four years was relatively mild. The presumptive reasons for the leniency (given above) are strengthened by collateral evidence such as the lament of the Speaker of the House of Commons at the end of 1563, on the want of schools and schoolmasters, and the contrast between prevailing ignorance and the flourishing condition of learning in the past. It is somewhat surprising, therefore, that the oath was clapped on all schoolmasters at this point, unless one bears in mind the plot of Cardinal Pole's nephews that preceded it, and the Privy Council's dismay when the returns to an inquiry about the justices of the peace revealed that so many of them were enemies of the new regime.[2]

The Act of 1563 extended the oath to 'all schoolmasters and public and private teachers of children and all manner of persons that have taken or hereafter shall take any degree of learning in the Common Laws'. Refusal to take the oath at the third time of asking was to rank

[1] Such information as has come to light about these men, and *all* other Catholic schoolmasters to be mentioned from here on, is in my *Biographical Catalogue of Catholic Schoolmasters at Work in England, 1558–1700, with an Index of Places* (*Recusant History*, 1964).

[2] In Shropshire all but six of the J.Ps. were. Durham replies added two special hindrances to the spread of Protestantism: 'Scottishe preistes that are fledde out of Scotland for their wickednes and here be hyred in parisshes on the borders bicause they take lesse wages than other'; and 'the grete number of scholars borne hereabout now lieng at lovan [Louvain] without lycense, and sending in bokes and letters which cause many tymes evill rumours to be spredde and disquiet the people. They be mayntained by the hospitals of the newcastell and the wealthiest of this towne and this shire.' (Text in *Camden Miscellany IX*, Camden Soc. vol. liv, *passim*; 1895.) For the plot, see Conyers Read, *Walsingham* (1925), ii. 273.

as treason. No special machinery was established to enforce these provisions; and, on the assumption that it was left to the Ecclesiastical Commission and the bishops, the fact that Norwich provides the only diocesan injunctions issued between then and 1570 shows the enforcement to have been very slight until the excommunication of Elizabeth seven years later.[1] It is indeed inherently probable that the oath would be tendered to all newcomers to the teaching profession, but much less often to existing masters unless they had made themselves individually objectionable to the bishop.

Thus far, then, the policy of the State towards the Catholic schools seems to be defensive. Regulations were enacted, but held in reserve, not demanding more than outward conformity, and fairly easy to evade. Catholic masters in 'lenient' areas could still give a Catholic education; Catholic parents accordingly were still using the grammar schools; and the new State policy had little effect at all as yet upon the Catholic nobility, who in any case educated their children at home by means of tutors.

What changed this situation suddenly and radically was the impact on the Government of two events within one and the same year 1569–70: the rising of the Northern Earls and the excommunication of Elizabeth. The first of these alone would have provoked a blaze of recusant-hunting. The second made it determined, and became the basis of Elizabeth's later policy of treating all Catholics as potential traitors. It also divided the Catholics, for they were left in doubt for years to come how far Pope Pius V expected his Bull 'Regans in excelsis' really to be acted on.[2] When the Ridolfi plot broke less than a year later, repression turned to persecution.

The cues for the repression from now on lie in the new Anglican Canons of 1571 and the new (fourth) penal Act of the same year. The Government had crystallized a threefold policy: to enforce conformity, to stamp out Catholic schools at home and to prevent any leakage abroad to the colleges the exiles had begun to create.

The new Canons covered the whole country. The injunctions that followed them were accordingly more standardized and centralized than ever before. Dean Nowell's new *Catechism*, put into English by Thomas Norton the previous year, was prescribed for all schools.

[1] N. Wood, 274; and T. F. Knox, *Douay Diaries* (1878), xviii, on the contemporary evidence of the Bridgewater *Concertatio*.

[2] One of the best contemporary commentaries on this situation is the *Responsum* of Robert Persons, S.J. See also Pollen, 157, 297; Meyer, 124ff.

Henceforth, in some schools, it was a qualification for entry; and it was universally the basis for Anglican religious instruction in the grammar schools. Here, too, lies one of the clearest sources of the local Catholic resistance movement. Many who had been fairly content to conform outwardly by going to church, even after the Bull, now drew the line: especially since mere outward conformity was now incomparably more difficult to preserve, in terms of the new Canon making a knowledge of the Catechism a prerequisite for Communion. Grindal's injunctions at Canterbury ordered registers to be kept of all communicants, Sunday classes for all between the ages of six and twenty who proved defective in catechism, and punishments for their parents. Schoolmasters were to teach nothing derogatory 'to the religion now set forth by public authority', nor to use any books tending thereto; nor to 'propound to their scholars any themes, vulgar or subtle questions whereby matters of religion, concluded or established, might be made doubtful unto them, or they induced to deride or scoff at any godly order, rite or ceremony now set forth and allowed'. To the oath of 1563 was added complete subscription to the Thirty-Nine Articles.[1]

But the great portent was the Act of 1571 'against fugitives over the sea'. No more the freedom of travel throughout Christendom which had characterized medieval English scholarship. No one might leave the country without licence, on pain of forfeiting all property; and those already fled abroad must return within a fixed time and conform. This Act cut the bond between England and the Catholic exiles. They were excluded from all successive amnesties, and the Government began to compile lists of their names and habitats.

For the first time, in short, there was now a *general* hunt for papists, spurred on as regards the schools by the resistance to the Nowell *Catechism*, and as regards the universities by the electric effect of Sander's *De Monarchia*, with a background of fear created by the Massacre of St. Batholomew in France in August 1572. The queen immediately sent letters to the lords lieutenant asking for the names of *all* absentees from church: the beginning of the road that was to lead ultimately to the seizure of their children for forcible education at Protestant hands. The year after that produced the first Tyburn martyrs. The next added an astute move intended to disperse the exiles altogether. Elizabeth and Philip II concluded an agreement whereby they would expel each other's fugitives. The Spanish authorities in the

[1] Text of the Canons in Wilkins, iv. Cf. N. Wood, 63, 148, 172.

Netherlands began to act on it at once, by rounding up English Catholics, but a year later the Governor, Don John, allowed them to trickle back for lack of reciprocal action in England.[1]

The adroit idea of adding a fourth element to the royal sanctions of force, six years after the Act and Canons of 1571, seems to have come from the Bishop of London, John Aylmer. In June 1577 he urged Mr. Secretary Walsingham to supersede imprisonment by fines, since imprisonment, 'by sparing their housekeeping, greatly relieveth them'. A month later the Privy Council itself acted. Measures were taken to remove all 'corrupt schoolmasters', that every bishop should at once prepare a list of the recusants in his diocese, and that there should be an enquiry into the actual teaching of recusants' children.[2] It was these decisions that resulted in the great recusant 'census' of 1577–8, the first on a national scale and the most revealing single document till the Recusant [Fine] Rolls of 1592 onwards.[3]

By 1580, then, when a Catholic revival began upon the arrival of the Jesuit missioners Campion and Persons, the policy of the Elizabethan Court and Council was set. We turn therefore to inquire next how Catholic education in exile had fared: i.e. to the College Movement.

2. THE FOUNDATION OF THE COLLEGES ABROAD

The twin-founders of that movement are William Cardinal Allen and the Jesuit Robert Persons. Allen came of gentle birth, his pedigree drawn from Rossall in Lancashire and Westby in Yorkshire; Persons was the son of a Somerset blacksmith. Allen had been educated at home till he was fifteen; Persons had gone to the parish school at Stogursey and then, for three or four years, to Taunton School. Allen had graduated at Oriel under the tutorship of Morgan Phillips (still associated with him as late as 1579–80, in the founding of the English College at Rome), and had become Principal of St. Mary's Hall in 1556. He had resigned four years later and gone to Louvain. Persons, who also passed through St. Mary's Hall, becoming bursar and dean of the college in 1572, took the oath of supremacy twice. When he in turn left the country (1574) he was received into the Catholic Church at

[1] Guilday, 12.

[2] *S.P. Dom. Eliz.* cxiv. 22, xlv. 21, cxiv. 68. N. Wood's view (p. 290) that the immediate cause was the influx of seminary priests from Douay is hardly tenable, for only forty-four had yet arrived, too few to have prompted the large-scale enactment now made.

[3] The Returns of 1577 (*S.P. Dom. Eliz.* vols. 117ff.) are printed in *C.R.S.* xxii.

Louvain, and then continued on to Rome to enter the Society of Jesus.

The work of these two men was in fact the beginning of modern English Catholic education; the first step in a policy which, at the outset nothing more definite than one of training priests in exile to return to England as missioners, became through pressure of events an educational policy at large, for clergy and laity, supported in time by preparatory schools at home and abroad specially directed towards the higher education given in the colleges, and destined to have profound influence on Catholic education in the nineteenth century after the return home.

The guiding hand was that of William Allen himself, until his death in 1594: at all levels, from the preparation of the Rheims-Douay Bible as a counterblast to the English Protestant Scriptures, down to the education in preparatory schools abroad of exile boys arriving too young or ill-lettered for the colleges.

Allen's aim in founding the great English College at Douay in 1568 has been variously assessed, but all the assessments have been too sharp and too exclusive.[1] One reason for this is the absence of any statutes for this mother-college for some time to come. It is part of Allen's glory that he was able to govern the college for the twenty years of his presidency without Constitutions at all, though it was a pontifical college directly obedient to the Holy See. It had affiliations to Douay University, among the limiting conditions of which were that the college students should not take Douay degrees. For the rest, while the Holy See appointed the president and carried out visitations, it left the administration to the personal rule of Allen, who himself wrote that 'there is neither oath nor statute nor other bridle nor chastisement', since the very diversity of the students would have made any 'minute code of rules' impossible. There were none in fact till 1600.

The best evidence of his intentions is Allen's own, in his letters; and the most representative of these is a long draft of 'Instructions for the erecting Seminaries' which he offered to the Bishop of Tournai (Dr. Vendeville) some ten years later, in the context of the migration of

[1] E.g. an 'Oxford overseas' (B. Ward, *St. Edmund's Coll.* (1893), ch. iv, and W. F. Hastings, *Education of English Catholics*, Lond. Univ. thesis 1923, 15); a joint Anglo-Fleming seminary (Pollen, 246 and note); not intended to send priests to England (Persons, *Memoirs*, in *C.R.S.* ii. 190—contradicting ibid. ii. 96); 'centralization of all English scholars in exile' pending return or re-establishment of Catholicism (Guilday, 64–5); 'a seminary to meet the need for educating Catholic youth, the purpose of which gradually shaped itself as a training college for secular priests' (J. E. Neale, *Q. Elizabeth* (1934), 249); to provide priests against the extinction, in time, of the old Marian clergy (Deplace, 55).

Douay College to Rheims, and the creation of a second English College in Rome. Allen's letters leave no doubt that the college was a seminary for priests; that its products were destined for the English mission after ordination; that lay students were not excluded; and that it would continue the work begun at Louvain, of what he was to call later a 'College of Writers'.

At the start, it would have been impossible to formulate this. For the founders were at the mercy of circumstances. They had no power to limit the range of exiles arriving, some with vocations and some with none, all at intense personal risk from Elizabeth's pursuivants, all needing education, those able to pay acceptable more than ever, and few in a position to be turned away. The ultimate shape of the educational system in exile was to be determined as much perhaps by the needs of the entrants as by prior policy in the minds of the founders. How well this was foreseen by Allen is manifest in his letters. There were to be gathered, under one and the same roof, 'the choicest wits from the universities'; theological students; 'gentlemen's sons who were studying humanities, philosophy or jurisprudence and who . . . were moved by the fame of the seminary to seek here a Catholic education'; and even heretics.[1]

The first men who came to England from this college in the Rue Blanc-Rosier at Douay were the precursors of a total that was to comprise one cardinal, 33 archbishops and bishops, 169 writers and 160 martyrs.[2] In his dealings with the founder generations Allen consistently preserved a distinction between religion and politics. Even after the martyrdom of Campion (1582) and the later penal legislation, he realized that 'priests whom he was training for the English mission must keep altogether clear of political action if they were to win souls for God. . . . Accordingly, in their training for England, all questions relating to the Pope's power of excommunicating and deposing princes were wholly omitted from the college course.'[3]

[1] Allen's Latin Memorandum to Vendeville is in T. F. Knox, *Letters and Memorials of Cardinal Allen* (1882), 52–67, and esp. 54, 58, 61–2. His statement of 'intentions' (in English) is quoted in Southern, *Engl. Recusant Prose*, 18–20. The most accurate of the summaries in the monograph literature is that of C. J. Destombes, *Persécution Religieuse en Angleterre sous les Successeurs d'Elizabeth* (1864), 163.

[2] They have had no more moving tribute than that of the German Protestant historian A. O. Meyer (p. 110). For the location of the college in Douay see Dancoisne, xviii note. The house belonged to the Hospital of Notre Dame.

[3] Knox, *Letters and Memorials*, xxx. A letter from Sander to Allen in 1577 (in *S.P. Dom. Eliz.* cxviii) could imply that he had become a 'politician' as early as that. But not in the colleges. See Allen's *Apologia of the two English Colleges* (1581).

Such were the aims of the English College at Douay. That it was not the first of the Tridentine seminaries has already been demonstrated.[1] But its formative influence amongst them was profound. Philip II of Spain directed Vendeville in 1578 to model his own new seminary for the Netherlands upon it; more than one bishop wrote to the president for particulars of his Tridentine system; in 1579 letters arrived from the Bishop of Ross, in Scotland, asking for the college statutes so that he could use them in a project of himself and the Bishop of Glasgow for a Scots College in Paris; and Vendeville was hopeful that his own countrymen might be 'added to' the Douay College 'to get the benefit of the same course and the stimulation of their example'.[2]

Douay College meant that the Catholic educational counter-attack now had a base. How the college was organized and sustained, and how it ranks in the history of education, we have to examine later.

But as a base it was highly exposed: conveniently near to England, yet in danger of being destroyed amid the periodical turbulence of the Spanish Low Countries. Within ten years, indeed, it had to emigrate to France for a spell. For trouble began from a fresh quarter, the anti-Spanish insurgents in and around Douay, who first spread rumours of a sort to prompt the magistrates to search the college for arms, and then more insidious rumours (of Elizabethan threats to the Belgian bishops unless the college were expelled), so that Douay University ordered them away. They left, for Rheims, in 1578 in a most macabre Palm Sunday procession. Classes were re-opened at Rheims in the Rue Barbâtre. The pope promised to pay the cost of their return to Douay when times should improve. During the fifteen years the college stayed in Rheims its numbers soared, to 112, in its 'permanent' home of the Collège des Bons Enfants, whence issued the Douay-Rheims New Testament in English.[3]

Such troubles being not difficult to foresee, Allen had a still 'safer', if more distant base in mind from early on, in the ancient English Hospice in the Eternal City of Rome itself.

This hospice in Rome carried legends going back to King Ine of Wessex. Its career is documented by its foundation–deed of 1362 and

[1] See p. 15 above.

[2] See respectively Vendeville to Allen, in Knox, *Letters and Memorials*, 46; Guilday, 78; Second Douay Diary (Knox), 157; Vandeville to Viglius, 1568, in Knox, *Douay Diaries*, xxviii.

[3] Knox, *Douay Diaries*, passim.

charters running from Innocent III to Sixtus IV in 1478. It was known as the 'Schola Anglorum', and its obligation was to give hospitality to English pilgrims. Funds from England had been cut off in 1534 upon Henry VIII assuming the royal supremacy. Dr. Morris Clynog of Oxford and (nearly) the see of Bangor under Mary, became its 'custos' in 1565 under papal guardianship, with eighteen Marian refugee priests.[1]

Attempts had been made in the early Louvain days to turn this Rome hospice into a college; and again in the very year of Douay College, 1568, on the grounds that the revenues were now being depleted by very few pilgrims and that many of the exiles were homeless, wherefore the hospice should either become a college and take them in or else send funds to the Low Countries.[2]

Allen matured his plans—for the former of these two alternatives—when he was in Rome in 1576. On his return to Douay just before its exile to Rheims, he sent to Rome two men, William Holt and Ralph Standish, 'to join the proposed College'. By the end of that year there were ten there from Douay, and they were already being joined by other intending priests who had come direct. The Cardinal Protector of England, Moroni, issued an 'Instruction' for the reception of six students at the hospice, but eighteen months later there were twenty-six, a 'colony sent from the Douay Seminary'. The prefect of studies and the procurator were Jesuits, borrowed for the purpose by the pope from the Jesuit General.[3]

And therefore trouble. Allen himself was pleased. His relations with the Society, by contrast with those of Cardinal Pole, had been consistently cordial from the time he had first met Edward Mercurian (later the General) at Louvain in 1561.[4] But not everyone shared his satisfaction. Trouble between the Jesuits and the secular clergy—later to become the bane of English Catholic history in penal times to an incredible degree—was soon to erupt.

[1] Past studies of the English Hospice in Rome, Cardinal A. Gasquet's *Venerable English College* (1920) and H. E. G. Rope, *The Schola Saxonum* (1951), are now superseded by *The English Hospice in Rome*, Sexcentenary Number of *The Venerabile* (organ of the Ven. Eng. Coll. Rome), pp. 306 (1962).

[2] See letter, of either Allen or Clynog (?), 1568 from internal evidence, in *C.R.S.* ix. 49, 51, 61; and A. Kenny in *The Eng. Hospice in Rome* (*Venerabile*, 1961, 225).

[3] Knox, *Douay Diaries*, 25; J. H. Pollen, *Unpubl. Docs. of the English Martyrs*, ii. 462; Gregory Martin to Campion, quoted by B. Towers in *Ushaw Magazine*, March 1910.

[4] His letter of thanks to the General is in Deplace, 57. For his early friendship with the Jesuits see L. J. Hicks in *The Month*, clx (1932).

In the college now coming into existence in Rome the cause was at first a national feud among the students and staff. The student population in 1579 was thirty-three English and seven Welsh. The rector, Dr. Morris Clynog, a Welshman, had been appointed on the advice of Owen Lewis, another Welshman and Allen's right-hand man in the Roman project. Unsuited by personality for handling the different outlooks of the students, as Allen had been able to do so consummately at Douay, the rector showed an alleged partiality that provoked a memorial from the English students in which they went so far as to declare that it was 'as difficult for a Welshman to treat an Englishman fairly as it is for a Moor to act considerately towards a Spaniard'. They demanded a Jesuit rector in Clynog's place. Allen wrote to Lewis from Douay begging for some statesmanship in handling the situation. In default of redress the English students revolted and left the college. Townsfolk of Rome gave them large alms for their long journey back to Douay; the Jesuits appealed for them in the pulpits; the aged Dr. Goldwell, Bishop of St. Asaph, interceded for them with the pope. They had certainly put themselves in the wrong by revolting over a highly dubious issue—their support of a scapegrace visitor, Anthony Munday, who had outstayed his statutory eight days as a pilgrim and broken all the rules. In the end a settlement was reached by which the students themselves elected as rector the Jesuit Fr. Alphonso Agazzari and the pope appointed him. This gave great satisfaction to Allen. But the happy future he now foresaw did not materialize, through what can only be described as a Jesuit-complex, in which the historians have since joined.

On the one hand, the appointment of a Jesuit rector gave a handle to those who believed, with Owen Lewis, that the Society of Jesus was out to capture all the English colleges as fast as they were founded. The echoes of this charge were to reverberate for generations. Against it can be argued that the Jesuits did not want the rectorship, and that the fear expressed by others, that Jesuit control of the college would mean a loss to the English mission, is not borne out by the figures: for in the first seventeen years 303 students were ordained at the Venerable English College, of whom only thirty-one later became Jesuits—and of these, all but eight were sent to England.

In the second place, the episode produced an anti-Jesuit tradition especially in Wales. The college authorities, regarding Welsh students as fomenters of trouble, tended to look twice before admitting them. This meant a diminished output to Rome and Douay from an educationally handicapped Wales, whereby 'Wales was allowed to drift, by imperceptible degrees, away from the Catholic faith', and priests returning on the Welsh mission were regarded as trained 'after a foreign model'. Hence one reason for the capture of Wales by Puritan spirituality later. To some extent the friction against the Jesuits was inevitable. Every clerical student who entered the Society meant one fewer *certainty* for the English mission, since the Jesuits served all the missions of the world.[1]

This unhappy year 1579 is the official year of the *Venerabile*'s foundation. The Bull of Pope Gregory XIII established a minimum of fifty students, with the privileges of a Tridentine pontifical university, under the protection of Cardinal Moroni. Before the year was out the college had sent its first priest (John Askew) to England.

And now, just as the college in Rome had followed ten years after Douay because of Douay's insecurity, so a decade later again a third line of defence became necessary through the insecurity (above all, the financial insecurity) of both. The region chosen this time was veritably the national enemy's own home soil; and the two colleges set up in Spain, at Valladolid and Seville, were the work not of William Allen but of Robert Persons.

There was much to be said for bases in Spain, under the eye of their patron Philip II and remote from the theatres of war. There was much also to be said against it later, when the national spirit of the young students remained so embarrassingly English and rejoiced in every Spanish defeat. In the event, the Spanish foundations proved hardly a success. They began with a flourish, but settled down to obscure and leisurely vegetation till the nineteenth century.

They grew out of a mission of Persons to Philip II early in 1589, the year following the Armada, to settle a difficulty over the Spanish province of the Jesuits.[2] So well did he handle this that both the king and the General smiled upon the educational plan he then produced from up his sleeve. He therefore wrote to Allen's colleges, for a nucleus

[1] For the affair in detail see the authorities cited p. 43 note, and W. Llewelyn Williams, *Making of Modern Wales* (1919), ch. v. The contemporary sources for the foundation of the English College at Rome include a *Brevis Narratio* of 1582, in *Cod. Vat. Lat.* 3494, of which there is an 1878 transcript by Fr. T. W. Murphy in *Stonyhurst MSS.*, Anglia IV, 29a, pp. 2ff.; a Latin narrative of 1587, transcript by Fr. Christopher Greene, in *Stonyhurst MSS.*, Coll. C., Anglia IV, i. c., ff. 206–11. Persons' account is in *C.R.S.* ii. 83–160. The archives of the college itself are listed in Guilday, 73 note. They are gradually being published by *C.R.S.*

[2] See L. J. Hicks in *The Month*, May 1931, 410ff.

of students, Jesuit and secular, to come to Valladolid. He himself would board them with the bishop and elsewhere while securing funds from Philip to support a college. Of the five sent, three were set upon when they landed, being mistaken for members of Drake's expedition which had been marauding in Lisbon. But as they were found to be carrying letters to the rector of the Spanish Jesuits they were allowed to pass, reached Valladolid and began classes (in the university and in the Spanish Jesuit college). Persons canvassed his Spanish friends for a college, to replace their temporary lodgings in the Monastery of St. Clare. He then bought a house, and in September he issued his Rules for the college. By donations, and by dint of begging on the part of the students themselves, ten thousand crowns were raised. The English College of St. Alban, Valladolid, goes on record therefore as the first to be founded largely out of local subvention. The first rectors were Spaniards.

Persons' policy was to boost the new venture as founded to implement the decrees of Trent (since Spain had as yet few such colleges). The flow of students from England (Valladolid numbered seventy-five within three years) was greatly helped by Elizabeth's proclamation of 1591 against the seminaries, which mentioned Valladolid by name and thereby made its existence known to Catholics in England hitherto ignorant of it. At the end of its first year the college had already sent twelve men to England on the mission. Five of these went *via* Seville, and Persons who accompanied them found two other exiles, John Cecil and William Warford, from Oxford, attempting to found an English college in that city. He dissuaded them, till Valladolid should have become well established.

How wise this restraint was, the complications at Valladolid soon showed. In the first place, there was already on foot a project for an Irish college there. Persons preferred not to amalgamate with this, bearing in mind the unhappy legacy of English-Welsh life in the English College at Rome. In the second place, there were not wanting Spaniards suspicious of his new college, on the ground (and who could know?) that some of its inmates might be spies. Thirdly, there was strong opposition in England, led by the anti-Jesuit party at home. The colleges in Spain, they prophesied, would be used as bases for the invasion of England by Spain; as Jesuit colleges they would be *ipso facto* 'bad' in themselves; and it were better far to petition Elizabeth to tolerate a Catholic seminary on home soil! But in April 1592 St. Alban's was confirmed by Papal Bull, and its privileges were defined before the end of the same year. It was empowered to grant degrees in arts and philosophy 'equivalent' to those of Oxford and Cambridge.[1]

Two things remained. One was to strengthen the communications of the new Spanish educational theatre by setting up a *caravanserai* for students coming and going, on the coast, at the mouth of the Guadalquivir: the English Residence of San Lucar. The English colony's house already there since 1517 had decayed; in April 1591 it was handed over to Persons, as Allen's 'Visitor', and entrusted by him to Dr. Stillington as provost. Students passing through it received clothing and a *viaticum* of fifty crowns. It was also used for revision-courses.[2]

The other was to take up the suggestion made to him in Seville, for a college there. In this, Persons' hand was forced by Valladolid itself, where the rector, faced by 1592 with the problem of accommodating seventy-five students, felt 'colonization' to be the only solution. When King Philip visited Valladolid and the English students greeted him with speeches in ten languages, it was easy for Persons to secure letters of commendation. Armed with these, and with fourteen students, he repaired to Seville and in November 1592 opened his seminary. Within two years it had a papal confirmation and permanent quarters—in the

[1] *Douay Diaries* (Knox), 8 May 1589; More, *Hist. Prov. Angl.*, 157; Yepez, *Relación de Algunos Martyrios* (1590). For the students, L. J. Hicks, *The Month*, 1931, 505. The rectors were Caecilia (from Madrid, July 1589), Pedro de Guzman (autumn, with Fr. Flack as Minister), Juan Lopez Monçana (July 1590), Rodrigo de Cabredo (Oct. 1591). The text of Clement VIII's Brief is in *C.R.S.* xxx. 246–51.

[2] The details of all the political moves leading to the foundation at Valladolid are in *Stonyhurst MSS.*, Anglia VI. Contemporary sources for the foundation are listed in *C.R.S.* xiv. 2n. The *Register* of the College from 1589 has been printed in full in *C.R.S.* xxx. For the whole of the English College movement in Spain the major source is G. Panzani, *Relazione dello stato religione catholica in Inghilterra*, in the Vatican archives; there is a transcript of this in *B.M.Add.MSS.* 15389, and a poor English translation in J. Berrington's (1793) *Memoirs of Panzani* (see Meyer, 64n. and 119n.). The *Annals* of the Valladolid college, from 1598 to 1616, by Fr. John Blackfan, one of the original founders, are a contentious source; extracts from them appeared in *The Month* in 1898 (vol. xcii), and the *Revised Annals* are in *C.R.S.* xxx. 263–72.

The principal *Spanish* sources for the English Colleges are F. Sacchini, *Historia S.J.*; Diego de Yepez, *Historia Particular de la Persecución de Inglaterra* (1599); and Antonio Astrain, *Hist. de la C. de Jesús en la Asistencia de España.*

The original deed of gift for Sanlucar de Barrameda was destroyed in the Spanish riots of 1931. There is a certified copy in the archives of the English College at Valladolid. The other English College, St. George, at Madrid, 1611, was at times only a house for a procurator managing the pensions of the other colleges in Spain; and it was incorporated into Valladolid in 1768. See Guilday, 136; Foley, vii. lv–lvii; and Abbé Mann, in *Trans. Soc. Antiq.*, xiii. 251.

Calle Sierpes. It remained in Seville till incorporated into Valladolid in 1768.[1]

Seville was the fifth and last of the English colleges founded abroad during the reign of Elizabeth. But those established meanwhile by the Scots and Irish bring the total to thirteen.[2]

Well might Persons ask, in penning the most terrific of all his polemical works, the *Philopater* of 1592:

> Has history since the memory of man anything more wonderful to tell, than of youths nobly born and wealthy for the most part, who could live quietly and comfortably at home, and who solely from zeal for their faith have left parents and friends, and all that is dear to them in this life, in order to go into voluntary exile, with such greatness of soul, and stedfastness, that they fear neither spies nor prisons, neither executioners nor instruments of torture, for the sake of religion and the salvation of souls?[3]

[1] See L. J. Hicks, in *The Month*, Aug. 1931; Foley, vii. 27f.; and the *Annals* of the Seville College, written by Persons in 1610, in *C.R.S.* xiv. 1–24, which cover the first three years.

[2] See Appendix 4, p. 273 below.

[3] Para. 73. The work ran into seven editions in its first year.

IV

THE RESISTANCE 1580-1603

I. THE BACKGROUND OF REVIVAL: JESUITS AND DIVISIONS

THE English Catholic revival from the shock of the Elizabethan persecution is always dated from the arrival in the country of the Jesuits Campion and Persons in 1580. This was an 'invasion' comprising a dozen men. Their mission was spiritual ministration and the distributing of books. Persons alone among them was a 'politician'.

They found the ground prepared already by the formation of the famous 'sodality' of George Gilbert, consecrated to facilitating the journeys of priests throughout the country from the ports of arrival. In addition to Gilbert and the printer Stephen Brinkley, the personnel was drawn from young noblemen of the families of Vaux, Throckmorton, Tichborne, Abington, Fitzherbert, Stonor and others. The secret printing-press set up by these young men cost the Government vast anxiety, to trace it from Greenstreet, East Ham (where it began) to the depths of Stonor Park near Henley, where Campion and Persons found it a godsend.[1]

For our purpose the Jesuit mission was significant in distinct ways. Immediately it meant an influx of books of piety and apologetics from abroad systematically organized, with care that copies were placed in the houses and shops of Protestants as well, so that the queen's pursuivants could not arrest only Catholics for possessing them.

But above all the mission began a Catholic revival which could not be stemmed by anything short of complete eradication. 'Many innocent hands', wrote Campion to the Privy Council, 'are lifted up to heaven for you daily, by those English students whose posteritie shall never die, which beyond seas, gathering virtue and sufficient knowledge for the purpose, are determined never to give you over, but

[1] For the Sodality, see *S.P. Dom. Eliz.* cxxxvii, No. 128; Foley, *Records*, iii. 627; Gillow, *Bibl. Dict.*, i. 219, v. 470; Simpson, *Campion*; and Pollen in *The Month*, cv. 592–9 (1905). With Campion and Persons came Ralph Emerson (brother-coadjutor to Campion), five English College students and a few secular priests.

either to win you heaven or to die upon your pikes.'[1] At home the centre of strength was inevitably the gentry; for the peerage had been re-stocked with new men established on monastic spoils, and the Catholic rank and file in the towns lacked political experience. Through the seculars and regulars, then, coming in as 'seminaries' to hide in remote houses and replace the ageing Marian clergy in family chapel and schoolroom, the colleges abroad were now to rekindle in England its old Catholic spirit and zeal, and simultaneously recruit to these colleges, in a chain of interaction that was to last till their return during the French Revolution.

Today we know that 1580, politically as it seemed to so many the beginning of the end, was spiritually the end of the beginning. 'The Church here', said Campion, 'shall never fail, so long as priests and pastors be found for the sheep, rage man or devil never so much.'

Yet, at the time, the advisability of the Jesuit mission was hotly debated by Catholics: and far into the future. Certainly it meant more persecution for them, especially in the minds of those who, content (in Meyer's phrase) to 'compromise with conscience', had hoped to be left alone. It brought in, moreover, men not subject to any ecclesiastical authority *in* England, and in this way it helped to deepen the quarrel of seculars and regulars during the chaos; and as a result of that chaos the English Catholics were soon bitterly divided on crucial issues of even faith and morals.

This deep tragedy of cleavage among the persecuted themselves had begun with controversy over the succession to Elizabeth, until 1603. It then continued, over the general question whether the government of the Catholics in England should be by a bishop or not. Both the political and the ecclesiastical aspects were intertwined with the implacable issue of regulars versus seculars. By 1603 the record is stained by more than one denunciation, of priest by priest, to the English Government. Two centuries later the differences were still there.

'They wrote against the Jesuits', said an eighteenth-century Benedictine chronicler, 'and the Jesuits and those that adhered to them against them again; which miserable doings much rejoiced the enemies of the Church, and further contributed to their eternal ruin. And these miseries lasted all the rest of Queen Elizabeth's days and further.'[2]

Even today, on some aspects of this unhappy story, it is still a

[1] 19 July 1580. Quoted in Pollen, 352.

[2] Dom B. Weldon, *Chron. of Engl. Benedictines* (1709), ed. of 1881, 38.

matter of truce among even the pundits: the Jesuit historians discrediting the attacks of their detractors by proving in them anterior bad faith, the refutations nevertheless failing sometimes to convince the critic so long as the Jesuit archives in Rome (unlike the Vatican archives) should remain closed.

The Elizabethan succession question produced two parties in the ranks of the English Catholics. One, the Scottish party, supported Mary Stuart (until her execution in 1587) and thereafter her son James VI. The other party, the Spanish, preferring Philip II, was led by Allen and Persons and the colleges in exile.

The question of Church government, in abeyance because there were still members of the Catholic hierarchy alive in exile, and because the length of the queen's reign could not be prophesied, became acute immediately upon the arrival of the Jesuits in England. To ecclesiastical diversity, confusing in itself—with the Jesuits subject to their Father General in Rome and the secular clergy subject to the Cardinal Protector of England—was soon added a suspicion that the Jesuits would contrive to control altogether the Catholic life of the country. When the old hierarchy became extinct, on the death of Bishop Thomas Watson of Lincoln in September 1584 (in Wisbech Prison) and Bishop Thomas Goldwell of St. Asaph in April 1585 (in Rome), there was a gap of fourteen years, of acrimonious debate on the question 'Bishop or merely Archpriest?' before the Holy See appointed George Blackwell as 'Archpriest of England'.

The resultant Archpriest Controversy raged through three reigns: Blackwell till 1608, George Birkhead till 1615 and William Harrison till 1621, when the pope made a virtue of necessity and appointed a bishop with full episcopal faculties.[1]

Such is the domestic background till well after the turn of the century. It has constantly to be borne in mind.

In the eyes of the queen and her Council, however, the coming of the Jesuits was seen against the wider background of the Counter-Reformation at large: Spain, Mary Stuart (in captivity in England since twelve years ago) and the plots.

Hence a tightening of sanctions on all fronts against the Catholics, and against the Puritans as well when the leniency of Archbishop

[1] There is a discussion of these dissensions in Guilday, *Eng. Cath. Refugees*. The studies by T. G. Law—*The Archpriest Controversy* and *Jesuits and Seculars*, to say nothing of Charles Dodd's *Church History* (1737) and its nineteenth-century edition by M. A. Tierney—need incessant checking in the light of the *Letters of Fr. Robert Persons*, ed. for the Cath. Record Soc. (vol. xxxix) by L. J. Hicks, S.J.

Grindal ended suddenly upon the appointment of Whitgift to Canterbury in 1583. We have now to trace those sanctions in their several directions down to the climax-year of 1593, save as regards Catholic schools and schoolmasters at work clandestinely in England, which are reserved for separate consideration later.

2. THE GOVERNMENT'S FAILURE

(*a*) *The Universities*

Oxford and Cambridge had been neither effectively purged by the visitations, nor completely emptied of Catholics. There were conformers ('church papists'), there were complaisant Anglican and ex-Catholic dons; and there were therefore plenty of Catholic students residing in the two university towns and getting the benefit of lectures and tuition, though precluded (by the oaths) from taking a degree.

How far Cambridge was 'safe' is aptly illustrated by the fact that after the Master of Caius had been charged with Romanist leanings and had his 'popish stuff' and books burnt in 1572, his two successors Legge and Swayle were both found similarly disaffected. At Oxford the new statutes of 1576 had reinforced the rules as to the Thirty-Nine Articles, but they had to be extended again in 1581. The Earl of Leicester, as chancellor, tried to stem the evasions by ordering that subscription to the Articles precede *admission*. By the time of the Armada, Convocation was ordering that they be known by heart and defended (at graduation) before the vice-chancellor or proctors or regent masters.[1]

Catholics still came up. And Catholics still went away, taking to Douay and Rome an academic formation that would relieve those hard-pressed colleges from having to teach 'rudiments' to still more of their *alumni*. 'Most of the seminary priests which at this time disturb the church', wrote the Privy Council plaintively to the Vice-Chancellor of Oxford in 1581, 'have been heretofore scholars of [your] university.' Trinity, Balliol (Persons' college) and St. John's were especially notorious, in the decade 1580–90, for those they allowed to come and then to leak away abroad.[2] When the Privy Council in desperation ordered a simultaneous inquiry into both universities in 1592 they found at Cambridge more church-papists and actual

[1] Heywood, *Oxford Univ. Commissions*, 477; N. Wood, 279, 122. Dr. Legge at Caius was said to have brought Papist students with him from Jesus College. See Heywood and Wright, *Cambr. Univ. Trans.*, i.314.

[2] *Second Douay Diary* (Knox), 362–4; N. Wood, 295.

recusants than they had expected; Savage Hawarden of Lancashire actually became a fellow of King's in 1602. At Oxford more still, many of whom (like Persons before them) had indeed taken the oath and later lapsed from it: while anon a friendly administrator would even omit it from the degree ceremony.[1] It is no coincidence that the staunchly Anglican Trinity College in Dublin was founded at this very time.

Allen had long had it that the Government was 'tormented' by the Catholic traffic to and from the universities. In 1583 he recorded, in six months, as many as eighty going to him 'from the English universities and schools'.[2]

(*b*) *The Leakage Abroad*

It was manifestly unavailing to rely on proclamations and fines to seal the Continent off from recusant emigrants. Much had to be done along the supplementary line of discovering who *were* in the colleges in Flanders and Rome, to help in identifying them upon their return as seminary priests. The *State Papers Domestic* for 1580 are full of feverish activity along this line, culminating in a list of the papists known to be returning to England, a list of those who had children in the seminaries abroad or were harbouring priests, and a list giving the 'Names of all the Papist Pupils in the English College, Rome; of all English resident at Rome, Remes, Paris, Douay; all who left on April 18 with Edmund Campion and J. Persons jesuits.' Much of this information was reaching Walsingham through a spy in touch with an English lady staying at Dieppe who accommodated priests on their way to England.[3]

Betrayal was the surest line. It was for long to dog the colleges. One of the original forty-nine students sworn-in at the *Venerabile* in 1579, Gilbert Gifford, was to turn out a Government agent. At each college the hospitality afforded to visitors could be a risky affair: witness the case of Anthony Munday at Rome; the agent Solomon Aldred; and James Walsh of Magdalene College, Cambridge, who apostatized and 'undertook to spy upon Catholics for the Bishop of London because he could not get work as a schoolmaster'.[4]

[1] Pollen, 253; N. Wood, 279; Gillow, iii. 182.

[2] Knox, *Douay Diaries*, lxx–i; quoted in Mullinger, ii. 281 note.

[3] *Cal. S.P. Dom.* 1580, Nos. 129, 137; 1581–90, No. 61; also for 1579, Nos. 6 and 54; and for 1580, Nos. 20, 23, 31, 38, 59.

[4] These spies as follows: Gifford, *D.N.B.*; Munday, *Downside Review*, x. 214–36 (1891); Aldred, Conyers Read, ii. 425–32; Walsh, ibid. ii. 323 note, from Walsh's

The proclamation that accompanied the notorious Act of 1581 (the Act which instituted the monthly fine of £20 for non-attendance at church) is the prototype of an interminable series that lasted ineffectually till the middle of the eighteenth century. No one whatever, henceforth, save merchants, might leave the country without licence.[1]

Prosecutions began at once for 'persuading' to popery and for conniving at departures from the realm. Whitgift, as soon as he was installed in Canterbury, ordered an inquiry into how many recusants, of each diocese, actually 'have their children beyond seas'.[2]

The 'Act against Jesuits', passed soon afterwards, in 1585, was obviously bent at last on the 'extermination' of Catholicism. It was henceforth treason for a priest to be found at large. This is the clause of which Lord Chief Justice Mansfield said in the eighteenth century that 'it is death for a priest to be found alive in this country'.

(c) *Printing*

Bound up with the traffic to and from the Continent was a veritable Catholic printing industry to cope with. Campion and Persons had been hard at work on the press in Lady Stonor's Park near Henley, a few months after their arrival in 1580, with Stephen Brinkley as 'prefect of the printers' (till he retired to Rouen two years later to succeed the defunct Catholic printer George Flinton), and Fr. William Maurice as 'procurator to buy the paper'. Campion's *Decem Rationes* were printed at Stonor.

In London there were Catholic bookbinders available even in St. Paul's churchyard. Throughout the reign, as press after press was captured or dispersed, there were printers forthcoming to fill the breach. Some were executed: William Carter, taken to the Tower in July 1582; James Duckett, at Tyburn in April 1602; John Collins, at Tyburn in 1601. Some fled and resumed work abroad: John Fowler of

Report in *S.P. Dom.* clxx, No. 44. It is a grim comment on the times that eight men indicated in Persons' *Memoirs* as working for the Government included Munday and Nowall in the English College at Rome; John Peschall, lately a follower of Persons himself; John Nicholls, a scholar at Rome; Eliot, a Catholic in 'Mr. Roper's House'; and two Regulars—Langdale and Perkins. (Text of *Memoirs* in *C.R.S.* ii. 181f.) There is a detailed account of the 'Spies and Traitor Priests' in *Ushaw Magazine*, July 1934, 105–21.

[1] 10 Jan. 1581. In *Tudor & Stuart Proclamations*, i.81; Strype, *Annals*, iii (i), 57; *Cal. S.P. Dom. Eliz.* 1581–90, p. 42; Tierney, *Church Hist.*, iii. appdx. p. xxi f. For the distinction in the Act of 1581 between active and passive Catholicism, see Conyers Read, ii. 292, and Meyer, 148.

[2] From his MS. *Register*, i. f91, in Cardwell, i. 408; N. Wood, 67.

Winchester and New College (to Louvain to Laurence Kelham); Rowland Jenks (in Oxford as late as 1578); Stephen Brinkley, to Rouen when the press in Stonor Park ceased, when he went to replace George Flinton; Christopher Plantin at Rheims; Richard Verstegan at Antwerp; and Persons' own press at St. Omer.[1]

The most far-reaching of all the enterprises in this field was of course the Rheims New Testament of 1582. It crowned the work of that band of original founders from Douay College, now in second exile at Rheims: Gregory Martin, William Allen, Richard Bristow, John Reynolds. The quarto volume, prodigiously expensive, and issued from the press of J. Fogny, carried the 'approbations' of the archbishop, canons and theological professors of Rheims University. Though its completion by the Douay Old Testament was to wait another twenty-eight years, this first Catholic Bible in English was reprinted by Belgians at Louvain, Douay, Brussels and Antwerp; by English printers such as Plantin, Fowler's widow, Verstegan, Kelham and Persons himself. When the English war with Spain began, the Belgian taxes on these books, and State authorisation, were remitted.

Moreover the work was extended, in the vernacular, to Wales. In 1585 Griffith Roberts, of the English College at Rome, published at Rouen his *Drych Cristionogawl*; and Fr. Robert Gwynne's Welsh translation of the *Christian Directory, or Book of Resolution*, appeared six years later.[2]

The discreet size of individual operations can sometimes be gleaned from what was found on the *colporteurs*. When Peter Lawson, a layman, was caught landing at Dunwich from Le Havre early in 1583, he had with him thirty primers, 500 Vaux *Catechisms*, fifteen Latin Testaments and forty-five books of devotion. Together with the two priests who accompanied him (John Nutter and Samuel Conyers) he was 'examined' and sent to the Marshalsea prison, where he died three years later. Sometimes, as with Richard Lacey in the same year, the distributors were forced to betray others. Sir William Browne, at Flushing, sent home in 1598 detailed information on receivers, extracted by him from a *colporteur* he had caught. Sometimes, as with one Wibley taken in 1585 distributing Allen's latest book, they were

[1] Persons' *Autobiography*, in *C.R.S.* ii. 29. See Foley, ii. 589, from the Burghley Papers in the *Lansdowne MSS.*, for the 'two book-binders in Powell's Churchyard, called Cawood and Holder. . . . I am sure they sell Papistical books forbidden to be sold.' For the others, Tierney, iii. 155–7; Gillow, i. 414, ii. 133–5, i. 544, ii. 300, ii. 327, iii. 256, iii. 614. A biography of James Duckett the martyr, by M. M. Merrick, appeared in 1947.

[2] W. Ll. Williams, *Making of Modern Wales*, 206 note, 221 and sources; Gillow, iii. 70.

executed within twenty-four hours. But the penalties on private persons found 'possessing' these books were not at the fierce extreme of Queen Mary's closing year.[1]

(d) Schools and Tutors

Meanwhile, the country was infested with Catholic tutors in the houses of the rich, and now, illicit Catholic schools in the villages and even towns. What these amounted to, and how far it was possible to secure a Catholic education at home in England, we have to decide later. For the moment we are concerned with the Government's sense of their danger.

The first to act were the bishops. Edward Scambler (Peterborough) warned the Privy Council within a year of the oath being extended to schoolmasters in 1563. The bishops of Worcester and Chichester ordered detailed inquiries into the prevalence of tutors in gentlemen's houses who 'do exceeding great hurt as well . . . in the country round about'.[2]

After the excommunication of the queen in 1570 the attorney-general joined in, urging on the Government a searching inquiry into the qualifications and conformity of all schoolmasters. Typical of the procedure adopted is York, where in August 1575 the Council of the North sent round four sworn men to inquire after 'such as wander from place to place to teach or instruct . . . contrary to the laws and ordinances of this realm, and of all that receive, harbour, cherish or receive them'. The mayor and aldermen of York were able to send the queen within a year their first catalogue of recusants.[3]

The Privy Council did not move until the arrival of Campion and Persons. But it then acted at once (18 June 1580) by instructing the bishops to intensify their searches. Every schoolmaster was to be examined.[4] And by the Act passed next year (sect. 5) the penalty for an unlicensed schoolmaster became £10 a month for those who had kept him and a year's imprisonment for the man himself. This enactment has been described as of the highest constitutional importance, as it 'supplanted by implication' the common law of the kingdom

[1] For these see Gillow, iv. 169; Wood, 289; *C.R.S.* v. 73, xxii. 399; *Hist. MSS. Comm.* xiii, pt. 4, p. 334, and (1901) i. 69; *Hist. MSS. Comm.*, De Lisle and Dudley MS., ii. 335.

[2] For Peterborough, *Camden Miscellany*, ix. 35; Worcester, text in Frere iii. 225; Chichester, *S.P. Dom. Eliz.* lx, No. 71, and q. in *V.C.H.* Sussex, ii. 397.

[3] *Lansdowne MSS.* 155, cited in Birt, 542–3. Pollen, 262, from John Morris, *Troubles of our Catholic Forefathers* (1872–7), iii. 246–8.

[4] Dasent, *Acts of the Privy Council*, xii. 59; Cardwell, i. 393; N. Wood, 65.

whereby all persons had a right to teach the young.[1] Within a few years of Whitgift succeeding Grindal at Canterbury in 1583 there were eleven separate diocesan inquiries.[2] Wales was combed from end to end, as an area where the recusants 'swarmed' and were marrying and baptising in secret places, and their children 'be learned and bred by schoolmasters of theire own creed'.[3]

Wrote Campion, 'You may guess how great the Catholic *total* is, if so many offer themselves to suffering and ruin on its account.'

So widespread was the local habit of turning the blind eye in regions thickly Catholic, that the York Diocesan Court Books for the very active year 1596 seem to reveal only two presentments of unlicensed recusant teachers.[4] Nevertheless the closing years of the reign show that with Anglicanism as the established religion, and the Church of England a department of State, recusancy was a national and constitutional and political question in one. By 1601 it is the Council *itself* that asks 'what masters, mistresses or dames do retain or keep in their houses or service any schoolmasters or servants or other persons that forbear to come to the parish church or chapel . . . [and] how many schoolmasters are in your parish'.[5]

(e) *Seizing the Children*

Nothing more starkly reveals the Government's feelings of insecurity following the Jesuit 'invasion' than the decision taken to go to the extreme limit, and forcibly remove children from the custody of their parents in order to rear them in sound Protestant households.

Catholic historians have underestimated this fear. For in any case a Protestant education for a Catholic child was of course by then no rare phenomenon. There was widespread conformity; frequently there was no school available other than the local grammar school; and there was indifference and apostasy.

The cases of Fr. Edward Gennings in Lichfield, or John Laithwaite in Wigan, illustrate the many in which family Catholicism withstood

[1] J. E. G. de Montmorency, *State Intervention in English Education* (1902), 95, and 96 for text of schoolmaster's licence now issued. Whitgift tightened it further in 1599.

[2] The dioceses were: Chester 1581, Middlesex 1582, Bath and Wells 1583, Coventry and Lichfield 1584, London 1586, Hereford 1586, London 1581, Chichester 1585, Salisbury 1589, York 1590, Nottingham 1599. Kennedy, *Eliz. Episc. Administration*, ii. 248, 262, 323, 328. And Whitgift's MS. Register, i. f91, for 1583, in Cardwell, i. 408.

[3] C. A. J. Skeel, *Council of the Marches of Wales*, 101.

[4] *York Dioc. Ct. Bks.*, R. VI. A. 26. See details in J. Kitching, *Catholic Education in the N. and E. Ridings, 1571–1870* (Univ. Durham thesis, 1956), ch. 2.

[5] Morris, *Troubles*, iii. 292.

the atmosphere of the grammar schools. But 'little Jacke' Hilton in Cumberland typifies the indifference—he was given a Protestant schooling and sent to Oxford despite all that the priest Hopton could do to dissuade his father. Edward Walpole, brother of Henry, the priest-martyr, had to flee from his parents to avoid a Protestant schooling. Robert Walker likewise, on arrival at Valladolid, told how his lapsed father had been so incensed at his conversion to the Catholic Church by Fr. Blount that he had flown at him with a dagger and terrified him into leaving the country. A still worse case is that of John Maxey, whose father bided his time until the boy had returned to England as a priest from Spain, and then not only betrayed him to the Bishop of London, but had him transferred from the Gatehouse prison to Bridewell because the atmosphere of the former was too papist, and finally had him buried in the prison rubbish-tip.[1]

The kind and degree of education the Catholics were getting at home, which we are to examine later, is a complex issue. But at all events the Council were patently dismayed and alarmed.

The plan for forcibly seizing Catholic children originated with Secretary Burghley himself. He addressed a long memorandum to Elizabeth in 1581–3, entitled *Advice in Matters of Religion and State*. Good schoolmasters and diligent preachers, he insisted, were not enough. They were indeed failing—'the greatest number of Papists is of very young men'. The queen should do two things in addition, as a 'pious and godly means'. One, 'make their parents in every shire send their children to be virtuously brought up at a certain place for that end appointed'. The other, put in practice a 'noble stratagem' used by Sertorius in Roman Spain, whereby 'you shall, under cover of Education, have them as hostages for the parents' fidelities'.[2]

There we have the beginning of a thread in Government policy that was to thicken and coarsen for close on a century, long before it reached statutory force in Ireland. In so far as the device suggested amounted to a direct violation of the fundamental right of the parent, in conscience, to have his child educated in his own faith, a natural and theological right defended consistently before and since by Catholic and Protestant equally, it is fitting that the device was conceived in the mind of a man so dominated by 'reasons of State' as Cecil.

[1] *S.P. Dom. Eliz.* Add. xxviii, No. 59, iii; cf. *C.R.S.* v. 67; Gillow, ii. 415; Blundell, *Old. Cath. Lancs.*, ii. 52–3; *C.R.S.* xxx. 17, 72.

[2] The full text of Cecil's *Advice* is in B.M., *Somers Tracts* IV (1752), i. 101–8. At the end he refers back to this section as 'the School Hostages'. On Sertorius, see Plutarch, *Lives*, ed. Langhorne (1770), iv. 18.

Action on it began early in the following year. One of the seizures is a robust epic, as well as an excellent illustration of the method.

At 3 a.m. on 12 February 1584, four boys of the Worthington family, of Blainsborough, Lancashire, were seized at the house of a Mr. Sankey near Warrington, together with their uncle (the Rev. Thomas Worthington) and two other men. The boys, aged twelve to sixteen, had been brought up by an old Marian priest called Peel. Upon their seizure two were left in Sankey's charge, and the others taken to Wigan to be examined by the Earl of Derby and Bishop Chatterton of Chester.

To soften him up before this examination, John, aged twelve, was kept without food but plied with wine—at which he protested (and with some highly precocious remarks). Thomas, the eldest, refused a tempting bribe from the Earl of Derby that he should hear a Protestant sermon. The two other boys were then examined in due course, only to make replies so discomfiting to the inquisitors that thereafter the examinations were conducted in private.

All four were then confined in a house in Manchester and treated kindly for a month, when their food was suddenly reduced because of their obduracy. Ordered to church, they refused; and the magistrate actually pronounced them guilty of treason accordingly. Hereupon one Bull, assuring the bishop that he could bring them to heel, flogged all four in their cell and then separated them—two to separate cells, one to the house of a Dutch Puritan and John (the youngest) to the house of the bishop himself. Next day the two eldest were taken by force to a schoolmaster, but refused his catechism and set to work to 'infect' his other boys. The third stonewalled the Dutchman's efforts to dissuade him from his Catholicism, while the prodigy John engaged in disputations with the bishop, who was rash enough to argue that he himself would conform to a Catholic king if required, and was told that this would not lessen the 'avenging fires' already awaiting him in his hereafter.

In due course all four recalcitrants were taken back to the house in Manchester, and thence to a Protestant church under guard. They consented to walk obediently on this excursion, to avoid violence. But when this was construed as voluntary conformity they wrote letters insisting that they would never go again.

Then began the escapes. The first, Thomas, got away through the help of 'certain Catholic friends'. The second was liberated by two friends while on the road to Chester Castle in the custody of a constable. The third slipped away unnoticed. All three met further south, were recaptured, and at once released because the pursuivants were really hunting for their father. Soon after they reached London with their uncle, all were betrayed at Islington, and the priest and the boys' horses were seized. Thomas was sent to the Gatehouse prison, but the others escaped again. The priest was subsequently banished in January 1585. The fourth boy, Richard, was allowed by his Dutch mentor to go.

Three of the four Worthington boys accordingly crossed to Douay-Rheims. Thomas, after being quartered on the Lord Treasurer, was back in the Gatehouse by 1586. But he also contrived to reach Douay later. All four were ordained, John and Laurence as Jesuits. Two of them returned later on the English mission.[1]

Only two days after the start of this Worthington *saga* a second case had opened. On 14 February 1583 a York draper named William Hutton was imprisoned for having heard Mass. 'An order was made that his children be placed with their mother, unless he could otherwise provide for them, so that they be not suffered to go abroad.... It would appear that shortly afterwards even their mother was denied access to them.' This situation persisted for the best part of two years, till the Privy Council was induced to rescind the order by 'the murmuring of the people'.[2]

A third case, also in the North, occurred in 1589 on the death of Thomas Hoghton of The Lea (Salwick) in a feud. His son and heir, Richard, was given in ward by the queen to Sir Gilbert Gerard, Master of the Rolls, who brought him up as a Protestant and married him to his daughter while still a minor. The same thing happened soon afterwards to Sir Roger Bradshaigh, of the same neighbourhood.[3]

A further case is that of Thomas Singleton, born in 1573. His father died while he was a child, and he was handed by the Government to a Protestant schoolmaster, who by trickery married him to his daughter while he was still a minor. After a few years the girl died, and Singleton went abroad to travel. He was ultimately converted to Catholicism by an English Jesuit, and made straight for Rome, whence to Douay for

[1] The Worthington story is told in John Gibbons' *Concertatio* (1594), pt. ii, and Foley, iii. 116–133. The Government's own account is in *S.P. Dom. Eliz.* cxc, No. 25 (12 June 1586). See also Persons to Agazarri, Sept. 1584, in Brady, *Catholic Hierarchy*, iii. 48–50; *C.R.S.* ii. 245; Blundell, iii. 35–6, 157; and, for the boys' futures, Foley, ii. 134.

[2] Gillow, iii. 521.

[3] *C.R.S.* xv. 159; Gillow, iii. 328.

a year, and then to Valladolid in October 1598. It was here that he told the tale of his youth and wanderings.[1]

These cases have been cited because they illustrate the three different means by which the seizure of these children of Catholic nobility could be done constitutionally: the Worthington children—by the bishop and lord lieutenant; the Hutton children—by the Privy Council; the Hoghton boy—through the queen's right of wardship. All three devices sprang from the theory and fact of the royal prerogative. Parliament was not yet in the picture.[2]

The whole transaction is clinched in a memorandum of Walsingham to the Council in December 1586, on the reform of religion in England, which directs the prevention of further recusant education in 'erroneous religion' by ordering what Burghley had recommended four years earlier: 'the said recusants to be ordered by my Lords to send their children, by a day named by the bishops, to such place as by them shall be appointed'.[3]

Constitutionally, the importance of this document lies in its implication that degrees of interference with the conscientious rights of parents unattained yet by statute could be nevertheless secured by royal prerogative. Within seven years, however, the sanction of seizing the children was tabled in Parliament itself.

Now, this is a matter which has had insufficient attention from historians. More than one standard account of it leaves the impression that what was done to the Worthington boys, and to so many others afterwards, was by 'extension' of the laws already existing, and particularly that of 1585. Moreover, the authority for what happened in the baleful Parliament of 1593 is usually cited as a letter from the Jesuit Joseph Creswell, written some time after the event but undated,

[1] *C.R.S.* xxx. 36 and note, 54.

[2] This exercise of the feudal right of wardship was mentioned by J. R. Green, *Short History*, ed. 1874, 607; and by F. Adams, *The Elementary School Contest* (1882), 25. Cf. J. Hurstfield, *The Queen's Wards* (1959)—'The Privy Council itself . . . took a special interest in the guardianship of wards; but that was merely to keep track of the Catholics and their movements overseas.' This special use of the right will have given added point to Cardinal Allen's wish that, should the Armada succeed (ibid. 245), feudal wardship should be abolished.

[3] *S.P. Dom. Eliz.* cxvii, No. 89; *Lansdowne MSS.*, 97, f. 154; summary and quotations in Conyers Read, ii. 307–8, whose commentary is a superb *litotes*: 'It is clear that Walsingham was no friend of the recusants. He was completely out of sympathy with their religious views. . . . There can be no doubt that his influence was not exerted upon the side of leniency.' This memorandum of Walsingham is clearly the document referred to vaguely by Persons, in *C.R.S.* xiv. 11 and note, and not identified by Hastings, 353–4.

and from a copy in the Vatican archives and not the original. In 1593, too, Fr. Creswell was far from London: in Spain.[1]

In view of this, what did happen in the Parliament of 1593 is worth establishing, for the honour of Parliament itself. The evidence comes not from the *Commons Journal* (which has nothing for the reign of Elizabeth later than 15 March 1581), but from Sir Simonds D'Ewes, *Journals of All the Parliaments . . . of Queen Elizabeth*, and the contemporary letters of Persons and Creswell and the 'agents' of the English colleges.

The Parliament opened on 19 February (Old Style), a very important date.[2] A week later the Commons gave a first reading to a quite savage Bill. Recusants-convict were to have their children removed from them at the age of seven, by order of the Council or the local bishop or the judges of assize, and the children were to be given a Protestant education financed from one-third of their parents' lands.

In the second reading debate one speaker wanted the bishops deleted, on the score that so many of their chancellors were 'so much affected to the Canon Law that some are infected with Popish Religion'! Others were at pains to know how the guardian appointed would be able to extort the maintenance costs from the parents. The Bill was then committed—to the whole Privy Council and certain lawyers.

When it came back, the scruples of the House were sufficient to get it rejected as too drastic. A new Bill replaced it, in which the age of seizure was raised to ten (till sixteen) and the justices of the peace were added to the authorities to be empowered. Should a third of the parents' lands not suffice, maintenance was to come from their goods as well. This new Bill went to the same Committee as before, together with one for 'restraining Popish Recusants to certain places of abode'.

On 21 March the 'abode' Bill *only* went forward to be engrossed. We may therefore take it that the 'education' Bill had died before then. The Parliament ended a fortnight later. Thus the sole enactment of that session of 1593 was the 'Five Mile Act'. Parliament had not stooped so low as to authorize by law the inroads on parental rights already being made through the prerogative.[3]

[1] Cf. Meyer, 174–5, citing two statements, Cecil's *Advice* of 1582–3, and the Creswell letter; Guilday, 139 and note, also citing Creswell; M. V. Sweeney, *Engl. Cath. Education, 1580–1829* (Univ. Leeds Thesis, 1946), 95, which speaks of the practice 'as the law allowed'. There is in fact a far more definitive letter of Creswell's, written at the time (19 April 1593) to the Pope—in *Arch. Vat.*, Borghese III, 124 (P.R.O. *Roman Transcripts*, ix. iii).

[2] See p. 64 below.

[3] D'Ewes, ed. Paul Bowes (1682), 471a, 476, 477, 498b, 500–19 *passim*. For the 'abode' Act, Meyer, 149 and N. Wood, 294.

But, by the same token, Parliament's non-complaisance did not stop the practice. Just as children of the Jerninghams had been seized in January immediately prior to the session, so a girl of the Throckmortons was seized in June soon after it. These were leading Catholic families destined to give sons to the Church for a long time to come. The Jerningham boys (George and Edward) were caught on their way out of the country. The Throckmorton girl (Margaret) was entrusted to the Dean of Gloucester and forbidden any visitors.[1]

Small wonder, then, with these examples from on high, that local zeal should proceed even to the forcible baptism of a Catholic child in a Protestant church. Small wonder, too, that Catholics handed over their children, in advance of likely seizure, to Protestant kinsmen or others whom they could personally trust.[2] So that by the end of the reign the Privy Council was ordaining that *all* children were to be educated in the established faith, and that recusants and non-communicants should be prosecuted unless they bound themselves in stiff recognizances as to their children's education.[3]

Yet there were ways even of circumventing the threat from wardships. The classic case here is that of the Vaux of Harrowden Hall in Northamptonshire. Lady Elizabeth Vaux had to satisfy the Privy Council that the young lord was being brought up by Protestant tutors; but by dint of finding complaisant tutors she was able to make of her house 'a Jesuit College in the heart of England', in which priests found refuge, and the children of her retainers found schooling, and two tutors (Thomas Smith and his successor Tutfield) became Catholics. 'We had good store of books', says Fr. John Gerard, who was there, 'which were kept in a library without any concealment, because they had the appearance of belonging to the young baron....'[4]

Two summings-up may round off the reign from the standpoint of the State. One, a lament to Cecil in 1596 upon the country in general:

> The bringing up of recusants' children in their parents' errors is too general, and if not reformed will grow very dangerous. My Lord of Canterbury

[1] Dasent, *Acts of the Privy Council*, N.S. xxiv. 25, 56, 88, 279, 303, 346, 399.

[2] Cf. forcible baptism 1597 at Fullthroppes (Gillow, ii. 340). Protestant 'connivances'—cf. cases in 1593 (Richard Garnett: in *Stonyhurst Magazine*, iii. 333) and 1597 (Edward Barlow: in Blundell, ii. 16).

[3] Morris, *Troubles*, iii. 278–80; N. Wood, 299–300.

[4] Three of the boys schooled here became priests. See *C.R.S.* xxx. 85, 60, 91. For the schoolmasters, Gerard's *Life.* 351, and *Hist. MSS. Comm.*, Salisbury MSS., xvii. 528. Also G. Anstruther, *The Vaux of Harrowden*, 244–5.

cannot reform it, and the suffering of it offends God, weakens the Kingdom, and encourages the devilish attempts against Her Majesty's sacred person.

The other, upon the Catholic North in particular:

Small reformation has been made there by the Ecclesiastical Commission, as may appear by the emptiness of churches on Sundays and Holidays, and the multitude of bastards and drunkards. . . . The people lack instruction, for the preachers are few, most of the parsons unlearned, many of those learned not resident, and divers unlearned daily admitted into good benefices by the bishop.

The youth are for the most part trained up by such as profess Papistry; no examination is had of schools and schoolmasters. The proclamation for the apprehension of seminaries, Jesuits and mass-priests, and for calling home children from parts beyond sea, is not executed, nor are their Lordships' letters commanding the Justices to call before them quarterly all parsons, vicars, curates, churchwardens and sworn men, and examine them on oath how the statutes 1 and 23 Eliz. as to resorting to churches are obeyed, that at the next quarter sessions information may be given against the offenders . . . The Seminaries in many places have lately offered disputations against the settled religion: but nothing has been said to them.[1]

3. THE SCHOOL AT ST. OMER[2]

That year of the Parliament of 1592–3 is perhaps the greatest climax-year in the entire penal period; for it is the year in which also the mother college returned from its temporary sojourn in Rheims, to Douay; in which the second of the Spanish colleges (Seville) began; in which the first of a long series of fine-rolls, the Recusant Rolls, gives us something of a continuous census of the recusants. Finally, it is the year in which Persons established abroad the greatest of all the *schools* in exile, at St. Omer, the Stonyhurst of today.

A development in policy is involved here, stemming from what the Council of Trent, in legislating for ecclesiastical seminaries, had not foreseen.

[1] Dean of Durham (William James) to Cecil, 1596; *Cal. S.P. Dom. Eliz.* xlviii, No. 57, p. 95. And report to Privy Council 1591: ibid. ccxl, No. 188.

[2] The analysis which follows below was written from the Farm Street (London, S.J.) collection of transcripts of original documents, generously put at my disposal by Fr. Leo Hicks, S.J. It is independent of Fr. Hicks' own study of the problem in his *Foundation of the College of St. Omers* in *Arch. Hist. Soc. Jesu*, xix. 146–180 (1950), and of H. Chadwick, S.J., *St. Omers to Stonyhurst* (1962), which appeared as this book went to press. On the date of St. Omer, its relation to the Eu school, and how far it was a school, there is full agreement.

The English colleges at Douay and Rome and in Spain were seminaries. But not all the men and boys arriving at Douay and the *Venerabile* had vocations to the priesthood; and many of those who had a vocation arrived lacking any complete prior education in the humanities. On both these counts, then, of completing the 'grammar' schooling of those who did, and of meeting the demands of those who did not wish ordination, something else than seminary training must also be made available somehow. Scholastic enterprises in England were too harassed and too interrupted to count for overmuch.

In meeting this need the initiative came from where one would expect: from the Jesuits, who were *ex professo* schoolmasters, and (much more than the seminarians) were flexible on principle in all their strategy. The initiative came in particular from Robert Persons.

As so often with Fr. Persons, we have here an educational plan broached as by-product of a political project (as we saw in the founding of Valladolid in 1589). On a visit to the Duke of Guise in Belgium to solicit help for the captive Mary Stuart, in the year 1582, Persons retailed Allen's anxiety at the number of postulants arriving from England half-prepared, and the pressure being put on him by parents in England to do something for the schooling of Catholic children. The Duke at once promised money for a school; Persons begged from the Jesuits at Eu their older, disused buildings there, and a small school was opened with a Mr. Chambers as master, and the president of Douay College (Dr. Richard Barret) virtually 'patron'.[1] It lasted ten years.

This little school at Eu (it never had more than thirty boys at any one time) is important as being an innovation. Allen called Eu a 'novum seminarium'. He was thinking of the dire need for preparatory studies for emigrant boys. Persons called it 'a seminary for English youth', and wrote of Douay and Eu without essential distinction. The contemporary French documents called it simply a school. And the actual records of the ten years support this wider view.[2]

Records give us the movements of young boys to and from the

[1] L. J. Hicks, in *C.R.S.* xxxix (Persons Letters), 50; Guilday 129ff. The English ambassador reported this to Walsingham, and Elizabeth at once protested to France, actually before the school had opened: cf. *Cal. S.P. Foreign*, May-Dec. 1582, pp. 33, 150, 162. Philip II gave £100 p.a. See also Knox, *Allen*, 166, from Westminster Archives, iii. 159; *Stonyhurst MSS.* Coll. P, 229; and John Gerard, *Autobiography* (ed. P. Caraman, 1951) for a visit to the Eu school in 1588.

[2] Allen, in *Second Douay Diary* (Knox), 183; Persons, in *C.R.S.* xiv. 21. Also Pollen, unpubl. continuation of his *English Catholics in the Reign of Elizabeth* (MS. at Farm St., London, ch. 13), and in *Stonyhurst Magazine*, i. 285, xxvi. 178.

several institutions now existing in the region. There were four of them—Douay College (temporarily at Rheims), two Jesuit preparatory schools, at Pont-à-Mousson (Flemish) and Verdun (French) and Eu itself.

When boys arrived at Douay College insufficiently prepared, it had recourse to all the other three. In the decade 1580–90 it sent nine to Pont-à-Mousson, twenty-nine to Verdun and nine to Eu. The boys sent from Eu *to* Douay total thirty-two, of whom only three had originally been received *from* Douay (labelled *rediit*).

This traffic of boys shows that, on the one hand, Eu did not supersede the two Jesuit schools as preparatory schools for Douay. On the other hand, the roll at Eu was by no means confined to the postulants it did send to Douay. The remainder of its ten years' population can presumably have been lay boys.[1] It thus represents a broadening of the base of the exile education movement, albeit due to force of circumstances in that the *pueri* arrived and had to be schooled irrespective of lay or religious destination.

As to its fate, the view that the death of its patron Guise in 1588 doomed it[2] is untenable. It was still at Eu four years later; in those four years it sent twenty-one boys to Douay-Rheims; and Valladolid was expecting a party from it in June 1590.[3]

The link between the Eu school and the coming St. Omer school lies in that, by the time the latter was broached, the eight or ten boys living on the Guise pension at Eu had been transferred to the town of St. Omer. Dr. Barret of Douay, after application to the local magistrates, bought a house for them and others, opposite the Jesuit Walloon College, in September 1592, the magistrates' condition being that its rector should not be an Englishman, nor its numbers exceed fifteen.[4]

When Persons broached a plan for a Jesuit school in St. Omer early the following year 1593, Barret was suspicious of it. Not from any overwhelming predilection for 'our' school from Eu ('aedicula nostra' he had called it), but lest the granting of a pension by Philip II for a new Jesuit venture should still further retard the arrears of his pension due to Douay.[5] It has been said that Allen too was against the venture.

[1] *Second Douay Diary* (Knox); *Third Douay Diary* (*C.R.S.* x).

[2] Guilday, 130. Morris, *Troubles*, ii. 28, dated its demise at 1589.

[3] Cf. Pollen, in *Stonyhurst Magazine*, i. 284–5.

[4] L. Willaert, *Coll. Anglais de S. Omer*, in *Recueil de Travaux* of Catholic Univ. of Louvain, fasc. 40–1 (1914); Pollen, in *C.R.S.* xiv. 11 note, and sources; St. Omer Municipal Arch., M. f. 14 (transcript at Stonyhurst, p. 45); *Stonyhurst Mag.*, iv. 932–4.

[5] Pollen, *MS. Continuation . . .*, ch. 13, p. 45.

There is no evidence, however, that his hesitations were due to anything more sinister than lack of information about it, owing to some of Persons' letters to him at the time going astray. But until Allen, as leader of the whole College Movement, approved it, the Jesuit General (Aquaviva) likewise hesitated: i.e. till the end of that summer 1593.[1]

The new venture had been put by Persons to Philip II in March. Philip's first letter on it (13 March) was favourable: that there be a school 'for sixteen young English children', whom he would himself support. Persons invited the Flanders provincial (Oliveira) to appoint a rector, and offered himself to supply a minister and master of studies. This last fact alone shows that he had in mind something very much more ambitious than the half-dozen Eu survivors and the St. Omer magistrates' sixteen. At the start, he added, the other seminaries could help support the new one financially; for would it not 'send them subjects to study philosophy with them'. Fr. Garnett in England had said, already, that there would be no lack of boys from home to fill it.[2]

In July Persons (still in Madrid) sent Fr. William Flack to St. Omer 'to begin to assemble such young men as may be there and are suitable'. Fr. Flack arrived there on 27 September, with Fr. Henry Walpole—whose knowledge of the Colleges was to be extracted from him later, in London, by torture.[3] Within a week the St. Omer sheriffs reported a score of English boys, and the Flemish rector said: 'In God's name when there be means let them come an hundred.'[4]

The St. Omer roll began with boys arrived from England. They came by escaping to the coast, the passages of some paid by the Spanish government; or some of them disguised as mariners, by way of Scotland or Irish ports. From interceptions and captures the Government soon had a shrewd appraisal of what was afoot, but nevertheless by the end of the first term there were thirty-three boys, in a house rented by Fr. Persons' brother George. By the end of the

[1] For Allen's (suppositious) opposition, see More, *Hist. Prov. Angl. S.J.*, 162; Knox, *Letters & Memorials*, 358; Tierney-Dodd, ii. 162, ii. 178 note; Dodd, *Secret Policy of the Jesuits* (1715), 64, 66. For the approvals, Pollen, *MS. Continuation*, 48 (Aquaviva to Manares, 31 July, and Persons to Aquaviva, 16 June). For the lost dispatches, Persons to Aquaviva, 15 July 1593—see following note.

[2] For King Philip's letter, *C.R.S.* xiv. 24. Persons to Aquaviva, 22 March 1593, in *Arch. S.J. Rome*, transcripts at Farm St. (London); and again 16 June; and General's reply, 10 May.

[3] Cf. *Cal. S.P. Dom. Eliz.* 1591–4, pp. 483–539 *passim*.

[4] MS. Diary of the Flemish S.J. College at St. Omer, in St. Omer Municipal Arch., transcript, p. 135; Walpole to Persons, 13 Nov., q. in *Stonyhurst Mag.*, xxiv. 177.

first full year there were fifty, in a larger house in the Rue Tenne, till palatial permanent quarters became available a year later in the Hotel de Licques; and when the century ended six years later there were a hundred.[1]

We shall have later on to examine the internal work of this remarkable school, in relation to education at large and the college movement in particular. Meanwhile, the lengthy narrative of events above settles two points: St. Omer's date, and its relation to Eu. The date is clearly 'Winter Term, 1593.'[2] The relation to Eu may be a continuity of personnel, but not of foundation. Both schools had been Persons' contributions, but St. Omer was a new foundation. Its date, however, raises a third issue. Was there any connection between the St. Omer enterprise and the abortive Education Bill in the 1593 Parliament?[3] Given the juxtaposition of these two events, a Bill to seize Catholic children and a school founded abroad to receive them, was there more than coincidence? The Bill in the Commons in London—26 February (O.S.); King Philip's approval in Madrid to the St. Omer project—13 March. Was one cause and the other effect?

It is thoroughly in character, that what Fr. Persons did, in effect, forestalled the Bill. His first intimation of his St. Omer project to the Jesuit General, Aquaviva, was before the end of February. As he was in Spain at the time, he cannot have yet heard of the actual Bill, however. As soon as he did hear of it, he went at once to King Philip.

Persons' chief source of information on events in London was Richard Verstegan, a Londoner of Dutch extraction who had left Christ Church rather than conform. His public reputation today is that of an antiquary, and a friend of Sir Thomas Gresham, who was Elizabeth's ambassador in Antwerp, where Verstegan went to live soon after 1576 and set up a printing-press. It was from Antwerp that he served as a clearing-house for Catholic letters and information passing between London and the exiles. His *Advices from England* were one of the very lifelines, through Persons, of the whole exile movement.

Verstegan sent off his first news of the February Parliament four days after it opened, forecasting 'severe laws' against the Catholics. His final account of the Education Bill, ending 'but this Bill did not

[1] *Simancas Archives*, and *S.P. Dom. Eliz.*, in Guilday, 141ff.; *Stonyhurst Mag.*, iii. 336.

[2] *Pace* John Gerard's monumental *Stonyhurst* (1894), 2, whose '18 Sept. 1592' is actually the date of Barret's successful application to the St. Omer magistrates for the transfer of the Eu boys.

[3] See p. 61 above.

pass', was sent on the very day the Bill was dropped.[1] And at the end of the month he sent the full text of the Act of 1593, and Persons made a long summary of the whole business in Spanish. This is presumably how the Spanish Governor of the Netherlands, in describing the St. Omer project to the local magistracy, was able to adduce 'the suffering English, escaped from the heretic Lords that are forcibly separating them from their parents'.[2]

Persons' own account, in his long disquisition on the colleges delivered in 1610, implies that he had not had advance notice of what was brewing in the Commons. But the dates show that once he heard he lost not a single moment in bringing to birth the St. Omer 'idea' already in his mind.[3]

There is one final matter—the purpose of St. Omer. This too is settled by the contemporary documents (against some of the historians). In intention it can be described as 'Eu writ very large'.

A priori, it could have begun as a *petit séminaire* and have become mixed by dint of lay boys arriving, thus marking no step forward in policy since Douay in 1568.[4] But the second rector, Schondonck, speaks of all the students, *alumni* (foundationers) and *convictores* (fee-payers) alike, as being there to escape a heretical education in England:[5] which suggests that, while the Jesuit founders would naturally expect many vocations to their Society from the school, it had from the start that 'mixed' character which we have traced back to the *Constitutions* of Cardinal Pole.[6]

Persons himself once speaks of St. Omer as 'a fifth seminary'. But much more often he is describing how it will feed to all the other seminaries 'picked men'; and this precludes the rigid view that in St.

[1] 6 or 17 Feb. (o.s.)—cf. L. J. Hicks, p. 62, n.2. The originals of Verstegan's letters are in *Stonyhurst MSS.*, Collectanea B. esp. ff. 75, 79. There are transcripts at Farm St. They have been edited for *C.R.S.* (lii, 1959) by Anthony G. Petti.

[2] Quoted by J. J. E. Proust, in *Messager des Sciences Historiques*, 1861, p. 300.

[3] 'Valde saeviebat in Anglia persecutio hoc tempore contra Catholicos, ubi inter cetera constitutum fuerat ut filioli deinceps parentum catholicorum praesertim nobilium a teneris annis praeceptoribus traderentur hereticis pestilentissima haeresi Calviniana imbuendi; cuius rei indignitate impietateque motus, P. Personius ad aulam regiam statim se contulit, scelerisque immanitatem Majestati regni aperuit, obtinuitque commiserante rege tantae calamitate, ut aliud adhuc Seminarium Puerorum Anglorum Audomaropoli in Belgio instruerentur.'

[4] 'Nettement ecclésiastique'—the view of L. Willaert, S.J., in *American Catholic Quarterly Review*, xxx. 745–58 (1905) and his *Collège Anglais de S. Omer* (1914). Thus also R. Lechat, S.J., *Refugiés Anglais* (1914), 215–17—'only intending priests'.

[5] In a *Responsio* of 1609, in Royal Archives at Brussels, *Varia S.J.*, carton, 31, q. by Willaert (1914), p. 6.

[6] See p. 24 above.

Omer we are dealing with a kind of pre-novitiate. His monumental speech on all the colleges, when he was in the *Venerabile* in Rome in 1597, refers to it in patently general terms, as a college:

to receyve the first frye that cometh out of Ingland, which before must eather have stayed there and bene in deanger of infection, or else lose there tyme and lack maintenance on thys syde of the seas, for that there war no fyt place for to receyve them here.[1]

In short, St. Omer provided Jesuit vocations, but it was for others as well.[2] Eu writ *very* large—for by the end of the century it held one hundred pupils: larger than the Elizabethan grammar schools. What is most to the point is *how far* it was lay. But while for the seventeenth century we have evidence enough to divine the proportions,[3] for the sixteenth we have not.

These conclusions are strengthened, lastly, by what happened a few years later when the Scots College was founded in Rome (1600). This college was *expressly* for lay as well as ecclesiastical students. Its purpose was that of the medieval universities. Ironically enough, the *lack* of boys eager to become priests—as shown by the number who would take no oath to return afterwards to the Scottish mission—was a prime reason why the college languished so soon and for so long. The Jesuit leader in Scotland, Fr. William Creighton, wrote to encourage the Cardinal Protector (Caetani) in a quite mistaken belief that boys from all three Scottish universities would now flock to Rome. In 1615 the Scots College was placed under Jesuit control by Paul V. Early in the following year the decision was taken to make it a clerical seminary pure and simple. The boys were given three months to decide whether to enrol for ordination or depart. All of them chose the former; and Jesuit rules came into force.[4]

[1] In his Life of Campion, in S.J. *Letters & Notices* (London). The speech is in *Stonyhurst MSS.*, Coll. N. ii. f. 125 on. Cf. his letters of 22 March, 19 April, 12 July and 7 Sept. 1593, to the General.

[2] A view cautiously allowed by Foley (*Records*, vii. xxxvii–iii) and Thomas Glover, S.J. (q. ibid., xxxix, from *Stonyhurst MSS.*), and definitely adopted in Burton, *Challoner* (1909), ii. 41–2. Its earliest expression is in Dodd's *Jesuits* (1715), 64, 66—'the mainteigning of hopeful Youths, and in order to give them some tincture of Catholic Learning, that they might be qualified for more Noble Studies, and here and there are pick'd out to be incorporated into the Society'.

[3] See p. 167 below.

[4] A. Bellesheim. *Hist. of Catholic Church in Scotland* (1889), iii. 386–7; Meyer, 115ff.; Creighton to Caetani, 7 Sept. 1595, in Meyer 524–6; Statutes of the College in *Bibl. Vat., Barb.* 8629, ff. 9–22 (based on the English College, Rome); and *History of the Scots College, Rome*, by W. E. Brown (1930), 2, 6–8, 11, 14–15.

But at all events the original setting of the Scots College at Rome was that of a mixed institution and without postulant bias. With St. Omer, it reflects a broader educational outlook than would have been likely earlier, when so many of the exiles had expected to return home in triumph on the queen's death. This is made nowhere more clear than in the statutes drawn up for St. Omer itself in the same year 1600, which we shall have to examine in due course.

V

CATHOLIC EDUCATION IN ELIZABETHAN ENGLAND

THE Catholic schoolmasters executed in England total twenty-three, all but two of them in the reign of Elizabeth. They were executed not as schoolmasters, for the maximum penalty for that was a prison sentence, but as traitors. Actually they were executed for being Catholics: as is shown so often by the offer of their life and sometimes their freedom, on the scaffold, if they would assert the royal supremacy. The list is as follows:

PLUMTREE, Thomas (Lincolnshire)
Corpus Chr. Coll. Oxford. Durham, 4 January 1570.
SHERT, John (Cheshire)
Brasenose, Oxford. Tyburn, 30 May 1582.
COTTAM, Thomas (Lancashire)
Brasenose, Oxford. Tyburn, 30 May 1582.
SLADE, John (Dorset)
Winchester and New College. Winchester, 30 October 1583.
BODY, John (Somerset)
Winchester and New College. Andover, 2 November 1583
FENN, James (Somerset)
Corpus Chr. Coll. Oxford. Tyburn, 12 February 1584.
MUNDEN, John (Dorset)
Winchester and New College. Tyburn, 12 February 1584.
GWYN, Richard (Llanidloes)
St. John's Coll. Cambridge. Wrexham, 17 October 1584.
WOODFEN, Nicholas (Herefordshire)
Leominster Gram. School. Tyburn, 21 January 1586.
DOUGLAS, George (Edinburgh)
Educated in Paris. York, 9 September 1587.
GARLICK, Nicholas (Derbyshire)
Gloucester Hall, Oxford. Derby, 24 July 1588.
LUDLAM, Robert (Derbyshire)
St. John's Coll. Oxford. Derby, 24 July 1588.
HOLFORD, Thomas (Cheshire)
Clerkenwell, 28 August 1588.

WIDMERPOOL, Robert (Nottinghamshire)
Gloucester Hall, Oxford. Canterbury, 1 October 1588.

CROCKETT, Ralph (Cheshire)
Chr. Coll. Cambr. and Gloucester Hall, Oxford. Chichester, 1 October 1588.

SUTTON, Robert (Leicestershire)
? Oxford. Clerkenwell, 5 October 1588.

GERARD, Miles (Lancashire)
Educated at Rheims. Rochester, 13 or 30 April 1590.

WELLS, Swithin (Hampshire)
Grays Inn Fields, 10 December 1591.

SWALLOWELL, George (Durham)
Educated Sherburn Hospital. Darlington, 26 July 1594.

FREEMAN, William (Yorkshire)
Magdalen Coll. Oxford. Warwick, 13 August 1595.

LINE, Anne (Essex)
Laywoman. Tyburn, 27 February 1601.

WELLBOURN, Thomas (Yorkshire)
York, 1 August 1605.

SOMERS, Thomas (Carlisle)
Educated at Douay. Tyburn, 10 December 1610.

Because of the inquiries and documentation involved in proceeding against them, these twenty-three are among the best known, in detail, of the period. They include both kinds of teacher, the unlicensed 'public' teacher of a school, and the private tutor. They include priests and laymen; schoolmasters who became Catholics, Catholics who became schoolmasters, and one woman. Those who became priests were apprehended in England after their return on the mission from Douay College. One of them, Robert Sutton, was at work ten years before he was caught; two of them, John Body and Nicholas Garlick, were at large five years; Thomas Somers, four years; John Shert, two years; but Thomas Cottam was arrested on landing at Dover. One of the laymen, too, John Body, had been at Douay, but had there realized his vocation was 'in the world'. Another of them, the Welshman Richard Gwyn, had had a Protestant education in both universities, till 'reconciled'. Twelve of the twenty-three were Oxford men.

All paid the supreme penalty of the law, with varying degrees of severity. For long they have been among the martyrs for whose canonization modern English Catholics have worked. They are the 'mentioned-in-dispatches' of an educational force whose strength can never be exactly assessed and has never till now been scrutinized as a whole.

At first there was no deliberately organized strength at all. The Catholic Church as a self-governing and dominant institution in England had disappeared, but the country was still overwhelmingly Catholic in religion, and though the new laws touched the clergy sharply, they left the laity comparatively alone. The Government was not immediately well equipped to molest. The measures taken to avoid a Protestant education, and the exile movement itself, were at first stop-gaps.

For those who could afford it, the readiest course was to substitute a private Catholic tutor for the public Protestant schoolmaster. In this way began a practice which, from having been the norm of aristocratic education in Catholic England, was henceforth the dangerous device of the Catholic minority throughout penal times, and the most important single means of maintaining wandering priests.

Some of these tutors, serving in families and at the same time teaching the children of the neighbourhood, were ejected priests. 'There is one', Parker was informed in 1564, 'comes hither [to Whalley, Lancs.] that has been deprived, and changes his name, and now teaches school. . . .'[1] At Preston, Nicholas Banester was reported in 1565 as an 'unlettered priest' running a school, and was haled off to Lancaster gaol. Ten years later he was found near Preston and barred from entering the town. Sir Thomas Petre in Essex had his own family priest-schoolmaster, Watham; Sir Henry Dury in Suffolk and the Verney house in Warwickshire likewise. Many of them were kept on the run—John Bolt migrated from the Petres to the Verneys.[2] Fr. John Gerard, of Gunpowder Plot fame, was tutored at home and even managed to have a Catholic tutor at Oxford (Mr. Leutner). Most of the old Catholic county families of today, indeed, owe the preservation of their faith to having been able to maintain tutors, clerical and lay, in the seclusion of their private mansions, from Elizabethan days onwards.

After 1571, stimulated by the excitement resulting from the excommunication of the queen by the pope, most of the bishops' injunctions refer directly to tutors as well as schoolmasters. This is a point of major significance, since it extends the term 'schoolmaster' to cover everyone who ordinarily should need a licence. More significant still is

[1] Parker *Correspondence*, 221, No. 168: and q. in Birt, 307. Wherever the schoolmaster or tutor is named, from here on, the relevant references are in my *Biographical Catalogue of Catholic Schoolmasters* . . .; see p. ix, preface, above.

[2] Foley, ii. 586–7 note, 590; *S.P. Dom. Eliz.* clxxv, No. 75; Lambeth, *Hussey MSS.*, 1577–88, ii. 45; Gillow, i. 257.

the light it throws on the royal policy of waiting for the Marian generation to die out. A contemporary draft of 'Regulations for Schools and Schoolmasters' puts it wryly: that three out of every four papists 'were not twelve years old when the Queen came to her crown, but have learnt it in the time of her reign. So it appeareth that the Queen's trust hath been deceived in the education of her subjects....' This is no doubt levelled at lenient local justices.[1]

Tutoring was of course the least risky of all the evasions. So rife was it, as the reign drew on, that even the Puritans, themselves under persecution from Archbishop Whitgift, complained of the slack enforcement of the laws against Catholic teachers, and 'the sufferance of corrupt private schoolmasters in houses whereby the youth of England hath been so corrupted without the prelates looking into it that if all the Papists in England be divided into four parts, three of those parts are under thirty-five years olde, and so learned their papistry in her Majesties own tyme'.[2] Likewise the travelling lay catechists, though these were the more easy to apprehend because more people knew of them. John Finch, of Eccleston in Lancashire, caught in 1581 and executed at Lancaster three years later, had been catechist and *liaison* man between the county families and itinerant clergy, while officially a clerk.[3]

Thus far tutors. But schools too were coming into existence for those below the ranks of the nobility. Some were able to continue for long periods before being broken up. At Tideswell (Derbyshire) Robert Pursglove, an ex-suffragan bishop, opened a Catholic school in 1560 and ran it for fifteen years, and his successor Nicholas Garlick continued it for a further six until he went to Rheims. Michael Tirrye maintained a school for Catholic children at Nisgarthes (Aysgarth?) and later at York, till 1577. At least six of such schools are on record as still surviving in 1584: Thomas Asmowe at Ormskirk, Humphrey Cartwright at Scarisbrick, John Burge, William Aspinhall, William Fletcher at Wigan and one at Farnworth. By dint of outwardly conforming, John Case was able to keep a Catholic school at Woodstock after leaving his Oxford college some time before 1570. There must have been many more of these new schools than the bishops' inquiries

[1] *Lansdowne MSS.* 155, No. 40, q. in Birt, 385 note. A report in *Arch. Vat. Misc. Arm. XI* (t. 94, f. 208; q. in Meyer, 211 note) relates both to the exiles and to 'Alii quoque [qui] se faciunt ludi magistros in familiis nobilium, ut semen catholicum spargant in Anglia.'

[2] Q. in N. Wood, 288.

[3] Gillow, ii. 258.

brought to light.[1] In view of the clerical tradition, and the legislation of Pole in England and Trent at large, the lay Catholic schoolmaster was also something of an innovation.

Nevertheless these were the years of Catholic decline, caused most of all perhaps by the perplexing question of how far they might legitimately 'conform'—avoid trouble by attending the Protestant services and schools (as the law demanded) and 'stopping their ears'. On the evidence of the phenomenal number of re-conversions in the first years of the Jesuit mission in England after 1580, and the fairly constant ratio between the Catholic minority and the total population in the following century, it has been cogently argued that the decade 1560–70 is the crucial period in the Catholic decline, on account also of the destruction of ecclesiastical organization, which left the people feeling forsaken by the Church in the years before the opening of the colleges abroad and the appointment of an archpriest in England.[2] It was easy enough to make a personal distinction between exterior and interior conformity; and to be swayed by the fact that no less a person than the Imperial ambassador went to church with Elizabeth; and to make use of a Bible in English available in the parish church years before a Catholic edition could be had. The Catholic heroine of York, Margaret Clitheroe, could resist unto death, even the horrible death by *peine forte et dure*, by pressing (1586); but her brother, John Middleton, had meanwhile conformed and reared his children in Yorkshire as Protestants. Ironically enough, the Catholic decline took place before the vigorous persecution of 1581 set in; and that persecution served indeed to check it. *Sanguis martyrum semen Ecclesiae.* Clandestine schooling and tutoring were increasingly to become a goal and a policy as the reign lengthened and hope of relief in one's own lifetime waned.

There was plenty of Catholic 'activity' also in some of the schools of the Establishment itself. When William Camden, the historian, became second master at Westminster School in 1593, the situation there was that the Queen's Scholars had to conform, as they attended the Abbey services, but the Town boys were under no such obligation. Camden claimed to have converted 'certain Irish boys of popish breeding and affection'. Richard Ireland, who succeeded him in 1599,

[1] The only attention to the clandestine schools under Elizabeth, hitherto, is the summary in W. F. Hastings, C.M., *English Catholic Education, 1580–1800* (Univ. London thesis, 1923).

[2] Meyer, 60–75.

himself became a Catholic and went to France ten years later to the 'College of Writers' then about to be established in Paris in fulfilment of a dream of Allen's. Just before the end of the century the headmaster of Worcester Collegiate Grammar School sent his own son Alexander to the English College at Rome 'for the purpose of instruction in the Catholic faith'. Similarly Francis Johnson, the son of the master of Winchester, was sent via Douay to the English College at Valladolid about the same date. As time went on, other licensed masters in prominent schools followed suit.[1]

Even in the prisons every opportunity was seized. 'Both in this [the Marshalsea], and other prisons', wrote Allen in 1583, 'many Masses are said daily, with the leave or connivance of the gaolers, who are either bribed or favourable to religion; people from without are admitted from time to time for conference, confession or communion; and, more than this, the priests are allowed to go out every day to different parts of the city and attend to the spiritual needs of the Catholics, on condition that they return to prison for the night. In this way the salvation of many persons is furthered quite as much as if the priests were at liberty.'[2] Wherever there were Catholic schoolmasters in leniently run prisons, as for example in Salford gaol in 1584 there were three,[3] it is at times a legitimate inference that they plied their craft among the children of the inmates. But lenient conditions in the Elizabethan prisons were hardly the rule. More than one of the forty-six Catholic teachers known to have been in gaol died there. The Carnarvonshire master William Griffith, committed to a dungeon by his keeper upon the uproar at the death of the Queen of Scots in 1587, died a fortnight later 'as soon as he came into the fresh air'.[4]

Wisbech Castle, commandeered from the Bishop of Ely in 1572 to serve as an additional prison for 'constant Catholics', became not only a disedifying centre of intrigue in the quarrel between the secular clergy and the regulars, but a notorious place of considerable informal education. Framlingham Castle was added to it in 1580, as a national

[1] Sargeaunt, *Hist. of Westminster School*, 53 f.; Foley, vi. 570; *C.R.S.* xxx. 66 and note. Cf. also Thomas Whitaker, master of Burnley Free School, whose son Thomas (*alias* Starkie) went to the Spanish colleges in 1634 (*C.R.S.* xxx. 153 and note), and his other son Humphrey to the English College at Lisbon, via St. Omer, in 1629 (Croft-Gillow, *Lisbon College*, 269).

[2] Allen to Agazarri, 14 March 1583, in Knox, *Douay Diaries*, lxix.

[3] Blundell, *Old. Cath. Lancs.*, ii. 10.

[4] Q. in Morris, *Troubles*, iii. 36.

and not merely a local gaol.[1] A few of the boys entering the colleges abroad disclosed that they had been actually born in gaol, while their recusant parents were incarcerated.[2] In York Castle early in the new century a regular Catholic school was suppressed that had been catering for the surrounding countryside as well as the city of York, and took in *boarders*, and ran a grammar curriculum that included music.[3]

It is possible, here and there, to catch the flavour of a given area over a period. Lancashire in particular, as always. Brian Cansfield, who went to Flanders at sixteen in 1597, to become a Jesuit, had been educated at no fewer than six different Catholic schools in Lancashire: at Lancaster, Tunstall, Blackburn, Urswick, Warton and Thornton.[4] In a report on the state of Lancashire in 1590 the Privy Council was told that 'the Papists everywhere are grown so confident that they contemne magistrates and their authoritie . . .', while the Jesuits behaved locally with 'confident ostentacion' and 'open disputacion' owing to the lukewarmness of so many J.Ps. There was 'no worse house in Lancashire', said Sir Robert Cecil in the same year, 'than Mr. Yates', the schoolmaster at Blackburn [Grammar School] whose wife, daughter and maid are recusants, and although the maid is known to have done much hurt amongst the scholars, he is yet suffered to keep her'.[5]

An apostate priest James Young, *alias* George Dingley, made Lancashire his hunting-ground in 1592. He listed ten of the leading Catholic estates in the county as keeping 'priests or recusants as schoolmasters'. Their names are of Catholic families that run through the annals of the penal centuries: Thomas Southworth of Samlesbury, Thomas Garrard of High Carre, Bartholomew Hesketh of New Hall, Skillikorne of Preese, Houghton of the Lea, Houghton of Park Hall ('I think this twenty years he hath had one after another'), Blundell

[1] Pollen, 255, 357. The records of Wisbech Castle are vol. li of *C.R.S.* (*The Wisbech Stirs*, ed. P. Renold, 1958). The young George Muskett (later at Douay) found there in 1595 'imprisoned priests secretly instructing a number of youths, who, under the guise of servitors, were permitted to reside in the prison'.

[2] E.g. Thomas Macclesfield, born in Stafford gaol in 1585 when his parents had been there a year. Educated in the prison and at the local grammar school, and to Douay in 1603 (Gillow, iv. 312).

[3] J. Kitching, 18 ff., citing York *House Books*, 1605–12, fols. 269–72. Also Foley, iii. 187, 205 for the families of two boarders there, Cater (later S.J.) and Constable (later at St. Omer).

[4] Gillow, i. 396. His *Responsa* at the *Venerabile* are in *C.R.S.* liv. 106.

[5] *S.P. Dom. Eliz.* ccxxxv, No. 68; ibid. ccxl, q. in *R.H.S. Trans.* vi. 196.

of Crosby, Haydock of Cottam (a kinsman of Allen), Blundell of Ince Blundell, Massey of Rixton.[1]

For all his cunning, Dingley seems not to have got wind of the school of Thomas Somers at Grange-over-Sands, nor another that was certainly flourishing about the same time at Much Woolton, near Liverpool, where one John Almond had his early education before going to Rome in 1597.[2]

But Dingley was not the only Government agent in that part of the country. Another of them keeping watch from 1580 onwards throws much light on how the landed families, who were to be the mainstay of the faith in the depths of penal times later, contrived to be so. He instances the Catholic tutor Robert Dewhurst as having taught a whole tract of families—the children of Alexander Rigby at Ormskirk, Sir William Norris at Speke, Sir Richard Shirburn at Stonyhurst, the Standish family, the Huttons, the Rigbys of Harrock and the Molyneux of Hockley.[3]

For many of the thirty-two schools so far known to have been at work in Lancashire before 1600 these two spies are a major source. Indeed, reports of this kind light up odd corners of what is otherwise, from prison lists and fine rolls, a very shadowy picture of the whole country.

London itself, for example. After the vivid episode at St. Paul's school in 1561, when the ejected High Master, Freeman, is told that he can save his post by taking the oath, and his wife cries that she will beg in the streets for them both, we find little of London schools in the documents. John Shert of Brasenose is teaching there about 1570, Robert Sutton till just before 1577, a layman Monkaster in 1584, and another layman Sanford, in Fetter Lane, in 1597. Into this bald catalogue comes an informer (the priest Dingley again), telling the much he can remember of his Catholic friends in the days when he was himself on the run: how he 'went [again] to [Thomas] Wiseman [near the Inns of Court] for two days, and by this means was tabled with Cole, a schoolmaster, at the upper end of Holborn, but as he got into trouble was again forced to repair to Wiseman. . . . Was visited [at Cole's] by Mr. Stamp of Derbyshire, to whom, and to Mary Felton of Highgate and Mr. & Mrs. Cole, he said Mass', and so on. From this piece alone

[1] This lengthy report is in *S.P. Dom. Eliz.* ccxliii, No. 52. For Dingley see *C.R.S.* xiv. 15 note, xxx. 7 and note, and Foley, vi. xix note.

[2] Gillow, i. 127.

[3] *S.P. Dom. Eliz.* cxlvi, No. 37.

the Government got five names, and we a glimpse of that 'upper end of Holborn' which was to be two hundred years later the first seed-plot of the Catholic charity school movement.[1]

As the reign closes, the only other pedagogue we can document in London is the heroic woman Anne Line, of Dunmow in Essex, who had had charge of the house which Fr. John Gerard, S.J., established as a refuge for priests in the metropolis. She taught children. In 1600, under the Act of 1585, she was executed at Tyburn for 'harbouring'.

But we catch the flavour of the period most intimately from what young Catholic men told of their past life on entering the colleges abroad.

> Was struck by the advice of his father when he was leaving London to study law—to remember Catholicism while living among Puritans, but to attend heretical churches for the sake of his career.

Or,

> Son of an obscure tanner and a mother of extinct nobility, whose name he used because less known, so as to spare his uncle, whom he left to come here, and because he wishes to follow its lustre. . . . Has mainly heretical and schismatic kinsfolk, except for the uncle aforesaid, an honest and industrious clerk of the Chancery Court. Studied dialectic at Oxford; proceeded bachelor after 16 terms and was intending to complete his examinations in the following Lent, but was persuaded instead to spend his money in crossing oversea.

Or,

> lived with heretics until fourteen; discussed religion with a young Catholic who took him to the Clink [prison: where there were priests]; was there reconciled by a priest; had all his Catholic books burnt by his mother and elder brother when they learned the news. . . . Was persuaded to go to heretical churches. After two or three years began to think again of Catholicism, but did not know where to turn, owing to the death of his Catholic friend. . . .

Or,

> was sent by his uncle to York, where, living in the prison with Catholics, he learnt grammar and religion from the confessor Clement Hodgson, gent.

There are hundreds of these. They give cumulatively a picture of varying steadfastness, and varying drift, amidst complete disorganiza-

[1] Cf. my 'Beginnings of Catholic Elementary Education', in *Dublin Review*, No. 411, 284–309 (Oct. 1939).

tion and chaos. To read them today is like walking an ancient battlefield.[1]

How widespread the map of clandestine schooling in Elizabethan England in fact was can be asserted with some confidence, but not (as yet) sketched with much assurance. It is quite impossible to regard the limits as being reliably measured by the proved *overt* totals of Catholic schools and teachers. And the size of the 'fifth column' implied by so much of the evidence can never be measured at all.

Qualitatively, there is plenty of evidence for every gradation that could be imagined. At one extreme are the men and boys who, on answering the biographical questions set them when they entered the colleges abroad, could say quite simply 'tota vita inter catholicos educatus'. At the other extreme are the families that conformed and then apostatized very early, and became lost to Catholic history altogether. Many of those who spent their childhood in Catholic homes, learning their faith and their letters from their parents or from tutors, went thence to the public grammar schools; and many of these went on to the universities or the Inns of Court. Many more, village children and the children of family retainers, were taught by the 'private' schoolmasters in the houses and halls and manors of the Catholic rich. Many others lapsed and were temporarily lost to the Church, till influenced by a Catholic relative, or by reading the controversial works of Robert Bellarmine or Robert Persons or books of Catholic piety, or (in London) coming under the spell of John Gerard, or meeting a wandering priest, and being 'reconciled'—a commitment which (after 1585) was high treason for both parties. Some were born in prison and more died there. Some were caught, stealing away to get their education beyond seas. Some grew up and had had manly careers in commerce, or in the foreign wars, before the trials of adult life constrained them to think of letters and the after-life at all.

All this could be asserted, qualitatively, without evidence. It is part of human nature in any profound crisis of conscience. Much more difficult is to see its proportions, to see it quantitatively, on the cumulative evidence we have. Not all of this has ever been examined. Nor could it be. The Anglican episcopal archives of the period, and the county archives alone, are material for a team of scholars for a lifetime: to say nothing of what has been lost. But some attempt can today be made, especially since none has been made before, to answer

[1] From the *Responsa* at the *Venerabile* in Rome. See p. 84 below.

such a central question as: what was the chance of a Catholic education for an ordinary Elizabethan?

The Government's own first attempt at a basis that would obliquely bear on this, the nationwide inquiry into recusancy in 1577, is of very little help. Altogether nine schoolmasters appear in the returns, and twenty-two Oxford men.[1] These of course can be only a fraction of the total number of recusants in academic life. The grand total of names for the whole country, indeed, is only 1,387, and for London only 99. An independent contemporary source for one county alone (Cambridgeshire) gives nineteen parishes having a schoolmaster and sixteen of them unlicensed; and in another (Durham) there were ten unlicensed, though not all of these can have been Catholic recusants, as two were the local curates.[2] The 1577 returns are clearly but a *ballon d'essai*.

Far more promising at first sight are the Recusant Rolls, the long series of eighty-three surveys, at yearly intervals, beginning in 1592. Few of these have as yet been systematically searched. They differ from all preceding lists of recusants in that, following the imposition of the £20 penalty for every month of non-attendance at church, the object was not only to count but to fine. The information is given parish by parish; it includes names, status, amounts owing, how discharged and '*fiat commissio*' (i.e. that payment was to be enforced).[3]

But while these Recusant Rolls are a superb source of evidence for the effect of fines and (later) double-taxation, and for assessing how far the leading Catholic families were or were not impoverished,[4] they are of hardly any service for assessing the prevalence of Catholic education. In the first roll, of 1592–3, only seven recusant schoolmasters are recorded by name, and all of them are in Lancashire.[5]

[1] These returns, with a critical Introduction, are in *C.R.S.* xxii. The teachers are Richard Powle, lately of Sutton; two other priests unnamed—also dioc. Peterborough; Tarry (Battle); Thomas Whistons (Stone, Staffs.); William Pylstone (at The Van, in Wales); John Fletcher; Michael Tirrye; Geoffrey Stevenson. The Oxford men are on pp. 100–1.

[2] Archdeacon's Visitation Book, Cambr. 1581–3, in *V.C.H.* ii. 238. The Durham [1578] lists are in Surtees Soc. vol. xxii (1850).

[3] The 1592–3 *Recusant Roll* forms *C.R.S.* xviii, edited by Hugh Bowler, O.S.B. There is a list of the same date, covering gentry and squires, in *Hist. MSS. Comm.*, Salisbury MSS., iv. 263 and xiii. 564.

[4] Cf. Brian Magee, *The English Recusants* (1938).

[5] Robert Whitfield and his wife, 'lately of Clayton-in-the-Moors'; John Butterfield, lately of Sutton, and owing £224; Richard Aspinwall of Lathom, owing £240; Peter Longworth and his wife, of Ballam, owing £224; Edward Waddington, of Church; Edward Sager of Dinckley; and Isabella Yate, wife of Lawrence Yate 'lately school-

There could hardly be a more telling example of how incomplete and misleading the official returns must have been throughout the entire penal period, for all the obvious reasons, of ignorance, bribery, collusion, complaisance and slackness. Wherever the rolls have been searched for particular areas, the verdict is the same.[1]

The fact that other sources can prove the existence of over 120 schoolmasters and tutors during the reign, and of over eighty places where there were schools,[2] shows the complex of negative responses the State's inquests always met.

And here once again, the historian is snagged by the very unevenness of the evidence. The dozen schools that can be named in Yorkshire cannot have been by any means all there were: for only a year after Elizabeth's death many more can be proved, from Peacock's *Yorkshire Catholics of 1604*. A contemporary local survey, or a spy's report, at any particular moment, can make all the difference.

The attested Elizabethan Catholic schools were (naturally) most numerous in Lancashire and Yorkshire and London. In two places there was continuity over twenty-four years: Ormskirk under Thomas Asmowe, Scarisbrick under Humphrey Cartwright. In two others, sixteen years: North Laffenham in Rutlandshire (George Douglas), Wye in Kent (Morland and later Clifton). At Tideswell in Derbyshire the record shows twenty-one years (Pursglove and Nicholas Garlick). In the decade that ends with Parliament's abortive Education Bill in 1593, close on forty schools can be found.

Of the attested schoolmasters, twenty-five had been dismissed before the year of the oath (1563) but many of them were back in other centres later. Twenty-three (besides the twenty-three executed) knew prison from the inside. Some, as Edmund Arthur, who went to Douay in 1587 but returned after the probationary week there, saw their apostolate to lie in the world rather than the cloister. Some, as John Case in 1570 in the city of Oxford, conformed themselves, but were sought by Catholics to teach their children. Some, like Ralph Crockett in 1586, arrived back trained from Douay to be immediately scooped into gaol. Where Catholicism was strong, the gentry could still go far

master at Blackborne'. From other sources, just on 40 can be documented; and these are only some.

[1] E.g. seventeenth-century Wiltshire, by J. Anthony Williams, summarized in *Newsletter for Students of Recusant Hist.* (ed. T. A. Birrell), No. 4 (1962), 21–2.

[2] In addition, the total of clergy in England by 1600 was about 350, of whom about one in seven were 'old' (Marian). The Government had lists only of those it could locate. Cf. *Hist. MSS. Comm.*, Salisbury MSS., vi. 311 ff., 561 f.

to get their way; when Madox was dismissed from Wolverhampton Grammar School, they induced the Merchant Taylors' Company to remove his successor. And the drain on the grammar schools, that had begun with the pre-1563 expulsions and departures of masters, had worsened. 'Ludi-magistri are very many; almost one half of our priests here [Douay] have been schoolmasters.'[1]

Thus the mustering of schools and masters gives many indications, but only a tentative picture.

By far the best evidence, both qualitatively and quantitatively, comes rather from the other end of the chain of events, in the records of the students who entered the English colleges abroad. This was a highly organized matter.

At Douay College the record was kept by the succession of college officers who produced the seven *Douay Diaries* that run from the beginning in 1568 till 1778. At the *Venerabile* in Rome the entrants were required to answer a detailed questionnaire, and their *Responsa* are extant from 1598 to 1685. Likewise at Valladolid, where the *Liber Primi Examinis* runs from the foundation in 1589 to 1862.[2]

The questions asked concerned each entrant's family, upbringing, education, health and religious condition. The answers form manifestly a historical document of the highest importance. The Rome and Valladolid *Responsa* are germane here for the light they cast on Catholic education at home under Elizabeth. The Douay *Diaries* will be examined in a later context, that of the colleges as educational establishments themselves: how and what they taught.

Of the 236 at Rome whose *Responsa* between 1598 and 1621 are complete, Lancashire, Yorkshire and London account for about one-third. Their distribution throughout the country is fairly even, though with relatively few in the West of England (12) and Wales (11). The youngest entrants are under sixteen (two), the oldest one is forty-five. Over half of them enter between eighteen and twenty-two. (This makes the fact that the replies begin in 1598 particularly convenient.)

Roughly two out of five say that they have always been Catholic,

[1] 1591. In a manuscript correction (in the hand of Fr. Henry Walpole) for the 1591 edition of the Bridgewater *Concertatio*. Transcript in *Stonyhurst MSS.*, Coll. M, f. 190, by Christopher Greene, S.J. (late seventeenth century).

[2] *Douay Diaries* 1 and 2 (ed. T. F. Knox, 1878); 3, 4, 5 and 7 are *C.R.S.* x, xi and xxviii; 6 is lost. Venerabile *Responsa* are *C.R.S.* liv (ed. A. Kenny, to 1621) and lv, to 1685 (1962–3). Valladolid *Liber Primi Exam.* is *C.R.S.* xxx (1930). The *Venerabile* volumes completely supersede the extracts in Foley, *Records* (*passim*), and the J. Stevenson *Roman Transcripts*, ix, x, xiv, in *P.R.O.*

the others (fallen into material 'schism' by conforming, or into formal heresy) have all been reconciled to the Catholic Church before (a few immediately upon) entering the College. Well over half have had fully Catholic parents. In all but three of the 'mixed' families, it is the mother who is Catholic (the father usually having conformed to keep his post). Less than a third can be said with certainty to have had a completely Catholic education. But those who have had a mixed, or a completely Protestant schooling, are fewer again; for not all the replies to this question are precise.

Of the forty-four brought up in Catholic families but sent to local grammar schools, nineteen have remained Catholics but twenty-five have had to be reconciled. Early on, there is plenty of evidence of Catholic families having recourse to the grammar schools, but as time goes on the word 'tutor' becomes more frequent. Where the father had conformed but the mother was a Catholic, the number of boys lapsing is three times those who have not (sixteen to five). Nor is Catholic family and completely Catholic education an automatic guarantee, since there are six such cases where the entrant had nevertheless lapsed at some time.

About one in four have had a higher education, at Oxford (38), Cambridge (19) or the Inns of Court (8). The Anglican grammar schools named number 33, including Eton (2), Westminster (3) and Worcester (5).

Less than a quarter have come from England direct, and of these only a handful after 1609. Well over half have come from the Jesuit school at St. Omer; after 1610 virtually the whole entry is from there. The others are from Douay (31) or variously from Europe.

The 145 Valladolid entrants in the last decade of Elizabeth's reign show a not dissimilar pattern. Always Catholic, one-half (Rome two-fifths); mixed or Protestant schooling, one-third; lapsing followed by later reconciliation, almost exactly one-half, of whom two out of every five have had a Catholic childhood.

From these *Responsa*, i.e. close on four hundred attested cases, it is clear than any romantic picture of the Catholics of England recruiting the future from within depleted but still solid ranks is wide of the mark: witness the proportion of entrants who are from mixed or schismatic families, and of those who have temporarily gone back on a careful Catholic upbringing. The erosion started by 'outward conformity' has been deeply at work. At the same time the depleted ranks are at last beginning to close: witness the increased recourse to tutors, and the steady rise in the number of those who can say 'always Catholic'. And this coheres with the Catholic schools in England demonstrable from other, independent sources, which are more numerous in the crisis year of 1592–3 than at any other time.

Now, in any society, the proportion of men who enter religion is small. And the Rome *Responsa* are from such a minority. But in so far as these 400 young men represent a cross-section of all ranks, their stories suggest that there was still an even chance for later Elizabethan children to keep the faith; a one-in-three chance for a Catholic schooling (or tutoring); a one-in-four chance of a higher education in the universities; a five-to-four risk of weakening in the atmosphere of the grammar schools; and a risk of lapsing, after a fully Catholic education, so slight as to be in startling contrast to modern times.

When the queen died, on 24 March 1603, the Catholic educational spring-boards across the Channel had been built, and, though their engineers neither wished nor knew it, had been built to endure. Their lines of reserve in Rome and in Spain, smaller but safer, would help to meet recurring periods of financial hardship by drawing off students from the bursar's rolls. In Douay and Rome lay the ecclesiastical power houses of revival. In St. Omer there was now an increasingly lay counterpart. These were all for men.

As for the English Catholic girls and women, whose story is omitted here because it has its own special monograph, the religious orders of women likewise were on the threshold of a continental makeshift policy destined to last them, too, till the French Revolution.[1]

At home, the Jesuit and the mission priest and the tutor and the parent, and that new major factor the lay Catholic schoolmaster, were consecrated to a double task: the basic schooling of those unable, and the preparatory humanities of those able, to go to the colleges abroad.

This was Catholic England's special adaptation to the crisis conditions peculiar to England, of what had been laid down for that country by Pole and for the whole of Europe by the Council of Trent. In that context these Englishmen are more than ordinarily typical of the Counter-Reformation, which here appears at its most deeply spiritual and its least political. Its wings are the politician Robert Persons and the martyr Edmund Campion. Central between them, and uniting in himself much of both, stands William Cardinal Allen.

[1] The study of the feminine side of the education movement, superseding the outline-chapters in Guilday's *English Catholic Refugees on the Continent* (1920), is W. J. Battersby, *The Educational Work of the English Religious Orders of Women*, to be published.

Allen's death on 19 October 1594, followed six months later by the death of the last of the old hierarchy, Bishop Goldwell of St. Asaph, seals the end of an age. For twenty-five years he had been the *de facto* head of the whole educational work of the *diaspora*, from its first organization after the 'Oxford' and 'Cambridge' houses of writers in Louvain. The college at Douay had waxed under his personal dynamism and indomitable missionary spirit, without as yet any written statutes. The college at St. Omer had not been sanctioned by the superior of its own Jesuit founder until sure that Allen himself approved it.

From now on, the Catholics abroad and at home were for a time without a unifying head nearer than Rome. There was a Cardinal-Protector; there was soon to be an archpriest. But the archpriest was to become the focus of domestic Catholic controversy, and Persons as the nominal successor of Allen abroad was too identified with some of the colleges in contradistinction to the others.

When Persons himself died, in Rome on 15 April 1610, there were still a few aged Marian priests alive in England, and a few venerable tutors who had been schoolmasters in their prime. But they were wraiths from a past now irrevocably gone. For after the accession of James I in 1603 no one could any longer regard the religious revolution in England as temporary, as it had been under Edward VI: though few dared speculate on how long the inevitable wait for a 'second Spring' was going to be.

PART TWO

THE SEVENTEENTH CENTURY

VI

THE STUART PARLIAMENTARY BATTLE

THE sabotage planned by Catesby's gunpowder plotters in November 1605 was to colour the attitude of Protestant to Catholic right down through the Fire of London, and Titus Oates, and the Fifteen and the Forty-Five, until exploited for the last time in savagery by Lord George Gordon's riots two years after the first Relief Act of 1778. The Catholic cause during penal times never recovered from the Powder Plot scare.

But the attitude consistently held to by all the Stuart Parliaments had in fact already been taken up by then. In James of Scotland's first year at Westminster the stage was set: by the universities in their address of welcome, by the Church of England in its canons, and by Parliament in the new oaths of allegiance and supremacy.

1. JAMES I

James' first penal Act was 'for due execution of the statutes against Jesuits, seminary priests and recusants'. Persons not returning from the foreign colleges within one year were made incapable of inheriting or holding any lands or annuities at all. Anyone acting unlicensed as tutor in the household of a recusant could be fined forty shillings per day.[1] Meanwhile the Canons of 1604 that emerged from the Hampton Court Conference showed that the Establishment and the secular arm were virtually one. Any *licensed* schoolmaster who should subsequently offend against anything he had *formerly* subscribed to was to be suspended: thereby closing up one more loophole in the law. General enforcement of all this was to lie with the school visitor, i.e. the bishop.

King and bishops thus made it plain that the educational system was to remain an exclusively Anglican preserve as to the appointment of teachers and the curriculum, no less than as to pulpit and press.

Early in 1605 Parliament went so far as to resolve on 'the taking of

[1] 1 Jac. I, c. 4. Full text of proclamations on it in Tierney-Dodd, iv. appdx. p. lvii.

Papists' children from them'.[1] When this failed, as the Education Bill of 1593 had done, they saddled a new oath on all schoolmasters and tutors instead, besides increasing the fines by substituting two-thirds of the recusants' estates in lieu of money should the king so choose, and adding a £10 monthly penalty on any servant or even visitor not conforming; and prescribed a fine of £100 if they neglected to have their children baptized as Anglicans within one month of birth. No man whose wife was a recusant could hold office unless he educated his children as Protestants and took them to church. The final turn of the screw extended the penalty on a married woman recusant to three months' imprisonment, or the forfeit of a third of her lands, unless her husband paid £10 a month. Thus was Parliament recognizing the key-position of the mother in Catholic education; thus also did Parliament strive shrewdly to weaken family solidarity by driving a wedge between husband and wife.[2]

There were special factors at work behind this increase in severity. The proclamations following James's first penal law had had little effect: at all events they had to be repeated in 1606.[3] The oath of allegiance was condemned by Pope Paul V in September of the same year, all the more an affront to the Government since the archpriest, George Blackwell, had accepted it in June. (He was deposed in the following February and succeeded by George Birkhead). Above all, there was the afterglow of the Powder Plot scare.

The pivotal year is 1610. In April and May of that year the Commons petitioned the king 'that all their children who, from their cradles, are trained up in hatred of the truth, [should] henceforth be educated in the knowledge of God and His Word, and in obedience to His Majesty and his laws, to which they are strange, many being carried beyond seas in their tender years, there to be corrupted'. James replied that he would fulfil all this, 'but of the tyme, and some other circumstances, he was not yet resolved'; he would consult with his Council.[4] This is the first of those temporizings which by 1621 were to rouse Parliament to fury.

[1] *Commons Journal*, i. 264 (Feb. 6); Tierney-Dodd, iv. appdx. p. xcvii.

[2] 3 Jac. I, c. 4 and 5; 7 Jac. I, c. 6. For the common informers who throve on these and later Acts see Havran, *Caths. in Caroline Engld.* (1962), ch. 7.

[3] Proclamation banishing priests and Jesuits, 10 July (text in Tierney-Dodd, iv. appdx. pp. cxxxii f.); proclamation forbidding women and children to cross the seas without licence, 23 Aug. (*Cal. S.P. Dom. Jas. I*, xxiii).

[4] Text in *Cal. S.P. Dom. Jas. I*, xxxix, No. 18 and No. 118 (p. 53). See also S. R. Gardiner, *The Debates of 1610*, in Camden Soc. vol. 81, pp. 43–4.

Difficulties of administration,[1] parallel with Parliament's doubts of the king's sincerity, at last came to a head in the session of 1621, as a cumulative result also of several other distinct developments which vexed the Court and Government. For by then the English Benedictines had emerged into the field of education, alongside the Jesuits; a Catholic 'College of Writers' had finally taken shape in 1611; an English Jesuit province had been set up throughout England and Wales; and there was plenty of fresh evidence of clandestine schools at home.

The King's own words in opening the Parliament, on 30 January 1621,[2] augured well for the papists, for he spoke in favour of religious freedom. This was taken by a very restive House of Commons as their cue to press him in the opposite direction. In his reply to this first petition the king came some way to meet them. 'If the seeds be Tares,' he admitted, 'the harvest cannot be good. To prevent the stealings of children beyond Sea, whoe are there brought up in superstition, as are many Noble mens sonns both of Ireland and Scotland, And to take order that they may be bredd upp here in our Schools not under the instruction of Papists, is a mayne poynte to be provided for.' But the House had now the experience of half a century of evasions to draw on. The Great Committee (i.e. Committee of the Whole House), debating the question of Catholic education at large, declared flatly that the failure of the Government to date was due to 'fayned conformity of Recusants', 'Corrupt Education of their children either under Popish wives or Tutors', and 'Negligent Education of Protestants children, who beaing weakely grounded in the Principles of Religion . . . are fitter matter for Preists and Jesuits to work upon.' Out of this debate there emerged a 'Committee to frame laws against the Recusants'. The attempt of 1593–1603 was about to be repeated.

We need not follow it. All the devices, by now long familiar, were gone over again. The only fresh element in the debates is a positive one at last, to meet the lack of Anglican religious instruction in the schools. A Bill 'for the catechising and instruction of Children' (26 April) was introduced ordering parish ministers to catechize for half an hour every Sunday afternoon, and to 'give notice, the Sunday before, what

[1] *B.M. Add. MSS.* 32,092, f. 219. Cf. Talbot (at Louvain) to Owen (at Eng. Coll. Rome), in *Arch. Vat.* Borghese III, 448 ab, f. 40; and *Cal. S.P. Dom. Jas. I*, vol. 80, p. 299; *Cal. S.P. Ireland*, 1615, p. 83; *Cal. S.P. Dom. Jas. I*, lxxx, No. 85, p. 285 (1615, April).

[2] For the various accounts of this Parliament see W. Notestein, *The Commons Debates of 1621.* (6 vols. 1935); also F. H. Relf, *Debates of 1621, 1625, 1628*; and Tyrwhitts' (1766) edition of the *Journal* of Sir Edward Nicholas.

children shall appear'. The parents, and the child's master, were to forfeit five shillings for non-appearance.[1]

For the rest, the House petitioned the king for some definite action. In a long list of 'causes' crying for remedy they included: 'The Education of their Children in many Seminaries and Houses of their Religion in foreign parts, the Grants of their *just* Forfeitures transferred or compounded for at such mean Rates as will amount to little less than a Toleration . . . the licentious printing and deciphering of Popish and seditious Books, even in Time of Parliament . . . the swarm of Priests and Jesuits (common Incendiaries of all Christendom) dispersed in all Parts of your Kingdom.'

The only remedies, James was told, were to execute the penal laws, to marry Prince Charles to a Protestant, to recall from overseas the children of the disaffected, and—'that the children of Popish recusants, and of such whose wives are Papists, be brought up, during their minority, with Protestant schoolmasters and teachers, who may sow, in their tender years, the seeds of true religion'. But the king evaded the issue once more. The Parliament was adjourned on 18 December.[2]

From that point onwards, for two whole years, his desire for a Spanish marriage for the Prince of Wales produced not the tightening of the penal laws but their virtual abrogation; wherefore it is no coincidence that the school activity we have to examine in England elsewhere is found at one of its peaks during that period, between the Parliaments of 1621 and 1624.

The Spanish marriage episode produced orders for release that actually covered persons imprisoned for recusancy, refusing the oath of supremacy, having or dispersing popish books, and hearing Mass. It is an astonishing relaxation of the penal code, and only heightened in dramatic value by a counterbalancing order given simultaneously by the king to the Archbishop of Canterbury that all the clergy must preach on a basis of the Thirty Nine Articles, and that Sunday afternoon services must be devoted to catechizing the children.[3] Of the Commons' two complaints—Catholic zeal and Anglican sloth—he would now, having winked at the one, chastise the other. He had gone over to the offensive. To leave no doubt, he took the occasion later, when the Spanish marriage-contract was in draft, to rest his recent

[1] This Bill was re-assigned on 18 November, and (presumably) guillotined by the session coming to an end on 18 December.

[2] For these prolonged deliberations see esp. Notestein, iv. 75, v. 471, ll. 274–7 and 285; iv. 215, iii. 269–270 and 283–4, ii. 461, iv. 447.

[3] 4 Aug. 1622; in *Cal. S.P. Dom. Jas. I*, cxxxiii, No. 85 (pp. 436–7).

toleration solidly on the royal dispensing power, by means of a 'Dispensation by the King, authorizing the Privy Councillors . . . thenceforward, neither personally nor by their inferior officers, to prosecute any law or penalty against Roman Catholics for religion, all statutes and ordinances to the contrary notwithstanding.'[1] This is unique in the history of English Catholic penal times until James II. But by 12 September the Court had news that Prince Charles was returning from Madrid *without* the Infanta. The King had upset Parliament for nothing after all, and was now to face a whirlwind.

When he opened the final session early in the new year (1624) he tried at first to gloss over the whole episode. Their accusation that he had neglected religion was false; he had never intended more than a temporary alleviation of the penal laws.[2] But he had by now shown his hand too far. The Commons denounced the English Catholics universally: the clergy as 'engines of Spain', the laity as traitors. And they went again to extremes.

On 5 May they introduced a Bill whereby *all* children of popish recusants over nine years of age were to be placed at Protestant schools or as apprentices or servants to known Protestants, 'at the discretion of the parents if they be willing'; if not, then at the parents' expense 'according to their position and means'. The bishops were to apprise the Privy Council of the names of *all* recusant peers, and their wives, with particulars of where their children were at present educated. The Council would prescribe the places of education. But, mercifully, as in 1593 so now again, this Bill went too far for the whole House to stomach it, when faced with the stark details. It did not pass, and within a month the royal evasion of the existing laws was beginning all over again: this time in virtue of a French marriage.[3]

By the time Prince Charles' marriage-treaty with Henrietta Maria of France was ready for ratification, at the end of the same year, the pattern of the 'Spanish years' just passed had completely repeated itself. Appropriately on Christmas Eve the King instructed Mr. Secretary Conway 'to convey his pleasure to the Law Officers of the Crown that all prosecutions against Roman Catholics for their religion be forborne'. The fine for non-attendance at Church was waived, the fines paid since the Trinity Term were actually refunded.

[1] 19 July 1623. Text in Latin, *Cal. S.P. Dom. Jas. I*, cxlix, No. 12 (p. 22).

[2] *Cal. S.P. Dom. Jas. I*, clix, No. 55; *Lords Journal*, iii. 209 (19 Feb. 1624).

[3] *Commons Journal*, i. 761, 766, 783; *Hist. MSS. Comm. IV*, Lords' Library MSS, p. 123a (1874).

By the following February Conway was sending for 'any of the Archbishop of York's officers complained of as too eager against Catholics', to 'warn them privately of the King's wish'. For the French ambassador was showing himself restive for results.[1]

Parliament was near to incandescence. Who can say what might have happened to the new Bill they now put up for the education of the children of recusants (15 February), sponsored by Prynne, Cage and Mr. Solicitor-General, still under discussion when on 6 April the King died.[2] The prince on whose behalf the nasty skirmish over toleration had been fought was now to face Parliament himself.

2. CHARLES I

At the coronation of Charles I 'all the recusant Lords . . . did ride to the church with the rest, but when they came there they all went away and heard not the sermon'.[3] The event is symbolical. It hints at the Catholic strength still surviving, at the hopes raised by the Henrietta Maria marriage, at the new king's known preference for not turning the penal screw any further. But the Catholic Lords once again reckoned without the Protestant Commons.

The King stood by his marriage treaty. The new Chapel at St. James's, the work of Inigo Jones, was staffed by the French Fathers of the Oratory. Somerset House became the queen's residence, served by Capucin friars, till a mob destroyed the chapel there and it was left abandoned till the Restoration of 1660. It was not long before the Secretary of State, Lord Conway, was being told of 'a place within the Savoy where Mass is usually said, with much resort of people', and gave orders that the priest was to be apprehended and the 'papish books and massing stuff' seized. By the time Charles had been on the throne ten years it was being said in petitions from London that the papists 'are so exceedingly multiplied that in . . . Bloomsbury there are as many or more than Protestants'.[4] The papal agent Panzani declared that the king was 'clement and averse to bloodshed, and albeit in want of money, does not enforce fines against Catholics'.[5]

[1] *Cal. S.P. Dom. Jas. I*, clxxvii, Nos. 10, 25, 28, 39; clxxxiv, No. 32; clxxxv, No. 46; 14 Dec. 1624–12 Mar. 1625.

[2] *Commons Journals*, i. 819, 826, 840.

[3] *Buccleugh MSS*, cited in *Dublin Review*, cccxcvii, 78.

[4] *Cal. S.P. Dom. Chas. I*, xx, No. 67 (10 Feb. 1626); lxvii, No. 8 (26 June 1627); cccxlix, No. 116 (15 Mar. 1636–7).

[5] 1631; quoted in detail in Brady, iii. 87.

Charles I's leniency has to be seen in terms of his French marriage, his personal character, and his desire for a religious understanding with Rome. The curve of toleration thus rose during his eleven years of personal rule from 1629 to 1640, and fell all the more steeply on the arrival of the Long Parliament.

When the Civil War came, the Catholics sealed their Royalist bond with their blood. Though we are concerned with only that part of the struggle between Crown and Parliament that turned on the education of the Catholics, concentration on that part does not distort the picture. For what exasperated the Commons was 'executive encroachment', the king by-passing statute law through excessive use of an ill-defined royal prerogative; and his Catholic policy was (to them) an aspect of precisely this, sharpened by their having been frustrated in all their Education Bills since 1593, and by the advantages manifestly seized by the English papists at home and abroad.

When, in the very first session (June 1625), they twice read a Bill to 'explain' the penal legislation they had forced on the king's father, with shrewd aim the House headed its list of remedies in the positive way *alone* likely to prevail: 'the well educatynge of the youth of this realm'. The king must order 'greater care . . . in the choice and admittinge of schoolmasters', and restore 'the ancient discipline of the two Universityes'. When the matter came before a joint conference of both Houses, there was one thing in all this that the Lords would not have: a clause for re-enacting all the penal laws. This was a reflection on the judiciary—'the law hath already trusted the judges and the justices with it [i.e. with enforcement]'. The rest went forward as a petition to the king.[1] For Scotland, similarly, the Privy Council ordered a list to be prepared of all Catholics in the country, the more effectively to prevent the harbouring of priests or the sending of children abroad.[2] Charles could not evade compliance, at least on paper. By 16 November the attorney-general assured Secretary Conway that he had presented in the courts of Westminster the king's commission for putting the laws into execution against recusants, and for watching all the ports to prevent the traffic of children.

But it was only compliance with the letter of the petition, for very soon the same attorney-general (Heath) was certifying particulars of 'moderation' in the execution of the laws; and the King's Advocate (Dr. Thomas Ryves) was informing Conway of rumours that since

[1] S. R. Gardiner, *The Debates of 1625*, in Camden Soc. vi (1873), 14, 18, 30.

[2] Bellesheim, iv. 10; *Tudor and Stuart Proclamations*, ii. 294 (2 Nov.).

the king's accession there had been *no* persons questioned by the High Commission Court for matters of religion, 'and only a few, very few, for conveying money for the support of seminaries, for sending children to foreign parts, for dispersing books, or using speeches contrary to the religion established'. The edicts seem to have been better enforced in Scotland, where we find so many Catholics attending the Protestant services, and so deliberately, that the wandering priests were loth to admonish them for fear of being barred from their homes and obliged to starve. But in England the proscription in 1625–6 was largely a mere façade. The Benedictine John Barnes, arriving from Salamanca, was able to live openly in Oxford University, for the purpose of consulting libraries 'to furnish himself with matter for works he intended to publish'.[1]

What goaded Parliament most, however, was the discovery of the famous Jesuit House of Studies at Clerkenwell, in the heart of London, only a few days before the session of 1628 opened. William Laud himself, the Archbishop of Canterbury, harangued the Upper House with some zest. 'The Papists have a Bishop here, and all officers, etc., *prout*. They holde intelligence at Bruxelles, Paris, Rome and Spayne, etc., as by a packett of many letters appeared. They have meetinges at this tyme also, as at all other tymes, to crosse our designes. Lately in London their convencions, houses of residence five, *vizt*, Southwark, St. Gyles, now at St. James a house for the Jhesuites, a house of Nunns at Knightsbridge, so lately at Highgate.'[2]

The Commons for their part concentrated on one precise Bill, and this time they passed it: a Bill (19 March) 'to restrain the passing or sending of any to be Popishly bred beyond the seas'. The committee that piloted it included Sir Edward Coke, John Hampden, and all the lawyer-members. The Archbishop of Canterbury was waited on by a Commons deputation led by Prynne demanding to know 'what had been done by the Bishops concerning Popish schoolmasters'. The Bill passed both Houses by the end of June. The penalty it enjoined for sending to—or supporting—the colleges abroad was to be forfeiture of *all* lands and goods, and disability from taking any lawsuit. Before

[1] *Cal. S.P. Dom. Chas. I*, xxxii. No. 80 (29 July 1626); and cccxcv, p. 435 for a catalogue of 'Popish Recusants who were committed and made composition' from 1625 to the end of 1642. An *Advice* of Oct. 1626, on the 'Present State of the English Catholics', is in xxxviii, Nos. 91–3. Ryve's report (28 July 1626) is in xxxii, No. 56. See also Bellesheim, iv. 77.

[2] F. H. Relf, *The Debates of 1621, 1625 and 1628*, 69. The house of nuns at Knightsbridge was that of Mary Ward's Institute.

the end of the year, too, a reprint of the Thirty-Nine Articles was ready, for use in the two universities, with disputations on the Articles flatly forbidden.[1]

How much the Commons supposed they had achieved is doubtful. In any case, when John Pym roused them at their next session the king sidestepped. Parliament was dissolved.[2] And the conclusion of a treaty of peace with France in May 1629 meant that, on the intercession of Queen Henrietta Maria, the penal laws continued at half-pressure, till the end of his period of personal rule eleven years later.

The real inspiration for all Charles' efforts to soft-pedal the penal machine is to be found of course in what was his deepest experiment of all—the effort of reunion with Rome. It was this that brought to England that most statesmanlike of Welsh Benedictines, Dom Leander Jones, and the papal agent Gregorio Panzani. The report sent back by Panzani to the pope has given us, as a by-product of the transaction, an invaluable cross-section of Catholic life in England at the time. Both men arrived in the second half of 1634. The king's High Churchmanship held out, however. Still more did Archbishop Laud's. And the onset of the Parliamentary struggle of 1640–2, and the Civil War, curtailed the discussions.[3]

Laud himself cannot be accused of undue complaisance in the matter of the Catholics. He could act in two capacities, as Archbishop of Canterbury and as Chancellor of Oxford University. In neither capacity did he relax his vigil.

As Chancellor he promulgated the Oxford University statutes of 22 June 1636, by which subscription to the Thirty-Nine Articles and the oath of supremacy was made a prerequisite for matriculation. Boys were exempted from both until the age of twelve, and from the oath until sixteen, but there had to be instruction in Catechism for all undergraduates once a fortnight. At Cambridge, where the oath obligatory on all resident members was frequently (and safely) declined, no less a person than Godfrey Goodman (later Bishop of Gloucester) was suspended, as 'a pervert to the Roman Church', till he subsequently submitted. The Jesuit William Lacy walked into Oxford, put up indefinitely at the Dolphin, and by his poetic learning

[1] *Commons Journal*, i. 873–4, 877, 882, 889, 914–19; Relf, 221, 227 note; Statute 3 Car. I, c. 2; *C.R.S.* i. 104; G. L. Young, 32 f.

[2] Notestein, *Debates of 1629*, 67.

[3] See Gordon Albion, *Charles I and the Court of Rome* (1935), ch. vi—vii.

contrived that 'his company was desired by certain scholars of the university'.[1]

As archbishop, during the same years, Laud tightened up the watch on schoolmasters. His Canterbury visitation articles of 1635 demanded of his clergy whether there were 'unlicensed private or open teachers' at large in their parishes, whether they conformed and brought their children to church, and whether any unauthorized catechisms were in use. Bishop Wren of Norwich, who appears to have had many such, craved the archbishop's direction, in his reply, as to 'what to do with scholars, some in Holy Orders, kept by gentlemen in their private houses under pretence to teach their children'. Laud proceeded to tell him, and to commend him to the king for his zeal.[2]

But most zealous of all was the Privy Council, whose renewed activity over clandestine papist schooling was stimulated by spies' reports of how many priests had been released and how many schools identified. The documentation on this, for the one year 1635–6, is greater in fact than for any year before or since till the Catholic revival under James II.[3]

When the Commons finally reassembled in 1640, in first the Short and then the Long Parliament, Pym's draft speech for the opening made great play with the latest 'Innovations to Prepare us for Popery': divers books printed, questions published and maintained in the universities, popish seminaries introduced, 'discouragements upon the professors of the Protestant religion'—all this by the king. The House was not going to lose its advantage. Its hour had arrived. The king was bankrupt and must come to it cap in hand. Thus one more penal law reached the Statute Book.[4]

This is all the less surprising in that the winter of that year, 1641–2, was excited by a Popish plot scare of the same kind as the Powder

[1] All these events occurred in the two years 1635–7. See Mallet, *Hist. of Univ. Oxford*, ii. 319 f.; Mullinger, *Hist. of Univ. Cambr.* iii. 144–5; Gillow, v. 187; Wood, *Athenae Oxon.*, ii. 379; Oliver, *Collections S.J.*, 128 f.

[2] Laud, *Works*, V. 2. 427–8; Cardwell, *Documentary Annals*; *Cal. S.P. Dom. Chas. I*, cccxxxvii. No. 19 (7 Dec. 1636); Bishop. 75–6. But his proposed new canon, of 1640, prescribing a fresh oath for all clergy and divinity graduates and schoolmasters (Rushworth *Collections*, III, i. 112) was declared illegal by the Long Parliament, 16 Dec. 1640.

[3] For these schools see later. Cf. the 1635 report of the pursuivant Gray, that thirty-two priests had been set free (*S.P. Dom. Chas. I.* cccviii, No. 66); and the scrutiny of permits for foreign travel in 1636 (ibid. pp. 341, 452).

[4] D'Ewes, *Journal*, ed. Notestein (1923), p. 443; *Cal. S.P. Dom. Chas. I*, cccel, No. 108; cccclxxii, No. 45 (November); cccel, No. 122; cccclxxi, No. 50; *Commons Journal*, ii. 26; Camden Soc., lxxx. 80 f.; and Statute 13 and 14 Car. I, c. 1.

Plot scare.[1] The panic, so plausible against its Irish background, is itself the setting for the twenty years of Catholic repression now ushered in, at the hands of the victorious Puritan Parliament. The spearhead of their attack was to be directed against the popish schoolmaster. For the Puritans knew the tactics of resistance-movements from inside experience. Since the days of persecution under Elizabeth they had themselves been under fire. They themselves had known how to go underground; how to obtain itinerant preachers, if not how to contrive many schools. They knew, above all, the real strength of a resistance-movement welling from the spring of outraged conscience. The great irony of the Commonwealth period from 1640 to 1660 was to be that, in canvassing religious toleration as the only answer on such an issue, they excepted the papists, on the pragmatic principle that, *mutatis mutandis*, the papists would not have tolerated them.

How great their dilemma was, the more sanctified of them, was best brought out when the latest Bill for the forcible education of Catholic children in Protestant tenets was being debated in the Commons in January 1646, and the Committee drafting it was warned that it should apply to papists and popish recusants *only*.[2]

Till now there had been the hope that a royal Stuart, of High Church principles himself, and married to a Catholic wife, might continue to operate the laws to the letter rather than in their spirit. But the very tension with Parliament that made the Catholic county families more than ever desirable allies of the needy and unpopular throne, finally snapped. While the lull lasted, the Catholics had made the most of it. All they had asked—all that the Jesuits, certainly, had asked—was that their pastoral enterprises and their hole-and-corner schools should be winked at. Parliament's answer, for the next twenty years, was to be far otherwise.

3. THE CIVIL WAR

There were two educational fronts, and the Parliamentary leaders fought on both. The positive front, once the Anglican monopoly was breached after 1640, was that of building up a system of schools for the whole country, analogous in scope to what there had been before the Chantries Act of Edward VI. This offensive was opened in

[1] See B. Magee, in *The Month*, May 1940, 349–57.

[2] *Commons Journal*, iv. 332.

January 1641, with an Act abolishing the need for Oxford and Cambridge students to subscribe to the Thirty-Nine Articles; and later by abolishing the episcopal licence for schoolmasters. The climax of this aspect of the work was reached in the year of the king's execution, 1649, in a spate of no fewer than five educational laws covering the British Isles and the Colonies.

The negative side, the stamping out of Catholic education, was more immediate, and certainly more continuous. A *Protestation against Popery*, for adoption in every parish, drafted by the Commons in May 1641, went the rounds of the country in the short year that remained before the Civil War opened. The names of those who had refused to accept it were actually being scrutinised by the House when the outbreak of hostilities curtailed any further action.[1]

In each session, meanwhile, the matter of securing a Protestant education for Catholic children was attended to. A motion was tabled on 15 May 1641 whereby 'wards that are under the custody of Popish Recusants, and by name the young Lord Peters, under the custody of the Lord Herbert, might be considered of'. On 13 August the House resolved that an order of the Lords, 'concerning the *exception* of their [recusant's] children and servants from being proceeded against as recusants', be referred to the Committee for Recusants-Convict. Charles by edict ordered all priests to quit the country by April 1642, on pain of death 'according to the statute'. Those in prison were released, on condition that they left within a month. There came in yet another Bill 'for the Breeding of Recusants' Children in the Protestant Religion'.[2]

With the wind setting as it now was, the traffic of boys to the Continent swelled that year to proportions reminiscent of the foundation-years over half a century before; and the business of intercepting them was so brisk as to involve disputes among the port authorities themselves. Three of the 'searchers' at Gravesend petitioned the Commons that they were being ousted from their office by 'the present Port of London searchers'. The port of Dunkirk was full of 'youths and maidens brought over from England by every packet, the youths to St. Thomas' to the Jesuits, the maids to divers cloisters'.[3]

[1] Surtees Soc. vol. 135 (ed. H. M. Wood), 1922.

[2] *Commons Journal*, ii. 147–8, 254, 523; *Cal. S.P. Dom. Chas. I*, ccccIxxii, No. 96. Edward Nicholas (at Westminster) to Sir John Pennington, 29 July. In December, seven priests were condemned, but reprieved by the king (ibid. ccccIxxxvi, No. 63). See also Gillow, iii. 37.

[3] *Hist. MSS. Comm. V*, Lords' Library MSS., pp. 9b, 28a (1876).

In Scotland simultaneously the Presbyterian General Assembly (abolished on the accession of James I to the united crowns in 1603, but revived in 1638 on Charles I's trouble with the Scots) ordered that henceforth every parish must have a reader and a school, for reading and writing and the elements of religion. The Privy Council ordered home, by January following, all the children of Scottish noblemen at present abroad, their parents or tutors to be surety for them.[1]

The War began on 22 August 1642. For Catholic schooling it was to mean much: the denuding of the colleges abroad—at times they were near to extinction; the establishment of new schools for boys; and the removal from London of the one seed-plot of girls' education, when Mary Ward withdrew her London community to the safety of Hutton Rudby, in the North, and thence to York in 1644.[2]

Parliament proceeded, as in 1624, and this time effectively, to devise an 'automatic' test of religious safety. The new oath, ordained in April 1643, was an Oath of Abjuration—denying the distinguishing tenets of the Catholic faith. Recusancy, from now till the Restoration of 1660, meant simply and straightforwardly the neglect to take this oath.[3] The sequestration of Catholic estates had already been under way since the preceding Christmas, at least in London and its hinterland. England had been scoured from end to end by Commissioners for Plundered Ministers. By the end of 1643 these were told also to 'inquire after malignant Schoolmasters', since in many places the *entourage* of the Stuart bishops were suspected of being 'confederate' with the 'Roman Party'. In quiet corners the edicts were indeed being evaded,[4] and so much so at the universities that by the end of 1647 every Oxford College except three (Oriel, Lincoln and Queens) had changed its head as the result of a visitation—though a reputable estimate of some 400 displacements of Fellows is probably too high.[5]

[1] Strong, *Secondary Educ. in Scotland*, 89; *Tudor and Stuart Proclamations*, ii. 318 (5 July 1642).

[2] In 1650 it migrated to Paris, till the return of Frances Bedingfield and the permanent settlement of the school at Hammersmith in 1667.

[3] *C.R.S.* xxxiv, p. xlvi. This oath, and an Act for educating Catholics as Protestants, formed part of the Parliament's 'Newcastle Proposals' in 1646; text in Sir. C. Petrie, *Letters of Charles I* (1935), 185.

[4] Cf. the Darells in Kent, in *Commons Journal*, ii. 892; iii. 280 (18 Oct. 1643); *Camden Soc.*, lxxx. 28 ff., 76–8.

[5] Mallet, *Oxford*, ii. 371, 381; Mullinger, *Cambridge*, iii. 349. Among the prominent converts to Rome during this period, whose example was being followed, is the poet and dramatist James Shirley.

What was particularly exasperating, all along the front, was that Parliament had left a vacuum. It is well illustrated in the Commons' instruction to the solicitor-general to bring in an 'Ordinance for the supply of that defect which is occasioned by reason Bishops are taken away [they had been abolished in 1642] and cannot give certificates of the conformity of Papists'.[1]

But while the war was still undecided there began a transaction that reflects small credit on its Catholic authors and only served, in the end, to prolong the bitter dissensions that had never ceased inside the Catholic body itself. This was the attempt to secure toleration from Cromwell, by one party in the Church at the expense of another: the affair of the 'Blacklow Cabal'.

A party led by the priests Dr. Blacklow (*vere* Fr. Thomas White) and Dr. Henry Holden, and the layman Sir Kenelm Digby, made overtures to the Cromwellians as early as 1647 or thereabouts, for toleration in return for Catholic support at home and abroad. They rested their case on the distinction between loyal and disloyal Catholics; between those who asserted that the pope had no *temporal* jurisdiction whatever over civil sovereigns, and those who maintained that he had; between those who would, and those who would not, have acted on the excommunication of Elizabeth; between those whose Catholicism was 'religious' and those whose Catholicism was 'political': in short, to use the labels long since familiar, between 'Catholic' and 'Papist'. The case was well argued later in Blacklow's *Grounds of Obedience and Government* (1655), condemned in due course by the Inquisition.

The 'Blackloist' plan as put forward by Dr. Holden centred on the Catholics being allowed, by the Government, a hierarchy of bishops independent of the pope, and on 'what course is fit to be suffered for the education of Catholic children in learning, or other qualityes, that they may not be sent over see to be brought up amongst forraines and strangers, maintained upon the Pope's and other Princes pensions which draw many inconveniencyes into their dispositions'.

But there was a more than disedifying side to the scheme. It amounted to 'appeasement' with a vengeance. As divulged by Dr. John Sargent in 1652, it boiled down to toleration for the 'Catholics'; the total expulsion of the Jesuits, as 'Papists'; and banishment to America of every layman who dissented from the Blackloist views.[2]

[1] 23 Nov. 1647. *Commons Journal*, v. 366.

[2] See R. Pugh, *Blacklow's Cabal* (1680), 39 ff.; M. V. Hay, *The Jesuits and the Popish Plot* (1934), 37 ff.

Though it never came to anything, this Blacklow Cabal intrigue is part of a thread that runs right through the history of the penal days, from the divisions over loyalty to an excommunicated Elizabeth, to the acrimonious disputes between 'Cisalpines' and 'Ultramontanes' in the years before Catholic Emancipation in 1829. Had it succeeded, it would perhaps have solved for both sides the problem of exile education. Thereby it might have antedated the return to England of the colleges abroad. But the long-distance results, on English Catholic solidarity, would have been disastrous, above all morally.

4. THE INTERREGNUM 1649–60

Upon the execution of the King (30 January 1649), and with the House of Lords abolished, as well as the bishops, the Commons in the Long Parliament began to legislate along the constructive lines of Comenius and Hartlib. Their five educational statutes of 1649 do indeed amount, on paper, to the outline of a national and imperial schools system. They reflect a clear sense of responsibility in the public authority for the schooling of all children: an idea in England born two hundred years prematurely. But, while in so far as they stood for religious toleration they upheld the fundamental right of a parent's conscience to have his child brought up in his own faith, in so far as they excepted the Catholics they violated it.[1]

The key, as always, was the schoolmaster's licence. For Catholics there was a categorical ban, authorized in the two leading constitutional documents of the period: the Instrument of Government (1653) and the Humble Petition and Advice (1656). The Church was still a department of State, as Henry VIII had made it.

Eloquent appeals for toleration of Catholics were forthcoming at intervals from Protestants. There were John Goodman's *Plea for Liberty of Conscience*, Roger Williams' *Bloody Tenent*, and Jeremy Taylor's *Discourse on the Liberty of Prophesying*—two of these as early as 1644. But the Tudor theory of the State remained the title-deeds, now they were in power, of men whose fathers had suffered under it alongside the fathers of those same proscribed Catholics. For the modern theory of the separation of Church and State, and of freedom in education, lay within a category of ideas not by then accepted wholeheartedly by any of the parties at all.

[1] There is a study of the period in the unpublished London Univ. Ph.D. thesis by E. W. Bishop, *Education under the Commonwealth*, 1942. See also W. A. L. Vincent, *The State and School Education, 1640–60* (1950).

When the returns were finally in, district by district, concerning the estates of Recusants sequestrated, Parliament consolidated its wishes into the comprehensive 'Act c. 16' of 1656.

This is the Act, 'for the suppression of Popish Recusants', that made the Oath of Abjuration (passed in 1643) the automatic test. It was to be presented at quarter-sessions, before the justices of the peace. Defaulters would be taken as having refused. Suspects would be bound over. On conviction, two-thirds of all property would be confiscated, and heirs could inherit only if and when they took the oath, their guardian profiting meanwhile. Anyone marrying a recusant-convict would be subject to like penalties unless he/she took the oath. No one might take it, moreover, until after having attended church on Sunday regularly for six months. The penalties for 'concealment'—including connivance by the justices themselves—were heavy, and half the fine was to go to the informer. The penalties for hearing Mass in the Embassy Chapels in London, finally, were £100 and six months' imprisonment, half the fine going to the informer. The lure of this vast sum would lead obviously to a toll of betrayals.[1]

From now on, furthermore, the Catholic resistance was to be without a visible head for thirty years. The Vicar Apostolic, Richard Smith, in impotent exile at Paris, died in 1655. Once more there was no English bishop to consecrate oils, etc., for the liturgy. The clergy had to have recourse to Irish or continental prelates. From now on till the reign of James II, while the regulars were ruled by their own provincials, the secular clergy on the mission were ruled by the 'Old Chapter', the advisory body which had been set up round the archpriest. If we bear in mind the Blacklow controversy, by now in full swing, and the fact that most of the chaptermen were 'Gallicans' or 'Jansenists' of the Blacklow kind, then we can appreciate something of the blow dealt at English Catholic fortune for a generation, by the death of Bishop Richard Smith.[2]

Of the most significant features of these Interregnum years as regards Catholic schooling at home, one is the changed system of controlling the schoolmaster. On the ruins of the Anglican system of episcopal licences the Long Parliament erected in March 1654 commissions of 'Triers'. Any minister presented to a living had to undergo

[1] Firth and Rait, *Acts and Ordinances of the Interregnum*, ii, 335; H. Scobell, *Acts . . . 1640–56*; *Cal. S.P. Dom. 1652*, xxiii. 15, 47 f.; *Commons Journal*, vii. 244; *B.M. Add. MSS.* 34, 242. There is a list of the estates confiscated, in *Catholicon*, i. 178–9 (1815). Text of the 1656 Act in Scobell, *Acts . . . 1640–56*, ii. 443–9; and cf. *C.R.S.* xxxiv, p. xxxix.

[2] See Brady, iii. 104 ff.; and cf. Guilday, 250–1.

a scrutiny as to his 'holy and unblamable' conversation and fitness. In the following August a commission of 'Ejectors' was set up, with power to expel ministers and schoolmasters who should be proved 'scandalous in their lives and conversation', and also those proved guilty of 'holding or maintaining such blasphemous and atheistical opinions as were punishable by the Blasphemy Act of 1650', together with (and this repeated the Ordinance of 1643) those who 'hold, teach or maintain certain specified Popish opinions' such as Transubstantiation, Purgatory, the veneration of crucifixes and images, and salvation by works. Anyone who maintained an ejected schoolmaster was liable to a fine of ten shillings a day, to be used for the poor of the parish[1].

The machinery did not, however, work well enough to obviate the Protector having to remind the country by proclamation a year later that many schoolmasters ejected under this Ordinance were still in possession of their posts, and must go within a month.[2] There had been plenty of connivance at 'concealment', particularly (as always) at the universities. John Bassett, a Catholic who went up as a sizar to Gonville and Caius in 1657, contrived discreetly to became a junior fellow by 1664 and a senior by 1667. (Under James II he was to be Master of Sidney Sussex College, and have Mass celebrated there publicly.) Sir Robert Throckmorton had his own Catholic tutor at Cambridge. More famous than either was the lawyer, Richard Langhorn, future victim of Titus Oates, who was admitted to the Inner Temple in 1646 and to the Bar eight years later. The fact that his wife was a Protestant helped his career considerably.[3]

The most doleful feature of the entire twenty years of the Long Parliament is the resolute seizure of Catholic children, a practice now extended beyond the nobility to commoners fighting in the Civil War.

The Bradshaigh family, of Haigh Hall, near Wigan, actually lost the faith in this way, when the infant heir of Sir Roger Bradshaigh, who died in 1641, was given into the custody of the Earl of Derby, lord lieutenant of the county, and brought up as a Protestant. The Jenison family, of Walworth Castle, Co. Durham, were more robust; for

[1] Mullinger, iii. 545; Bishop, 134–5; Gardiner, *Commonwealth*, ii. 322–3; *Cal. S.P. Dom. 1654*, pp. 190, 308; Scobell, ii. 335–47.

[2] *Cal. S.P. Dom. 1655*, pp. 224–5 (3 July). Henry Hills, who printed the Lord Protector's proclamations, himself became a Catholic, but managed to hold his post till the reign of Anne.

[3] Gillow, i. 153; Barnard, *A Seventeenth-Century Country Gentleman*, ii. 43; Gillow, iv. 128.

though the heir Thomas, born in 1643, was educated as a Protestant, they retained the faith unbroken through penal times, this Thomas Jenison himself becoming a Jesuit. Roger Downes, again, whose father had recovered the head of Ambrose Barlow after his martyrdom at Lancaster in 1642, was taken from his parents when a few months old (in 1643) to be educated in a Protestant household.[1]

During the Civil War the seizures were more frequent than ever before, through the heads of Royalist families falling in battle. When Thomas Eccleston of Lancashire was slain at the Battle of Warrington in 1646, his two sons, Henry and Thomas, aged nine and three, were put into the guardianship of Col. Ireland, whom the commissioners told to 'see them placed with godly persons to be educated as Protestants. If he do this, he may have the rents of their estates to provide for their expenses.' When Robert ap Rhys (Price—the Welsh martyr) was captured at the Siege of Lincoln in May 1644, Parliament took possession of his estates and his son, and brought up the boy under appointed Protestant guardians.[2] In the same year it was represented to Parliament that Sir Edward Hungerford had 'been at the charge of' keeping Lord Arundell of Wardour's children for fourteen months. In this case the House resolved that he might release the children as soon as he were 'satisfied the charges'.[3]

One case involving girls has survived in detail, in the account of her childhood given by Alethea Anderton when she entered the English Convent of St. Monica at Louvain in 1658. She was one of fourteen children born to her parents, who 'both suffered very much in their conscience in the time of the Parliament. Their goods were plundered, and . . . they took away three of her children, one son and two daughters, and . . . there was taken for these three out of their parents' living more than was left them to maintain all the rest.' The children seized were so effectively conditioned, by cruelty and starvation and bribes alternatively, that when ultimately Mrs. Anderson contrived to get them back they refused Catholic prayers altogether, and were long in being won back to their religion.[4]

Mercifully the word 'Parliament' has not perpetuated in the

[1] *V.C.H. Lancs.*; Blundell, ii–61–2; Gillow, i. 238; iv. 244. This younger Roger became a baronet in 1679, 'as was customary in the case of Protestant converts from Catholic noble families'—*C.R.S.* iv. 208; Gillow, iii. 611; Blundell, ii. 23.

[2] *V.C.H. Lancs.* 364; Blundell, iii. 108; T. P. Ellis, *Cath. Martyrs of Wales*, 100.

[3] *Commons Journal*, iii. 553.

[4] Narrative in *Chronicle of the Eng. Aug. Canonesses of the Lateran . . . at Louvain*, ed. Dom. A. Hamilton (1904–6).

descendants of those Catholic families of England the baleful ideas that the word 'Cromwell' is still apt to excite in Irishmen. One effect on them, however, was to make them more staunchly royalist than ever when the Stuarts were restored in 1660. The political attitudes that the next generation of Catholic children glimpsed in the characters of those priests and lay schoolmasters who taught them their Catechism and their letters will have been overwhelmingly royalist and in due time Jacobite.

5. THE RESTORATION 1660–85

'King Charles II halted between two opinions, and a stream of popery went between his legs.' So said Titus Oates,[1] speaking better even than he knew. For the remark epitomizes the entire reign.

On the one hand, Charles was returning as king to an England set in the Church-State theory of Henry VIII. On the other hand, Charles was soon to be betrothed to a Portuguese Catholic wife, Catherine of Braganza; his years of exile had been spent as a pensioner of Catholics abroad; his very flight in 1651 had been facilitated by those English Catholic families who had rallied to his father so staunchly; his own brother James, Duke of York, was 'infected'; and his own increasing penury made him more and more dependent upon the purse, and therefore the policy, of the Catholic King of France. The tradition of his crown and the tradition of his family thus pulled him in opposite directions. In so doing, they fought their struggle publicly in the arena of religious toleration, Charles stretching the leniency of the law to its limit, as his father and grandfather had done (and with him it was more deliberate still), constantly checked by the Whig-Protestant elements in his successive Parliaments.

At the moment of the Restoration in 1660 'toleration' was in the air. There were so many Puritan restrictions that one and all were anxious to throw off. Currents of opinion were articulate that had departed so far from the doctrinaire positions of the Reformation years as to be almost purely scepticism. A fleeting freedom had been won, during the Puritan Interregnum, that was not to be entirely lost during the reimposed Anglican monopoly of education after 1660. This was the 'liberty' of schoolmasters unlicensed by the Established Church. The episcopal 'licence to teach' was certainly revived, but cases in the courts, such as those of Bates in 1670 and Cox in 1671,

[1] The speech is in *State Trials*, x. 1097–1132.

continually restricted the field of schoolmastering to which it could be said unequivocally to apply. To some extent this very fact may have helped Catholic schools to flourish, un-denounced to the authorities. But the presumption is a weak one, since not only was there a tempting reward awaiting informers, but the popish schools were outside the law altogether. The freedom of printing, moreover, which had prospered since the abolition of the Star Chamber in 1641, was soon hedged about by the Licensing Act of 1662. Here both Papist and Puritan were to suffer alike.

Charles's own position emerged in the Declaration of Breda which he sent to England in April 1660 before his return. 'We do declare', he said, 'a liberty to tender consciences.' It is significant that the Parliament which received this declaration had recently passed an Act for enforcing all the laws against papist recusant delinquents, with a £20 reward for the apprehension of priests and Jesuits.[1]

The 'Cavalier' Parliament's riposte to Breda was the Clarendon Code, subtended from the Act of Uniformity put through in 1662. There was fierce opposition to this in the Lords, where numbers of peers pleaded for pensions for the ministers and teachers whom its terms would expel, and even for exempting schoolmasters from the need of subscribing to the formulas laid down. For the king's word was at stake. Clarendon went so far as to press for a clause that would enable the crown to grant dispensations from compliance. When Charles signed the Bill he intimated that he would mitigate its severities by using his prerogative.

In its sections on education the Act of Uniformity forbade any teaching without licence, 'in any private house or family' as well as in schools, on pain of three months' imprisonment for the first offence and a £5 fine in addition for each subsequent offence. All masters in 'public or private' schools, and all family tutors, were to subscribe to the oaths by St. Bartholomew's Day (24 August). All clergy and fellows of colleges were to do likewise.[2]

The main impact of all this was upon the parties of the 'late Parliament men', the Dissenters from now on. For the Catholics there was nothing novel in the enactments. The Conventicle Act alone (1664)

[1] Text and Declaration in *Commons Journal*, viii. 6. 'The religious toleration which it held out was complete, and the terms in which it was expressed were unequivocal'—Charles Butler, *Hist. Memoirs*, iv. 121 (1819–21); *Commons Journal*, vii. 862, 871–2 (5–12 March).

[2] 14 Car. II, c. 4.

had any new element of legal penalty for them, in its prohibition of any meetings numbering more than five persons.[1] This was the education code of which it was said that 'the thirst of the Archbishop [Sheldon] for information [on evasions] was the thirst of the Sahara: unlimited, unquenchable, unproductive . . .'.[2]

Charles had nevertheless done what he could, outside Parliament, to live up to his Declaration of Breda. His marriage-contract with Catherine of Braganza followed closely the lines of his father's with Henrietta Maria. He saw fit in 1662 to prohibit *English* Catholics from frequenting either of the queen's chapels, at St. James's and Somerset House, or the Embassy Chapels, save officers and families of the two households; but a report sent to Rome at this very time had it that he was contemplating suspending those parts of the penal code which bore upon non-attendance at the Anglican churches, and had already abolished the oath exacted from Catholics on entering or leaving the country.

He had indeed already set up a committee to investigate the penal laws with a view to their abolition, and the 'chapter-men' among the Catholic clergy were petitioning him that the Jesuits be excluded from toleration.[3]

In this climate a number of Catholic plants began to blossom. The first periodical in England since the Reformation, *The Catholic Almanack*, appeared in 1661–3, produced by Thomas Blount of Orleton.[4] Controversialists emerged into the open in large numbers—men whose works belie the gibe of Macaulay that they had never been to the English universities, and were bad stylists and outmatched: John Sargent, Thomas Godden, the Jesuits Laurence Worsley and John Warner, the Benedictines Cressey and Canes, and the layman Abraham Woodhead. Charles was meanwhile relaxing the laws as he had promised. He remitted fines. There was widespread suspicion in the country at the rarity with which Catholics were actually

[1] 16 Car. II, c. 4; 17 Car. II, c. 2. Scotland and Ireland suffered too. The Scottish Estates in Feb. 1661 ordered sheriffs to search for all suspected papists; 'the education of their children is to be committed to some well-affected and religious friend'—*Acts of the Parlt. of Scotland*, vii. 26; *Tudor and Stuart Proclamations*, ii. 359. The Act of Uniformity for Ireland was passed in 1665 (17 & 18 Car. II, c. 6).

[2] J. E. G. de Montmorency, *State Intervention in English Education* (1902).

[3] For the marriage-treaty (signed in Paris, 23 June 1661), *C.R.S.* xxxviii, p. vii. See also *Cal. S.P. Dom. Chas. II*, lvii, No. 33, and for re-issues of the proclamation by Order in Council, ccxvi, p. 456 (11 Sept. 1667).

[4] It was revived under James II as *Kalendarium Catholicum* (1686), and then with its original name (1687).

prosecuted.[1] And there was a Catholic infiltration following his Declaration of Indulgence.

But the turn of the tide came in 1670, when Charles's secret Treaty of Dover with Louis XIV pledged him to declare himself a Catholic at some convenient moment in the future. Parliament was already dissatisfied with his leniency, and already frustrated by its own policy; three years previously it had discussed its doubts whether the oath of allegiance was not so harsh in penalties as to make vast numbers of papists 'accept' it, thereby denying the Treasury even composition-fines![2]

Charles's Second Declaration of Indulgence (March 1672) overcalled his hand. By the summer he realized as much, and the following March he paid the penalty—Parliament forced him to sign the Test Act, brought up to him post-haste from its passage through the Lords.

It was called an Act against the dangers from popish recusants. It enjoined the oaths of supremacy and allegiance on office-holders of every description. It enjoined a bishop's licence on every person presuming to 'instruct youth', even in a private family. Persons not reared as papists who should breed up *their* children as papists, or allow them so to be brought up, would be disabled from office also, till reconciled to the Established Church before the justices of the peace.

With the passing of the Test Act the king's policy of toleration failed. Henceforth the Catholics must look to his brother the Duke of York. Henceforth the king himself, who was thought to be using toleration for Nonconformist Dissenters as a stalking-horse for his 'Romanizing' ends, left the Nonconformists also to the Parliamentary wolves.[3]

Though he tried to mollify the Commons by a proclamation in February 1675, along the old dreary lines of giving priests a month to leave the country, and banning the sending of anybody to be educated abroad in a popish college, Parliament, faced with the alarming list of proclamations of a like nature littering past records, proceeded to a 'Test Act Explanation Bill', particularizing the persons engaged in education who were to take the oaths: to wit, professors, readers,

[1] *Cal. S.P. Dom. Chas. II*, lxiii. Nos. 47–8; Sheldon Letters in Bodleian, cited in Bate, *Declaration of Indulgence*, 53; *Cal. S.P. Dom. Chas. II*, lviii, No. 83 (27 August 1662).

[2] *Cal. S.P. Dom. Chas. II*, 1667, p. 149.

[3] 25 Car. II, c. 2., c. f. *Cal. S.P. Dom. Chas. II*, 1673–5, pp. 27, 57, 102, 128, 151, 280, 549–51: period from 1 Nov. 1673 to 10 June 1674.

masters, heads, fellows, chaplains and tutors in the universities; deans, canons, prebends, parsons, vicars, curates and lecturers in the Church; and 'any schoolmaster keeping any public or private school, and every tutor in a house or private family'. The Duke of York at this point threw down the gage by ceasing any longer to attend services at the Chapel Royal, so leaving no doubts of his Catholicism. By March 1677 the Lords were in the throes of yet another Bill for the forcible education of Catholic children as Protestants,[1] while the coming storm of Titus Oates' Popish Plot was already gathering.

At one extreme, that 'Plot' involved the judicial murder, on perjured evidence, of the leading Jesuits in the kingdom; and this was irrevocable. At the other extreme, of the rank and file of the masses, Lord Shaftesbury and the Whigs worked might and main to close every loophole in the law and to succeed (where only the Long Parliament had yet succeeded) in extending the law to cover the forcible education of Catholic children by Protestants. This enterprise ultimately failed.

The excitement hotted up outside Westminster rather than inside. At Oxford the pope was burnt in effigy, and the heads of several colleges, including with some truth Obadiah Walker of University College, were alleged to be papists.[2] A welter of anti-Catholic newspapers appeared, under beguiling titles such as *The Weekly Pacquet of Advice from Rome*, and *The Catholic Intelligence*.[3] One patriot, eager to prove the plot no mare's nest, produced detailed suggestions for attacking Rome and carrying off the Vatican Library.[4]

The abortive Popish Recusants (Children's Education) Bill on 7 December was the fiercest that Parliament was ever to see. There was to be a fine of a thousand pounds, half of it to the king and half to the person prosecuting, for any boy under twenty-one years of age (or any woman at all) sent abroad in the care of any popish recusant. The boy or woman concerned was to forfeit all property to the next

[1] *Tudor and Stuart Proclamations*, i. 437; 3 Feb. For the list, see *Cal. S.P. Dom. Chas. II*, 1675–6; Feb. 1675. For the Draft Bill and Lords' amendments (April), *Hist. MSS. Comm. XI*, Lords' Library MSS, pp. 50–1 (1883). 'They went into a Grand Committee on the Popery Bill, and ordered a clause to be added to supply the defects therein as to the disposal of the Children of Popish Recusants'—22 March 1677. *Cal. S.P. Dom. Chas. II, 1677–8*, pp. 45, 57.

[2] The Warden of Merton maliciously listed Anthony à Wood, the Oxford historian! (Mallett, ii. 444 f.).

[3] Copies in Burney Collection, British Museum, vols. 79a and 81a.

[4] Giles Vanbrough to the Bishop of London (28 Dec. 1678), in *Cal. S.P. Dom. Chas. II*, ccccviii, No. 106.

of kin Protestant. Should they later conform, the lands would be restored to them but not the profits of the intervening period. Should the forfeited estate be worth less than £20 a year, the penalty instead would be seven years' imprisonment (or till conforming). All popish recusants were to register the names, ages and places of education of all their children, once every year, at general and quarter sessions, with a penalty of £50 to the king and £50 to the person prosecuting. Finally, the exportation of money to help the colleges abroad would mean a fine of £500—half to the king and half to the prosecutor likewise.

This, and two other Bills, seemed to close every loophole: except one—the Catholic Duke of York was heir-apparent. Hence the climax, the Bill to exclude the king's brother from the throne altogether. When this passed its second reading in the Commons on 21 May Charles saved the situation by first proroguing and then dissolving Parliament. The majority against him had been seventy-nine. When the 'Oxford' Parliament revived the Exclusion Bill next year he abruptly dissolved it for good, and called no more Parliaments for the rest of his reign.

The *rationale* of this prolonged and embittered Parliamentary battle had thus become ominously apparent. James I and Charles I had wanted the laws relaxed for reasons of expediency, partly dynastic, partly financial. Charles II had the added motive of honest conviction. This trend in the personal policy of the Stuart kings is the measure of the Commons' intensity. Where the 'seize-the-children' Bills under James were but an afterglow of 1593, in a generation still preoccupied with nothing more doctrinaire than the security of the realm, those of both the Puritan and the Cavalier Parliaments were directed to the final eradication of Catholicism completely, once and for all. Everything depended now on whether the king's brother and heir would realize this and tread accordingly. But before we come to that final debacle we have to inquire how the proscribed Catholic schooling had fared both abroad and at home.

VII
EARLY DAYS OF THE COLLEGES ABROAD

FEW colleges can have begun with a population of such established eminence as Douay.[1] And therein lies its uniqueness as an educational centre. For while its students during the first ten years were all mature scholars taking courses in theology, either in the house itself or in Douay University, on its removal to Rheims in 1578 it received an influx of younger students, needing instruction in philosophy and in the grammar school course, of humanities. It thus goes on record as a school that 'grew downwards' from the top. The circumstances of the time made this inevitable; students fleeing into exile half-way through their course at university or school must first be able to complete their preparatory studies before proceeding to theology and the priesthood. Douay College began with theology, but in time it learned to begin with 'rudiments'.

The professional studies, however, were but the surface. Beneath them there lay the personal, spiritual formation of the missioner and teacher. Allen set himself to impress upon the students the grim contrast between their sheltered life in the seminary and the hunted existence they would ultimately have on the English mission. He interpreted this latter as punishment for the sins of their generation, and their own, to be expiated only by a consecrated career of penance, study and endurance. The spiritual formation, from the start, was intensive.

There was the explanation of a chapter of scripture daily at dinner and supper; dictation of passages on all points of theological

[1] Cf. names in Guilday, 65; Knox, *Douay Diaries*, xxixf. The main sources for the history of the college, the *Douay Diaries*, are as follows: First and Second (ed. T. F. Knox, 1878), covering the period to 1593 and, thereafter in a fragmentary way, the whole history till the return to England; Third (1598–1633), Fourth (1641–7) and Fifth (1647–54), ed. for *C.R.S.*, vols. x and xi (1911); Sixth, which is lost, covering the period 1676–92; Seventh, covering 1715–78, ed. for *C.R.S.*, vol. 28 (1929). There is also a *Douay Diary* kept by Edward Dicconson for the years 1704 ff., which has been edited for *C.R.S.* but not yet published. The gaps in the extant *Diaries* are therefore 1633–41, 1654–1715 and 1778–93.

controversy rife in England; weekly disputations on these; sermons in *English* every Sunday and feast day: to such purpose that the Old Testament was covered twelve times every three years, and the New Testament sixteen times, with supporting courses in Greek and Hebrew. There were two lectures weekly on the *Summa Theologica* of Aquinas, and a disputation. 'Pastoral matters' for professional instruction included the breviary, rosary, catechism and confessions, in the light of the Tridentine decrees. All this was in addition to their academic course and the enduring character-formation of the liturgical and community life. At the end of it, none was sent on the English Mission till aged at least thirty, and till academically able to have taken 'any degree in divinity' at Oxford or Cambridge.

By the time the first six ordinations had been carried out and the first seminarian (Louis Barlow) had left for England (1573–4), laymen had begun to arrive, a dozen of them in one ship, half from Oxford. Within three years of that, the Douay men in England numbered forty-four, and two had already become martyrs (Cuthbert Mayne and John Nelson). The Government in London believed that there were now at least forty-five youths in the college.[1]

From the time of its trek back from Rheims in 1593, till its removal to England during the French Revolution, the college remained firmly rooted in Douay. The town was thus showing a vast concentration of Catholic higher education from the British Isles. For in addition to Allen's college and the Flanders Jesuit College there were the Scottish Jesuit College from Paris (transferred in 1593) and the Irish College for secular clergy (from 1594). Elizabeth's Government had cause for particular alarm. Douay was an enemy town, under Spanish government; and, as a clearing-house for the disaffected of three parts of the British Isles, it was uncomfortably near. The implications of this, however, cut both ways. It was the constant fear of the exiles that sudden changes in the political alliances might mean their having to pack and trek at short notice.

From the beginning, as a wise precaution, admission was granted only to boys bringing recommendations. When four Englishmen arrived in 1578 who were known to nobody in the College, 'die sequenti discesserunt'. When one Johnson, an actor, arrived in 1580, and, besides knowing nobody, fluffed his preliminary interlocutory, 'pecunia donatus, statim discessit'.

[1] *S.P. Dom. Eliz.* cxlvi, No. 137; cited in Birt, 555.

As we have seen, the college began its career as a graduate finishing-school, and was forced by circumstances to 'grow downwards'. The curve of the admissions of little boys, *pueri* in the *Douay Diary*, rises steeply after each new penal Act in England. At the other end of the age-scale there were veterans. Henry Chaderton arrived from Southampton in 1581 as old as twenty-six, and 'began rudiments with the boys. This astonished not only the students but likewise the townspeople, who saw me, a man of twenty-six years of age, with a beard, going in and out of the schools with the numerous scholars, all of them lads of between seven and twelve years of age.' In three and a half years he worked his way from rudiments to the top of humanities.

The college of course had to take what came. Now it would be a *librarius* from England; now two men and 'mulier quaedam', of whom one stayed but the other and the woman had to go. Sometimes a boy would return to England 'for his health', but be back ere long because the persecution was too hot for him, or even before he had left the Continent—plundered on his way to the coast. One arrived from England to get as many Catholic books as he could carry, and then doubled back with them—'hos ut saepe antefecerat cum seipso transportabat'. Others would bring with them bundles of letters recounting the harrying of their predecessors, now in England, at the hands of 'the Biteshipe of London'. Richard Baron, a man 'totally illiterate', came to Douay not for study but because 'he wanted to see the Mass celebrated publicly'.

Many priests arriving, or returning in banishment after a spell on the mission in England, brought boys with them; sometimes as many as seven, and once twelve. It was thus, accompanied on the journey, that the scions of so many noble families slipped out of England: the Gifford boys, the Throckmortons, and so on. The *Douay Diary* is punctuated with the comings and goings of at least one regular 'courier', Richard Hargreaves, never empty-handed. And this traffic in priests bringing boys, too, was always greatest after each new penal Act. In 1580–1, seven boys reached the town of Douay only to find that they had to pursue the college across another frontier into its second exile at Rheims. From time to time there were bumper harvests, as in 1585 when seventy-two priests arrived almost together, exiled and deported from various prisons in England under the latest proclamation; or in 1603, when ten arrived from Framlingham Castle together after being deported a second time.

The first two *Douay Diaries* are not precise on all the matters relevant to educational history. For particulars of ordinations, for the comings and goings between Douay and the other colleges, for the total roll at intervals, and for the counties of origin of the students, they are magnificent. They distinguish between *vir*, *juvenis*, *adolescens* and *puer*; usually too between *nobilis* and *pauper*. But the organization of the college, and its curriculum and teaching methods, have to be read between the lines; for (after all) these were not the express purpose of the *Diary*.

There was too little continuity of teaching staff till after the removal to Rheims, when the names begin to appear of scholars drawn from the English College at Rome, men destined to fashion the very life and atmosphere of the community over long periods. The theological studies were in the hands successively of William Gifford and Richard Barret, Thomas Stillington, John Vavasour, Matthew Kellison. Philosophy was in the hands of Gilbert Gifford, Christopher Hodson and John Hargrave. While on the one hand 510 Englishmen matriculated at Douay University (the papal university) before 1612, only seventeen took the Douay University doctorate in divinity after the foundation of the English College. Curiously enough the *Diaries* are meticulous as to the degrees held by the students on entry, but the rectors paid no attention to their degrees in placing them for studies —a cause of sharp discontent later.

The full course of study, characteristic of all the colleges, developed not so much from a pre-conceived prospectus, as to meet needs. At first, Douay was to all intents and purposes a substitute for Oxford and Cambridge. By 1580 a distinction in organization is clear, between the upper and lower—*communia superiora* and *communia inferiora*, and the entries reveal the form the organization was taking, till it became at last stereotyped. As regards their communal life and their meals, the students were organized in upper and lower hall, corresponding to the difference in their studies as between higher and preparatory: philosophy and theology on the one hand, the humanities on the other as *prolegomena*. So far as can be gleaned, the method of instruction for the philosophers and theologians was by dictated notes and discussed commentaries and glosses. The juniors were taught humanities by the methods already established throughout Europe in Jesuit schools; and the organization of the curriculum approximated to that of the ordinary grammar school.

Thus arose at Douay, as in Jesuit schools earlier and at St. Omer later, the division into classes ranging from a sixth form to a second, but called respectively Rhetoric, Poetry, Syntax, Grammar and Rudiments. In time to come there would be gaps—as during the English Civil War, when, for lack of recruits, the lower grades went temporarily out of existence. At other times, through a sudden vast influx resulting from the political situation at home, there would be a Rudiments I and II and even more.

At first, until the use of the preparatory schools at Verdun and Pont-à-Mousson and Eu (and later St. Omer) was regularized, much of the class-teaching was done in the local schools. The sequence of works read aloud at meal-times is revealed now and again. Allen himself taught the priests the rules of catechizing, and of discussing with anybody so as the more easily to convert or strengthen him. Saturday disputations, the *Sabbatinae*, began as early as 1579.

The College had been possible financially through the charity of Dr. Vendeville and others. Allen's salary as professor of divinity at Douay University had been added in 1570, and later he threw in also his stipend as canon of Cambrai. There was a monthly subvention, also, from the Jesuits. The papal Brief of 1575, making Douay a pontifical college, added to it an annual pension. This produced thenceforth an important distinction of students, between *alumni*, supported out of the papal pension—which maintained forty of them, and *convictors* supported by their parents or by other private persons. When the pope increased the pension a few years later, Allen ordered at once a new coat for every student. A pension from Philip of Spain was added in 1582. If he hoped thereby to render the English exiled students pro-Spanish, the king failed most miserably: as their impudent acclamations, all over his dominions, at English victories, were to show. (In any case his pensions were always in heavy arrears.) The papal and Spanish pensions never sufficed. Moreover, balance or no balance, there was 'journey money' (*viaticum*) to be found for every priest leaving the college to go on the mission. Allen even contrived at times to pay the passages of boys from England. Donations from England itself fluctuated with the political situation. Sales of the Rheims Bible helped, and sales of Persons' books.

At the end of 1584, when the college was in actual danger of closing down, Allen warned Rome. The Cardinal Secretary of State replied that it could—and should—be saved, by reducing its numbers. This Allen refused to do. Some could be sent to Rome, but the college must not turn its students away, especially orphans and those who had come in defiance even of their parents' wishes: and especially as so many arrived without resources and could not be kept waiting for vacancies.

Despite propaganda-drives all over England, and Persons' output of pamphlets in various languages to commend them to Catholic Europe, it was more the financial duress than any other single cause that had sent the college back to Douay in June 1593. At the time, the professors were unpaid. Allen's death a year later was thus a fateful blow at a critical moment.

The curve of numbers at Douay, then, does not accurately reflect its fortunes. In 1582 the number that left England for Rome was itself eighty, despite the proclamation of that January. By 1584 the Douay population had reached nearly 200.

Immediately upon Allen's death, Persons, having to act quickly, proceeded to send students to Douay Jesuit College for lectures, as a means of avoiding increases in staff. This became a source of bitter recrimination, in that the arrangement put these students under a Jesuit confessor. Moreover, Richard Barret, who succeeded Allen, gave place five years later to the worst president in all the history of the college—Dr. Thomas Worthington—during whose term of office the interplay of rumour and scandal between Jesuits and seculars was virtually to ruin the prestige of the college at home.[1]

Accordingly the Holy See asserted itself. Dr. Thomas Worthington's appointment was accompanied by a visitation from Rome, thorough in intensity and grievous in results. The visitors' report was directed to remedying things likely to cause 'the complete overthrow of the College': finance, commisariat, discipline. Since numbers must be reduced, and since *convictors* were (in theory) self-supporting, the reduction must be made among the *alumni*—to sixty. All existing *juniors* who could not pay must be dismissed, and none admitted for the future unless qualified to begin in the class of rhetoric (sixth form). Only students approved by the archpriest in England, or by the English Jesuit superior, were to be accepted; and, at the end of their formation as priests, only those who would take a prescribed oath of obedience to the archpriest were to be sent *to* England. The confessor of all students was to be a Jesuit, resident in Douay Jesuit College.[2]

The effect of these rulings, on the minds of those already prone to detect Jesuit plots, was lamentable. Numbers were reduced at once to sixty, and ten servants. Educationally, the restriction of admissions

[1] Cf. Guilday, 107 f.

[2] For details of the visitation, *Third Douay Diary*, 7 ff.

to nominees of the archpriest and the Jesuit superior meant that others could come only as *convictors*, at their own expense. (One of them took lodgings in the town till his uncle could send his fees, and another, sent from Rome, and by no less a person than Fr. Robert Persons, was refused 'propter inopiam Collegii', and duly departed.)

There was little the visitors did not think of. New arrivals were not to be contacted by students till they had been seen by the president or vice-president; *alumni* on arrival must give their own money to the college; servants who married must leave; and the latrines must be moved further from the front door.

'It is more expedient for the English cause', wrote the visitors, 'that fewer and more carefully chosen men should be educated for that end, with decency, decorum and the proper Collegiate observance, than that a promiscuous crowd should be admitted to share in destitution.' Perhaps they wrote well; there was only one Allen, and he had gone.

Douay, then, was a concentration-point of colleges. But throughout the entire exile period the meeting-place *par excellence* of all the currents in English Catholic thought, political and pastoral, was the *Venerabile* in Rome.

The Venerable English College was not alone as a power-house of the English mission, nor was it the largest, but it was a base at the very centre of Catholic Christendom. All roads led to Rome, and all the currents of English Catholic life flowed through the English College, by virtue of scholastics arriving, priests leaving and visitors great and small.

Moroni, the Cardinal Protector of England, issued its first statutes in the June of its first year, 1579. No student could be admitted younger than fourteen or older than twenty-five, nor with insufficient Latin to begin philosophy. For the first eight days of his course, to enable him to settle-in and meditate, he was to be separated from the other students. Every day he was to attend Mass and Vespers, and recite the Office of the Blessed Virgin Mary. Every month, at the least, he was to go to Confession and Holy Communion. The general rules as to obedience towards superiors applied to all, and there was much detail in the strain of 'tum etiam extra seminarium neque cibum capere neque pernoctare nisi concessu superioris'. Classes were to take place in the Jesuit *Gymnasium*. The art of disputation was to be cultivated as a means of mastering the faith. All conversation, indoors and out, was to be in Latin or Italian.[1]

[1] Full text in Meyer, appdx., 481–5.

From the end of 1579 onwards each student took the 'College Oath', by which he pledged himself that at the end 'I shall return to England for the salvation of souls whenever it shall seem good to the Superior of this College to order me to do so.' Not that all in fact complied.

The 'formation' of these students, as priests and teachers, was based on Jesuit practice and on the theory that lay behind the decrees of Trent. Each day's life was a dedication. Throughout the seven years of the course—three for philosophy and four for theology—the morning was devoted to lectures, the afternoon to an hour's recreation followed by study, the evening to domestic duties, supper, litany and final examination of conscience. From the start the careful supervision, of almost every moment and act, was as close as that which Worthington clapped down on Douay during its first visitation. Only thus, as the Church knew from experience, could a real dedication of the personality to the service of God be perfected: by a life which proved itself by unquestioning obedience to superiors and by complete self-renunciation, even at the cost of frustration and distress when individual superiors misjudged their office or succumbed to the taste of authority.

At the end of his Roman formation, and on the eve of his departure for the hazards of the English mission, each man had an audience of the pope, and was accompanied by his own colleagues beyond the confines of the city as far as the Milvian Bridge.[1]

During its second year, a devotion was founded in the college, later to become universal in Jesuit schools: the Sodality of Our Lady. This was not the first occasion, for the sodality had been established as early as 1559 at Syracuse, by the Sicilian Jesuit Cabarrasius, and at Rome four years later by John Leunis. In membership it was perforce exclusive, since it was confined to intending Jesuits. For this particular reason it was attacked as unjustly privileged. The first visitation of the college both confirmed it and sponsored a non-Jesuit parallel sodality.[2]

Financial poverty dogged the *Venerabile* from the start, hardly less than Douay. Dr. Owen Lewis had launched the college with his own furniture and books and money; Gregory XIII had given one hundred crowns a month; but numbers soon outran the papal pension, even

[1] For a masterly account of the formation in the *Venerabile* see Meyer, 101 ff.

[2] *Stonyhurst Mag.* vii. 568–70 for origin of the sodality. Meyer, 112 and appdx. xix for its Constitution.

before the new Pope Sixtus V curtailed it for reasons of economy (he called for alms for the college as a consolation).

The students, for their part, were fretted more by the domestic tensions that accrued from their being under Jesuit control, and having a Jesuit confessor. Indeed the first visitation, in 1585, was carried out primarily because of this; and while it upheld authority to the hilt, finding no fault with the Jesuit management of the college, condemning complaints in general, and criticisms made in particular to anyone but the rector, the commission did hear the grievances they had come to investigate, and gave the dissidents eight days' grace to depart (should they wish) to Rheims, where there were no Jesuit superiors. The second visitation, nine years later, confirmed all that was done here and added an order for separate cubicles, to prevent secret conferences among the *alumni*.

If the Society were to give up the *Venerabile*, wrote Persons, then in the existing state of affairs, and that of England, 'that band of young men is bound to be completely ruined', and the college would become a 'perpetual seed-bed of licence, factions, enmity and hatred of the Society and of all the other Seminaries under the Society's government'. Instead, he urged that a more resolute rector be installed, with two or three other Jesuits, if available, and a stricter choice of prefects. Barret at Douay likewise deplored any suggestion that the General should wash his hands of the college at Rome. 'Call to mind', he wrote, in a remarkably frank outburst, 'who else but you labours with us in the English Mission? . . . To whom can we send our students?'[1]

Three years after this, the *Venerabile*, which had begun with such high hopes, surrounded by giants of the eminence of St. Philip Neri and Bellarmine, and had now fallen so low, was welcoming as rector Fr. Robert Persons himself. Its numbers had fluctuated from seventy to eighty so far. Its output to England was just short of a hundred—twenty-one of them Jesuits. From now on, till the suppression of the Society in 1773, the rector was always an English Jesuit.

The Spanish colleges, by contrast, managed to avoid at first the constitutional troubles, arising from this dual or mixed government, that plagued Douay and Rome. Moreover, they were specialized

[1] Persons to General, 2 and 9 Dec. 1595, in *Arch. S.J.* Rome, Hisp. 139, f. 122 (Farm St. transcripts); Barret to General, 8 Dec. 1595, q. Foley vi. 53 and Gasquet, *Ven. Eng. Coll.*, 99.

colleges for higher studies, philosophy and theology. As such they recruited from all the others.

Each of them, Valladolid and Seville, had its own (Spanish) rector, with the roving authority (at first) of Persons, as Allen's 'Visitor', guiding both of them. To allay any risk of clashes, the post of 'Prefect of the Missions' was created in 1598, covering the two colleges and the two residences (San Lucar and—1593—Lisbon).[1] Prestige was high, as Spain had as yet no comparable Tridentine seminary. Combined numbers in 1600 were over a hundred.

None the less the English colleges in the Peninsula had particularly detergent growing pains of their own. These were two: personal differences, and the loss of students into the various religious orders.

At Seville the rector, Francis Peralta, did not see eye-to-eye with Creswell, who was procurator. Nor did the minister, Charles Tancred. Creswell was not, in fact, an easy man to live and work with, unless one had the psychological insight of Robert Persons. He had already been removed from one office on grounds of temperament. At Valladolid, similarly, there was friction between the rector, Cabredo, and the English Fr. Gibbons.[2]

The more serious trouble, however, arose from defections to the orders. A report by Cardinal Sega in 1595 gave the leakage as 31 to the Jesuits, 17 to the Benedictines, 14 to the Dominicans, 10 to the Franciscans, 10 to the Carmelites, 4 to the Carthusians: i.e. 86 in all, from all the colleges. This drain was felt most at Valladolid and Seville. It was the old quarrel revived. Vocation to the orders might well mean fewer men on the English mission (especially the contemplatives). It would certainly mean a loss of income to the impoverished colleges every time a *convictor* left. It would also mean that the orders would receive men whose education had in fact been paid for by the colleges. 'The English Students of these former Colledges', wrote one who detested all the orders indifferently, 'notwithstanding the oath of obedience as they termed it, ranne away (like Sheepe to the water) to bee Monks. Yea, many Schollers and Gentlemen; nay, roaring Boyes and Whoremongers rid Post from England thither, to wear Saint Bennets Cowle.'[3]

[1] Foley, vii. 27 f. *C.R.S.* xiv. 8–9. *Brussels Arch.*, cited by Hicks, *Month*, July 1931, p. 34. The *Annals* of the Seville College, written by Persons in 1610, and covering the first three years, are in *C.R.S.* xiv. 1–24.

[2] *Arch. S.J. Rome*, Hisp. 135, ff. 187, 306, 136, 362 (Farm St. transcripts).

[3] Lewis Owen, *The Running Register* (1626), 88.

The Annals of St. Alban's College, Valladolid, by Fr. Blackfan, offer a vivid *crescendo*, beginning with the violence of the Jesuit superiors towards one student, Mark Barkworth, in 1599, and mounting by way of six defections (three of them in flight) to a climax four years later, exacerbated by Fr. Creswell's relations with the Spaniards.[1] On the Jesuit side it was said that the Benedictines were 'enticing' students away with copies of their *Rule*. Open trouble broke out, and the 'rioters' went off to the Benedictine Abbey of San Benito. The abbot reported to the papal nuncio. So did the rector. The nuncio's first reaction was to order the rector to be put in irons, but instead he ordered him to leave the town. During the next five months St. Alban's lost twenty-five students to San Benito's. In the end the Holy See stepped in, and with ineffable impartiality forbade the Benedictines to entice or the Jesuits to desert (10 December 1608). Spies meanwhile took the scandal to England.

The whole episode has to be seen in perspective, however. The background to these personal outbursts was (as always) a complex of exile, nostalgia, poverty and want of fixed traditions. When everyone fretted, a remark like Creswell's to the nuncio, that the Society of Jesus was 'the only bulwark of the Church against her enemies', could go far in its effects.

The English Government, all the time, was very well informed indeed on the Spanish college situation. A report to the Privy Council from William Vaughan, in July 1602, gives a full and graphic description of the personnel at Valladolid—'Caterpillars I mean Jesuits and seminary priests.' Vaughan had been on the trail of these men at least ten years, to judge from his comments on one whom he found there. This was William Robins, one of four boys who had been captured in 1592 on the Holyhead road, en route for Valladolid *via* Ireland. All four had been imprisoned, with the priest William Davis who was with them, for over a year. Fr. Davis had then been executed at Beaumaris, and the boys had escaped. Their narrative is an epic comparable to that of the Worthington children. They reached Ireland, spent a year there until their money ran short, were then joined by five other lads, and paid a ship-master to take them to Spain. But he first of all ignored them once the money had been passed to him, and

[1] Fr. Blackfan's *Annals* are at Ushaw. These Valladolid troubles of 1599 and 1603 have been examined by Dom Bede Camm, O.S.B., and J. H. Pollen, S.J., in *The Month*, 1898 and 1899. There is a letter on the affair, from the Spanish council, 18 Sept. 1603, in *Arch. West.* viii, No. 59.

then threatened to betray them if their protests persisted. Their plan leaked out in any case, however, and they were arrested by the Viceroy's constables. On being set the usual test—go to church—they refused. All of them were committed to Dublin Castle except the youngest, who was put under the tutelage of the Protestant Bishop of Meath. When he wept for his brother, the Bishop contemplated having both boys in his house. But the elder refused to come, and the younger could be pacified only by being sent to join the rest of them in Dublin Castle prison. Two months later, after further examination, they were all sent in custody to England, on a Privy Council order, together with a page-boy who had meanwhile crossed to Dublin to find them.

Their journey was broken for some time at Chester, where they were befriended in the gaol by a Catholic who had himself been there twenty years. On their arrival in London they were examined by Cecil in person and then sent to the Bridewell prison (June or July 1594). When nothing could be extracted from them by examination there, they were set to strenuous labour, and even incarcerated with real criminals. It was this last that provided them with the means of escape. Three of them got away and scattered,one to St. Omer and Valladolid. Subsequently four more escaped, by means of a rope, from the prison roof, and one of this party also reached St. Omer.[1]

It is not surprising, then, that populated by generations of boys like these, the College of St. Omer itself soon had the reputation of being no less hardy than it was uncompromisingly English. These were the boys that cheered the English victories during the Marlborough wars, stolidly anglicized the pronunciation of the name St. 'Omers', went to untold hazards in escaping from their motherland and yet were ready to return to it deliberately, sometimes in the midst of their studies—as for example the sixteen who came to London in 1679 to testify that Titus Oates was a perjured liar.

In their distinctive dress[2] they were soon known about the town. Local opposition was considerable. The Belgians 'would have much preferred [for financial reasons] that these English boys should be

[1] Cf. Yepes, 652, 806; Bede Camm, O.S.B., *In the Brave Days of Old*, 31, 137; *C.R.S.* xxx. 34 note. On the numbers in Spain there is remarkable agreement between an anonymous report to the Government in 1601 (*Cal. S.P. Dom. Eliz. 1601–3*, p. 181) and the report of Henry Tichborne, S.J., to Fr. Darbyshire at Pont-à-Mousson in 1597 (*Cal. S.P. Dom. Eliz. 1595–7*, p. 356).

[2] There is no certainty about this. Cf. H. Chadwick, *St. Omers to Stonyhurst* (1962), 233 f. But the *Stonyhurst Mag.* (iii. 336) suggested that 'If we imagine a blue coat boy, under one of those large hats which students use in Rome, we shall have a very fair idea....'

brought up in the Flemish schools and students' hostels, or at least that they should live within the College of the Fathers and not have a separate house'. The area, moreover, was swarming with English spies, to such an extent that the magistracy insisted on passports for all English nationals coming into the town, even the refugee boys.[1] The frenzy with which the Government of Elizabeth sought to assess the danger from St. Omer is well illustrated in Fr. Henry Walpole's torture by the Privy Council.

There were inevitable disagreements, also, over the actual government of the college. Aquaviva, the General, took it that the rector appointed would administer the institution, and not be dependent on 'our [i.e. the Flemish] College'. This, he said, was 'the usual custom of the Seminaries with which we are charged'. The rector would consult with the Walloon rector at his discretion, but his responsibility lay direct to the provincial (until the establishment of the English province of the Jesuits in 1620). The Belgian Fathers, on the other hand, wanted the college to have merely a superior (with the title of President) and be altogether subject to their own college. Persons (in Madrid) wanted it fully independent, 'like the one in Rome and these two in Spain', especially as rector and president would clash. In the event, the Aquaviva-Persons view prevailed. The rector governed the college, and he himself delegated to the prefect of studies full academic control of the boys' work. Father Flack, the procurator, was in a real sense an ambassador also between the rector (a Belgian—Fr. Foucart) and the boys' parents in England.

A third source of friction was the internal discipline. Discipline was maintained by three prefects, one for each of the large rooms. One of the three was a Belgian; further, he was not a priest, and he was young. The question of the prefects' authority in 'correcting' the boys therefore became electric, until settled through the good offices of Fr. Holt, by a rule that punishment should be given by the rector. By 1600 the Netherlands provincial, Oliveira Manares, was reassuring the General that 'the boys are highly satisfied, and more obedient than they ever were before; I hope that Ours [the Jesuit term for Fathers of the Society] will take care not to disturb these youths by any words of theirs'.[2]

[1] Persons to the General, 20 Mar., 18 Apr., 4 and 16 June 1594, in *Arch. S.J. Rome*, Hisp. 136.

[2] Aquaviva, 19 June 1594, q. in Willaert (1914), 10; *Arch. S.J. Rome*—Anglia 30, ii. 328–31—Flands. Belg. 1, ii. 692—Gall. xliv. 55—Germ. clxxviii. 744—Hisp. 137, 164, 138, 122 (all from Farm St. transcripts).

So far so good. But much depended on Persons' own pre-eminent position in the college movement being preserved. Indeed, it was a curious roving commission he held, and he was far away in Spain. Much was already settled, but there were many hazards outstanding. Of these, three were ever-present, poverty, disease and capture.

A plaintive letter by Creswell in 1599 pointed out that the income originally given to support a college of eighteen boys would not go far among 107. Plague in the province, though it did not reach the college, impelled the rector to evacuate sixty boys to Courtrai early in 1597, for a whole term. But the greatest anxieties were those caused by the Government at home. Early in 1595, six boys who had left St. Omer for the college at Valladolid were intercepted in the English Channel, taken to England, brought before the Privy Council, and confided to the Archbishop of Canterbury for apportionment among approved Protestants who would see to their schooling. Fourteen others were caught in England in 1601 and imprisoned. The evidence of a spy shows, however, that by 1603 there were a record of 140 in the College.[1]

By the end of the century, then, the colleges abroad were in full swing. If we assume, as is surely warranted, that official Catholic reports to Rome on the numbers in the colleges, and spies' reports to the Government, represent the best information that could be got, and that neither side had any motive for minimizing, then it appears that by 1600 there were about seventy students at Douay, seventy at Rome, eighty at Valladolid and from seventy to ninety at Seville. At St. Omer there were over 120. A total of well over 400.

[1] Narratives in Foley, i. 186, iii. 502, vii. 1154; *Stonyhurst Mag.* iii. 336, 357. Cf. *C.R.S.* xxx. 37–8. For the spy, *Cal. S.P. Dom. Eliz. 1601–3*, No. 91, p. 45.

VIII

THE SEMINARIES ABROAD

THE colleges overseas had in common their spiritual purpose, their internal discontent arising from mixed government, and their penury arising from delays in the Spanish and papal pensions. But by 1620 they could all regard themselves as part of a missionary enterprise that had become permanent This was due, negatively, to the collapse of any hope that Stuart England would speedily return to the faith. Positively it was due to the reconstitution of the orders. The rise of the Anglo-Benedictine Congregation after 1606, 'from the ashes'; the establishment of the English Franciscan province in 1618; the erection of the English Jesuit province in 1620—all these were portents. All of them, too, made the neighbourhood of Douay the educational centre of the English Catholic resistance as never before.

When the president of Douay College reported to Rome on the whole movement in October 1622 he particularized seven colleges for boys and men in the vicinity. There were his own college (that of Allen, dating from 1568); the Jesuits at St. Omer since 1593, with a college at Louvain and a house of professors at Ghent and a house at Watten and a novitiate at Liège; the Benedictines at St. Gregory's, Douay; the Franciscans at St. Bonaventure's; and the Carthusians at Bruges and then Mechlin.[1] If we add to these the University of Douay itself, and the several Augustinian and Dominican and Premonstratensian colleges,[2] the academic aura of Douay becomes impressive. The various traditions, monastic and secular, have each their uniqueness and peculiar 'spirit', which emerges only from prolonged study of their archives and is for ever too intangible to be formulated exactly in words. Together, they represent one unitary educational stream.

[1] 3 *D.D.* 195 f., 391 f. Cf. Lewis Owen—'They have another faire Colledge two leagues from Saint Omer, at a place called Watten, the revenues whereof are worth about five hundred pounds yearely; which they got (by their cheating and policie) from an old doting Fryer that owned it' (*Running Register* [1626] 11–13). Watten became the great novitiate of the English S.J. province in 1622.

[2] Cf. Guilday, 227.

1. THE ENGLISH COLLEGE, ROME

The *Venerabile* was expressly a seminary for the training of priests. George Gilbert, who finished his days there as a lay pensioner in 1583, emphasizes this by his very loneliness in the lists. The English spirit of the place was manifested from the start, and perpetuated from the moment when its Italian rector (Agazzari) was succeeded by William Holt.

What weakened the college, even had its finances not been precarious, was that it became inevitably caught up in the dissensions of the Catholics at home over the archpriest controversy and the Blacklow controversy in turn. The great probability that the Jesuit leaders were reluctant to have control of the *Venerabile*—they had certainly not sought it—made no difference to the odium cast upon the place by the very fact of Jesuit control. It was only too easy to regard the college as an instrument of power for an order which served a quarter of all the mission-stations in seventeenth-century England.[1] Parents accordingly tended at times to send their boys to Douay instead. And as the Jesuits at St. Omer, for their part, were sometimes very hard up for boys wanting to go to Rome, the *Venerabile* was obliged increasingly to admit boys less well grounded educationally than hitherto: sometimes indeed not certain of their vocation at all. Hence the paradox of the best-endowed college having sometimes the smallest population: for which, albeit exaggerated, there was also a more elemental reason. 'Our English Students', wrote a Protestant in 1626 after touring some of the seminary towns, 'when they come to Rome doe die, like so many rotten Sheepe, by reason of the unwholesomenesse and putrifaction of the ayre; so that they are not able (God be blessed) to send so many Locusts into England.'[2]

In the eighty-five years between the death of Elizabeth and the fall of James II some 600 students entered the *Venerabile*, the majority of them from the English middle and upper classes and the nobility. Most of them arrived already determined to be priests and to return to England on the mission: though the minority was substantial—seventy-four in doubt as to a vocation on arrival, thirty-four quite definitely not intending to enter religion.

With few exceptions they were all proficient in Latin, but few had very much Greek and none had any Hebrew. The overwhelming bulk

[1] Cf. Gasquet, *Ven. Eng. Coll. Rome*, 113 f.

[2] Lewis Owen, *The Running Register* (1626), 21.

of them, from soon after the beginning of the century, had completed their humanities at St. Omer. And while a few had gone back to England for a spell, most had come to Rome direct, with an attestation from the St. Omer College rector. From Douay College, apart from a batch of five coming together in 1601, the arrivals were intermittent and totalled fewer than thirty throughout the whole period, very few of them after 1610. This is only to be expected, bearing in mind that Douay College and the *Venerabile* were both pontifical seminaries, and that by 1610 the pattern of inter-relationships was stabilized.

Of those whose *Responsa* state their ages, well over half were between eighteen and twenty-one on arrival. This means that most of them would be close on thirty when they returned to England as ordained seminary priests, and many of them (the St. Omer boys) might then have been away from their native land for a dozen years and more, with palpable effects on their outlook and their command of English.

Their course of study, and their formation, was that of all the new Tridentine seminaries. We can take the course at Douay, which is better documented, as speaking for them all.

2. THE ENGLISH COLLEGE, DOUAY

Rome was the focus. But no other single institution can compete with Douay College in its influence among the English Catholics of penal times. Douay College educated, that is to say, the vast majority of those parish priests who were to be the backbone of such Catholic popular education as England was to know in the generations preceding Emancipation. There was a ready market for calumnies about it, no doubt in proportion to the chagrin of its various enemies. The traveller Lewis Owen wrote of it in 1626 that it 'was wont (and yet doth) receive all manner of persons, specially our hackney and Apostate Ministers, and all such discontented persons, who are within a yeare after made Priests and sent into England. . . . I have knowne many men made Priests there, that never learned Grammar.'[1] What Allen was to the college movement abroad, Douay was to the education movement at home. It furnished a constant flow of missionary teachers. And it is typical of that college that it nourished the first, and the last, of the English martyrs: Cuthbert Mayne in 1577, and Thomas Thweng during the Oates panic in 1680.

[1] *Running Register*, 80.

In 1602 the English College celebrated the tenth year of its return from Rheims by laying the foundation-stone of permanent buildings, centred on a chapel dedicated to St. Thomas of Canterbury. The whole of the new college was in use before the end of 1604.[1]

As it was among the first Tridentine seminaries north of the Alps, its daily timetable of devotions and studies became a model—save in so far as later benefactors elsewhere may have ordained minor modifications in their deeds of gift. The students rose at 5 a.m. From 5.30 till 6 there was mental prayer, in church, where at 6 they were joined by the juniors for litanies and for Mass. An hour of study followed, before breakfast at 7.30. From 8 till 10 they had classes, and thereafter study till 12 noon. After dinner there was recreation till 2, schools from 2 till 4 and study from 4 till 6, when litanies and prayers and spiritual reading followed till supper at 7. They were then free till 8.30, when the final night prayers and examination of conscience took place, with meditation to complete the day before retiring. There is no reason to suppose that that *horarium*, as reported to Rome as late as 1741 in answer to *quaesita* addressed to the president, had changed at all since the time of Allen.

The new student was plunged into it after his first few days, which were always allowed him unfettered, so that he could settle into the college easily. During those opening days he would have his first interview with the procurator, answer his *Interrogatory* in writing, have his name and *alias* noted, have his fees paid in advance, by prior arrangement with the college's agent in London, and submit himself to a test of proficiency in order to decide the class in which he must start.

The course of study began with a class called variously Rudiments, Elements, Figures and Little Figures. Its content was in fact the first elements of Latin. The terminology for this class varied among the colleges. At Douay the first mention of a class of *Figuristas* is in 1615. Two years later there were classes in both Figures and Rudiments. But a scrutiny of the circumstances reveals that this was a freak year; there were three entrants who knew little or no Latin, of whom two were boys of thirteen and sixteen and the other a man of twenty-five. These could not well be taught together as one class. In the next two years the lowest class was called Rudiments. For ten years after that

[1] *Menology of St. Edmund's College* (1909), 11. There is a plan of the buildings at Douay, with photographs, and an inventory of relics translated to England in 1793, in *The Edmundian*, No. 19, pp. 160–9.

THE ENGLISH COLLEGE, DOUAY

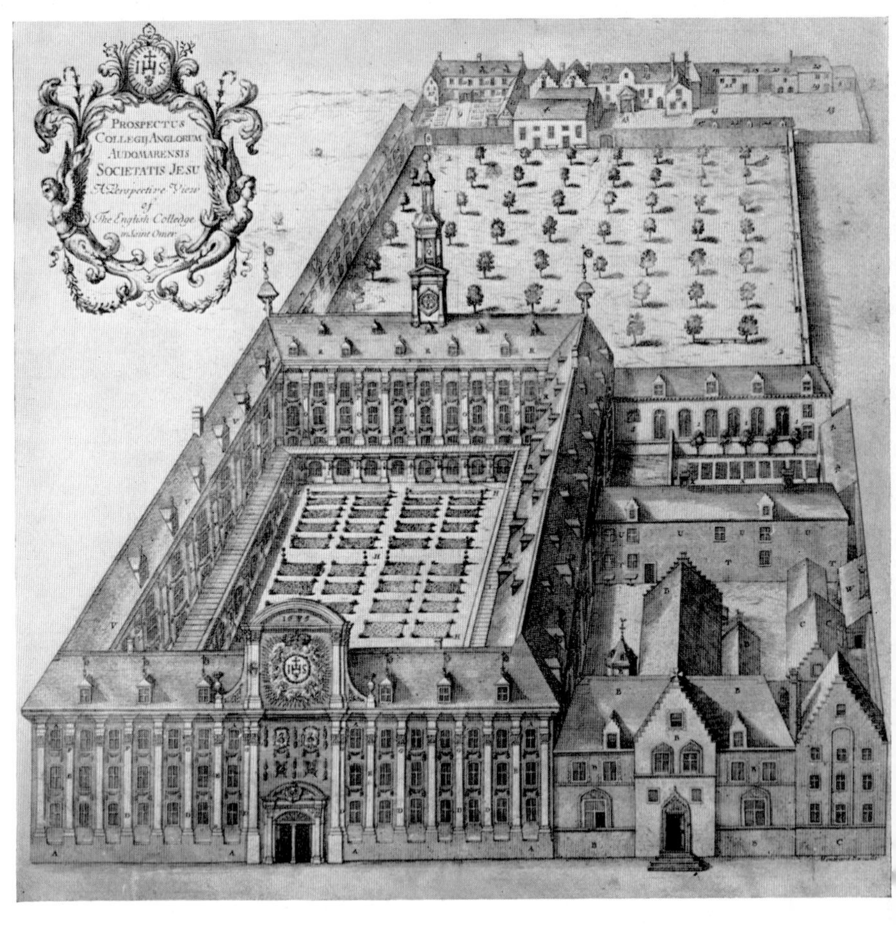

THE ENGLISH COLLEGE AT ST. OMER

there were no beginners at all among the admissions. From then onwards the class was called Figures.

The second class, Grammar, began with a three weeks' revision of the elements and then settled down to two grammar lessons per day and a study of authors: usually Alvarus, Terentius, Christianus and the *Epistles* of Cicero. The rudiments of Greek were introduced at this stage. The boy's 'themes' prepared in the morning were examined in the afternoon. The programme on Saturdays was largely revision.

In the third year, Syntax, they finished the *Epistles* of Cicero and went on to the *De Senectute* or *De Amicitia*, together with formal Greek grammar. The rules of poetry and metaphor were added in the fourth year (Poetry) through the medium of the sixth and twelfth books of Virgil's *Aeneid*, together with Claudius, the *Odes* of Horace, and the prose of Sallust's histories, Caesar's *Gallic War* and a few Ciceronian speeches.

The fifth and final year of the course in humanities was Rhetoric. Here they read Virgil's *Bucolics* and *Georgics*, the satires and epistles and *Ars Poetica* of Horace and the satires of Persius. Roman history was studied as ancillary.

These five grades, through which the boy completed his humanities, were universal throughout all the colleges. They were indeed the course established by the Jesuit system, on the model of the pre-Reformation grammar schools. They made up that classical education without which the postulant could not begin his priestly studies.

The formation for the priesthood started with logic as the threshold of a full course in philosophy, and was completed by four years of theology. Here the routine method of instruction was by dictated notes on texts and commentaries.[1] During this lengthy academic formation, which has to be visualized as taking place inside the daily framework of spiritual exercises which we have already outlined for the early days of Douay and Rome, the minor orders of sub-deacon and deacon would be taken. Ordination as a priest came usually at the very end of the course, which would have had in mind his future on the English mission to the extent of giving him a year of study in controversy, and a thorough training in preaching.

Douay College, then, had been obliged to grow downwards over the whole scale of schooling. The other colleges strove always to take

[1] The libraries of the two English seminaries to which Douay gave rise after 1793, Ushaw College (Durham) and St. Edmund's (Old Hall, Ware), contain many of these seventeenth-century 'Dictates'.

humanities for granted and confine themselves to philosophy and theology, while the Jesuit School at St. Omer and the later Benedictine schools at Douay and Dieulouard provided the humanities course only.

Such was the curriculum as described in the *Rules of Douay College* in 1640. French was added in 1648. Dramatic performances were frequent, on sacred and historical subjects, the *libretti* written usually by Douay professors and in Latin verse.

The examinations, at fixed intervals, were always oral, and two hours in duration. They took place each time a book was finished, the examining board comprising the prefect of studies (headmaster), the president and vice-president and the tutor. The spirit of the place went on, unspoiled by attempts at innovations, and enriched by some of them—the 'Treat' on the president's feast-day, introduced in 1650, and the special festivities put on if an old boy were visiting the college.[1]

In the academic work of Douay College the only hard and fast distinction was between the lower and higher studies. This had shown itself visibly in the division into lower and upper dining-halls as early as 1580. In the field of teaching it meant a staff for philosophy and theology (the seven years of the priest's formation) separate from that of the school of humanities (the preparatory five years, from rudiments to rhetoric).

Theology was usually taught by the president and an assistant, and philosophy and logic by senior professors, subject to variations whereby a man went up with his class. During the Civil War, when the college was so small that in 1646 there was only one master (John Singleton) required for humanities at all, he accompanied the whole group in due course as far as the end of their first-year philosophy.

This 'form-master' device, as against the subject or grade-master, was frequently adopted in the humanities school. There were few difficulties attending it in the contemporary 'grammar' course, and it made for close contact between master and boys. Edward Pigford began with a class of syntax in 1622 and took them through poetry and rhetoric to the end. John Hawley took the syntax squad of 1649 as far as the end of rhetoric, and then began again with a Greek class in 1652. A special class in Greek, additional to the foundation-work in

[1] The Douay *Rules*, of 1640, are at St. Edmund's College. For a description of them see M. V. Sweeney, 55–63, and 247–50 for the detailed syllabus.

rudiments and grammar, features in the lists from 1619 to 1629 and for a few years following the Civil War.

The class-master element was not sufficiently constant to have been a matter of general policy. Few men are found with the same boys for more than two years. Often a subject in humanities was taught by one and the same man over a longish period. Sometimes a master had two classes in the same year, as when William Hart took the rhetoricians of 1623 and the Greek class as well. The closing decade of the century shows further refinements still, with Edward Hawarden inheriting a class of first-year philosophy in 1692, taking them right through to theology, and remaining as one of the two teachers in theology from then on. William Crathorn took the 1693 syntaxians to the end of rhetoric, then the 1696 poets, and then began again with the syntax class of 1697. Anthony Jackson took the 1693 grammarians right through their humanities.

We can say, then, that the class system was flexible, that it tended to seek the personal contact of master and boy over longer periods than one year, and that it was obliged to adapt itself to the changing demands of numbers and personnel.

The college once reached a total of 130 students and seniors—a very high figure indeed, exceeded only by the phenomenal numbers at St. Omer. This was in 1624, at the height of James I's relaxation of the penal laws. The numbers were over a hundred till after the first Parliament of Charles I. They then fell gradually, rose again during the years of the king's personal rule, fell catastrophically during the Civil War—to thirty in 1645, fluctuated thereafter according to the trend of political events in England, and by 1676 stood again at 105.

The age of entry varied very widely. Of some 200 documented cases given in the *Diaries*, during the thirty years following the death of Elizabeth, the youngest admitted was ten years of age, and the oldest thirty-three. The fourteen-to-eighteen age group accounts for over half, with a slight preponderance of the younger half of that group. But the diversity of age in a class at any one time was severe, when a boy of thirteen arrived fit for the class of poetry (George Fortescue, in 1617), and a man of twenty-five fit only for rudiments (Gilbert Andrews, same year). In lean years, when admissions were few, a boy whose age was well below or above the normal age for his attainments could be fairly easily assimilated, as classes were small. In bumper-years it was a different story. The lowest class, figures, had for example during the peak-years 1629 to 1632 an age-range of 13–21,

12–21 and 11–18. The third form, grammar, had a range, during the same period, of 13–19, 12–25, 14–20 and 16–22.

During these same thirty years (1603–33), for which the *Diaries* are most forthcoming, it is possible to discriminate the good entry years from the bad. In 1628, for example, none of the entrants were below the standard of poetry (fifth form), whereas in 1621 none had been above syntax (fourth form). As was to be expected, the great majority entered at third or fourth form level (grammar and syntax): 120 out of 200 clear cases during this period. Of the remainder, no fewer than forty-seven had to start in the lowest class of all (figures). These proportions thus throw additional light on the extent of schooling it was possible for a boy to secure beforehand in England. Yet (again) conclusions must not be pressed too far. If seven of the fifteen entries in 1629 were ready for the third form, and three for the fourth, two years later nineteen had to be 'put to' figures, out of forty-three. In thirty years only ten boys entered qualified for the top form (rhetoric), and only twenty-five with their humanities altogether completed and ready for philosophy or theology.

Statistically handled, these heroic boys lose their colour. To come upon them one by one, however, in the *Diaries*, is to follow the career of 'Jacobus Britonus parvulus' (aged thirteen), or Nicholas Waldegrave, aged fifteen, but 'scribere nescit', or the convert Thomas Read of Hampton after twenty-eight years of study at Oxford, or John Yeatman, aged seventeen, but 'in fidei Catholicae rudimentis non instructus', or the infant Thomas Short, '*alias* Peregrine', aged ten. It is to watch, too, the journeys back and forth of priests, returning to Douay upon banishment from England, bringing boys with them.

There were also expulsions. Not every postulant's vocation was firm. Nor his character. Three had been dismissed for indolence in 1599. Four went together in 1602. One from Spain in 1601 left within four days because 'not apt'. Thomas Hamilton was expelled in 1605 'ob malos mores', Jasper Garnet in 1610 for 'scurrilia verba'; one unnamed in 1623 'huic vocationi plane ineptus' and another 'cum nullum in studiis fecerat progressum'; one in 1629 because he insisted on proceeding from poetry to logic, thus by-passing rhetoric; one in 1632 on account of 'taverns'; one in 1648 'quia nec regulas observarat nec penitentias subiret', one in 1651 'lassus hic studendo'; and so on. From time to time boys had to be dismissed because their pension was so long in arrears. Now and again a boy would be recalled by his parents, following a royal proclamation against the exiled colleges, or temporarily upon 'family business', or expressly to collect his fee-money from his sponsors and bring it back with him. Occasionally a boy was sent home to England because his health broke down.

There was a considerable traffic in students throughout, between Douay and the other colleges in Spain and Portugal and at St. Omer. It is not always easy to descry a pattern in the movements as recorded in the *Diary*, though at times what was happening is clear enough.

The college at Valladolid, as we saw, had begun with a substantial filiation from Douay. In the first year of the English College at Seville, Douay sent sixteen senior students. From then onwards, however, the departures for Spain are less easy to classify, with the exception of the squad of twenty-four put into one house at Douay under Roger Ridley (Easter 1600), to prepare themselves for migration. A few left nearly every year down to 1611, after which none are mentioned till 1626, and after that none at all. Admittedly the *Diary* varies in completeness from compiler to compiler. Admittedly, too, there was a fairly constant connection also between Douay and Lisbon after the founding of the English College there in 1627–8. The fact that the *Diary*, which is so detailed for Lisbon, is silent on departures for Spain, may be evidence that the Spanish connection did indeed cease.

The arrivals at Douay *from* Spain have no direct bearing on this. There were one or two nearly every year down to 1630. Some of them were merely calling, on their way to England to serve on the mission. As many as seventeen, out of sixty-nine, came for reasons of health, owing to the heat of the Spanish summers.

As Valladolid and Seville were colleges for the final studies, the vast majority of the men who came thence to Douay were put in the corresponding classes, theology or philosophy or logic, to resume at the point where their studies had been interrupted. Occasionally there was an exception, as when Peter Chambers was accepted from Spain in 1603 and put to grammar, serving Douay in a novel way by undertaking to act as teacher of music at the same time. All this certainly confirms that the Spanish colleges and Douay lived their own life without any degree of interpenetration that could be called a policy. Nor, in view of the background, is this surprising.

Similarly the colleges of Douay and Rome were severely separate. During the period of the *Third Diary* only six students were sent on to Rome for study (four in 1609, two in 1621), and only sixteen came from Rome to Douay (two of them expelled) down to 1653. We have already seen that the Jesuit *v.* secular feud was tending to draw off to Douay a good deal of patronage hitherto centred on the *Venerabile.*

Relations were the least complicated between Douay College and the St. Omer school. Those of the St. Omer boys who developed a vocation to the priesthood went either to the Jesuit novitiate itself, or to Douay for training as secular clergy. The pattern is not, however, consistently as straightforward as that. In 1621, after 'several years' at St. Omer, James Watkins was admitted at Douay to the class of grammar! Nor did boys always complete their humanities before moving from St. Omer to Douay. Edward Belson in 1627 entered poetry; John Pickering and James Ironmonger in 1628 entered syntax; Thomas Waldegrave in 1630 entered grammar (at the age of twenty-five); Robert Bowerman in 1632 was put into rhetoric—and also used as a teacher of singing and the violin. But usually the students arrived at Douay ready for logic. The total from St. Omer in the first half of the century, as recorded in the *Douay Diaries*, does not seem to have exceeded twenty-six. The few boys sent from Douay *to* St. Omer are obviously exceptions to a traffic that was all the other way. There were only seven of them down to 1630, and there were usually special personal reasons.

Throughout the whole period Douay was governed from Rome as a pontifical college. This meant a series of visitations after the style of that of 1599, some of them routine visits, some of them *ad hoc* for a special purpose, as when the visitor of 1607 came expressly to find means of reducing numbers on account of expense. After 1625 the president sent a progress report to Rome every year. It was a system that should normally have meant government by 'remote control'. But Douay College was seldom normal, life was a progression from crisis to crisis, dogged by poverty, chagrined by calumny from outside.

While Richard Barret followed out the lines laid down by Allen, the domestic life of the college prospered. But Thomas Worthington, who succeeded Barret in 1599, was an innovator, and a difficult man. Both these characteristics combined to prompt him to do away with the system of *Lectors* teaching their classes in the house, and to substitute for them class *Repetitors*, whereby the students were sent for lectures to the public schools of the Jesuits. Of all the causes of domestic stress in the seventeenth century this was the deepest. It lasted for twenty years.

A further source of friction arose in 1604 with the defection of boys from Douay to the Benedictines, as we have already seen was happening in Spain. Six students left. Letters were given by the president to all six, but money to only two, 'for we did not think that this impoverished College ought to bear the expense of those who, leaving us and our vocation, departed to wealthy monasteries'. When the papal visitor arrived in May 1607 to reduce numbers because of the growing impoverishment, he formally dismissed the Benedictines; and when they complained to the rector of Douay University itself, Worthington declared tartly that that dignitary would be ignored.

Yet again, there was deep discontent about Douay doctorates. When Richard Smith went to Rome in 1609 to canvass a revival of Allen's dream of a College of Writers, this doctorate issue was high on his agenda. His memorandum to the pope argued that while no one could deny that a doctor's degree was an incentive to study and a means of livelihood, Pope Clement VIII had seen fit nevertheless to make such an attainment impossible for English scholars, by forbidding them to take doctorates (at Douay University) till four years after leaving the English College—by which time they would be in England on the mission. Clement VIII's Brief had, moreover, made their promotion depend on the judgement of their rector, who was a religious, rather than on that of the head of the secular clergy, the archpriest in England. Smith pleaded that they be allowed to proceed to doctorates as soon as Douay University, or the archpriest, should consider them individually ready. The papal reply, as so often in a dispute between senior authorities, was to canalize the procedure through the Cardinal Protector of England in Rome. The Brief was not recalled, but the archpriest was told to notify Rome of such students as he proposed should be allowed to go on to the doctorate, and the Cardinal Protector would arrange it. A cumbrous procedure, but the necessary price to pay for saving faces all round.[1]

Meanwhile, too, the financial crisis had come urgently to the fore. We have already met with the drastic reductions ordered by the visitors in 1599. When John Wright arrived as papal visitor in 1607 there were four boys admitted who had to live outside in the town for some months. In the next five years the papal pension was covering only one-fifth of the expenditure.

[1] The documents are in *C.R.S.* xli, 141 ff., where the editor, L. J. Hicks, S.J., comments that some students were in fact already taking Douay university doctorates, and that of course the problem had not arisen earlier because in Allen's day there had been far too few men for *any* to be delayed in returning to England.

But if in addition to all this the English secular clergy were distrustful of the college on account of its having a Jesuit confessor—and distrustful is a mild term—the flavour of the Douay *Diary* suggests that that situation was the contriving not of the Jesuits themselves but of the unhappy third President, Worthington.

What actually brought matters to a head was Worthington's change of attitude on the archpriest question. In 1612 he decided to support the 'Appellants' in England in pressing the pope to appoint a *bishop*, with jurisdiction over regulars as well as seculars. A conference on this being held in the college, Worthington's personal shortcomings as a negotiator and a president brought him to a standstill. He was opposed by both his vice-president and his prefect of studies. The only way out of such an *impasse* was by means of a visitation.

The new ordinances which the visitors duly read to the assembled staff in November concern these scholastic struggles very closely. Any student should be free to take Douay University degrees, provided he did so at his own expense. No *alumnus* might be admitted in the future younger than sixteen, or not well advanced in humanities. Boys under age, or insufficiently educated, or not intending to become priests, must enter as fee-paying *convictors*, and their pension must be kept up continuously six months in advance.

There was wisdom in this. On the one hand, every student not in the main line of the college purpose, as a seminary for priests, must be altogether self-supporting. On the other hand, by insisting on a high minimum attainment for the intending clergy on entry, the decrees hoped to make their course at Douay shorter and therefore cheaper. The papal pension for *alumni* would go further by dint of speedier changes. At the same time, in so far as the prior education in humanities would have to have been provided somewhere, these ordinances must be regarded as passing the burden on to St. Omer and to such Catholic schools as could be set going in England. We have here, then, a collateral reason for the periodic multiplication of schools at home whenever the penal laws were temporarily relaxed.

This was the climax of Worthington's presidency. A year later he was succeeded by Matthew Kellison (November 1613), whose reversion to the Allen tradition, as reformed by the visitations, was to last for thirty years of heartfelt academic stability.

President Kellison's own first crisis arose on the wings of rumours, coming from St. Omer, that Douay was suspected of favouring the new oath of allegiance prescribed in England by King James I. This was a damaging allegation; for the pope had not only condemned the oath but had deposed the archpriest for taking it. Kellison dealt with the calumny adroitly. He assembled all the Douay staff and senior students and asked for their individual views. All but two uncompromisingly denounced the oath.

He then had to meet an epidemic of plague. It is typical of his balanced and vigorous mind that he turned the dangers to the advantage of the college by using this crisis to put an end to the unpopular Worthington policy of sending the students outside for lectures.

He had already taken a first step to reverse this by himself taking classes in scholastic philosophy inside the college in 1616, on the Third Part of the *Summa Theologica* of Aquinas. When plague swept over the province in the following July, all schools had to be discontinued. The boys were set to private study. When by the opening of the next academic year there was no sign of any abatement of the scourge, humanities classes were opened in the college as of old. The next session opened with the boys going again to the Jesuit schools, but a recrudescence of the plague forced their recall within a few weeks, and the classes in rhetoric and poetry were run inside the college for a month. The final return to the traditional system of inside-lectures came about through a dispute. In 1619 a Douay scholar, affronted by a boy while attending the Jesuit classes, struck him and was sent for punishment to the Jesuit prefect of studies. The Douay boy asked that he be punished by his own head, Kellison. This was agreed to, but another Jesuit master intercepted him. His Douay classmates rallied round and released him, and reported to Kellison, who, failing to persuade the Jesuits to forswear punishing any Douay boys in future, categorically withdrew his scholars from the Society's classes and set up his own. And he stood his ground. For when the Jesuit version of all this reached Rome, and the nuncio to Flanders conveyed severe orders for the Holy See in vindication of the Jesuits, Kellison expostulated so smartly that Rome concluded the matter to his entire satisfaction. From this time onwards, the classes in humanities at Douay continued inside the college till the suppression during the French Revolution in 1793.

When Kellison reported to Rome in 1622 on the whole College Movement, he took pains to recall what Douay had so far stood for, amid its poverty and arrears of pension. It had become the model for nearly all other foundations since. It had sent close on a thousand priests to England since its first *alumnus* landed there in 1574; and 111 of them had been martyred. There had been over a hundred Douay seminarians in England before any Jesuits arrived. And there were now a hundred in the college waiting to tread the same *via dolorosa.* He ended with a frank account of the pauperization that had set in, with the papal pension difficult and the Spanish pension quite impossible to collect, and *convictors*' fees in arrears because, statutes or no statutes, the charity of the college tended to outrun its means. In the following year Kellison went himself to England, despite his sixty years, to plead this cause in person.

The two troubles, the financial situation and the resentment against the religious orders for recruiting students from Douay, virtually resulted in a new College Oath being ordained by Rome, whereby every *alumnus* over fourteen years of age, and future boys reaching that age, must pledge themselves not to join any order without the express leave of the Holy See. This oath was enjoined on all the pontifical colleges in Christendom. The shade of Worthington, who had written so scathingly on the defections to 'wealthy monasteries' after the struggles of Douay to educate the deserters, must have rejoiced.[1]

But relief was needed immediately. It becomes noticeable in the *Diary* from about this time that more and more of the fees of *convictors* are insisted upon in advance, at the rate of 60 florins (£25) a year. Some boys on arrival are found paying in 600 florins. About this time, too, there is recorded the first of those testamentary 'Funds' which were to mean so much to the college later. Richard Todkill arrived in June 1626 under the terms of the will of the Rev. Robert Tempest (and took as his *alias* the name of his benefactor). By the end of the century there were several of these funds. The Tempest bequest endowed a place at Douay until such time as England should return to the faith and Douay be disbanded, when the place should be transferred to Oxford University. The Lancaster Fund, set going by an agreement with the secular clergy of Lancashire in 1628, was the second of the series, and John Bisley the first boy to benefit from it. The Thimbleby Fund followed. They were godsends. Apart from them, the only solace to a college perpetually in debt was the intermittent financing of a particular boy (not a series) by some wealthy patron.

While his envoys were begging in England, Kellison received the

[1] For the oath, see 3 *D.D.* 240 f., 408; and Foley, vl. 127. For a Benedictine reaction see p. 178 below.

sharpest affront of his career, following the visitation at the end of 1626. It served to bring out his fighting qualities to the full, in defence of Allen's college that had once stood so high.

The visitor appointed by the Pope, Archdeacon Stravius of Arras, was thorough. What the college anticipated from him is to be seen in the *Diary* entry that recorded his departure: 'After so careful an examination, nothing could be discovered or found out worth telling, nor had he found dissensions or jealousies amongst us, but peace and harmony; he said to some that this was a College of angels not Angles, but to others he said that they had all made an agreement to hold their tongues and conceal anything that they knew.' He seems also to have broken the rules of etiquette that govern visitations, by reporting to Rome the snap answers of the Collegians and not allowing them time for mature reflection when he returned later with the Holy See's decisions.

President Kellison held his hand until the new papal decrees, based upon this visitation, arrived in August 1627. Then he struck. Gathering his staff round him, he set down their matured reflections himself. They could *not* continue to make their meditations in the college church so long as that church remained as small and damp as it was; the hardship was too great. Those dispensed from fasting during Lent could *not* sit at separate tables from the rest, as that would create distinctions of class which the college to its credit had never tolerated as yet. The continued restriction on doctorates was 'a disgrace to the whole nation, [in] that the English, who have defended the authority of the Pope not only by learned writings but also with their blood, should be prevented by that very authority from those degrees to which all learned men through the whole of Christendom are freely admitted'. The decree on doctorates had been obtained from the pope by men hostile to the secular clergy, while 'certain rectors of seminaries, members of the Society [of Jesus], are allowed to promote whom they will to these degrees within their own walls'. As to the mission, Douay *must* send priests to England without the leave of the nuncio; they had to seize what chances offered—the enterprise could not be timetabled or staggered. As to discipline, the president *must* be allowed to expel on his own authority—the alternative was chaos. And he threw in that visitations, being very costly affairs, should be few—and conducted by an English visitor, sent from England.

The decrees were promulgated, all the same, to the dismay of the students, whose only hope now was that Kellison would mitigate their operation. This in fact he did, by suspending the decrees altogether until their ratification reached him at the very end of 1629.[1]

Douay College thus continued to suffer academically through the fears entertained in Rome—and plausible fears—that higher degree study would weaken the English mission by slowing up manpower. For the rest, a Douay president found his constitutional power eroded by the student's oath, and his authority over his men after they had gone on the mission usurped by the chapter in England.[2] Kellison was fighting on a slippery slope. He was without further shocks, however, till his death in January 1641, on the threshold of the Civil War.

His successor, George Muscot, was in prison in England for the past twenty years at the time of his appointment, and only the energetic good offices of Queen Henrietta Maria could ultimately secure his release. When he at last arrived at Douay, Muscot found five major posts vacant through resignations due to exhaustion; a debt standing at nine times the yearly revenue; and only eight of the twenty *convictors* not in arrears. There thus fell to him the utter chagrin, bearing in mind the size of the college in the past and the needs of the English mission, of reducing its numbers to twenty.

The reduction of debt during the next ten years, under Muscot and his successor William Hyde, was a major surgical operation, with no alternative save extinction. It was largely the achievement of Edmund Ireland, the procurator, who had begun to take the thankless task in hand before Muscot's arrival from prison. As the Spanish pension was no more likely to be paid now than at any time since it had fallen into arrears years ago, and as the era of endowment funds was only beginning, Douay could count firmly on nothing but its permanent revenue from the lands it held in the neighbourhood. Retrenchment could come therefore only from economy. Within a year Edmund Ireland had paid off 6,000 florins of the 45,000 debt. By the end of his procuratorship, five years later (1647), he had paid off a total of 30,000. But it had meant his being ruthless in dismissing students whose pensions were in arrears; obliging visitors to the college to eat outside; and even sending a priest to England before he had completed his theology. The next president, William Hyde, was even reduced to selling 350 of

[1] 3 *D.D.* 267, 415. In 1647 the President of Douay, then William Hyde, was allowed by the Cardinal Protector to proceed to the doctorate in divinity. But the grand total of Englishmen who took the Douay University D.D., or taught there, from 1568 to 1750, was only seventeen.

[2] Cf. Guilday, 322 note.

Kellison's books. But by dint of such distasteful measures the college was restored to temporary solvency.

When the town of Douay fell into the hands of France in 1667, the president (George Leyburne) petitioned Louis XIV to take responsibility for the Spanish pension, outstanding since 1625. Nothing came of this, very naturally, and ten years later the arrears of pensions still amounted to £7,429, and the outstanding debts of past scholars totalled £3,240.[1] The total of priests sent to England was by then well over 1,600.

For the period of Charles II and James II the history of the college is far less definitive. The Sixth *Diary*, covering the years from 1654 to 1715, has not survived. Comparatively little is to be known, therefore, of the events leading up to the open rebellion of the students on the fall of James II in 1689. A new president had been installed in the previous year, Dr. Edward Paston, who decided to break with tradition by introducing the French Sulpician method of discipline, already made famous in Paris and elsewhere from its great exponent Jean-Jacques Olier, who had founded the Seminary of Saint Sulpice in 1640 on an austere monastic basis. The insurrection flared up over an individual case of punishment, when rumours got about that the prefect of studies was going to flog a rhetorician. The boys downed tools, refused to go to bed but lit fires in the quadrangle instead, and constrained the new president to call in troops.

The whole episode illustrates the extent to which the Douay tradition rested on 'the custom of the house'. They had resisted innovations before, under Worthington. Under Kellison they had resisted them in the face of Rome itself. Even in the present deplorable insubordination it seems that what rankled was not so much the Sulpician discipline—for postulants to the priesthood were never likely to revolt over matters of that order—as Paston's decision to seat the *convictors* apart from the *alumni*: a class distinction, the thin end of who knew what wedges, and in any case foreign to the college. Furthermore, he had dropped music from the curriculum and discontinued the dramatic performances.

This time the custom of the house was to take fifty years to re-assert itself. Pastons's decrees, confirmed in new Constitutions sent by the Cardinal of Norfolk (Philip Howard), endured till 1741. It must have been a proud moment when the president of Douay in that year, replying to Rome's question as to what distinctions among students

[1] *Ushaw MSS. iii.* 190, cited in Sweeney, 54 f.

were enjoined in the college, could again say succinctly 'none whatever'.

Douay College at the very end of the seventeenth century is nowhere better described than in the pages of an exceedingly rare book by the Church historian Charles Dodd (*vere* Hugh Tootell), who was there from 1688 till 1698 and had taught rudiments. To adduce Dodd on Douay will startle those who know his resentful mind and his unscrupulous habits of suppressing what his sources say against his case. But his *History of Doway College* is tolerably safe on the one point of straight description of the place as he saw it: though the moment he moves from that he becomes partisan and poisonous.

The College, as to the Building, is very mean, and low (excepting the Refectory, or Romm where they dine, which is a large cheerful structure) but this Defect is abundantly recompensed with other Conveniences of Chambers and Offices for Servants, with a large Extent of Ground, employ'd in Gardens, of which there are three or four in Number. A private one for the President's Use, a common one for the Scholars, another for the Students in Divinity and Masters, a fourth for the Use of the Kitchen. The Church is but small, proportion'd to the rest of the College; 'tis dedicated to *Thomas Beckett*, whom the Papists number amongst their Saints, as having lost his Life in Defence of the Immunities of the Church.[1] It is beautiful with a fine Organ; and (as I was inform'd) not many years ago, they did not want several very able Musicians; but of late, they have very much laid that Study aside, upon Pretence that it called the Scholars from applying themselves to things of greater Moment. The Church is not unprovided with Relicks of Saints (as they esteem 'em). . . . The College has two Libraries, one for the Students in Divinity, the other is chiefly made up of Classick Authors. I was amaz'd to see such a Number of Books of Controversy about Religion, chiefly published by Members of this College, which shows how indefatigable their Ancestors were in endeavouring to make up the Breaches of Henry VIII, and stemming the Tide of the Reformation. But what I mostly admir'd was, that the greatest Part of these Works were printed when the Authors labour'd under the very Extremity of Poverty; and yet Money was never wanting to carry on the Press: but now of late they have found another Use both for their Money and Learning, than to scatter 'em in the way of Contention. I will not say they have lost their primitive Zeal.

Every Scholar (excepting they are very young) has a private Chamber to himself, notwithstanding which several Prefects and Superiors have an arbitrary Access to, by means of a Common Key. There is a very decent Infirmary for the Sick, at some distance from the College, with a Prefect and Servants to attend 'em, a Physician and an Apothecary. I had not the

[1] Dodd was a Catholic priest, writing for a rather wider public.

opportunity to be an Eye-witness to the Order of their Studies, and the Oeconomy of the House: the Siege having driven away most of the Masters and Scholars, and interrupted the usual course; but by the Relation I have from 'em.[1] Their way of living appear'd very edifying, and the Order of their Scholars very methodical. I have frequently heard some in our Universities repine at their Happiness in this Respect, and earnestly wish something of that Regularity might be established amongst us. They don't run headlong upon their Studies. The Progress they make is slow and gradual, and by consequence must be solid. They are obliged to hear nine different Masters before they can compleat their Studies. Five Masters are allotted for what they call Humanity; two for Philosophy, and two for Theology. What we call Accidence they call Figures, which they devide into two years, one for the lower, the second for the higher, the third for Grammar, the fourth for Syntax, the fifth for Poetry, the sixth for Rhetorick, which with two Years Philosophy, and four years Theology, make up twelve years.

They have different rooms for their Schools, which they every Year remove into, according as they advance in their Studies. They have daily, monthly, and yearly Exercises, or Experiments of Learning, both private and publick, which provokes the Scholars with a laudable Emulation to run with Courage thro' the tedious Paths of Learning. They are oblig'd to about an Hour's Devotion every Morning, and every Day is in like Manner finish'd by Publick Prayer; and, as I take it, their Hours of Rising and going to Bed, are five and nine. This College entertains no Foreigners, yet there are a Mixture of *English* in it; some design'd for the Church, other Persons of Figure and plentiful Fortunes in their County, some of mean Parentage, others of prime Nobility: and yet the Discipline of the College runs so, that there is not the least Distinction observable either in Dress, Diet or Apartment. If there is any Preference, or Partiality, 'tis only when singular Progress in their Studies recommends 'em. The House is govern'd by a President, who is constantly nam'd by the *Pope*. He enjoys his Place for Life, and his Power is arbitrary in punishing or rewarding, tho' he governs according to the standing Rules of the College, and seldom acts in Matters of Moment without the Advice of a Council of Seniors. The next in Dignity was the Vice-President, a Procurator, a General Prefect, a Prefect of the Infirmary, a Prefect of the Wardrobe, a Prefect of the Kitchen, and (as I said before) nine Masters. All these Offices depend entirely upon the President. Besides, they have a Gardener, Cook, Brewer, Taylor, *etc.*, all within the Precints of the College, and maintain'd by yearly Salaries. Their Dress is uniform, black Cossacks, Surtouts placed upon the Shoulders, and Collarbands. They eat thrice a day. Their Breakfast is Bread and Butter; at Dinner they have half a Pound of Meat; at Supper the same, with double the

[1] The book was published in 1713. The siege of Douay is that during the Marlborough wars. Dodd was chaplain to an English regiment. From his text no one would infer that he had in fact lived in the college for the best part of ten years before this visit.

Quantity upon Sundays and Holidays. Their Bread and Beer is oft the best Sort, and of this they may have at discretion. . . .

I did not think it Manners, to call them Rebels, who are presented to me as Saints, and Martyrs, and whom they make Account of as the greatest glory of their College. So I disturb'd not their Devotions, but left 'em in a quiet Possession of their Opinions.

Not many years after Dodd published his account, the total of priests sent to England from this Mother-College of 1568 reached 2,000. They included the three archpriests, one cardinal, two archbishops, fourteen bishops (twelve of them Vicars Apostolic in England) and a hundred and forty martyrs.[1]

3. THE COLLEGES IN SPAIN AND PORTUGAL

The colleges in the Peninsula were never to have, after their inaugural period under Robert Persons, anything like the focal importance of Douay. Numerically they were annexes. Politically they were too far away from the centre of English Catholic strife and suffering. Life moved more slowly for them. They were base camps rather than action-stations. Should the Low Countries be devastated, and Douay and St. Omer be rendered untenable, the Spanish colleges would indeed be due for a spectacular future, as the last strongholds of the education movement in exile. Till then they would go about forming their own modest quota of priest-students with unhurried devotion and (towards the end of the century) unimaginative repetition. When the blow ultimately fell, in Catholic Europe, and the colleges of men and women in France and the Low Countries were expelled during the French Revolution after 1789, their *alumni* fled not to Spain and Portugal but home to England, where the generation of Edmund Burke had begun to prune the penal laws from the Statute Book, and a tolerated future seemed assured.

The English colleges in the Peninsula in the seventeenth century were four: Valladolid (1689), Seville (1692), Madrid (1611) and Lisbon (1627–8). We have no need to follow their political fortunes, since the issues were the same as at Douay and Rome and the scale and the repercussions so much smaller. Seventeenth-century Valladolid had never more than twenty-two students after the peak year of 1604, and the others never as many. Indeed, like certain English grammar schools which can validly claim continuity despite periods of complete

[1] Cf. *Ushaw Magazine*, xiv. 36; and St. Edmund's Coll. *Menology*.

THE VENERABLE ENGLISH COLLEGE, ROME

Jesus Maria

Annales Colleg. Pars Prima. Nomina Alumnorum

Anno Domini M.D.lxxviij Die 23 Mensis Aprilis quesitum fuit coram R^mo Dño Spettano Mediolanensi vices Ill^mi Cardinalis Moroni tenenti, et RR. PP. N. Cola Provinciali, et Ruberto Bellarmino Societatis Jesu ab omnibus Infrascriptis Scholaribus, An sint parati vitam ecclesiasticam ducere, et in Angliam proficisci quotiescumque Superioribus visum fuerit. Et responderunt ut Infra.

1 Pater Rodulphus Sheruinus Annorum 29 Sacerdos Sacrae Theologiae studens dixit, atque tactis scripturis iuravit, se potius hodie quam cras paratum esse ad nutum Superiorum in Angliam ad animas iuvandas proficisci. Missus fuit in Angliam, et factus est MARTYR. — martyr

2 Pater Richardus Hadocus Annorum 27 Sacerdos, Sacraeque Theologiae dans operam, idem iuramento promisit. Missus fuit in Angliam ad animas iuvandas. — confess. in carc.

3 Pater Martinus Araius Annorum 28 Sacerdos, sacraeque Theologiae dans operam idem iuramento promisit. Missus fuit in Angliam ut supra. — confess. passus carceres

4 Pater Ionas Meredith Annorum 31 Sacerdos, sacraeque Theologiae dans operam idem iuramento promisit. Missus fuit in Angliam ut supra. — confess.

5 Pater Joannes Hoseus Annorum 33 Sacerdos, Sacraeque Theologiae dans operam idem iuramento promisit. Missus fuit in Angliam ut supra.

6 Pater Leonardus Hidus Annorum 29 Sacerdos Sacraeque Theologiae dans operam idem iuramento promisit. Missus fuit in Angliam ut supra. — confess.

7 Pater Lucas Kirbeus annorum 30 Sacerdos Sacraeque Theologiae dans operam idem iuramento promisit. Missus fuit in Angliam ut supra. — martyr

8 Pater Gulielmus Harisonus Annorum 26 Sacerdos Sacraeque Theologiae dans operam idem iuramento promisit. Missus fuit in Angliam ut supra. — confess.

9 Pater Eduardus Rishtonus Annorum 29 Sacerdos Sacraeque Theologiae dans operam idem iuramento promisit. Missus fuit in Angliam ut supra. — confess.

10 Pater Georgius Birkettus annorum 29 Sacerdos Sacraeque Theologiae dans operam idem iuramento promisit. Missus fuit in Angliam ut supra.

THE VENERABLE ENGLISH COLLEGE, ROME:
THE FIRST PAGE OF THE LIBER RUBER (1579)

desertion, Valladolid occasionally had no students at all.[1] But both Valladolid and Lisbon have endured to the present day, and there are those who in 1940 were tempted to foresee for them possibly as significant a future in a twentieth century of totalitarianism as Persons foresaw in the sixteenth century of campaigning Protestantism.

St. Alban's, Valladolid, was beset as all its fellow colleges. There was plague at frequent intervals, from 1607 onwards. The strife over defections to the Benedictines dragged on till 1608.[2] In 1613 a conference was called, of English and Spanish Jesuits, as to how to save the college from its debility. They decided (as elsewhere) to transfer the lectures from Jesuit schools to inside the college. Next year a roll of sixteen students was contrived—by bringing reinforcements from St. Omer. Classes were begun in controversy and casuistry. These courses came in for much debate elsewhere later from those who regarded the seminarian's education as not fitted for his missionary future. There was even one open rebellion at St. Alban's, as at Douay. It came, however, much earlier (1636) and was quelled by the police and not the military.

The college at Seville found it necessary to perpetuate the technique of street-begging by which Persons had partially established it in 1592. Lewis Owen's account of this is embellished with a colourful malice, but is no doubt reliable as to bare facts:

> They have an English Youth, that walks up and down the Citie in a Gowne, and a Boxe in his hand all day long, and begs from doore to doore, for the English Colledge. . . . They have also a great Boxe in every Ship, that saileth either from Sevill, Saint Lucas or Cades, to the West India. . . . The Rector of the English Colledge hath the Key of this Boxe, and promiseth to have a world of Masses said for the prosperous and safe return of the ship and the passengers. . . .[3]

St. George's College at Madrid, the third English college in Spain, was not a creation of Robert Persons. When it began, with the arrival of Fr. Thompson and a contingent of twelve students from St. Omer in April 1611, Persons had already been dead a year. Its inspiration was Joseph Creswell, and its financial sponsor was an Italian, Caesare Borgacio.

[1] Years 1638–40, 1670 (Apr. to Sept.) 1685, 1692 (Mar.–Nov.): see the Valladolid *Register* (*C.R.S.* XXX).

[2] See p. 125 above. The settlement of the disputed points is given in documents in *Stonyhurst MSS.*, Anglia III.

[3] Owen, 68.

Until its records were published in 1929 this college was thought to have been 'little more than a residence'. It was 'to lodge their Agents, Collectors, Sollicitors' and others, and was 'not built for to bring up any young Schollars, but for Courtlike Jesuitas . . . maintained by the other two [Spanish] Colledges'.[1] But from the start it was a counterpart of Valladolid and Seville. The students from St. Omer who founded it had finished their humanities, and in fact the first batch went on from Madrid to Valladolid at the end of their philosophy, in June 1614. St. George's maintained them during their course, and during the century was wont to pay 1,400 *reales* a year to Valladolid for Madrid students' courses there.[2]

There was resolute opposition to them at first. Not only was it curious to find English students coming to the capital when the Spaniards were in the habit of sending their own sons away from it, to the universities; and not only were the English students likely to meet English Protestants in Madrid and thus run the danger of being recognized later on the mission in England, but Fr. Creswell saw fit to encourage them with printed pamphlets describing the worst excesses of the persecution at home. James I accordingly protested to the king of Spain, and the students were expelled from Madrid. Creswell took them to Alcalá. He then secured permission for them to return to Madrid for the summer months each year—the thin edge of a successful wedge whereby, 'little by little gaining ground' as a later rector put it, he could extend the indulgence tacitly to the winter as well.[3]

Thereafter its existence was fairly placid. The pope removed it from the jurisdiction of the Archbishops of Toledo and governed it as a papal college (July 1612 onwards), which meant that it was free from episcopal visitation. Once it seemed likely to be made into an exclusively Jesuit college, at the hands of its rector Francis Forcar in 1622, but the Jesuit General in Rome condemned the notion. More than once the college was nearly merged with one of the others, yet (such were the narrow margins of subsistence on which these seminaries persevered) in 1637–8 Valladolid itself was nearly closed and transferred to St. George's at Madrid. The one revolutionary change that occurred

[1] Owen, 73–5; cf. Foley, vii. p. iv, and Guilday, 136. The question is fully discussed in *C.R.S.* xxix.

[2] *C.R.S.* xxix. 100–1.

[3] The history of the college, by Juan de Cabrera (Rector 1718–27) is in *C.R.S.* xix. 1–76, trans. 77–142. The question of a *Scots* College for Madrid was discussed in Rome in 1642—see *Innes Review*, V (1954).

during the whole history of the college was the substitution of Spanish Jesuits for English Jesuits as rectors, in 1669, owing to the 'calamitous administration' of rector William Sankey. Spaniards continued in charge from thence onwards till the end.

The college went out of existence in 1767, upon the expulsion of the Jesuits from Spain by King Charles III. With Seville, it was merged in Valladolid, which was conducted by seculars: by direct intervention of the great English eighteenth century bishop, Richard Challoner.[1]

Lisbon College, the last English foundation in the Peninsula, was opened in 1628. Portugal was then a part of the Spanish dominions (1580–1640). The first step had actually been taken at the very beginning of the century, when a Valladolid student, Nicholas Ashton, of Staffordshire, bought a house in Lisbon. When he died in 1605, as chaplain to the English colony in Lisbon, he gave the property to his successor, William Newman (*vere* Sleighford), who in turn secured a promise of funds from a Portuguese nobleman, Don Pedro Coutinho, subject to a condition insisted on by Don Pedro that no Jesuit should have any part in the new college. Newman went in 1621 to plead his cause in Rome, where the case against any Jesuit participation was pressed energetically by the agent of the English secular clergy, John Bennett, who was himself an old student of Valladolid. These intrigues prevailed to the extent that in 1626 the English Bishop, Richard Smith, nominated as president of the proposed college a London secular priest, Joseph Harvey (*vere* Haynes), and sent him to Lisbon to complete the negotiations with Don Pedro.

Fr. Harvey duly arrived in the Portuguese capital in November 1628 with a party of ten students from Douay, accompanied by a staff of three besides himself to teach them their theology. But he died on the same day as the opening of the college, 22 February 1629.[2]

A political 'climate' emerged in this English College at Lisbon under its second president, no less a person than Thomas White, better known by his *alias* of Blacklow, the inspiration of the party of intriguers among the secular clergy who carried on in mid-century a veritable vendetta against the Jesuits and were themselves distrusted

[1] *C.R.S.* xxix. 100, 192, 213, 227, 306; and E. H. Burton, *Challoner*, ii. 100–2.

[2] For the negotiations see Croft and Gillow, *Hist. Account of Lisbon Coll.* 2, 252–3, 212, 230; *C.R.S.* xxx. xii note, 181 and note; and 3 *D.D.* 270, 418. For the founder-personnel see Croft and Gillow, 4–5; 3 *D.D.* 270; and Oliver *Collections*, 282. The papal Bull of approval was dated 22 Oct. 1622 (*Lisbonian*, xi. 292). There is an article on Don P. Coutinho in *Lisbonian*, xvi. 22 ff. (1932), and studies of the early students in vols. viii–x.

throughout much of Catholic Europe and suspected of Jansenism, on account of their complaisance towards the oath of allegiance in England.

From the circumstances of its origin, and now by its Blacklow statutes, the college was constitutionally unlike any of the others. It was not a pontifical college such as Douay, governed from Rome; nor a Jesuit college like St. Omer, governed ultimately by the Father General of the Society; nor, as with the *Venerabile* and Valladolid and Seville, was it a college for seculars under a Jesuit rector. Its president had been appointed by the Vicar Apostolic of England, Richard Smith, and it continued to be governed by the London Vicariate till the thirty years' hiatus in that office set in (1655). Under the Blacklow constitution the president had to work with a council of the other superiors. Academically, the college shared with Rome and the others the intention of confining itself to the higher studies of philosophy and theology. In practice it very soon shared with them likewise (all of them except Rome) the necessity of instituting preparatory classes in the humanities.

The studies were carefully prescribed in the printed (Latin) Constitutions of 1635. In philosophy they took their students steadily through Aristotle. The first year read the *Physics* and the first book on Generation and Corruption, with the *Organum* and Topics in the afternoon. The second year—the three books on the Soul, with *Physics* books 7 and 8, the second book on Corruption and the four books on the Heavens. Third year—the *Metaphysics*, *Ethics* and *Politics*. For all this there was no 'textbook' apart from the text of Aristotle itself; nor for a century later.[1]

The relations of Lisbon with the other colleges as regards students and staff cannot be defined with any precision. Douay sent a further contingent of seven, after the first batch, four from rhetoric and three from poetry, in 1633. Occasionally students went from Lisbon to Douay for one or another of the reasons we have already noticed. When Lisbon wanted to send Fr. Starkey in 1646, Douay declined, because of 'defectis unius tibiae quem in bello Anglicano [the Civil War] amiserat'; for the Douay Rules precluded the admission to the community of anyone not physically whole. In 1650 the late president of Lisbon himself, Edward Daniel (*alias* Pickford), went to Douay to teach theology. In the following year Douay took in three students

[1] There are extracts and citations from the Constitutions in *Lisbonian*, xiii. pt. 3, pp. 4–6 (1926).

who had left Lisbon for England before the end of their philosophy, and had now crossed the Channel again to complete it, together with one who, having finished his theology before leaving Lisbon for England on business, came to Douay for the ceremony of ordination. These cases, with one other at the end of 1652 (a Lisbon logician going to Douay to finish) are the only ones clearly traceable down to the end of the fifth *Douay Diary*.

From the Lisbon College *Register* itself comes evidence of teaching staff sometimes recruited from ex-St. Omer boys who had gone on to distinction in one of the other seminaries. The career of Peter Clarence, who came in 1638, had lain through St. Omer, Seville and the *Venerabile*; William Hargreaves, through St. Omer, Valladolid, Rome; and Humphrey Whitaker, through St. Omer, Rome direct and the mission.[1] Cases like these are important because they are exceptions to the traditional policy of these colleges, which was normally to recruit staff from their own interns.

The other main characteristic which Lisbon shared with all the other English colleges was inevitably its financial straits. The first president, Joseph Harvey, had buttressed the gifts of Don Pedro Coutinho by bequeathing 800 crowns, half to the college and half to his friend and colleague Dr. Mayler. But Mayler was soon obliged to throw his 400 into the pool. Blacklow, the second president, went to London in 1632 to beg in person, and it was his failure in this that led him at once to resign. The third president, William Hart, had to be deposed in 1637 by the English Vicar Apostolic for mismanagement.

Small wonder that the living conditions of the Lisbon students were the most pinched and Spartan of all the colleges, and their premises for long in a tumbledown state. The seventeenth-century archives of the college show that meat for supper was in practice a luxury and an event.[2] Never were students better hardened for the rigours of the English mission.

In proportion to its size, indeed, the college figured more than well in the missionary work. It gave martyrs to the cause: Thomas Blount, who died in gaol in 1647; William Floyd, who died in gaol during the Oates Plot. Three of its ex-students nourished schools in eighteenth-century England: Peter Goodwin at Aldcliffe Hall, Daniel Fitter at Stafford and Christopher Tootell at Ladywell, Fernyhalgh. Of the controversialists, again, who flourished in the reign of James II, three

[1] Croft and Gillow, *Register* (printed alphabetically).
[2] Ibid. 54 f.

were trained at Lisbon: Thomas Godden, who had been its eighth president, John Gother himself and Richard Russell. And in the realm of Church government, finally, the Lisbon college contributed during the century thirty-eight priests to the Old Chapter of the Secular Clergy, dating back to the time of the three archpriests.

These, however, were the high lights of an existence normally drab and precarious, in which the one material solace was their distance from the battlefield while preparing themselves for the front-line. In their quiet backwater the Lisbon collegians whom George Borrow visited in 1835, when he went to spread Protestant Bibles in the Peninsula, were pursuing unchanged, in both essentials and accidentals, the vocation laid down for them by Harvey and Blacklow two centuries earlier.[1]

4. THEIR JOINT EDUCATIONAL SHORTCOMINGS

In all this intense scholastic formation there was a danger, always latent, and by the end of our period actual and chronic. It affected the colleges abroad rather than the schools, for the products of the schools left earlier, they were not conceived as 'scholastics' unless they showed a vocation for the priesthood, and even then their humanities course was not in the least 'orientated' towards their priestly career. The danger was one inherent in all clerical education based on a transcendental reverence for custom and tradition and canon law: insulation.

During the foundation-period, under Allen and Persons, this risk had been small. Allen's mind was clear on the purpose and practice of his Douay seminary and the *Venerabile*. Persons' mind had been as clear in the direction on which he set the colleges in Spain. They were training priests for the special circumstances of the English mission then still young: that is to say, men who would need, in addition to the formation laid down by Trent, a technique of catechizing, and an acquaintance with the chief sources of theological difficulty likely to be met with in the minds of lapsed Catholics about to be reconciled to the Church. For this reason the study of 'cases of conscience' (casuistry) loomed larger at Douay and Rome, from the start, than would have been necessary had they not been specifically Counter-Reformation colleges.

As late as the middle of the eighteenth century the president of Douay was conceiving his task in precisely these same practical terms,

[1] *Bible in Spain*, ch. 5.

directed to a situation in England still essentially the same, still shrewdly adjusting the labourers to the vineyard.

There can be little doubt that the instruction here given to the youth of England is of great advantage to the Catholic faith; for not only is it practically impossible to obtain a classical education in England, without danger to faith and morals, but this method of educating the sons of the higher classes brings patrons to the missionaries in England, friends and benefactors to the Colleges, and . . . many an excellent *alumnus*.[1]

No attention was paid in the seminaries to the particular necessities of individual towns and regions. 'If he who asks for the Oath [i.e. asks to be allowed to take it] is judged by the Superiors . . . capable of the labours of the Vineyard in England, he is allowed to take it, be he rich or poor, noble or commoner.' His work in England was decided for him, upon his subsequent arrival, by those on the spot.

But while the theory of the mission remained unaltered, the practice was ceasing to be fully related to the needs of the moment. We get a foretaste of this in the 'marvelling' recorded when the aged priest William Wright, S.J., a man of 'great age and consummate learning, a professor of philosophy and theology in the most celebrated Universities', condescended 'to teach little children the lowest rudiments'. This was in or about 1606.[2] Given that such was the need in the Leicestershire to which he ministered, there need have been nothing remarkable in his fulfilling it: as in fact they all did, whether in a private house or instructing the children born in Wisbech Castle and the other prisons.

When the drawback became manifest later, it was not from slackening vocations but from a training which had become stereotyped and academic: Catholic theology and philosophy in its classical forms, as in the textbooks, but not adequately 'mediated' for the minds of those to whom the priests would have to teach it. This was in fact manifest by 1650.

When the provincial carried out a visitation of the English College at Valladolid in 1656 he did not mince matters.

I disapprove of the students not being given lectures or exercises in the theological questions of the day, because the scholastic theology they study is of no practical use over there [England], and what is of use over there they do not study here. Therefore, while we are getting to know what is

[1] In replies to the *Quaesita* of 1741: 7 *D.D.*, reprinted in *Ushaw Magazine*, xiv. 31.
[2] Foley, ii. 285.

the custom at the German and English Colleges in Rome, and await the orders of our own Father General on the subject, I order that some compendiums of Fr. Martin Becano be bought.[1]

Similarly with the Scots.

There is no more certain nor more immediate cause of our present evils [wrote Alexander Leslie in his report to Propaganda in 1681] than the bad administration of our Colleges [abroad] and the inadequate and unsuitable education of youths resorting to them. . . . We look for the fitting remedies from you, whom the Holy Spirit has appointed to rule God's Church.

This was strong language indeed.[2] He urged that

Your Eminences will deign to provide masters for the schools in the Highlands, so that youths well versed in humane letters may be chosen for the foreign Colleges, and others may be instructed in the faith. It is probable that, when the allocation of priests is once made, the inhabitants of the Lowlands will send their children to be educated in these schools

—a consummation which had not come about by the end of the century, however, for the area was honeycombed with garrisons and the mission priests had to be constantly on the move.

By 1693, in the Scots College in Rome, the students themselves were to complain. They were getting no training to fit them for controversies with Calvinists in Scotland. They were getting no education in the use of their own language, as (by the statutes) all conversation had to be in Latin or Italian. The visitation of this college in that year therefore resulted in an order that the supper reading in the refectory should henceforth be in English.[3]

Cardinal Philip Howard confided his own fears to the Anglican historian Gilbert Burnet, who visited him in Rome in 1685. He said, records Burnet,

that they [the Colleges] had not instruments enough to work with: for though they were sending over all that were capable of the mission, yet he expected no great matters from them. Few of them spoke true English. They came over young and retained all the English that they brought with them, which was only the language of boys. But their education being amongst strangers they had so formed themselves as upon that model that really they preached as Frenchmen or Italians in English words, of which

[1] *C.R.S.* xxx. pp. xxix–xxx. The book ordered was Becano's *Manuale Controversiarum hujus temporis*. Lectures in controversy had been introduced at Valladolid in 1613–14.

[2] Quoted in Bellesheim, iv. 356–64.

[3] W. E. Brown, *Scots Coll. Rome*, 18–19.

he was every day warning them, for he knew this could have no good effect in England.[1]

There is much irony in a training which left the national sentiments of the exiled scholastics so virile that they affronted their Spanish and French protectors by cheering at British victories, while contriving that sometimes their mother-tongue atrophied away. The case of James Ravenscroft of the Inner Temple, who asked at his trial during the Oates Plot to be allowed to defend himself in Latin because he 'had lived so much out of England',[2] is an exaggeration of the typical. What is significant is that it was typical. Halting English, and the inevitable aura of 'foreign' that surrounded it, as still today does the wearing of a *soutane*, was detected even in the sermons of Andrew Poulton when the Jesuits held the Savoy Chapel under James II. For priests who had studied hard, to come 'home' and work amid the hazards of outlawry, this gibe of 'foreign' must have been a bitter pill. There is no denying that, inevitably, their manner of education was in part to blame.

[1] Burnet's *Own Times*, ed. of 1809, ii. 353. Personal friendships between Catholic and Protestant leaders, illustrated by that between Cardinal Howard and Burnet, were not uncommon despite the political background. Cf. also the visit of the Principal of Glasgow University to the Scots College in Rome (before 1690), whither much of the archives of the pre-Reformation university had been taken by the first exiles, and the amicable correspondence that went on about this down to 1738.

[2] Gillow, v. 393.

IX
THE SCHOOLS ABROAD

BECAUSE of its size, and still more its prestige, St. Omer throughout the seventeenth century was the supreme symbol of Catholic persistence. It did not long remain the only school of its kind, for the revival of the other religious orders banished by Elizabeth began the moment she was dead. The Benedictines very soon, and the Franciscans and Dominicans later, were its colleagues and even rivals on the educational front. But because St. Omer was so much larger than any of the other schools, and because it had behind it a Jesuit tradition of secondary education reaching back over much of Europe to the time of Loyola, it was St. Omer that loomed largest in the minds of English Privy Councillors and Members of Parliament in their paper war on the exiles by statute and proclamation.

I. THE COLLEGE AT ST. OMER

Oh fie upon him, how he wears his clothes!
As if he'd come this Christmas from St. Omer
To see his friends, and return after Twelfthtide.

Massinger, in putting those lines into his play *The Fatal Dowry* (ii. 2) in 1632, suggests that the presence in London of St. Omer boys on holiday in their 'blue-coat' dress was by no means uncommon in the 'thirties, during the personal rule of Charles I. It was a paradoxical situation. The penalties on the Statute Book were mounting, the repetitions in the collection of *Stuart Proclamations* take on the air of a litany or incantation, and the College of St. Omer was coded in Catholic documents, for safety, under the name of 'Flamstead'. Yet the English ambassador was hosted in the college in 1604, the boys could walk the streets of London on occasion, and twice a whole contingent of them came to testify in Court. 'He has made himself liable to a penalty by being in that Seminary', cried Titus Oates, when they were giving evidence in 1685. But Oates had been a St. Omer boy too, and 'I hope a man may be at St. Omer', said the Lord Chief

Justice to him pointedly, 'and yet not be punished for it, Mr. Oates.'[1]

An aura of security, efficiency and daring surrounded the college. It stood uninterruptedly high in the favour of both Rome and the civil governments of the Netherlands. When Artois was ceded by Spain to France in 1659, there was a special clause in the treaty guaranteeing the college's security and the continuation of its pension from the Catholic King of France on receiving the territory from the Catholic King of Spain. Had the payments thereupon become regular, St. Omer would have been unique.

With the local authorities, also, the relations of the college were normally close and amicable, after the early years of suspicion and insistence on passports. The magistrates contributed towards the new college chapel, the college contributed towards strengthening the city fortifications. After the fire that destroyed the college in 1684 the civic authorities laid the foundation-stone for the rebuilding. But on occasion the irrepressible English outbursts of the boys strained good-will severely. The magistrates were vastly annoyed when the college bells were rung to celebrate the birth of the Old Pretender in the summer of 1688—for by then Louis XIV, rebuffed in his offers of help to James II, had decided not to oppose the Orange landing in England. The ringers were fined, and the rector had to apologize.[2]

The *Constitutions* of the college (dated 7 July 1599), promulgated by Pope Clement VIII, clarify much that might otherwise, from the earlier letters and documents, be only guesswork.

> The end and purpose of this Seminary at St. Omer is that primarily those youths and boys of tender age shall be nourished in it who are not unsuitable and cannot be admitted to any other English Seminary or College to perfect their learning. It is therefore necessary that those admitted be English, chosen from the kingdom of England or those born outside England whose parents are Catholic.

They must be not less than fourteen years of age, so as to move quickly to pass through the college. None must be admitted who are 'literarum penitus rudes' or have not learnt Latin. They must be 'of whole and sound body', of good character, and in good health, 'ut studiorum labores possint tolerare'. Above all, they must be boys most likely to profit from instruction in 'Christianis moribus, disciplina

[1] For 'Flamstead'—*Notes and Queries*, July 1934, and S.J. *Letters and Notices*, l. 85 (1935). For the trial in 1685, *State Trials* x. 1105.

[2] *Arch Vat.*, Prop., *Visite a Collegi*, t. 36, f. 375—in Guilday, 143 note; and J. Gerard, in *Stonyhurst Magazine*, i. 282–3 (1884).

doctrinaque catholica'. Each entrant must furnish a signed statement as to his name, parentage, places of birth and education, domicile, condition of his family and friends.

The answers to this *Interrogatory* on arrival, as at the *Venerabile* and Valladolid, are one of the most precious sources for what little can be reconstructed of Catholic education in England during the century.

Section Two of the Constitutions, *Observanda ab Omnibus circa Pietatem*, prescribes morning prayers; a fifteen minutes' examination of conscience every evening; the litanies and silence-periods; daily Mass; the divine office in chapel on feast days; literature for meditations, in each boy's cubicle in the dormitory, for nightly reading; instruction by their confessors in things spiritual; Confession and Communion monthly and on feast days.

Section Three, on Studies, lays down that work must follow the directions given by Superiors, and that 'nemo suum sensum et voluntatem sequatur'. The boys are to speak in Latin at all times, except during recreation or when the superior may allow. Outside the college they are not to speak at all unless absolutely necessary, and then in a low voice and in Latin (an order that recalls to mind the precautions necessary to Douay in the troublous weeks before its expulsion to Rheims in 1579). Apart from college textbooks they are to have no books of their own without leave from superiors.

The final section, on Domestic Discipline, enjoins community life at all times. They sleep in dormitories, partitioned off into separate cubicles as in the Roman and Spanish seminaries, with a ban on inter-communication or conversation without leave. No letters may be sent or received without leave from superiors. Any crime 'quod pacem, bonos mores, et disciplinam Collegii perturbat' may be punished by expulsion.[1]

These remained substantially the norms of St. Omer life throughout its two hundred years on foreign soil. A revision in 1623 did no more than define certain points more sharply in the light of experience. The fees, minimum £25 yearly as at Douay, must be kept up six months in advance. They will be sent home the moment their pension is six months in arrears. Holidays away from the college, 'to see ye country', are deprecated, and the *viaticum*, or journey-money home, must be paid in advance.[2]

[1] The text of these Constitutions is in *Stonyhurst MSS.*, Anglia II, no 67 (20 pages).

[2] Revisions of 1623 are in *Stonyhurst MSS.*, C. II. 19, the *St. Omer Custom Book*, transcribed from MS. 160 of the Louvain Catholic University Library (destroyed in 1940).

These *Constitutions* thus conformed to Jesuit tradition. To set them beside the tradition of Allen at Douay, or the Douay or the *Venerabile* statutes, is to appreciate at once the difference of spirit and atmosphere: a modicum of freedom on the one hand, careful provision on the other hand for every moment of the St. Omer day. The difference is not to be explained by the obvious fact that these boys were younger than the seminarians of Douay and Rome and Spain. It goes deeper than that, as the concrete details of St. Omer life show. The boy entrusted to the Jesuits was to have his mind formed on the active self-educational lines of the *De Magistro* of Aquinas, but his will meanwhile trained to complete and unquestioning obedience. Nevertheless 'the custom of the house' counted for much at St. Omer, no less than at Douay, and has been pleaded in modern Stonyhurst, by boys against masters, without damage to authority or to respect. The Jesuit system had the secret of divorcing rules and restrictions from personalities; notably in the provision whereby he who administered a punishment was not he who had ordered it.

The St. Omer boys lived a sixteen-hour day, from the moment when, upon arrival, they were 'stript of all their brave apparell and cloaked with a habit like to that of lame Ignatius'. They rose at 5 a.m. and retired at 9 at night. It was a Spartan day, practically without break, and (till 'bread and beer' at mid-afternoon came in later) no food from 11 o'clock dinner time till 6 o'clock supper. But across the Channel the schools of St. Paul's and Eton had a schoolday hardly less severe.

There is no seventeenth-century evidence surviving of the diet, but it can be inferred backwards from the account given on the college's migration to Bruges in 1762.[1] The quantities and variety of food were roughly the same as at Douay.

The most intimate account we have of the college in the early seventeenth century comes from the spy James Wadsworth, the St. Omer boy who left in 1622 for Seville and apostatized on the way.

Wadsworth recounts how the rector (Creswell) interviewed him on arrival, clothed him in the distinctive St. Omer dress with its 'stockings that had not troubled the weaver with over much pains', etc., and sent him to a prefect (Fr. Thunder) to allot him his study room and dormitory-cubicle, whereafter he was 'promoted to the first form, called the Figures'. He described the hierarchy of staff (uniform in all Jesuit Colleges): rector, minister, the three prefects (of studies, of

[1] By Charles Plowden, S.J., in *Stonyhurst MSS.*, Anglia II, 29, No. 18.

discipline and of the Sodality of Our Lady), the boys' confessor or 'ghostly father', the bursar and the five masters of the schools (classes) together with the army of lay-brothers who ran the printing-house, bakery, bootshops, infirmary and clerical office.

He takes his reader in graphic detail through the scholars' day, from 'the fifth hour summons' in the morning. Whosoever is absent from Mass 'shall be sure to have the unwelcome presence of Father Thunder'. When they file into the refectory two by two, rhetoricians first, 'the loss of breakfast is their punishment whose names have been given up to the Prefect for having spoken English the day before'. At dinner their 'mouths are shut, not from eating but speaking, bestowing their ears upon six others of their companions, disputing three against three in two pews, one overthwart the other, of such things as may rather help digestion to the Fathers than benefit their own understandings'. Music follows the midday meal, and after that they 'recreate' themselves till one, whence to classes and study till supper, at which six fresh disputators perform, and the martyrology is read in Latin and English. At the end of the day, last thing, 'while they are disrobing themselves, one amongst them reads some miracle or new book until sleep close up all, and Father Thunder's noise [a rattle] wake them in the morning'.[1]

There is extant a manuscript list of the college staff about 1620, headed by a note in a later hand: '? compiled from Wadsworth . . . if so not reliable'. Such a man—judged in the light of his book—could hardly hope for a milder epitaph.

What meagre leisure this formidable timetable left them on Tuesday and Thursday afternoons was spent in a series of vestigial games out in 'the Line' (the playground) which survived into modern times at Stonyhurst: nine-pins, trap-bat and ball and a form of football which reached its annual climax in the 'great matches' just before Lent and has been extolled in St. Omer Latin verses. From the Oates trial boys we also learn of the mid-Lent diversion of 'sawing the witch', a boisterous rite adopted from contemporary Spanish practice in the Low Countries, in which the sawing of a dummy into two equal parts symbolized that the austerities of Lent were half over.

The monthly holiday, in these centuries when few of the boys went home, was normally spent at a small country property purchased by

[1] Wadsworth, *English Spanish Pilgrim* (1630), ch. iii, pp. 11–32. Extracts from it in J. Gerard, *Memorials of Stonyhurst* (1881), 5–11; and Bede Camm, O.S.B., 'An Apostate (Wadsworth) at St. Omer, 1618–22', in *The Month*, xciv, 162–70 (1899).

the college in 1649 at Blandyke, some three miles away. These 'Blandyke Days' kept their name throughout all the later migrations of St. Omer—to Bruges in 1762, Liège in 1773, and Lancashire in 1794—whereby at Stonyhurst today Blandyke is no longer a place but a holiday.

From the early days, too, dramatics were an integral (and a famous) part of every boy's formation. 'A neat domestic theatre', wrote Fr. Hawkins in 1762, 'served for their diversion, or to teach them a genteel way of behaving, and carriage, and to break them of that bashfulness so natural to ye English.'[1]

The greater part of their waking hours, then, was devoted to academic work, in the hierarchy of forms from rudiments up to rhetoric. The first Stonyhurst lists, after 1804, called the pre-grammar class neither figures nor rudiments, but elements. Under whatever name, however, the function of the bottom class was always clear enough.

The whole of the teaching itself was integrated round Latin, and Latin taught not for the manufactured reasons of a later age but as a practical instrument of culture, indispensable by 'existing custom and definite utility'. The objective was personal mastery of the language, as with Cicero and Quintilian. This had been clearly stated in the passages of the *Ratio Studiorum* which dealt with the highest form, rhetoric.

By the beginning of the seventeenth century the Jesuit practice had already been reformed. Sánchez of Salamanca, echoing Vives, urged that the reading of authors should begin before any attempt to speak the Latin language. Fluency in speech should be taught as a result rather than a means. Hence the importance, in written compositions, of keeping close to the author's text. Hence the stress, in Jesuit advice to their teachers, on setting concrete rather than abstract subjects for composition: the themes of his work must come from within the boy's own range of knowledge, experience and interests. The texts of Cicero used in the grammar classes of the Jesuit schools were in fact 'adjusted' with these pedagogical maxims in mind; and the art of Latin conversation was approached through real models—the written dialogues of the authors. Verse-competition was not introduced until

[1] *Stonyhurst MSS.*, Anglia III, 20; and quoted in Gerard, 30. For the early days of St. Omer dramatics, L. J. Hicks, *Foundation of the College of St. Omers* (*Arch. Hist. Soc. Jesu.* xix. 178, and sources there); and the chapter in H. Chadwick, *St. Omers to Stonyhurst* (1962).

the class of poetry. It occurred to nobody to teach the vernacular language (English) as a subject. The desire to do so 'would presuppose a degree of use for the vernacular in the professional life of Europe which was then far from being realized'.[1] But we have seen that practical utility did bring French into the English exiles' curriculum as early as 1654.

There was certainly rigidity in the classroom technique. Facility in Latin composition was trained by a systematic, orchestrated procedure. The regent (master) explained the text; the boys read it; they performed disputations on it, and declamations in it every week. At the end they understood the difference between what Jacques Maritain has called 'knowledge about' and 'knowledge into'. Latin was an instrument. They had mastered the use of it.

At intervals throughout the school year, often as many as nine times in a year, the examinations known as 'Compositions' were held. On these depended seniority in class, made manifest in the special seating of the boys in the pattern of a Jesuit classroom. The two top boys were Imperators, the next two Praetors, the next two Tribunes; and these 'first six', liable to be unseated at the next Composition, had a 'good day' (special holiday) to mark their success.

This internal organization of the scholars' work was not the situation at the beginning of the century. In the early years, as we have seen, the boys went for lessons to the Flemish Jesuit schools in the town, till 1614 when the General in Rome (Aquaviva) consented to a separation 'for the good of the youths and to console their parents'. From thence onwards the St. Omer Jesuits taught their own boys on their own premises. Whether this meant that philosophy classes formerly held for the senior boys were now dropped, or that such classes were now added to the curriculum but only for a short time, or that no such classes had been, or were to be, instituted at all, until the Liège period of the college after 1773, the college at all events became from now on the English Catholic classical school 'par excellence'.

One other innovation, of immense significance, occurred soon afterwards—the appointment of a rector who was an Englishman. Under the original leases the rector had to be a Fleming. Of these there had been three: Foucart, Schondonck and Dentiers. But in 1621–2 the General in Rome appointed as fourth rector Fr. William Baldwin. When the St. Omer civil magistracy protested to the Spanish Infanta

[1] T. Corcoran, *Studies in Hist. of Classical Teaching* (1911), 233.

(Governor of the Province), and she replied that she would allow the appointment to stand but 'as an exception', the English Jesuits decided to press their advantage. The provincial, Fr. Henry Blount, appealed to the Infanta through the General that the rector of the English College at St. Omer be henceforth an Englishman always. She agreed, and the Spanish Privy Council in Madrid ratified the change.[1] Thus ended a dualism of government which, though it had irked the school to a less extent than Douay College, had meant obvious anomalies. Henceforth the school was to be homogeneously English, with all that implied in endearing it to parents and families far away.

The climax of each academic year was the classical and dramatic display known as 'Academy' (the term still in use). There have been those who argued that the word did not exist at St. Omer at all: that it arose only after 1773, at Liège, when the whole college was known as an Academy. But if this were so it would make St. Omer unique among Jesuit schools, for they were all administered on the same lines and with the same elemental vocabulary; and in the Western European schools in particular the term Academy applied to both the examinations and the community.[2]

The dedication of these boys, as part of the Catholic lay apostolate, was consummated in that Sodality of Our Lady which we have already met in the sixteenth-century *Venerabile* and seventeenth-century Douay. The sodality was introduced into St. Omer in 1609. The *Custom Book* defined it as consecrated to making its members 'fit instruments to co-operate with Almighty God for the reducing of our poor afflicted country . . . unto the true knowledge and sincere service of God'. Through weekly Communion, through special devotions and through mutual 'admonitions', and under rules almost as austere as those of a novitiate, they were formed to meet the tests of the mission. The initiative came from below, from the boys themselves; and the later rules (1629) were largely a codification of twenty years' assured custom. As a secondary function, the sodalists served as a 'prefect system' in the sense in which that term has established itself in the public schools in England. Its officers were elected; membership was open to all (on entering the class of grammar) who would freely and solemnly undertake the spiritual obligations. (Even Oates

[1] *St. Omer Town Archives*, transcript by John Harris, S.J., 22, 24; quoted in *Stonyhurst Magazine*, i. 282 (1884).

[2] Cf. the discussion by C. F. Cordell, with reference to the Jesuit College of La Flèche (founded 1603), in *Stonyhurst Magazine*, iv. 515 (1890).

could get into it, on trust, though how he got elected is incomprehensible.) The Sodality of Our Lady at St. Omer thus enshrined the best qualities of Catholic education: voluntary dedication and hard conditioning.[1]

St. Omer was a very large school indeed, by all contemporary standards. Even taking into account its shrinkage during the Civil War, and again after the fall of James II, its *average* roll for the seventeenth century was over a hundred.

As early as 1604 the college accommodation was already so stretched that when three Potinger boys were brought from England by their elder brother Nathaniel, on his own way to Douay, the Fathers had to refuse them on account of 'numerosum multitudinem qua Collegium illud praemitur'. They therefore continued on to Douay—only to find that their ages were below the minimum laid down there by the statutes. Foreigners were coming as well as English, drawn by the fame of the teaching. In 1610 the parents in England were sending boys of such distinction and promise, and so *jucunde* despite the danger to their own families, that the lack of available places was heartbreaking; 'familia nescio an unquam major'—it stood then at 180, with twenty recently sent on to Rome or Spain.

The curve of numbers followed the same general shape as in the other colleges, while always well above the rest. Throughout the century the staff-ratio steadily increased: 8 to 120 in 1602, 31 to 124 by 1677. Over the whole period there was an average of about 22 priests on the staff. The community of 180 'nunquam major' of 1610 was well eclipsed by 1635, when the total was 200 boys and 25 Fathers. This was the peak year. The roll never reached 150 again till 1670 (the year of the Treaty of Dover between Charles II and Louis XIV), nor 180 again till 1684.

After each tightening of the penal laws at home the numbers tended to drop: after James I's proclamation of 1615, during the Civil War, and during the Oates plot especially. In 1624 the *Annual Letters* record a drop, only thirty new boys coming from England, six or seven others being captured at sea on the way, some departing because recalled by their parents, eleven leaving for Rome and thirteen for Spain, and others to the Jesuit novitiate at Watten. The total was down

[1] Text of Rules in Custom Book (*Stonyhurst MSS.*); cf. *Stonyhurst Magazine*, iv. 302 f., 339 f., 368 f., 415 f. The sodality was not introduced at St. Gregory's School, Douay, till 1678.

to 124. In 1636, after the Government's descent on Jesuit schools in England, the college fell to 115.

Most critical of all was the Civil War period. Nearly all the rhetoricians and poets were called home, being old enough to fight for the king. The annual prize compositions could be organized in only the three grammar classes. In 1645 these were the only classes functioning. They became the syntax and poetry of 1646 and were still the only classes till 1647, when enough boys arrived to sustain two classes of figures. The three classes of 1648 comprised only sixteen boys altogether. But by 1653 the college was well on the mend again. There were then twenty-seven priests, seven temporal coadjutors (lay brothers) and one hundred and twenty-six scholars. The Latin and Greek were 'very promising', the choral music in full swing under two masters 'ex Anglia', and the public dramatic performances revived.[1]

If the output of vocations to the other colleges be tabulated—so far as the incomplete figures deducible allow—something of an answer emerges to the question of how far St. Omer was a 'lay' school.

Over certain periods we know both the intake, and the output to Rome, Spain, the Watten Novitiate in Flanders and back home to England. It appears that new admissions nearly always filled the gaps caused by the leavers, and that the number of vocations represent about a quarter of the total roll.[2] The output to Valladolid can be calculated for thirty years down to 1625. The maximum in any one year was fourteen, the grand total one hundred and sixty-three. But after 1625 the figures are fragmentary.

Reliable figures for recruitment from St. Omer into the Society of Jesus itself do not begin till after 1660. Thence onwards, to the end of the century, the total of boys sent on to the Watten novitiate (averaging

[1] *Stonyhurst MSS.*, Anglia IV, 13.1, 297 f.

[2] The vocations to Rome and the Spanish colleges can be sampled from the St. Omer *Annual Letters*, the *Valladolid Register* (*C.R.S.* xxx), the *Lisbon Register* (Croft and Gillow) and the Rome *Responsa*: but only for limited periods. For example:

	To Rome	*To Spain*	*To Watten*
1605	6	13	—
1607	5	12	—
1610	10	10	—
1620	——— 13 ———		
1621	14	10	—
1624	——— 24 ———		
1653	5		—
1676	3		13

the gaps in the records) is nearly 300, with ten novice masters sent during the same period.[1]

But in addition to serving as the regular nursery of the seminaries, St. Omer more than once contrived to fit them out completely. We have already seen that the College of St. George at Madrid was started with a party of boys from St. Omer (1611), that another party saved Valladolid from temporary extinction three years later, and that the St. Omer scholastics went at times as staff to Lisbon. Wadsworth was in the contingent of twelve who had finished their humanities and left for Seville in August 1622, and were captured by Barbary pirates and sold into slavery, till later ransomed.[2]

Later in the century a connection sprang up between St. Omer and the New World. A Jesuit had gone with Lord Baltimore in the expedition that founded Maryland in 1634, and Jesuit enterprise at last secured the establishment of a college in 1676. Say the Maryland *Annual Letters S.J.* for 1680:

> a school for humanities was opened by our Society in the centre of the country, directed by two of the Fathers; and the native youth, applying themselves assiduously to study, made good progress. Maryland and the recently established school sent two boys to St. Omer who yielded in abilities to four Europeans when competing for the honour of being first in their class.

By 1690 the Protestants in Virginia were petitioning William III for counterbalancing advantages: 'Jesuits and seculars priests are the only incumbents [here], for which there is a supply provided by sending

[1]

1664	3	1680	9	1695	5
1668	7	1681	10	1696	6
1669	7	1690	7	1697	7
1675	11	1691	7	1698	8
1676	13	1692	5	1699	7
1678	6	1693	8	1700	6
1679	6	1694	4		

From lists in *Stonyhurst MSS.*, Collectanea N. II, No. 45 (for period from 1664), Anglia IV, 13, iii, 1060 f. (for period from 1690). The Report on Watten for 1679 says: 'Dec. 6: Twelve of ours sick, and 13 of the servants. The House was smoked with pitch, to purify the aire. Four hogs dyed drunk with Beer' (Coll. N. II, No. 45).

[2] This saga is recounted in a MS. *Relation of the Journey* . . ., by one of their number, William Atkins (later a Plot victim—see *State Trials*, vii. 725). The *Relation* is in the Papers of Francis Whitegrove of Burton Manor (publ. *Hist. MSS. Comm.*). See also J. Wadsworth, *English-Spanish Pilgrim* (1629), 32; and J. Stevenson, in *The Month*, xxxvii. 535 f. (1879).

over Popish youth to be educated at St. Omers.' By 1685 they had sent two to the Watten novitiate.[1]

Though it was an exaggeration, therefore, when the *Annual Letters* of the English Province in 1697–8 called St. Omer 'the source of all the others', the mixed seminary that Robert Persons had started a century earlier had nevertheless become the keystone of the educational arch. It built upon such rudimentary studies as its scholars had received in the schismatical grammar schools of England, the dozen or so Jesuit schools functioning intermittently, and the other Catholic schools at liberty at any one date. In time it sent men on to Rome, Douay, Valladolid, Seville, Lisbon, Madrid and Watten, and later to America. But these vocations seem to have been only one in four of the school roll. The rest presumably remained laymen, to found families, or filter into the professions, or become 'teachers in corners' as the Elizabethan prison-lists had called their fathers. Of these we know far less than of the documented careers of those who became priests, of whom indeed St. Omer produced nearly as many as Douay.

The disproportionate size of the college was due partly to the Jesuit 'connection' that naturally grew up in those parts of England where, after the constitution of the province towards 1620, the Society established missions and schools. In addition to this, the prestige of Jesuit education stood universally high. Its adversaries within the Church had no pedagogical fault to find with it.[2] Even its Protestant adversaries feared it most because what it did it did so thoroughly. If efficiency means the proper relation of means to a given end, the Jesuit system was the quintessence of efficiency. Again, there was no student oath to be taken on entering St. Omer. It was not a pontifical college, and therefore was not affected by the oath enjoined by the Holy See in 1625—in sharp contradiction to all the other seminaries. This is part explanation of its high lay element.

There was probably no greater blaze of publicity for the college than when a squad of its boys testified at the Old Bailey during the Popish Plot trials: in June 1679, at the trial of the five Jesuits and that of the lawyer Richard Langhorn, and in May 1685 when Titus Oates himself was up for perjury.

Their evidence was needed for one crucial date in the history of the Oates plot: 24 April 1678. This was the day on which the famous

[1] See Foley, iii. 394; T. Hughes, *Jesuits in N. America* (1917), ii. 136–7; *Stonyhurst Magazine*, iv. 732 f. (1891).

[2] Cf. Dodd, *Church Hist.*, ii. 16 (1739).

'Jesuit consult' had been held in London, at which, according to Oates, it was decided to kill the king, Charles II. There was no dispute that a meeting had been held. What they did protest was that the charge rested on Oates's testimony that he was personally present at the 'consult', whereas in fact, for some time before and after that day, 24 April, he was at St. Omer, as a student-spy in the college

They did not save the five Jesuits, nor Langhorn. As the law stood at the time, a Catholic might testify but could not be sworn; and testimony not upon oath, on the other hand, need not be believed. Lord Chief Justice Scroggs ruled the trials of 1679, in an atmosphere so charged with the effects of Oates's 'revelations' that the verdicts were foregone conclusions. Lord Justice Jeffreys ruled the trial of 1685, in an atmosphere pro-James II and equally vitiated. None of this travesty, however, alters the straight fact that Titus Oates, on the day he professed to have witnessed in the Strand the fatal meeting that sent these papists to their death, was in the English College at St. Omer.

Some of the boys came to say so at great risk. Three of them were arrested by Sir William Waller, under the proclamations, the moment they reached London. They were needed by the defence, because documents offered from St. Omer, under seal of the college, proving the point of Oates's whereabouts, had been refused as evidence by the prosecution. Not all the boys had crossed to England in 1679 specially for the trials. Some had been home over a year.

Glimpses of St. Omer school life that punctuated the evidence are refreshing:

L.C.J. (Scroggs): Young man in what quality are you there?
Parry: I was a student there—a Poet.
Scroggs: When did *you* see Mr. Oates?
Fall: I saw him in my Syntax, and now I am in Poetry.
Scroggs: When did *you* see Master Oates?
Palmer: On the first day of May . . . Master Oates and several other boys played at nine-pins in the afternoon. I saw them.
Scroggs: Why! You did not count Master Oates a *boy*, did you?
Palmer: He was none of the Religious. He sat indeed at a table by himself, but he went to school with the boys, and we called all the scholars boys.

Their general opinion of him is best brought out in the passages which describe how the boy Billing 'throws up Mr. Oates his heels', and how another was 'one of these that broke a Pan about his head for recreation'.[1]

[1] *State Trials*, vi. 358–78, 448–60; and see J. Gerard 'Titus Oates at St. Omer, 1677–8', in *The Month*, cii. 133–43 (1903); and the chapter in H. Chadwick (1962).

At Titus Oates's own trial, on 8 May 1685, there was Samuel Morgan (now reverted to Anglicanism) who had played ball with him in the garden on the fateful 24 April itself; and there was Clement Smith, who had been visited by him in the college infirmary that same day, and to whom Oates had addressed the words 'Si placet Dominatio vestra'—a solecism so barbarous, from a rhetorician, as to be quite unforgettable.

But the unmasking of Oates could not bring back the men whose lives he had sworn away. St. Omer had had six of its old boys hanged at Tyburn before the time of the Oates Plot. One other had been hanged at Lancaster, and four had died in prison. The perjury of Oates sent seven more to the gallows: all of them leading Jesuits of the period. These seven were the five condemned together—Thomas Whitbread (provincial), William Ireland, William Harcourt, John Fenwick (the London agent for the college) and John Gavan; and Thomas Thweng (executed at York) and Philip Evans (Cardiff).[1]

During the years between the two trials the college had nearly gone bankrupt. Not for lack of numbers—there were a peak of 180 there in 1684—but from the inability of many parents to keep up the fees. Its funds had never been so low since the 'poverty year' of 1627. Then came a disastrous fire in 1684 to destroy a large part of the buildings. For some years afterwards it was impossible to rebuild, 'since the parents of the scholars were so reduced in fortune through the troubles of the Orange Revolution as to be scarcely able to subsist themselves, much less to pay their sons' pensions'. Nor did the possession of large quantities of real property elsewhere, for example the College at Madrid, help the St. Omer community in their immediate emergency.[2] By 1697 their debts in Flanders had mounted to 10,000 florins, a whole year's revenue.

The seventeenth century ended, then, with St. Omer affected by the backwash of the English Revolution no less than were the other colleges. But its resilience was greater than theirs, as its rapid recovery after the Civil War had shown. Moreover it was still the only school in exile for lay-boys from families not connected with the Benedictine or Dominican missions in England—neither of which were anything like as numerous as the Jesuits. It is curious that though the Society of

[1] St. Omer honours twenty-two martyrs altogether: these eighteen and four others who died in prison. See *Stonyhurst Magazine*, xx. 423–4.

[2] These possessions, listed by Christopher Mendoza, S.J., in *Stonyhurst MSS.*, Anglia IV, 13.iii.649 f.; and printed in *C.R.S.* xxix. 361 f.

Jesus had its implacable political enemies among the secular clergy and the English Catholic laity, educationally all were ready to learn from it: just as the *Spiritual Exercises* of its founder have since become the basis of the devotional practices of so many others. Educationally St. Omer had a long start, before the other orders entered the field. And St. Omer had not only a start but a tradition, which the others had still to make. Today Stonyhurst and Downside and Ampleforth can claim traditions going back for centuries. But in 1650 they were all very modern, and the Jesuits alone could begin to celebrate centenaries.

The core of St. Omer life is seized in a paragraph written some time later by Fr. R. Hawkins.

> Each School has its particular Master, who ascended gradually up every year, with his own scholars. Thus ye student, accustomed to ye same Instructor, imbibes an early love and esteem for ye person with whom he is to spend six years, and avoids ye many great and disagreeable difficulties which attend ye frequent change of Masters. This method of teaching is uniform in great measure among ye Jesuits.[1]

When we add to this the practice of staffing the college from among its own former scholars, avoiding the risk of narrow inbreeding by sending them far afield for higher studies and missionary experience beforehand, we can appreciate how the tradition actually grew. The college was always under the working trusteeship of men whose practice both cemented the past, by having grown up in the ways and thought of the place, and brought the present generation into the closest possible relationship with it.

There was at least one sturdy English Protestant pedagogue in the century who could penetrate to the essence of this 'system', despite his scorn of the popish religion, and offer it to his own fellows for emulation. Not as 'the Jesuit system' by name, for that would have been to put it out of court in advance, but by detailed description, down to even a plan of a Jesuit classroom. He was John Dury, famous in Cromwellian England. His account (1645) was called simply *Description of a Transmarine School*. Though it cannot be said that he had studied the *Ratio* as well as visited the school, 'more than a hundred passages are to be found in the *Ratio Studiorum* which afford exact parallel for the facts and methods indicated by Dury'.[2]

In short, the spirit of St. Omer was 'preventive', in the positive sense of preventive medicine. That simile is indeed apt, for it recalls

[1] *Stonyhurst MSS.*, Anglia III, 20, 4–5.

[2] *Corcoran*, 231–2, also for Dury's text, from Sloane MSS. 649, in the British Museum.

the analogy used by Aquinas himself in the *De Magistro*. Certainly in their methodology the Jesuits were voluntaryists; the will had to be curbed and broken-in. But the best answer to strictures on this, by critics old and new who conceived it as merely negative, is the pragmatic answer which judges by the products.

2. THE BENEDICTINE REVIVAL

At the start, the Holy See had given the Jesuits the management of every pontifical English college except Douay. This had been partly because of their experience as a teaching order, but also because the other English orders had practically died out and were not in the field. It was during the reign of James I that they revived: Benedictines, Dominicans and Franciscans. Of these only the Benedictines took to schooling early, but ultimately all three were the resorts of lay boys in exile, and the Franciscans actually essayed a footing on home soil.

The English Benedictine Congregation expelled from Westminster by Elizabeth had come near to extinction when Dom Robert Sigebert Buckley, in the Gatehouse prison in London, the only survivor, over ninety years of age and blind, professed two young novices some three years before his death, and the continuity was thus secured (21 November 1607).[1]

The urge to produce recruits for the English mission came, however, from the English Benedictines of the Spanish and Cassinese Congregations, who foresaw an extensive field, incidentally, among young men not anxious to be drawn into the quarrels of Jesuits v. seculars that threatened every postulant who went to Douay or Valladolid or Seville. Periodically the Benedictines petitioned the pope for a seminary in the Low Countries. Each time the plea was resisted by the Jesuits, notably Creswell, as likely to drain the English colleges in Spain already so penurious. We have already seen the discord produced in Spain, as a result, by defections to the Spanish Benedictines. All the anti-Jesuits were of course solidly behind the Benedictines, in order to break the 'Jesuit net' that was being drawn round the clergy. Clement VIII gave the desired permission for a Benedictine foundation in the Low Countries in March 1602.[2] The enterprise that followed produced the two Benedictine schools known today as Downside and Ampleforth.

The founding of St. Gregory's at Douay (now Downside) as

[1] Almond, *Ampleforth College*, 12–16; Gillow, i. 333–6.

[2] *Downside Review*, xvi. 34; E. L. Taunton, *English Benedictines*, ii. 67.

described in detail by Brother Benet Weldon, in a *Chronicle* of 1709, reveals that it was Fr. Austin Bradshaw who secured, towards the end of 1605, a dormitory in the Anchin College at Douay for the use of English students. Eighteen months later he was able to hire a house and begin conventual life, with five Benedictines and a lay brother. The Spanish governor of the Netherlands meanwhile conveyed to the Walloon Benedictine abbot his king's wish that they be encouraged, whereupon the abbot gave them a house and grounds. They took their lessons from 1610 onwards in the Marchiennes College, sending to Spain for brethren to come and teach the novices. In this way arrived Dom Leander Jones, one of the greatest of his generation, and a leading figure in Charles I's abortive discussions for reunion with Rome.[1]

Since much of the early records has been lost, the date of this first Benedictine *school* has had to be established by working backwards. A report of a Government spy in 1626 remarked on 'scholars', eating in the cloisters but separately from the monks. A letter of 1624 refers to 'a room for fifty monks and as many youths of good family who come to learn singing, Latin and music and then return to their own country'. An inventory of 1622 speaks of the 'scholars' refectory' as against that of the monks. In 1619 Leander Jones is writing of twenty-four monks and 'forty countrymen exiles for the Catholic faith', and of how 'necessity compels us to have as boarders with us some English youths committed to our care, whom their parents confide to us solely for the purpose of being brought up in good manners and learning'. The title of rector of the 'College' is used by Dom Thomas Green in a document of 1614. And as Dom Paulinus Greenwood is recorded as being given the Benedictine habit in 1611, it is argued that the school must have been started as early as 1608.[2] St. Gregory's thus conformed to the pattern foreseen by Cardinal Pole's decrees and acted on by Fr. Persons at St. Omer. It was seminary and school; and the school was ecclesiastical and lay, distinct but not separate.

[1] Bro. Weldon's Chronicle (publ. 1881), pp. 62–4, checked by Edmund Bishop in *Downside Review*, xvi. Papal approval of St. Gregory's was given on 10 Dec. 1608 and confirmed in April 1609.

[2] The case is thus argued in H. N. Birt, *Hist. of Downside College*, 7–13. The surviving archives, now at Downside, are listed in *Downside Review*, ii. 173–82; iii. 85–8 and 245–50; iv. 79–84, 132 ff. 197 ff.; v. 39 ff., 127 ff.; vi. 47 ff., 126 ff.; vii. 127 ff. See also Edmund Bishop, in *Downside Review*, March 1897; Stephen Marron in *Douai Magazine*, July 1922; and Hugh Connolly, *Some Dates and Documents for the Early History of our House*, Downside 1930.

The Benedictine educational stream that was to produce the second school, St. Laurence's at Dieulouard (now Ampleforth), began a year later than St. Gregory's, though not for many long years was it to have its school.

St. Laurence's arose from the eager desire of the English Benedictine monks, now three scattered groups—in Spain, at Monte Cassino in Italy, and elsewhere in their vagrancy—to secure a united house. In December 1606 the Bishop of Verdun made over to them an 'empty cloister and church' at Dieulouard, in Lorraine. He put it into the custody of the English 'Spanish' monks, but on the clear understanding that it was for the use of all three streams. For a time its fortunes fluctuated. 'The Spanish monks held it first; then it was seized by Fr. Preston, the Cassinese Superior; afterwards it passed into the keeping of the Westminster monks; later it belonged to the three parties conjointly; finally it was the proud possession of the one perfected, solidified English Benedictine Congregation. This was the monastery of St. Laurence, at Dieulouard.'[1]

Although three other Benedictine houses were started in the next few years, they never rivalled the original two. The house of St. Malo (1611) was ultimately abandoned after sixty years, having professed only fourteen monks in its whole history. The house at Chelles (1611) was small. The one in Paris (St. Edmund's, 1615) lived quietly till the French Revolution, when of course it was expelled with all the others (it is now Douai Abbey, Woolhampton).[2]

The great landmark in all this English Benedictine development was the final achievement of unity in June 1617. There had been several abortive attempts, and Pope Paul V himself had 'ordered unity'. It was now secured on a basis of the full independence of the revived English Congregation, though to placate the 'Spaniards' the Spanish habit was to be worn. The five Benedictine houses of the English exiles were henceforth organized in two functional groups (ratified August 1619). Three of them were monasteries: Dieulouard, Paris and Chelles. Two were colleges, or houses of studies: Douay (St.Gregory's) and St. Malo.[3]

From this it is clear that St. Laurence's at Dieulouard, though later it developed a school, had none at the start. Thus the origin of Ample-

[1] Almond, 273; Weldon, 66: *Downside Review*, iv. 205–15; J. I. Cummins, in *Ampleforth Journal*, iv. 14–28; and (for the buildings) i. 77–85.

[2] Guilday, 230, 234–6; and (for Paris) *Downside Review* xxxii. 125–47.

[3] Almond, 105–6; Guilday, 237–8; B. C. Butler, *Notes on the English Benedictine Congregation* (1887), 3–4.

forth College is an exception to the Tridentine conception which had produced St. Omer (Stonyhurst) and St. Gregory's (Downside).[1]

By the end of the reign of James I there were about sixty exiled boys preparing for the English mission in these five Benedictine colleges abroad, and as many again had already completed their studies and arrived back in England.[2]

St. Gregory's at Douay was a predominantly lay school from soon after its beginning. By 1626, it could claim 'many gentlemen's sons, who are their friends and benefactors in England'. These, said Lewis Owen in his *Running Register*, 'doe diet in their Cloister, but not in the same part where the Monks live, but in the other side of the Cloister; for they, and all other Monks and Fryers, will not have any Secular man to know of their private knavery. . . .'[3]

Conducting their own school was not, however, the only educational work of the monks. For when the abbot of St. Vaast at Arras (who had given them the house in 1608) donated them a permanent annual revenue for the support of twelve choir-monks, in September 1619, he stipulated that they should supply teachers of philosophy and theology for his own college; and they also gave public lectures in the town. Under this charter of 1619 the monks were to take an oath to go to England on the mission. Each new prior of St. Gregory's, moreover, was to appeal to the abbot of St. Vaast upon his election, for a renewal of the vows *et habitatio* at Douay. The abbot made it clear that he did not conceive this proviso in any arbitrary way.[4] Nor was the community limited to the original twelve *alumni*. But the rest, reaching a peak total of thirty-eight monks in 1625, and averaging seventeen to twenty-five for most of the century, were fee-paying *convictors* sometimes endowed as an act of piety by benefactors in England.[5]

[1] The first united Benedictine Chapter was held at Douay on 2 July 1621; and all was confirmed by Bull on 12 July 1637. The English Benedictine Congregation of women dates from the same year 1637.

[2] Letter of Rudesind Barlow, President-General of the English Benedictine Congregation, 12 Dec. 1624, in *Harleian MSS.* 4147; copy at Downside. See *Downside Review*, iii. 85.

[3] Weldon, 62; Birt, 8–11; *Downside Review*, xxxiii. 15; Owen, 94.

[4] Text of the charter is in *Downside Review*, xliv. 286–7, and lvi. 193–211. It named individually the first twelve monks covered by the pension.

[5] For the numbers, see Weldon, 152 note; *Downside R.* xi. 31. Cf. the endowment of a student in 1659: 'The Benedictine monks at Douay agreed with James Wolfe (called De Lupe), his heirs, exors. and assigns, for £400 rec$^{d.}$ of him to keep a scholar for ever at his or their nomination, advancing him through all his studies, making him a priest, and keeping him afterwards two years in their house.' (*Downside R.*, from Archives, iii. 250).

Atmospheres are difficult to catch, and more difficult still to define and portray. The spirit of St. Gregory's was ultimately a fusion of at least four contributory elements: the English 'Spanish' Benedictines with their austerity; the Vedaast monks, who shared the church though not the house; the spirit of the Rule of St. Benedict itself, and the aura of Douay, 'city of the martyrs' long since.

In the observance of the reformed Rule the monks of St. Gregory's 'tempered' their austerities by 'practical discretion'. (They normally ate meat on three days a week.) In the celebration of the divine office there was utter solemnity and precision. Their interior life is best seen in the manuals of piety it produced—above all in Dom Augustine Baker's *Sancta Sophia*. Their academic distinction was high enough to sustain them in the theological chairs they held at St. Vaast, and to make possible Dom Leander's *Biblia Sacra cum Glossa* (1617). With this went a skill in controversy typified in Rayner's *Apostolatus Benedictinorum in Anglia*.[1] Which of these eminent men taught in the school we do not know. For not till after the Restoration does the school figure at all prominently in the surviving archives. Dom Benet Weldon, visiting St. Gregory's in 1700, found the monks' day in full operation unchanged since the Charter of 1619 which had laid it down. 'Fr. Barnes taught casuistry in the Cathedral', writes Weldon of these early years, 'and the others sweated in the Confessional and pulpits; and as it began in drudgery, so it continued on.' But the coloured words are to be taken technically rather than editorially, for he also put it thus: 'The better to maintain themselves and prepare themselves for the English Mission, [they] exercise themselves continually in hearing confessions, preaching and pious examples in the places where they live, and are wonderfully profitable to those who are under their care.'[2]

In view of the controversy which arose in the nineteenth century on the question whether the English Benedictines were a missionary order *ex professo*, the matter of the missionary oath is important. It originated among them at Dieulouard, in 1613—they were to go to England, and to come from it, as and when told by their superiors. The forty-three professed during the first twelve years at St. Gregory's after 1619, however, took no such oath: probably because they had already been on the English mission. The Holy See itself had been reluctant to sanction a Benedictine mission on English soil, and had taken eight

[1] See the analysis of the St. Gregory atmosphere, in *Downside R.* xxxiii. 5–17.
[2] Weldon, 81, 89.

years to answer the appeal for one made in 1594. The Benedictine Chapter of 1625, too, undoubtedly thought of the house as a congregation first and a body of missioners only secondarily. The evidence suggests that the Benedictines accepted the need for missionary work *de facto*, and as only temporary, pending the return of normal Catholic times in England. 'We may and ought to exercise parochial duties', said Barlow's *Letter to the Provincials* after 1620, 'so long as our missionary state lasts (durante missionis conditione).'[1]

The other oath, that enjoined by the pope in 1625, is piquantly dealt with by Weldon: 'The Cardinals de Propaganda published an oath to be taken by all seminarists at the age of fourteen years old, that they will not enter any monastery till they have spent three years in the mission. This oath hath since been extended to all their lifetime, all the world standing astonished, even the learned, at the tenor of such a strange oath; and the other priests and Jesuits who tutored the seminaries maintained it was unreasonable that they who had been brought up at the cost of the Church left her service to hide themselves in cloisters; and yet the English [Benedictine] Congregation stands bound to the mission as much as they.'[2]

How devotedly they laboured on the mission is proved not only by their captures and sufferings amid their sixty missions in England, but by the extent to which certain tracts of England 'became Benedictine' in their sympathies, and sent their sons almost invariably to St. Gregory's at Douay and later to St. Laurence's at Dieulouard. Typical of these in the seventeenth century are the family ramifications of the Thornton–Swinburn–Englefield–Salvin–Meynell tradition, the Lawsons of Brough in Yorkshire and the Middletons of Stockeld.[3]

As the *School Chronicle* is scanty, and references to the school in the *Council Book* of the monastery are few, it is impossible to draw anything like a continuous picture of St. Gregory's. An inventory of 1622 reconstructs for us the boys' separate refectory, with its two long tables and one short, its cupboard and three forms, and its twenty-four cups, thirty spoons, five salt cellars, lamp and four trenchers. There is also extant an inventory of 1636. But as many of the boys had their own private cups and spoons, and these are not listed, the most reliable indication of numbers is always the quantity of beds. During

[1] Cuthbert Butler, *Notes on the Eng. Ben. Congregation*, pp. 35, 42, 44, 54.

[2] *Chronicle*, 147.

[3] Details in Birt, 20 ff., where it is cogently suggested that research into family papers might do much to fill out the lists of all the schools and colleges in exile for this period.

the fifty years after 1620 the total roll fluctuated between thirty and forty. From then till 1688 it rose as high as fifty, followed by a sharp fall at the Revolution, and by the end of the century was little short of sixty, though this was the peak figure and exceptional.[1] Materials for a regular list of the scholars do not exist for years earlier than 1666.

So slowly did the domestic conditions change, that descriptions of the school available for the early eighteenth century can safely be read back into the middle-seventeenth. It had the typical school *horarium*. The records show that its austerities put a premium on bread-smuggling and on raids on the woodshed. Occasional items in the inventories remind us, too, how English the climate of the place was: as witness the two leather beer-jugs of 1624—'Duo pocula quae vulgo Black Jack nuncupantur.'[2]

The custom at St. Gregory's of choosing a 'Christmas King' must have begun very early. Gilbert Langley in 1725 described it as reaching back to 'time immemorial'. No doubt it was invented originally to enliven a holiday which could not mean home. These boys never went home at vacations at all. The ceremony of electing the Boy King, the holding of his Yuletide Court,[3] the inordinate feasting that sublimated all the suppressed nostalgia from Christmas to Twelfth Night, were St. Gregory's counterpart to the impudent journeys to England undertaken at Christmas by the St. Omer boys.

On the devotional side, the Sodality of the Blessed Virgin, which had begun at Rome in 1580 and at St. Omer in 1609, was erected at St. Gregory's in 1678. Its enrolment book (the *Matricula*), complete from 1695 down to 1828, is no guide to the total number of boys in the school, for membership was voluntary and selective. What the book does show is that four out of every five members of it were lay boys.[4]

Lists of masters become available similarly from the reign of Charles II onwards. The whole of the humanities course was taught by one man (Wilfrid Reeves) between his arrival in 1675 (on his resignation of the mastership of Magdalen College School) and his return to England after the accession of James II. At this period the prefect of studies seems to have changed every year; and the changes in the assistant staff are too frequent for us to suppose that the Benedictines at Douay used the form-master system of St. Omer and the English

[1] For the roll, Birt, 32; *Downside R.*, xi. 32; and Almond, 187 note—for a 1709 list of Catholic colleges as presented to Parliament.

[2] See the early eighteenth-century account in Birt, 46–8.

[3] Cf. description in Birt, 90.

[4] Only 112 of the 553 names are those of clerics.

College. In any case the numbers on the roll were rarely above thirty. In 1684 the classes of rhetoric and poetry were fused.[1]

Constitutionally there should have been no danger of falling numbers. The chapter meeting of the whole Benedictine Congregation had decided in 1661, and repeated thereafter, that St. Gregory's was to be the college that should educate *all* postulants in humanities and in philosophy. The president of St. Gregory's would then apportion them, at the end of their course, between the three monasteries (St. Gregory itself, St. Laurence at Dieulouard and St. Edmund at Paris). But under the presidency of Dom William Gregson (1697) these decrees were violated. Boys had long been sent to other Benedictine colleges for their education—a collateral factor, incidentally, in the rise of St. Laurence's school. Prior Hesketh had protested roundly as the violations reached such proportions that by 1685 the annual pension at St. Gregory's had to be reduced from £25 (the standard rate throughout the colleges in exile), in order to attract more boys. By the end of the century there was lively fear that the school would no longer pay its way, and Prior John Philipson reduced the pension to as little as £16. It was not back to £25 for thirty-six years.[2]

St. Laurence's at Dieulouard, meanwhile, had moved from its original intention. When Fr. Bradshaw had taken possession of the church and house at the end of 1606, and when the rector of Rheims University had helped in installing the monks there, it had been with no idea beyond that of a monastery. Fifty choir-monks had been professed in the first twenty years. During the 'thirties, when Lorraine was troubled by political events and scourged intermittently by plague, the postulants had fallen off. Only four novices were admitted during the two decades 1636–56. It was in this situation that the president of St. Laurence's, Dom Paul Robinson, decided in 1658 to establish a college as such, hitherto eschewed as likely to be a distraction from the monks' main work.[3]

Therein lies the origin of the *school* at St. Laurence's. Therein lies too a patent reason for its smallness until the following century. For the decrees of 1661, after a fruitless discussion on the possibility of setting up two Benedictine schools in England, declared for a policy

[1] *Prefects of Studies*: 1685 Charles Sumner, 1686 Joseph Hesketh, 1696 Gregory Greenwood. *Humanities*: 1685 Wilfrid Reeves, Bernard Greaves, Edmund Taylor; 1686 Maurus Barber, Cuthbert Hutton, Benedict Hemsworth; 1694 Gilbert Knowles.

[2] Birt, 37–8; Guilday, 253 note.

[3] Almond, 184 ff.; *Downside R.* iv. 205–15.

of enlarging St. Gregory's at Douay and making that the only school for postulants to the order. Dieulouard's handful of boys (never more than ten in number at any one time till nearly seventy years later) thus personified a constitutional 'poaching', connived at by Dom William Gregson, the provincial president. That tiny establishment, reminiscent of the first school of all, at Eu in 1582, maintained but a shadowy existence until well into the eighteenth century.

One final 'St. Gregory' foundation calls for mention—the seminary established in Paris in 1667—for it revived Allen's original project of a College of Writers. The express purpose was to enable English priests to follow the full theology course at the Sorbonne. St. Gregory's was a power-house of picked men, never more than six or so at a time, living in the Rue des Boulanges. They took first a lower degree in divinity; then held three disputations, minor and major and Sorbonnick, lasting five, ten and twelve hours respectively; and finally took their doctorate.[1]

3. THE FRIARS: FRANCISCANS AND DOMINICANS

The English Franciscans, likewise, had nearly died out. Early in the new century there was only one survivor of the pre-Reformation English province, Fr. William Stanney. It was he who, by receiving into the order John Gennings, preserved the continuity, and it was Fr. Gennings who took the first practical step, about 1614, to restore conventual life, by establishing a Franciscan house at Gravelines. Within four years recruits had become so numerous that he sought permission to set up a house at Douay, and with the approbation of King Philip III there began St. Bonaventure's. Fr. Gennings ruled as its first provincial for ten years.

For a time the students attended the classes of the Douay Benedictines. In 1622 they opened their own 'Schools' for theology, and a year later a school for lower studies. But this was for postulants only. So were the residences they subsequently established on English soil, at Greenwich and near Reading. Two friars are found catechizing in

[1] Cf. *C.R.S.* xix. 93 f. The Irish College in Paris was founded in the same year 1667. There is evidence that the Benedictines in 1669 did plan two schools for England, one in the north and one in the south. Next to nothing is known of them. If they developed, they were no doubt swept away in 1689 at the Revolution. See A. Allanson, *Hist. Eng. Ben. Cong.* ii. 471–2. The plan was revived by the Chapter in 1713 and 1717.

London some time afterwards, but the first schools for lay boys were not to appear till 1672.[1]

The English Dominican Province had actually become extinct, when Fr. Hargreave died in 1566, though Englishmen had become Dominicans since then, and there had been as many as twenty in England in 1635, mostly at the London Embassy Chapels. The English Dominican house at Bornhem, near Antwerp, was established (December 1657) at the instigation of Fr. Philip Howard, later Cardinal, exactly a century after the Elizabethan suppression. A novitiate was opened at once, to provide friars for the English mission. In 1660 a school for boys followed that was quite distinct from it. This is a significant event, because what happened completes the evolution of the college 'idea'. It began with six boys and grew. In 1666, when Howard left for England, it was closed and remained so for four years. It was closed again in 1672, by his successor, but reopened the following year with Flemish boys, whereafter it flourished. No evidence has been adduced to suggest that this boys' school was in any way preparatory to entry into the order. It was not a juniorate. Where Allen and Persons had accommodated lay boys as circumstances increasingly made necessary, and where St. Omer had been preponderantly lay but (at first) clerical as well in *clientèle*, Bornhem was a school for the laity, and as such, the 'culmination of the foundation-movement'.[2]

Fr. Howard, as provincial, recruited three young priests to start this 'secular college': Thomas Molyneux from Toulouse, Thomas Fidder from Bohemia and Vincent Torré from Brittany. He tried to buy a house for the school (The Delft) but its owner held out for 3,000 florins more than the 20,000 he could find.

Though we know the names of a few of the early pupils,[3] and that some of them did become Dominicans, we know little else of the first years. How far the personality of Fr. Torré, who became superior in 1663, was responsible for the wilting of the school before it had fairly got going, can only be conjectured. Certainly his rule produced general dismay. The college was discontinued in 1663 and the boys

[1] Guilday, 286–90, 302 f.; *Franciscan Centenary Pamphlets*, ii. 2–3; *Douay Diary* (*C.R.S.* xi. 395–6) for report by Dr. Matthew Kellison. The English Franciscan 'Blue Nuns' were founded in 1621.

[2] *C.R.S.* xxv. (Dominicana), 101; Palmer, *Bygone Colleges*; *Bornhem and Carshalton*, in 'Merry England', xii (1889); Bede Jarret, *English Dominicans*, 182–3.

[3] 1659–60; Edward Williams, Cottington, Fortescue, James Goodlad [O.P.], Charles Veymas, Charles Atkins [O.P.], Esme Howard [O.P.].

sent to the Brabantine Dominicans at Vilvorde, Bornhem paying their expenses. Perhaps the misfortune might not have happened but for the long absences, in England and elsewhere, of the founder, Philip Howard.[1]

In 1671 the college was revived for a year and a half, till Christmas 1672, with (at most) five boys. The financial accounts for this period give sidelights on their life. We learn that a 'bow an Arrowes' cost seventeen pence, a sword and belt just over three florins. 'Oneal Bayles came hither to study ye 27 of July 1671 and returned to his Mo. at Brussells ye 17 of August 1671, for this we receaved nothing.' From it, however, the friars at least learned something, for there is the following sequence soon afterwards: 'Mr. Pegg came to us ye 27 of July 1673. Augst 27 *Nota* Harry Pegg is indebted to us for six weeks yt he dyeted at Bornhem. Mr. Pegg went.'[2]

Undoubtedly the college was revived again at times during the rest of the century, for the names are extant of some twenty-three boys who passed through it between 1672 and 1694, and one of these (Henry Smith) was there four years (1575–9). Whether it was serving now as a school for postulants we do not know. At all events by 1700 there were only eight Dominicans on the mission in England, only eight friars and four lay brothers at Bornhem, and only ten other English Dominicans altogether. Some of these were at Louvain, connected there with the university; some were at Rome, till the house there was given up in 1697; some were at Tangier.[3]

It is not until 1703 that Bornhem School can be firmly documented. Thereafter its history is clear. On 12 November of that year Fr. Antonius Thompson revived it, for both English and Flemish boys, postulants as well as lay. From thence until the French Revolution it flourished.[4]

By the end of the seventeenth century, then, English Catholic youth had at its service on the Continent a substantial supply of seminaries and schools.

Boys with a vocation to the secular priesthood going abroad would

[1] Dominican Archives, *MSS. Hist. Records* (Ed. Palmer), ii. 2. 497ff.

[2] *C.R.S.* xxv ('*Dominicana*'), 9506, 139–40, and lists of students after 1763, at pp. 164–71.

[3] Guilday, 411. The Irish Dominicans had founded a College in 1667 in Madrid, confirmed by Pope Clement IX for English and Scots as well; see Dominican *MSS. Hist. Records*, v. No. 444.

[4] See *MSS. Hist. Records*, ii. 2. 527; and Palmer, *Bygone Colleges*.

make for the English College at Douay, or the *Venerabile* in Rome, or any of the four in the Iberian Peninsula—Valladolid, Seville, Madrid, Lisbon. If they had not 'made their humanities' already in England their *entrée* into those seminaries would usually be by way of the English Jesuit College at St. Omer.

Boys risking the journey to sojourn abroad in search of a liberal education for itself, to be followed by a lay career in Europe or more hazardously at home in England, had St. Gregory's at Douay, St. Laurence's at Dieulouard, and the Bornhem school as alternatives to St. Omer; and each of these had its *clientèle* of families in England, determined by the movements of the regulars on the mission.

Postulants to the orders themselves now had available the seminaries that had been started immediately upon the resurrection of the orders 'from the ashes'.

Compared with this situation, the supply of schools and convents abroad for English girls was munificent. But the total of boys at any one time, in their few schools, outnumbered the girls in their many. And whereas at home in England there were only two schools for girls, at Hammersmith and in York, for boys there were—albeit often shortlived and always precarious—dozens. To this domestic end of the problem we now turn.

X

CATHOLIC EDUCATION IN STUART ENGLAND

I. INTRODUCTION

THE religious climate of the country in 1603, even after forty years of the Elizabethan regime, may still have been anything from one-third Catholic (as Fr. Roger Gwyn claimed in 1603) to one-half (as the Spanish ambassador reported). The evidence of Catholics in positions of authority under James I (including 81 J.Ps.), and of the debates in Parliament in 1605 and 1621, tends to strengthen these estimates. What the persecution had done was to drive the Catholics underground; and the measure of this was 'the contrast between the handful of officially earmarked recusants and the belief of contemporaries that nearly half the country was Catholic at heart'. The lists of recusants-convict in 1650 add up to some 54,000—only one per cent of the population. A petition sent to Propaganda in Rome in 1669, asking for a bishop to be appointed, gave a figure of 200,000, served by 800 priests. The considered estimates of Brian Magee go higher.[1]

Apart from periods of ease and security, the incidence of the penal laws from now on was to follow a fairly consistent pattern. They 'weighed less heavily than has been supposed', for they were sapped by undervaluations, evasions, leases of Catholic lands to Protestants at low rentals by the Crown and composition fines. The recusants paid less than they were legally bound to; and not all they paid reached the Exchequer. Sir Henry Spiller, Fines Officer to James I, was himself a

[1] Brady, *Hierarchy*, iii. 107; B. Magee, *English Recusants*, esp. 100ff. and ch. vii; D. Shanaham, 'List of Priests in England in 1610', in *Clergy Review* xlvi. 659ff. (1961). Agretti's report said there were 230 secular priests, 120 Jesuits, 80 Benedictines, 55 Franciscans, a few Dominicans and a few Discalced Carmelites. Birkhead told the pope in 1608 that there were now nearly 500 seculars on the mission, and that the number of regulars was bound to increase after the Benedictine and Franciscan revival. See *Westminster Arch.* viii, No. 64 (1608); ix, No. 78; viii, No. 164; xii, No. 233; *C.R.S.* xli. 121. In Scotland there were only six or seven priests in 1610 (Nat. Lib. of Scotland, *Dennistoun MSS.*, xi, No. 4, ff. 646, 652). See also Havran, *Caths. in Caroline Engld.* (1962), 80f., for a useful discussion of lay and clerical population.

Catholic. Under James I the number of recusants convicted trebled, but the number paying only doubled; and the majority of convictions were not fully followed up. As under Elizabeth, so in the seventeenth century, there were cases where the faith was preserved without any interruption at all in the daily celebration of Mass: the homes of the Blundells of Crosby, the Langdales of Holme in Yorkshire and Houghton in Lancashire, and the Levesons of Willenhall, Staffordshire, amongst many.

But the change from Tudor to Stuart sovereign was in fact to alter the Catholic ethos. Politics from now on loom less and less in their campaigns, religion and education more and more. The revival of the religious orders was the most immediate earnest of this. We have met that revival already where it produced its first schools, on the Continent. But the Jesuits, already fully stretched in those areas, took the creation of their own particular English province in 1620 as a call to organize their scattered missions at home.

Their English novitiate began in 1607, through the exertions of Fr. John Gerard, at a hallowed centre, Louvain, made over to them by the generosity of a Spanish noblewoman whose name the English exiles had great cause to bless in so many other contexts—Luisa de Carvajal.[1] After seven years they moved it to Liège, to be near their higher classes in philosophy and theology. This of course produced chagrin throughout the universities of Liège, Douay and Cologne, for it meant a loss of students from their own classes. It also stimulated the Government in London to thunder out the proclamation of 1615 against the seminaries; for already the Society was building gradually a complete 'English' organization from bottom to top. When the novitiate moved finally to Watten in 1622, the top had just been fashioned—a house of 'third probation', for professed Fathers, at Ghent, men who had behind them their two years of novitiate, five years of teaching and seven of seminary studies.[2]

And as an earnest that the English Jesuits were ready as a province of the Society, they now took on such organization. In 1619 the mission was made a vice-province, in 1620 a province, under Fr. Henry Blount as provincial.

England and Wales were divided into twelve districts designated

[1] There is a life of her by Lady G. Fullerton (1873).

[2] *Stonyhurst MSS.*, Anglia II, 29, Nos. 16 and 17, for a memo. on the property, and a note in the hand of Charles Plowden, S.J.; No. 20, for the opening at Liège on 1 Sept. 1614; No. 22 for its change to a college of higher studies in 1622. For the 1614 protests, Guilday, 151–2.

'Colleges', each with its 'Residence'. Only rarely at first was there anywhere a school to substantiate the first of these high-sounding titles, or more than the pack-horse of an itinerant, hunted priest to substantiate the second. But such was the organization. It meant that from now on the whole country was to be taken into account systematically, by men who had reached the peak of education and were spiritually tempered, and could act as one united wing of a world movement. The older men would find rest in a Catholic family and nurse a neighbourhood. The younger men would be constantly on the move. Recruits to the Society came in a constant flow from the landed families: 11 Petres, 9 Plowdens, 10 Poles, 16 Poultons; and Bedingfields, Stourtons, Keynes, Tichbornes, Mostyns, Cliffords, Talbots, Gerards, Walpoles, Welds.[1]

Not all these 'Colleges' were organized at once. The first three, by 1622, were London (St. Ignatius College), Lancashire (St. Aloysius) and South Wales (St. Francis Xavier)—the three most densely populated Catholic areas. The Welsh district, with its 'Residence' at Cwm in Monmouthshire, took in also Somerset and Gloucestershire. Six other areas had been covered by 1633. The rest followed by 1670.[2]

Within a few years the annual average of Jesuits active in 'the English Vineyard' was about 150. They had the signal advantage, over the 'shepherdless' secular clergy, of a full-scale territorial organization. The seventeenth century in English Catholic education is still supremely their century. Their schools, at one time and another, long before the revival under James II, were widespread: in the North, at Ormskirk, Berwick and the 'Mannor'; in the Midlands, at Wolverhampton, Stanley Grange, Spinkhill, Carlton (Yorkshire) and in Leicestershire; in the South, at Chideock, Dorchester and in Suffolk. These we shall have to notice in their proper place in the developments.

What is of supreme importance is that the English Jesuits were now in a position to face the problem of English Catholic education at all levels, from the clandestine village school taught by an itinerant priest —through the colleges of the Society abroad or the school at St. Omer—and so back to England either as missioner or as layman. In this sense were their schools in England 'preparatory schools'.

[1] Guilday, 147–8, from Foley.

[2] They were: Midland (Immaculate Conception), East Anglia (Holy Apostles), Durham (St. John the Evangelist), Yorkshire (St. Michael), Hampshire (St. Thomas of Canterbury), Worcestershire (St. George); and Oxfordshire (St. Mary), Staffordshire (St. Chad) and North Wales (St. Winifred). Their annals make up the middle volumes of H. Foley's *Records*.

The year 1622, in which all this was completed, is indeed a landmark year, for it saw also the beginning of that mighty organ of Rome's Counter-Reformation policy, the *Sacred Congregation de Propaganda Fide*, set up with a jurisdiction covering 'all lands not bound to the Holy See by political and religious ties'. The English educational enterprise was immediately affected by two of its very first decrees. The rector of every Pontifical College (that is, a college receiving an annual papal pension—for us Douay pre-eminently) was to make an annual report direct to Rome on all entrants and leavers; and (to avert the risk of colleges finding that boys whom they had educated as *alumni*—free—deserted them at the end and joined one of the orders) the 'student oath' was enjoined, whereby the student pledged himself not to do so without the express permission of the Holy See.[1]

A pyramid was thus formed, Propaganda at the apex, and the revived orders and the new 'seminary' clergy at the base. If anything were wanting, to show that the death of Elizabeth marks a change in the Catholic attitude, the proof is manifest in the Benedictine and Franciscan revival and the formation of the Jesuit province.

Certainly Parliament took it as such, and took the king's political temporizing accordingly as exasperating, particularly as James I, himself a scholar, was not too bigoted to encourage popish scholars at Court. It is typical of the Stuart objectivity about Catholicism, outside the political arena, that James could favour individual cultivated Catholics as persons while mounting a 'higher education offensive' against all they stood for. On the one hand Tobie Mathew; but on the other, Chelsea College, a thread that runs through the period till the time of his grandson Charles II.

2. HIGHER STUDIES

While Allen's educational practice had been forced to build downwards, his intention of building upwards had not weakened. The library that he took to Douay typifies his aspirations. Somewhere about 1580 he had begun to project a 'College of Higher Studies' to forestall any possibility of there being, later, a dearth of front-rank Catholic English scholars and apologists of the calibre of Sander, Vaux and Persons. The shortage of priests in England had already meant that some men's studies at Douay had had to be telescoped. In any

[1] For the beginnings of 'Propaganda' see J. A. Griffin in *American Catholic Hist. R.*, xli. 289–327 (1930).

case, Douay as it then stood was obliged by all the prevailing circumstances to restrict itself to training for the mission. Allen's idea, though it lived on, came to nothing in his lifetime, for several reasons, none more decisive than finance.

In 1602 the English ambassador at Paris got wind that 'our English priests' were about to bring it to a head again. The idea seems to have taken preliminary shape four years before, when the Cardinal Protector of England (Cajetan) was sounded on it. The ambassador's information was that there was to be a college, called Mignon, in no less a place than Paris.[1]

The fruit of all this came very soon. That the English Catholics felt the need of it shows how far the intensive curriculum of the seminary colleges made them unfruitful places for the extended detachment necessary for meeting the leisured intellectual output of the Anglican universities at home.

Given the writers, there were plenty of presses and distributors to hand, as in the days of Campion and Persons' printing-press in Stonor Park. A secret press was working in Lostock Hall, Lytham, Lancs., in 1604, from which Fr. Lawrence Anderton, S.J., turned out 'innumerable books' till the press was seized by the Bishop of Chester nine years later.[2] The Privy Council was warned by Sir Clement Fisher in 1605 that one Henry Tailor, a renegade printer, was ready to give information as to others, and that he (Sir Clement) awaited instructions on what to do with the 'prisoned printers in Warwick gaol'.[3]

The most famous of them all, that at St. Omer, started by Persons, had gathered strength since Francis Bollet was licensed to print there in 1602. It printed exclusively English works, for English readers. From its first mention, in the Jesuit *Annual Letters* of 1608, it ran for over a century and a half: down to the suppression of the Society in 1773. Under its first director, John Wilson, its output of pure controversy included Bellarmine's *Responsio* (1609, to James I), Persons' *Judgment of an English Catholic* and Brereley's *Apology*. Its early devotional and liturgical books included the 1610 *Spiritual Exercises* and the 1615 *Ordo Baptizandi*.

Despite their high prices these St. Omer books 'circulate throughout England with the happiest results. They effect what could scarcely be

[1] *C.R.S.* xli. 52 note.
[2] *C.R.S.* xvii. 422.
[3] Hist. MSS. Comm., *Salisbury MSS.*, xvii. 328–9.

done by priests; for to persuade a Protestant . . . is a capital offence . . . but nothing is easier than to call their attention to a new book, which they eagerly accept and devour.'[1] Spirited attacks were made on the St. Omer press by John Gee, in his famous *Foot Out of the Snare* in 1624; by Lewis Owen's *Running Register* of 1626, which estimated their profits at £400 a year; and by even the English Catholic secular clergy, led by the Bishop of Chalcedon (Wm. Bishop), in that it was a press 'unauthorized'.[2]

The culminating work of the period is the Douay Old Testament of 1609–10, completing the Bible in English begun by the Rheims New Testament twenty-eight years earlier.

A college of Higher Studies would be, then, a fitting climax to all this enterprise. The project, dormant for a time after the English ambassador reported it in 1602, was raised afresh when Dr. Richard Smith (later to become Bishop over the English Catholics) went to Rome in February 1609 at the behest of the new Archpriest Birkhead. The seven matters he was to ventilate with the pope included 'how some of the more learned of our priests may be supported abroad in order that they may write against the heretics, and try to get them appointed as lecturers in theology in the College of Douay as used to be done'.

The major argument used, the enormous value of the Catholic books in making converts, was strengthened by reflections on the lack of libraries in England, the frequent searches of Catholic houses by the pursuivants, and the dearth of financial help for English Catholic scholars and printers on the Continent. A papal brief authorizing Smith to set up in some Catholic country a house where 'five or six learned priests may live together for this purpose', on a papal stipend, 'however small', was all he asked.

But this was never the way the mind of the Holy See worked. Rome had a tradition of acting not to innovate but to ratify. Loyola had found this in the early years of his Jesuits after 1540. The same principle was at work in the drafting of the educational decrees of Trent in 1563. The English teaching nuns of Mary Ward found it, also. Dr. Smith was told that it was up to him to launch this apostolic House of Writers and begin work. Thereafter the pope might subsidize it.

[1] S.J. *Annual Letters*, 1615.

[2] There is a study of the St. Omer press in the Jesuit *Letters and Notices*, vols. 37 and 38, *passim*, with lists of its output at xxxviii. 308–11, 456–71.

Of this the sponsors of the scheme were not so sure. Fr. Thomas Fitzherbert, who was with the Smith mission, warned the Archpriest Birkhead that a like attempt, the 'Mignon College' in Paris, had recently been 'frustrated by the dissention of those who should have created and upholden it, yet amongst whom none would be subservient to other; and I fear me the lyke will fall out in thys, if it be granted'. But after all, Smith was the clergy agent in Rome and representative therefore of all the English seculars, the front-line men on the mission. The venture had, too, energetic support from leading lay exiles. So the scheme went ahead.[1]

The plan to which it was a counterblast, King James's own Chelsea College, was also taking shape simultaneously. A letter of May 1610 shows very clearly that the plans for this were already well under way.[2]

The traditional view of the Chelsea project is valid. It was to be 'a spiritual garrison, with a magazine of all books for that purpose, where learned divines should study and write in maintenance of all controversies against the Papists'. Anglican divines and teachers were to take a leaf out of the Papist book. The Catholic Church did not saddle *all* tasks on every priest, but used a specialized apostolate, 'reserving' some for 'polemical studies'. These would need refuting on terms of equal scholarship.[3] But the perspective of this was historically quite sharp. One has to see it against a background of Oxford and Cambridge denuded since 1568, already buffeted by the controversial skill of the exiles, and at the mercy also of Puritan and Brownist and Archpriest pamphleteers of no mean eminence. This very situation, moreover, meant that a scheme set up in default of the two universities was unlikely to endear itself to them: with all that that implied—for the political influence of the universities was still high.

At Chelsea six acres of land belonging to the Earl of Nottingham became the chosen site. King James gave £2,000 and timber from Windsor Forest; the Archbishop of Canterbury gave £100 and a library. Two thousand pounds were also paid in by the rector appointed, Matthew Sutcliffe, Dean of Exeter, who had already crossed swords with the Catholic exiled divines.[4] The king's patent of incorporation provided for a rector, seventeen divines and two historians, 'for the defence of true religion now established within this realm of

[1] *C.R.S.* xli, *Fitzherbert Letters*, 141–3, 51–2; Gillow, iii. 550–1; Guilday, 105 and note.

[2] Beaulieu to Turnbull, in Sir Ralph Winwood's *Memorials* (ed. 1725), iii. 160.

[3] Cf. Fuller, *Church History*, 1845 ed., v. 387.

[4] His works had been answered by Richard Walpole, S.J., at Antwerp, in 1605.

England and for the refuting of errors and heresies repugnant to the same'.[1]

The Catholic counterpart to Chelsea kept pace with it. As the Belgian Jesuits were averse from seeing it established in Douay, the English seculars contrived, through the Benedictine Prior of Douay, to have it set up in the Arras College of Paris University. It has accordingly gone down to history as the Arras College. Six months after it had opened, regulations were issued (28 April 1612). Its men were to be writers primarily, and some of them were to be men 'perfected' at the Sorbonne. The course of study, and the precedence of the staff, were to be settled by the Archpriest of England. Future admissions were to be agreed between the initial staff, the archpriest and the founder (Thomas Sackville). All were to be secular priests. Politics were barred from their terms of reference, and nothing was to be written against the Crown.[2]

Its team of men was formidable. Dr. Richard Smith severed his personal connection with the English mission to come and preside over it, till he became a bishop in 1625. Richard Ireland, headmaster of Westminster School for twenty years previously, was specially appointed; he died in the College in 1636. The others included William Bishop—made Bishop of Chalcedon in 1623; and Anthony Champney —later vice-rector of Douay College.[3]

The issue between Arras and Chelsea was very soon joined, when the Archbishop of Canterbury's chaplain, John Mason, published a book on *The Consecration of Bishops in the Church of England* (1613). Fr. Fitzherbert's immediate reply to it, in his *Addition to the Supplement of Fr. Robert Persons*, served to canalize the main battle for a long time to come—on the central question of Anglican Orders.[4] Within two years the king was issuing letters patent to the Archbishop of Canterbury to 'stir up all the clergy' in support of Chelsea College, and the Archbishop himself was flaying them because 'the idolatrous and superstitious papists are more forward to advance their falsehoods than we are to maintain God's truth'.[5]

[1] *Tierney-Dodd*, iv. 133–9, and appdx., p. cclxviii. The staff, appointed by the King on 8 May 1610, are listed in Fuller, *loc. cit.* They included the Deans of St. Paul's, Winchester, and Gloucester. The two historians were William Camden and John Haywood. There is a brief history of the college in J. Crossley, *Diary and Correspondence of Dr. J. Worthington* (Chetham Soc., 1874–6, xiii).

[2] Texts in *T.-D.* iv, appdx. p. cclxix.

[3] For these see Gillow; *C.R.S.* xxviii; Foley; Dodd, ii. 379. Also *Westminster Arch.*, x–xii (1609–13); and P.R.O. *Roman Transcripts* 9, bundle 118, for letters of nuncios.

[4] Details in Destombes, chap. vi.

[5] Quoted in Fuller, *loc. cit.*

Thus was resumed a scholastic war, among the rarefied heights of theology and canon law, whither we need not follow it. The close affinity of purpose and context between Chelsea and Arras is illustrated best by the fact that, having been born simultaneously, they fell into a common obscurity, and finally disappeared together.

It is during the Commonwealth that the last is heard of any reputable apologetic work from Chelsea College, which by then had been languishing for some time. The only dynamic personality at work in it was Matthew Sutcliffe, its original provost. The king's support dwindled to merely passive approbation. The finances, weakened by this, fell still more through the jealous opposition of university men—'two breasts, Cambridge and Oxford [wrote Fuller] being counted sufficient for England to suckle all her children with'. Towards 1640, also, the college was suspect in the eyes of Parliament, as being too 'courtly'. At large it was no more popular than other royal 'monopolies'.

By 1636 it had fallen into such virtual disuse that the Catholics themselves were actually trying to buy the property for use as a Catholic school. This prompted certain people to press Charles I to restore the place to its proper purpose, but 'this I will not do', he replied; 'too much time is spent on controversies which displease me. I would rather study were devoted to Reunion.'[1]

A revival of Chelsea naturally figured amongst the grandiloquent plans of the Anglo-Pole, Samuel Hartlib, in his *Reformed Spiritual Husbandmen, with an Humble Memorandum concerning Chelsey Colledge*, in 1652, till Parliament seized the foundation, to devote it to other uses. After the Restoration Charles II offered it to his newly-created Royal Society, but they found it 'ill adapted' to their scientific purposes. The Earl of Newport urged that it be made into a royal hospital. Far-sighted men in the Established Church pleaded that the college be reinvigorated. 'Bishops are gone, Deans and Prebends', it had been said during the Cromwellian interregnum. 'We had need to look out for some to stand in their places, that cordially fought the Lord's battles. The time is most seasonable, whilst war is preparing, and defiance proclaimed to the sword-men of Rome, to encourage a Society which are to take the pen-men to task.' But the college did not

[1] P.R.O. *Roman Transcripts*, Panzani to Barberini, 20/30 Sept. 1636; and Gordon Albion, *Charles I and the Court of Rome*, 187. The statement in S.N.D., *Life of Viscount Stafford* (1929), 16, that 'the King himself subscribed to the support of a school at Chelsea, where Catholic professors taught Catholic boys to know and practise their religion', is a curious garbling of this episode.

survive the death of its fourth provost, Dr. Samuel Wilkinson. Several attempts to have it transformed into queer shapes—a 'place of retirement during the plague', a prison, a brothel, a stable—failed. In February 1682 the Chelsea Royal Hospital was founded on its site.[1]

To return. By one of those ironies that litter the record of penal times, a plan for a royal 'College and Senate of Honour' at home in England, sponsored by *Catholics* under Crown patronage, was actually set on foot about the same time as the original Chelsea College. The details were clear by 1617. Assuredly was there truth in the allegation, by Dr. Benjamin Carrier of Corpus, when he resigned from Chelsea College to become converted to Rome, that King James was even prepared for a 'kind of coalition' between Canterbury and Rome,[2] and this well before the period of the Spanish and French royal marriage schemes, and longer still before the efforts at Reunion by Dom Leander Jones under Charles I.

The two chief sponsors of the 'Royal Academy or College and Senate of Honour' were Catholics. One was Edmund Bolton, aged about forty, of Trinity Hall, Cambridge, and the Inner Temple. The other was Henry Ferrers, the antiquary, by now getting on for seventy. Associated with them was one whose fame they never had—Sir Tobie Mathew, the friend of Francis Bacon, ordained a Catholic priest already (in Rome, May 1614).[3]

King James himself backed the scheme. So did George Villiers, Duke of Buckingham. By 1624 it was arranged that the College should have a royal charter, a seal and £200 annually. There would be three classes of members: 'Tutelaries', the Lord Chancellor, the Knights of the Garter and the university Chancellors; 'Auxiliaries', the flower of the nobility and the professions; and a body of eighty-four 'Esentials', hand-picked individuals—of whom Sir Tobie Mathew was one. These last were to bear the brunt of the work, which would concentrate on reviewing all English translations of secular books and preparing digests of them for ordinary people.[4]

Edmund Bolton, who sponsored it, fell on evil days, albeit he was the *protégé* of Buckingham and the friend and collaborator of William

[1] *Worthington Diary*, Chetham Soc., xiii. 74–5, 215; G. H. Turnbull, *Hartlib, Dury and Comenius*, 48; Tierney-Dodd, iv. 133–9. D. Lysons, *Environs of London*, ii. 89–93, from *Tanner MSS.* in Bodleian.

[2] Foley, i. 622–3.

[3] See Gillow, i. 258; ii. 252; iv. 537. Cf. David Mathew, *Sir Tobie Mathew* (1950).

[4] The motion on these lines is in *Harleian MSS.* and in West's *Collection*; cited in Gillow, ii. 252.

Camden. Free-lance literature, to which he had taken as all the professions were barred to his religion, did not sustain him. Four years after the abortive college plan he was convicted for recusancy and thrown into the Fleet Prison, whence he was transferred five years later to the Marshelsea and died about 1633. The voluminous works of his pen remain. His other dream—of a National Historical Library—had to await the founding of the British Museum. Henry Ferrers, who was of Camden's circle also, and known to the antiquary as 'very commendable and my special friend', died in the same year.[1]

How far the rank-and-file membership was to be Catholic, basking in the comparative toleration of James's last years, does not appear. Nor did the college. For the politicians round the throne would have none of it. It remains as only a hint of how Catholic scholarship might have been harnessed to its country's advantage in these ambivalent days of the early Stuarts.

There is a further direction, too, in which Catholic pedagogy made an impact on its Protestant fellow, unclouded by political or clerkly bitterness. This was the matter of how to teach Latin.

The most famous seventeenth-century work on the teaching of languages, until teaching through the vernacular was made the staple method of John Baptist De la Salle and his Institute of the Brothers of the Christian Schools, was that of the Czech Protestant Bishop, John Amos Komensky (Comenius). Long before Comenius visited England in 1641 his fame as a classical teacher was known all over Europe. But in so far as all new ideas have roots and sources, Comenius was anticipated, as he himself made clear, by two Catholic scholars, one an Irishman and a Jesuit, the other an English layman: William Bathe (Bateus) and Dr. Joseph Webbe.

William Bathe had been brought up a Protestant in Ireland, but was converted to Rome by his tutor, and went to Oxford. Thence, 'weary at the heresy' as Anthony à Wood says of him, he crossed to the Low Countries, became a Jesuit at Courtrai, and after higher studies at Louvain and Padua was made rector of the Irish College at Salamanca in Spain. Of his six major works three dealt with Christian doctrine, one with music and two with Latin. Of these last, his *Janua Linguarum* of 1611 ran into twenty editions, one of them in eight languages. Its English edition appeared soon after 1611. The other book on language-teaching, *Mercurius Bilinguis*, did not appear until 1659.

[1] Dodd, iii. 74.

Comenius wrote later, of his own *Janua* (1633), that

it was published with a slight change of title. For I had been advised by someone that there was already extant such a book, containing the whole of the Latin language, called *Janua Linguarum*, the work of Irish monks [*sic*]; but when I had seen it, I perceived it to be written without orderly arrangement of the materials. . . .

Bathe's work, moreover, was intended primarily as a guide for the Catholic missionaries in the New World, in learning the native languages and teaching the Indians Latin. Its author died in 1614, aged fifty, at Madrid.[1] Comenius was not actually indebted, then, to Bathe. With Dr. Webbe he had no personal contact either.

Joseph Webbe, his other precursor, is a vague figure. The year of his birth is not known, nor are his universities, but his M.D. and Ph.D. may have been Padua. His first book, published in Rome in 1612, was an astrological treatise. In 1623 he was living in London, alongside the Old Bailey, where he ran a school, in which he tried out his 'new gayme way to learne languages, and by this occasion may inveigle disciples'.[2] Foster Watson, the historian of the grammar schools, endorsed Webbe's colloquial method of teaching languages, 'from clauses to wholes', and deplored the obscurity into which he had fallen.[3] In 1622 Webbe published, as his contribution to the 'grammar war', an *Appeal to Truth in the Controversy between Art and Verse*, and next year a *Petition to the High Court of Parliament in the Behalf of Auncient and Authentique Authors*. It was in the latter tract that he asked for a monopoly from James I for the right to use his method in schools.

These two men, Bathe and Webbe, were not the only Catholic classicists on the fringe of the English scene. Francis Hawkins, who became a Jesuit in 1649, translated from the French a classic manual of manners, *Youth's Behaviour*, which ran into four editions in five years. (In 1657 Israel Tonge, later to be the inspirer of Titus Oates' plot, was using the Jesuit methods in teaching Latin grammar to his own boys at Durham College, a newly-founded rival to the two older universities.)[4]

[1] For Bathe see Wood, *Athenae Oxon* (ed. Bliss), ii. 146; R. F. Young, *Comenius in England*, 27 and note, 61; Backer, *Ecrivains Jésuits*, i. 446; Foley, vii. 41; *Irish Eccles. Record*, x. 524–7; T. Corcoran, *Studies in Hist. of Classical Teaching* (1911); and *D.N.B.*

[2] Gee, *Foot out of the Snare.*

[3] *English Grammar Schools to 1660*, 285. See also W. H. Widgery, *The Teaching of Languages in Schools*, 21ff.; Foley, i. 683; and *D.N.B.* Webbe's manuscript letters and papers are in Brit. Mus., *Sloane MSS.* 1456—*not* the reference in *D.N.B.*

[4] See Gillow, iii. 190–1; Foster Watson, 112; J. Marks, *Sir Edmund Berry Godfrey*, 7.

But the Catholic impact on academic circles at home in England by direct personal and friendly exchange was to remain slight. The main currents were overseas indefinitely, where by the time of the Restoration in 1660 (according to a report sent from the *Venerabile* to Cardinal Barberini) fifty of their 410 priests so far sent to England had published books of controversy.[1]

We find a Jesuit admitted to the College of Advocates and living in Doctors' Commons (Thomas Reade); and another erecting a famous 'Dial' in Whitehall Palace and writing a treatise on the barometer and a refutation of attempts to square the circle, and enjoying controversy with Sir Isaac Newton on the subject of light (Francis Line). We find a Benedictine becoming the first philosopher to reduce 'the system of Descartes to the method of the Schools' (Anthony Bonaventure Le Grand). We find among the Catholic converts one of the first men to attempt dramatic music for the English stage (Matthew Locke, 1675).[2] But they are happy exceptions to the pattern of their day.

3. CATHOLIC SCHOOLS UNDER JAMES I

A major reason why the official Government sources of the period are unsatisfactory guides to clandestine recusant schoolmastering and tutoring, quite apart from their incompleteness and patchiness, is that so much that was prosecuted was listed under the general heading of Recusancy and not particularized.[3]

The one reliable 'regional survey' of Catholics at the beginning of the Stuart period, Peacock's *Yorkshire Catholics of 1604*, furnishes no fewer than thirty schoolmasters and tutors in that one shire alone in that year, of whom six were in Sheffield.[4] The recusancy of some of

[1] Brady, *Hierarchy*, iii. 104.

[2] Gillow, v. 399, iv. 253, 189, 294.

[3] Cf. the London Sessions Records, *C.R.S.* xxiv.

[4] The thirty are: Geo. Egleshame, M.D. of Louvain, tutor to the children of Sir Thomas Revesby at Triburgh; John Holland, William Sampson, Nicholas Beete, Richard Horner, Robert Geslyn and John Batley at Sheffield, Robert Wadeforth and Gregory Slater at Kirkby; Laurence Tailor and Stephen Morrell at Burnfall; Richard Hindle at Gargrave; Richd. Bowden at Thornton; William Brigg at Bolton; William King, Robert Bourne and Christopher Tailor at Slaidbourne, Richd. Lilburne at Fenton (and lately at Kirkby Wharf); Henry Lewis and one Bond at Ripon; Francis Borwick, a poor man teaching reading and writing at Mynskip; John Chapman and his wife at Dacre Pasture; John Whitfield, a music teacher at York; William Mease, tutor to Mr. John Girlington of Hackforth, at Hornby; Gerard Ffawden, tutor to Francis Tunstall's children at Barringham; Christopher Newstead, 'parish teacher' at Hutton Bonville; William Postgate, who kept a school for recusants' children in his daughter's house at

them is queried, and no safe generalizations as to the whole country could be made from the evidence for Yorkshire alone. But that evidence does impugn the value of the contemporary *Recusant Rolls*, which give only two schoolmasters in the whole of the rest of the country.[1]

There is eloquent testimony of the unevenness of the regular Anglican diocesan inquiries also. A Hereford search at Christmas 1604 revealed only two schoolmasters,[2] and the total of recusants for all Wiltshire was given in 1610–11 as only fifty-four, concentrated round the five families of Stourton, Biggs, Cuddington (Corrington), Mayo and Legat.[3]

Widespread outward conformity is of course the explanation of so many of the discrepancies. Typical of many cases is the master of the Royal Grammar School at Abergavenny at this very time, Morgan Lewis. He had five children. He himself conformed, and kept his post even after the House of Commons got on to his track in 1624. His wife brought up their four daughters as Catholics. The son, David, passed through his father's school and then went to the *Venerabile* in Rome, to become a Jesuit and end up as one of the Welsh martyrs, executed at Usk during the Titus Oates plot in 1679.[4]

This kind of episode lends added point to the special clauses about married *women* recusants in the Act of 1605. It was so easy for a man to conform, have his children taught their Catholic faith by his wife, and stultify the effects of the laws as well as fooling the Exchequer. The General Assembly of the Church of Scotland was studying the same feminine loophole.[5] On the other hand, the correlative of special

Egton; Lucy Scaife at Huntington; Cuthbert Belton, tutor to Ralph Creswell at Nunkerling; and William Reynolds at Spofforth. See Edward Peacock, *A List of Roman Catholics in the County of York in 1604, transcribed from the original manuscript* (Rawlinson MS., B. 452) *in the Bodleian Library* (1872), *passim.* Another Yorkshire lay schoolmaster at the time, not mentioned by Peacock, is Thomas Aske (*alias* Oldcastle), at Risby in Rowley Parish, convicted 1605.

[1] P.R.O., *Recusant Rolls*, 12 (Ap. 1604), 14 (Ap. 1605). The men are Henry Coppinger at Wiggenhall St. Mary, Norfolk, and Henry Hemos at 'Wyersdall' in Lancashire.

[2] Richard Hipson (*alias* Siloe) at Welsh Newton, and Richard Jepson. See *C.R.S.* ii. 293f.

[3] *Hist. MSS. Comm.*, Wilts. Quarter Sessions MS., i. 83.

[4] Gillow, iv. 205. The *Responsa* of David Lewis are in *C.R.S.* lv. 461. And see p. 302 below.

[5] Bellesheim, iii. 401 for 'certain women who tacks upon them to bring up the youth in reading, sewing and uther exercises in schools, under pretext and cullour whereof traffiquing Papists, Jesuits and seminarie priests has their appointed tymes of meeting, at the tyme they catechize and pervert the youth in their growing and tender age'.

severity for some was special indulgence for others. Lady Mary Lovel on entering a convent at Brussels in 1609 besought no less a person than Lord Salisbury (Robert Cecil) himself to look after her children: which he did.[1]

Moreover, schoolmasters could still manifestly hang on for long periods. We find William Allen presented at the Nottingham Sessions in October 1623, and an ejectment order issued against him, for 'keeping a writing schole' in the parish of St. Mary, 'for that he is a recusant'—and again presented fifteen years later.[2] More impressive still, Hugh Powell, who first came to light teaching in Brecon School about 1620, 'a very learned man, and one who had suffered much for his religion', managed to continue in his post till Cromwell's Triers ejected him over thirty years later.[3] Much depended, as in the crisis of the first *Recusant Roll* inquiries earlier, and in the solidly Catholic parts of the country all through, upon local personal relationships. This indeed is surely how it came about that in the North, at Preston, a small thatched building off Friargate, opened as a Catholic chapel, in the very year of the Gunpowder Plot, was to enjoy discreet continuity right down to the building of St. Mary's chapel in 1761.[4]

By the same token, when in 1619 there were reported to be 'Romish rangers' abroad in Essex, priests prosyletizing all over the extensive parish of Stamford Rivers, the rector Richard Montague found the local atmosphere such that the most appropriate method of tackling them was to challenge them to debate (on three propositions in theology).[5] In Northumberland there was actually a spiritual retreat-house built for hunted priests from elsewhere, at the instigation of Dorothy Lowson and with a ceremonial laying of the foundation-stone by Richard Holtby, S.J.[6]

But of all the 'evasions' that have come to light during the reign of James I the most enduring is that at Scarisbrick in Lancashire, where Catholics today can claim a tradition of schooling hardly broken since indeed the Elizabethan settlement.

Scarisbrick, a few miles from Ormskirk, boasts a pre-Reformation chapel in its Hall, licensed for Mass by the Bishop of Lichfield in 1447.

[1] P.R.O., *Flanders Corresp.* vii. 34; *S.P. Dom. Jas. i*, lviii. No. 2; Foley, iii. 518; Guilday, 360–1.

[2] *Nottingham Borough Records*, iv. 384, v. 192.

[3] Foley, vi. 321; T. Richards, *Hist. of the Puritan Movement in Wales*, 265–6.

[4] Blundell, *Old Cath. Lancs.*, ii. 137. The registers of the Preston chapel were burnt in 1768.

[5] Cf. Gordon Albion, *Charles I and the Court of Rome*, 182 note.

[6] C. 1622. See Gillow, iv. 162–3.

Throughout penal times Scarisbrick Hall continued as a centre of Catholicism, its owners sometimes outwardly conforming and sometimes not. The Scarisbrick family enshrines also the tradition of those with whom it inter-married: the Barlows and the Bradshaighs. Its list of priests, most of them Jesuits, has been reconstructed, almost unbroken since 1618, from the books they left behind them in the library at the Hall.

Under Elizabeth there had been a Catholic school at Scarisbrick run by Humphrey Cartwright, an M.A. of Cambridge, who crossed to Douay in 1576 and returned ordained in May 1579. His school at Scarisbrick did not endure for long. In 1582–3 he was brought up at Gloucester quarter sessions and sent to Salford gaol, where he was still lying ten years later. The entry about him in the prison list of January 1584 says that 'he became a papist in the Lord Buckhurst House. Being bayled out of the Gatehouse forfeited his bond and went to Rheims having been over before at Douay and there made deacon. Became a schoolmaster to Mr. Stopford's children in Lancashire'.[1]

But however shortlived Cartwright's school at Scarisbrick under Elizabeth, there is evidence from 1618 or thereabouts of a school in the neighbourhood running intermittently, and for long periods, well into the eighteenth century. In all probability it owed nothing to the first of the series of Jesuit priests listed by Blundell—Michael Alford (Griffiths)—since he does not appear to have arrived in England till 1629, and then lived in Leicestershire and not Lancashire.

Periods which have been suggested for the undoubted activity of this school are: 1618, 1628 till possibly 1639, 1648–52 and thence probably till 1679, 1698–1700, 1703 and possibly 1723. One of the scholars' books surviving, used by Edward Molyneux, bears the date 1639. Two others of the books belonged to boys being taught there in 1650: Thomas Banister and John Alcocks. Henry Lodge, who entered the English College at Rome in 1659, aged twenty-two, had also probably been schooled at Scarisbrick with his brothers. John Plessington, who went to Valladolid in 1650, aged twenty-three, had likewise come from 'the Jesuit school at Scarisbrick'. But the priest there, in the parish, from 1655 till 1680, was a secular, Christopher Bradshaigh.[2]

[1] *Douay Diaries* (Knox); *S.P. Dom.* lxvii, Nos. 40–1, and clxvii, No. 59; Blundell, *Old Cath. Lancs.*, iii. 169; *V.C.H. Lancs.*, iii. 324.

[2] Gillow, v. 322; Blundell, iii; *C.R.S.* xxx. 169 and note; Foley, v. 352, from *Blundell MSS.*

When the Lancashire recusants were listed in 1668 and 1671, three schoolmasters amongst those convicted came from this neighbourhood: Richard Norcrosse of Lathom, Ormskirk; John Bradley of Claughton, Garstang; and Henry Robinson of Broughton.[1] The region was still a solid Catholic enclave.

It is an index of how widespread the laws were being by-passed, and of how far Parliament was dissatisfied with even the Privy Council and the bishops under James I, that the Commons in their angry session of 1624 made time to deal with papist schoolmasters in person, by having them up before the Committee for Religion

One was Morgan Lewis of Abergavenny, whom we have already met. They could hardly dismiss him (a conformer) but they admonished him to 'catechize his scholars as by law required'. Likewise the second one, John Claydon. The third, Simon Dormer, master of Eye Grammar School in Suffolk, irked them most of all. He was petitioned against on 5 May. On the 20th, as the Bishop of Norwich had made no move to curb him, the House itself resolved that he was unfit to continue as schoolmaster, and 'this business' should be presented to the Archbishop of Canterbury, especially since Dormer 'confessed he had not received the Communion these five years before; hath some scholars which went to church before their coming to him but not sithence; maintaineth and sweareth his Popish tenets; catechiseth not; no prayers in his house'. He was accordingly removed.[2]

It was painfully apparent that the law could not convict all the men found. When the Parliament of 1625 hauled up four—from Lancashire, Buckinghamshire, St. Clether in Cornwall and York—the last of these 'had 56 scholars of which there were 36 papists'. But he was a licensed schoolmaster, the secret being that his licence came from an official 'who hath the keepynge of the scole duringe his life, without privitie of the Arch Bishoppe'.[3]

The treatment of discovered masters thus varied widely, from

[1] *B.M. Add. MSS.* 20, 739; pp. 97, 311; *C.R.S.* vi. 37, 104, 178, 282.

[2] For these cases see *Commons Journal*, i. 707, 783, 792, 852, 869 (28 Apr.–24 May); and *V.C.H. Suffolk*, ii. 338. It is probable that the 'Catholic master in Monmouthshire' who taught Thomas Carpenter (who recorded the fact on his entry into the English College, Rome, in 1625—*C.R.S.* iv. 379, and Foley, vi. 308) was Morgan Lewis of Abergavenny. All three—Lewis, Claydon and Dormer—were before the Commons again a year later; and see *S.P. Dom. Charles I*, clxxviii, Nos. 43 and 100 (1629) for Eye and Yaxley as a 'Jesuit' area.

[3] *Camden Soc.* vi. 26; Hastings, 377. In Cornwall in 1630 there was also a classical school (at Ratallock), kept by the recusant John Coode.

imprisonment, through dismissal and bail, to mere admonishment. So did the fortunes of the boys they trained for export to the colleges.

'Three boys and children, being taken going beyond sea, to be in some priory there, were by the High Commission Court, about Michaelmas last (1620), released for twenty pounds in money, upon bond, that they should not go beyond sea; which yet they did contrary to their bond, and are there now friars.' Some even bought themselves off and disappeared underground again, as one pursuivant, Harrison, reveals in his complaints about the felonies of other pursuivants in and before 1621: 'They tooke Mistress Smithes schoolmaster for a priest and let him escape for 150 *li*'—and they released another schoolmaster for £36.[1] These figures, even allowing for unctuous exaggeration, imply wealthy patrons and high devotion.

In the last resort, there was shelter and protection to be had in the half-dozen Catholic chapels of the foreign embassies in London. Two of the religious orders got a footing in Jacobean England, and one of them, the Carmelites, used this means.

The Carmelite mission was re-started, from exile in Belgium, by Fr. Simon Stock (namesake of the greatest Englishman of the order in medieval times—d. 1265), late of the English College in Rome. He came to England to open a house and so avoid the necessity of novitiates abroad—an audacious hope in penal times as they were. The nuncio's purpose in encouraging him was partly to secure reliable reports from England on how the laity felt on the question of a bishop as against an archpriest. Fr. Simon (Thomas Doughty) arrived in England in 1615, and the mission was recognized by Rome three years later. Its two leaders, Simon Stock himself and Eliseus (William Pendryck), lived mostly under the protection of the Embassy Chapels in London.[2]

This Carmelite mission is historically important as being the earliest attempt, apart from the Jesuits, to found a school for 'interns' on home soil by any of the revived religious orders of men. They opened a school in Herefordshire during the Commonwealth, in the hope of finding vocations. From this school the postulants went on to the Carmelite novitiates in Flanders, Paris, Rome and Venice.

[1] Account given to the Commons by the renegade Catholic Jo. Kendall, quoted in Tyrwhitt, *Jnl. of Sir E. Nicholas*, ii. 77; Alford Papers, *Harleian MSS.* 6803, f. 174; quoted in Notestein, vii. 599ff.

[2] Guilday, i. 348f. The Bavarian Embassy chapel was in Warwick St.; the Sardinian adjoined Lincoln's Inn Fields; the Spanish was in 'Spanish Place' off Baker Street. See J. H. Harting, *Catholic London Missions* (1903).

The other order to secure a bridgehead on home soil is the most famous of the seventeenth century—the 'female Jesuitesses' of Mistress Mary Ward.

This is not the place to set down the history of Mary Ward's 'Institute of the Blessed Virgin Mary'; nor of her educational work in detail.[1] What is of significance here is that this resolute and devoted Yorkshire woman, whose persistence amid adversity from without and resignation under bans from within were hardly to be equalled till the unhappy career of John Henry Newman over three centuries later, came to work in England in 1618. She had found her vocation at St. Omer as early as 1605; she had set up a convent for English Poor Clares (Franciscan nuns) outside Gravelines, of which the Government had immediately got wind; and in 1609, determined on a double mission, of education as well as contemplation, she had established her 'Institute', with five other women. Recruits were so numerous that filiations had to be formed; by 1630 there were a dozen houses with schools for English girls. These 'Mary Ward Schools' were not the first, for the Daughters of St. Agnes at St. Omer and elsewhere (1601), the Daughters of Notre Dame at Tournai (1598) and a community of women in Brussels (1600) were already teaching; to say nothing of the Ursulines (1537) and the Oblates of Torre di Specchi in Rome. Mary Ward's foundations were remarkable rather for the extent to which they provided *elementary* education, and for the *furore* caused inside the Church by the revolutionary character of her apostolate.

In both her day schools (for local) and boarding schools (for English girls) she demanded a freedom from conventual rule unknown since the early days of the Ursulines two generations before. Hence the cry of 'uncloistered clerics' and female Jesuits. For nuns living in community to be non-enclosed was a breach of the Tridentine decrees. For them to teach girls along the lines the Jesuits used for boys was also a breach of Trent. The religious orders of women were bound to take their pedagogical cue from the local bishop. For them to encourage dramatic productions in their school was horrifying. The catalogue of these and other irregularities was not complete till a few years before the suppression of the Institute in 1630, by which time Vatican documents were describing the venture succinctly as 'devout women

[1] For Mary Ward see the two-volume biography by M. E. C. Chambers (1885); M. Oliver, *Mary Ward* (1959); Guilday, chapter vi. For her educational work see W. J. Battersby, *Educ. Work of the Relig. Orders of Women.* The Government's first knowledge of her activities is in P.R.O., *Flanders Corresp.* ix. 1608–10, pp. 604–5.

gathered into little groups, living in common with no vows, under individual Jesuit direction'. Her backers included an impressive number of archdukes, nuncios and bishops, and many English priests wrote in her support. But her imitation of Jesuit methods was disliked; her refusal to adopt the rule of any of the other four female teaching orders was considered capricious and insubordinate; her cult of lay dress gave widespread offence; and before long, such was her notoriety, even the archpriest and his seculars, and the English Jesuits, were for once in agreement, against her.

Her own defence was practical. The girls sent to her from England might find vocations; but many of them would return home to marry, 'there to maintain what they have received'. A female was no less logical than a male Jesuit rule: the Canons of Trent on enclosure had not foreseen female teaching orders, but that must not be suffered to weaken the Church by 'inhibiting schools'. Above all, her apostolate *must* be 'active', since it lay among split families and untended orphans, and she desired 'to enable women to aid, as far as possible, in the conversion of England'. All this she put into a memorial to Pope Urban VIII in January 1616, which was duly approved. Five years later she went to Rome in person to see Gregory XV. This was the beginning of her fall. Her costume scandalized the Romans; by 1630 detraction and calumny did the rest.

Her visit to England in 1618 produced no immediate institutional results. It did, however, sow the seeds. To avoid the pursuivants she travelled about in fashionable dress, she visited the imprisoned priests in Wisbech Castle, and she drew up a plan of educational action for her English Institute on English soil. The work did indeed spread, from London to various Catholic centres. But her enduring monuments at home, the Bar Convent School at York and the school in 'Pope's Corner' (Hammersmith), had to await both her own restoration and that of the Stuarts.[1] There is no evidence available of any sort of Catholic school in England expressly for girls until a plan of the Franciscan nuns in 1638.[2]

Mary Ward's importance for the future lay in what she symbolized. Educationally it was essential that teaching-nuns should be freed from the rule of enclosure. An enclosed nun, so tempted to visualize all her

[1] Cf. Chambers, i. 185, ii. ch. 2; and p. 226 below.

[2] The principal schools of the other English nuns in exile were those of the Austin Canonesses of St. Monica at Louvain (1609); the Benedictines at Brussels (1609 or earlier), Ghent (1624), Pontoise (1659), and Dunkirk (1662); the Carmelites at Antwerp (1619).

pupils as novices, destined for the stern discipline of her own life, might not be resilient enough in educating the mothers of families. On the other hand, while the Trent decrees held fast they had to be obeyed.

The clandestine schools traceable in England during the first quarter of the seventeenth century can be listed. From the evidence adduced above it should be clear that they are of course a fraction of the real total. The forty-two that have been documented are the following:

Abergavenny (c. 1624), Bolton, Yorks (1604), Brecon (c. 1620), Burnfall, Yorks (1604), Chideock, Dorset (since before 1600), Dacre Pasture, Yorks (1604), Stanley Grange, Derbyshire (before 1621), Egton, Yorks (1604), Eye, Suffolk (c. 1624), Fenton, Yorks (1604), Gargrave, Yorks (1604), Garstang, Lancs (before 1625), Holland, Lancs (1607), Huntington, Yorks (1604), Hutton Bonville, Yorks (1604), Ilton, Yorks (1619), Kirkby Ravensworth, Yorks (1624), Kirkby Wharf, Yorks (1604), Knaresborough, Yorks (after 1600), Loughborough, Yorks (1614), London (writing-master, c. 1610), London (Holborn, 1605), London (Old Bailey, 1623), 'The Mannor' (c. 1618), Masham, Yorks (1619), Minship, Yorks (1604), Nottingham (1623), Pately Bridge, Yorks (1604), Richmond, Yorks (1623), Risby, Yorks (1605), St. Chalher, Cornwall (1625), Scarisbrick (c. 1618 and intermittently for over a century), Sheffield (1604), Slaidburne, Yorks (1604), Spofforth, Yorks (1604), Swine, Yorks (1615), Thornton, Yorks (1604), Welsh Newton, Herefordshire (1604), Wiggenhall St. Mary, Norfolk (1604), Wyresdale, Lancs (1605), York (1604), York (Ouse Bridge Prison, 1610).[1]

4. BEFORE THE CIVIL WAR

Catholic London, under the very eyes of Council and Parliament, continued to show the same daring that had ventured, towards the end of Elizabeth's days, to place copies of Campion's *Decem Rationes* in the choir-stalls of St. Paul's Cathedral. Despite the names of recusant printers identified for the Government by Gee in his *Foot Out of the Snare*, the Bibles from Douay flowed in steadily, and while discreet persons followed the line of the titular Duke of Northumberland (Sir

[1] My *Biographical Catalogue of Catholic Schoolmasters at Work in England from 1558 to 1700* (*Recusant Hist.*, 1964) has an Index of Places, with cross-references from each place to the masters concerned.

Robert Dudley), who went to write and print his *Catholicon* in Italy, some were bold enough to print a *Life of Our Lady* in London; and others to publish an edition of *The Behaviour of Youth*, a Jesuit manual on education.[1]

In Pope's Head Alley, near Lombard Street, lived the stationer Henry Overton, who managed to keep going for decades, though sometimes on the windy side of the law. Twenty or thirty popish books, said his charge-sheet in 1630, 'were left at his shop by a strange porter, most of which he sold to persons coming to his stall, and the rest he brought into court'. He denied knowledge of the author or printer. Some two months since, two men had come and demanded money for these books. He asked who had sent them. 'They said that was all one.' And though, soon after this, the Commons charged him anew, with the unlicensed printing of a subtle book entitled *Rome's Ruin*, he was still at large in 1643 and issuing a newsletter.[2]

It fell to John Seldon, in his *Table Talk* after the final collapse of James II, to put the neatest gloss on this Catholic book-trade in London:

> Popish books teach and inform; what we know, we know much out of them. The Fathers, Church story, Schoolmen, all may pass for Popish books, and if you take away them, what learning do you leave? . . . These Puritan preachers, if they have any things good, they have it out of Popish books, though they will not acknowledge it.[3]

It was also the London of the schoolmaster-dramatist, James Shirley, whose success in England was not dimmed by the fact that he was a papist. He was an old Merchant Taylor, and an Anglican parson. His conversion to Rome cost him his headmastership of St. Albans School (1623–4). During the Civil War he returned to London and opened a school at Whitefriars, where he 'not only gained a comfortable subsistence but educated many ingenious youths', among them

[1] 1635 and 1640 respectively. Gillow, iv. 56; *C.R.S.* i. 109.

[2] *Cal. S.P. Dom. Chas. I*, cxlii, No. 20 (3 March 1630). The recusant printer Robert Gurney was also operating in London about 1632 (ccxxix, No. 131).

[3] Quoted in Mullinger, ii. 513. This book-trade continued unbroken. In the summer of 1676 Turner of Holborn Turnstile had his shop searched and nine popish books brought to light, and Anthony Lawrence came before the Privy Council for printing *The Great Sacrifice of the New Law*, a warrant from the Lord Chamberlain of the Queen's Household availing him nothing. Another, by name Dates, functioned in a joiners' shop in St. Alban's Street. Even Protestant printers would take risks. Nathaniel Thompson went to Newgate in 1684 for printing popish books—'a mercenary fellow for any side that pays him well'. See *Cal. S.P. Dom. Charles II*, 1676–7, pp. 138, 237; 1684–5, pp. 183, 187, 224, 228; *Hist. MSS. Comm.*, Duke of Leeds MSS., xi, pt. 7 of appdx., p. 17 (1887–8).

the antiquarian Thomas Dingley. Shirley's ushers at the Whitefriars school were a young Scot, David Whitford, who taught Greek, and John Leckonby, later jailed for hearing Mass and for being a recusant schoolmaster.

During the lulls in the penal laws London was a not unduly difficult centre in which to operate. In the first decade of the Restoration a school was kept fairly openly, off Jermyn Street, by a Scot, Alexander Gordon, for some six years. For greater safety his wife petitioned for an order to the Bishop of London, about 1669, to license a 'Protestant and conformable' schoolmaster to teach in the house of her husband, 'and for leave that her husband, though a Roman Catholic, may teach under him'.[1]

But what alarmed the Commons was the London Jesuits. There was

> a house taken by the Jesuits (at Newington) and kept by two women, who had three or four young children who were thought to be of good sort, and brought up by these women under the government of the priests. There was a fair Massing furniture found in the house, and all things thereto belonginge. A priest was in the house when the messengers entered, but escaped their hand.

This was 1626. The upshot was that one of the women was arrested, but a letter came from the Treasurer of the Household of the Catholic queen (Henrietta Maria) and she was set free[2]—only for the House to find, within a year, that this modest academy for children 'of good sort' at Newington was cover for something vastly more dangerous. For there came the startling discovery of the Jesuit 'College at Clerkenwell'.

What was most shattering about this place was the revelation that it had been quietly functioning for some five years. The Society had had a 'quasi-novitiate' out at Enfield Chase since the constitution of the English Province. Banking on the coming lull, during the French marriage negotiations of 1624, they had moved it in on London, first to Edmonton, then to Camberwell (1625), and at last in 1627 to the house of the Earl of Shrewsbury 'at the corner of the Broadway, above Clerkenwell'. A multitude of Fathers gathered here in March 1628, for a novena of prayer leading up to the Feast of St. Joseph on the 17th. The unprecedented orders for provisions started rumours; tradesmen gave these currency; and on 15 March the house was raided.

The haul of persons was rich, and of documents richer still, in that

[1] *Hist. MSS. Comm.*, *Leybourne Popham Papers*, Dr. Clarke's Diary, p. 260; *Cal. S.P. Dom. Chas. II*, cclxx, No. 29.

[2] Secretary Coke to Lord Conway, 5 Aug. 1626, in *C.R.S.* i, 96.

it proved the stages of a concerted plan to establish a novitiate in the capital, revealed the accounts audited by the provincial (Richard Bankes), and included papers on seeking relief for the college at St. Omer. The historian of the whole episode, J. G. Nichols, says of these documents that they 'throw far less discredit upon the Jesuits than they do upon the unworthy statecraft with which it was attempted to convert the "Discovery" into an engine of political influence upon the Parliament'. The engineer was Sir John Coke. The arrested Jesuits lay in Newgate till December, when three of them were indicted for being priests, and one was condemned to death on this count but reprieved. All this in turn was debated when the Commons reassembled for the New Year, and the House was engaged on it till the much more shattering episode of Speaker Finch and the Petition of Right (2 March) drove it from their major preoccupations.[1]

With Parliament in abeyance after 1629 for the eleven years of the king's personal rule, the other spectacular searches and suppressions on record are the work of the Privy Council. Three of them in particular, during the year 1635, are worth recounting for the procedure they so graphically illustrate. They are quite distinct from the individual cases under Council warrants and wardship disposals that had continued at intervals since the original case of the Worthington boys in 1584, for they involved disposing of the population of three whole schools.[2]

[1] *Camden Misc.*, ii. 64 (1852), iv. 10 (1859). Cf. the Government's tactics over the Gunpowder Plot earlier and the Popish Plot later. In addition to Nichols the sources for the Clerkenwell affair are mainly W. J. Pink, *Hist. of Clerkenwell* (1865), 258–67; Jesuit *Letters and Notices*, liv. 47ff. (1939), for the site; J. G. McLeod, in *Month*, xxxi. 220 (1887); Foley, i. 97–141; *Hist. MSS. Comm. 4th Report*, p. 596 (1874); *Cal. S.P. Dom. Chas. I*, xcvi, No. 8 (names); xcix (Sir John Coke's account); c, No. 41; cxxxv, No. 40; *C.R.S.* i. 104; and Notestein, *Debates of 1629*, 249. Before the middle of the century, and apparently unknown to the Government, the Jesuits founded a 'parish' just off Lincoln's Inn Fields; Mass was said 'in the house of a widow on the left-hand side of Duke Street'. Cf. J. H. Harting, *Catholic London Missions*, 2, 9.

[2] Charles I despite his leniency, when he was under pressure from Parliament in 1628 told the Court of Wards, through its Master, Sir Robert Naunton, that the wardship over Christopher Lord Teynham had been asked for by Mary Lady Teynham, Henry Earl of Worcester and Lord Petre, but that all three of these, as recusants, were incapable, and that he had therefore conferred the wardship on Mr. Secretary Conway, who would pay the usual fine and rent involved. As to the other device, disposal by Privy Council order, two earls in Scotland lost the custody of their own children in 1628. The Earl of Huntly was ordered to appear before the Council to witness the 'sequestration' of his daughters 'for their better breeding and instruction in the grounds of the true religion'; and the Earl of Angus was told to commit his son, James Douglas, to the Principal of Edinburgh University (Dr. Adamson) 'for the settling of his religious doubts'. See *Cal. S.P. Dom. Chas. I*, 1628–9, 419; and Bellesheim, iv. 17, 24.

The first school discovered in this busy year 1635, in Derbyshire, was in Jesuit hands. In July 1635 the Privy Council instructed a messenger, Lumley, that they had been apprised of 'a school kept at the house of Mrs. Anne Vaux, called Stanley Grange, co. Derby, where sons of persons of quality are brought up under the tutelage of the Jesuits'. This was the Vaux family which had kept a small school in its house at Harrowden, Northants, in the time of Fr. John Gerard before 1600. The messenger was

to repair to the said house and there to apprehend any Jesuits, and bring them to be examined, with all such children as he shall find there; and, if the children be dispersed, to inform himself whose sons they were, how long they were there, and where they now remain; as also to seize upon all books, papers and massing-stuff, and locking them up in a chest cause them also to be sent up.

Lumley was favoured enough to find the school in full swing, at Stanley Grange, six miles outside Derby. He reported that the boys there included Lord Abergavenny's grandchild, a Mr. Fossiter's son and eleven or twelve more. He added that a similar school existed near Wolverhampton, at the House of 'Mr. Luson'.[1]

The Jesuit *Annual Letters* state that the priest and pupils were roughly handled in the search before being taken to London. Two chests of books were seized, as well as religious articles. The priest was clapped into prison. Subsequently the boys were restored to their parents.

From the evidence available we are able to trace the career of this school, and its purpose as a preparatory school for the Continent. The *Annual Letters*, which give it as founded in 1633, are wrong. Not only had Fr. William Wright, S.J., who founded the Derby and Leicestershire mission, ruled it for twelve years before he died in 1639, which makes it inherently probable that the school had been running more than two years when it was discovered, but one of the boys, Edward Thimbleby, was at it as early as 1626. He was a Lancastrian, taken as a baby to Leicestershire by his grandmother, Mrs. Eleanor Brookesby, reared there by Fr. William Wright and put by him into the Vaux house at Stanley Grange for four years (1626–9), 'under the tuition of several Fathers of the Society of Jesus'.[2]

[1] *Cal. S.P. Dom. Chas. I*, ccxiv, No. 74; ccxix, No. 36—Report of Lumley's information by Edward Nicholson, Clerk to the Privy Council, 8 Oct. Also Foley, ii. 316–17.

[2] His *Responsa* at the Ven. Eng. Coll. Rome (1636) are in *C.R.S.* lv. 448–50.

Oddly enough, the Government had discovered the school themselves as early as that, and had evidently forgotten the fact. A report of the Secretary of State, Sir John Coke, towards the end of 1625, tells how

> At Stanley Grange, a house standing alone in Appletree Hundred, the doors were at first shut against us, but after a little while opened, where we found only two women in the house, who gave us to understand that the Grange House belonged to one Mrs. Vause, a farmer thereof to Mrs. Powtrell of West Hallam, dwelling within a quarter of a mile of the said Grange, both the one and the other being notorious recusants. Upon search of the said house we found so many rooms and chambers as I have never seen in so small a content of ground, and amongst other there was two chapels, one opening into the other, and in either of them a table set to the upper end for an altar, and stools and cushions laid as though they had been lately at mass. Over the altar there were crucifixes set, and other pictures about it. There were *beds and furniture for them in that little house to lodge 40 or 50 persons at the least.*[1]

From that report it was clearly a flourishing school fully ten years before the Council fell upon it.

We can in fact push it back to 1621, from the mission lists of the Jesuits, under the brothers Gervase and Germanus Pole. In 1625 George Lovett is listed; in 1633 Francis Johnson is added, with two others—Robert D'Arcy who 'modo docet Gram' till he went to London three years later, and Michael Gray who 'docet'. In 1636 Father D'Arcy is replaced by John Stafford, who is still teaching humanities as late as 1639, when the school had been surreptitiously reassembled. Father Sulyard is listed as 'Mag. Gram.' as late as 1645.[2] The school is thus authenticated from 1621, or even earlier, down to the middle of the Civil War.

The purpose at Stanley Grange is clear enough from the curriculum, which was Greek and Latin, and from the subsequent careers of its boys. Edward Thimbleby went on to St. Omer for four years and then to the English College, Rome, as a *convictor*. Later we find him not on

[1] 17 Nov. 1625 (Italics mine). *Hist. MSS. Comm.*, 12th Report, appdx., 1888, Earl Cowper MSS. at Melbourne Hall, Derbyshire, i. 226; also q. in J. C. Cox, *Three Centuries of Derbyshire Annals*, 284 (1890).

[2] The *Mission Lists* (copy at Farm St.) feature these eight men as follows: Geo. Lovett (b. 1582), 1625, 1633, 1636; Bro. Francis Johnson (b. 1582), 1633, 1636; Gervase Pole (b. 1581), 1621, 1633, 1636, 1639; Germ. Pole (b. 1578), 1621, 1633, 1636, 1639; Robert D'Arcy (b. 1588), 1633; Michael Gray (b. 1603), 1633; John Stafford (b. 1604), 1636, 1639 and till 1658; Andrew Sulyard (b. 1606), 1639, 1645.

the English mission but Provost of Cambray.[1] George Simeon, likewise, went to St. Omer and on to the English College, Rome, in 1645. He became a Jesuit.[2] Stanley Grange was manifestly a preparatory school for St. Omer.

The *Annual Letters* imply that its whereabouts had actually been betrayed to the Privy Council by an ex-pupil who had apostatized, and that after the raid the king himself intervened to prevent any further proceedings. If so, we have here the reason why in this case the boys were returned to their parents, and why the school did not in fact close.[3]

Whatever may be the truth about the king's intervention in this first case, the Privy Council went to the limit of its power in breaking up the second school they found, armed with a clue from Lumley's report on Stanley Grange that there was popish education going on 'near Wolverhampton, in the house of Mr. Luson'.

This was at Willenhall, the seat of the Levesons. The family were great benefactors to both Jesuits and Franciscans. They maintained a chaplaincy at Willenhall throughout penal times.[4] The original of the Stanley Grange search-warrant carries a marginal note in the hand of Mr. Secretary Coke that the same draft was used in ordering the search of Mr. Leveson's house soon afterwards.

How many boys were found here does not emerge, but a number of cases are well attested. Sir John Fitzherbert, of Norbury, Derbyshire, was made to give the Council an undertaking that the boy John Stanford, son of William Stanford, should be presented to the Bishop of Coventry and Lichfield, and the boy was given to be educated till further order by Sir John Persall, of Horseley, Staffordshire. John Blomfield, aged fourteen, was given to Sir Ralph Done, of Dutton, Cheshire, 'upon Sir Ralph's promise to see the said Blomfield brought up to the liking of the Lords, or else to remain with him as a servant'. Richard Wakeman, of Bickford, Gloucestershire, aged fifteen to sixteen, was handed to Sir Christopher Nevill, of Newton Sanclar, Somerset, 'on Sir Christopher's promise to place him in the University of Oxford'. William Andrew, of Denton, Northants, aged twelve, was handed to his Protestant uncle, Sir William Wilmer of Sywell. John Atwood, of Acton, Worcestershire, aged eleven, was given over

[1] *Fifth Douay Diary*, 538 (1667).

[2] *C.R.S.* lv. 490–1; Foley, i. 202, vii. 749.

[3] *Annual Letters*; and Foley, ii. 310; 312; viii. 749. For later events at Stanley Grange, see G. Anstruther, *Vaux of Harrowden*, 462.

[4] Gillow, iv. 201.

to Edward Newman of Gray's Inn, to be kept by him 'in his custody till further order be given for his education'.[1]

Among the boys who did not get into the Privy Council records was almost certainly Francis Fitter, born 1622, who said on his admission to the English College at Lisbon in 1640 that he had 'made his rudimentary studies at Wolverhampton'.[2] This suggests the conclusion that Willenhall also was a preparatory school for the colleges abroad, even though there is no conclusive proof that any of those captured by the pursuivant subsequently escaped from their new guardians, for none of these captured boys figures in the lists of Douay, Valladolid, Seville or St. Omer.

The presence of the school at Willenhall is not surprising, for the neighbourhood was as intensely Catholic, throughout the two centuries of penal times, as the Catholic parts of Lancashire. The difference is that some of the latter were more fortunate—witness the fair continuity of Catholic schooling at Scarisbrick from as early as 1618. The Wolverhampton papists were in trouble again from Cromwell's Council of State in the summer of 1654, when Sir John Worley and Captain John Stone were sent to quell 'meetings of Papists, Jesuits and ill-affected persons' there. For after all, not far away was the popish cell at Moseley Old Hall, where the Benedictine John Huddleston had started a school in 1650, whose boys watched from the windows while Charles II rested in the house on his flight after the Battle of Worcester. A generation later, the Wolverhampton recusants identified and listed included (of all persons) a gunsmith, John Pearson. And when the Jesuit John Gavan arrived in the district in 1671 he found it known locally as 'Little Rome'.[3]

The third school run to earth in 1635 was conducted by a layman, in Hampshire. He was William Hill, of Fareham, a popish recusant who, said the Court of High Commission in sentencing him, had 'taken upon him to educate at Fareham as a schoolmaster, presuming to teach them without any lawful licence, and that, upon search made, above twenty children, many of them gentlemen's sons, were discovered in his house kept secretly and never permitted to come to church. He had also entertained the two Frenchmen [charged with

[1] These orders are in *Cal. S.P. Dom. Chas. I*, ccciii, Nos. 73 and 88; cccv, Nos. 5, 70, 88.

[2] Croft and Gillow, *Lisbon College*, 197.

[3] *Cal. S.P. Dom.* 1654, lxxiv, p. 307; *C.R.S.* vi; Gillow, ii. 405. Fr. John Huddleston was the priest who subsequently received Charles II into the Catholic Church on his deathbed in 1685.

him], being Popish recusants, one under the pretence of instructing the children in the French language, and the other pretending that he came hither to learn English or to trade in merchandise.'

Hill appeared in the custody of a messenger (Wragg) on 16 April. He was remanded for examination, and until he should enter sureties of £1,000. The parents who sent children to his school were also to 'answer articles'. A fortnight later he was brought up again and examined, and ordered to reappear the following day for judgment. After postponements, and the hearing of his French assistants, judgment on all three was given, 'prout in acta' (according to the statute), on 18 June.

The Court actually 'fined Hill £2,000 to the King's use, and ordered him to stand committed till he make such submission as shall be prescribed'. He was 'further condemned in costs to be taxed next Court day, also disabled from teaching school in this kingdom, and committed to the Gatehouse till he give sufficient bond to perform the order of the Court'. As to the two Frenchmen, Amith Herbyn was 'adjudged a practitioner with Hill against Church and State and the religion here established, and was fined £100 to the King's use'. Nicholas Baillot was committed to the Gatehouse and condemned in costs.

From that point on the record loses direction. Hill's fabulous fine was respited at intervals, from 23 June till the following 18 February, at which date the account in the *State Papers* apparently drops him.[1]

William Hill had a son Augustine, who had not yet entered the Fareham school (he was only two years of age when the search was made). This boy subsequently studied Greek and Latin at home, then syntax at Claremont College, then poetry at St. Omer, and then (after a short return to England) went to the English College, Rome, in November 1649 as a *convictor*. Two years later he left the *Venerabile* for Douay, where he became a Franciscan.[2]

Such, then, were the hazards of being caught as unlicensed and recusant schoolmasters. Less risky was the Trojan horse technique of our fourth and last example of this year 1635, which escaped the Council's attention altogether. This was the simple device of infiltrating

[1] *Cal. S.P. Dom. Chas. I*, 1635, cclxi, pp. 182, 191, 197, 207, 214, 221, 228, 231; cccxxiv, p. 496; ccccxxxiv, pp. 398, 228. For the lurid career of Wragg the pursuivant, *Cal. S.P. Dom. Chas. I*, 1636, pp. 326ff., 498.

[2] Foley, vi. 376. His Rome *Responsa* are in *C.R.S.* lv. 516.

into an old established school: Kirkham Grammar School, in Lancashire.

Kirkham School had been founded in the reign of Edward VI (1551) by a 'kind of select Vestry' known as the Thirty Men. It appears that in 1621 a bequest of £30 was given to the reigning Thirty Men by Isabel Birley, daughter of John Coulbran of Kirkham, for the building of a school for poor children. Local subscriptions were added to it.

Now, Isabel Birley was a Catholic, and by the terms of her engagement with the Thirty Men she nominated the master of the school. Her first nominee, Thomas Armstead, held the post till 1628, when he was succeeded by one Sokell. Soon after this the Birley party persuaded all but one of the Thirty Men to leave the government of the school virtually in their hands. For the Catholic gentry (especially Sir Cuthbert Clifton, and Thomas Westby of Mowbreck) had been amongst the largest subscribers, and the Thirty Men were mostly their tenants. The bishop, when approached to make new orders on these lines for future elections of the 'feoffees', complied (31 July 1628). But the dissentient on the governing body, John Parker of Bradkirk, held out, and a Catholic-Protestant feud among the governors ensued. This seems to have reached a climax in the year 1635–6, when the third headmaster, Hugh Whaley, was locked out of the school by the vicar of Kirkham, Mr. Fleetwood, on suspicion of Romanism. What happened thereafter is obscure, save that Whaley was still master at the outbreak of the Civil War, when the neighbourhood was disturbed and he refused to go on teaching. The school then stood empty for some three years, till Prince Rupert's army had left the district.[1]

Underlying these four case-histories is the basic lesson of the penal times, the exploiting of all opportunities. The two classical preparatory schools in the Midlands took advantage of their isolation in the depths of the country. William Hill in Hampshire added French to his curriculum because he had two Frenchmen on his staff. Once again, how widespread these phenomena were cannot be known, though places and teachers can and increasingly are.

Catholic schooling in England under Charles I, down to the Civil War, is documented for the following thirty-one places, including known continuity from earlier:

[1] *V.C.H. Lancs.*, ii. 604, from a 1798 copy of a contemporary MS. (now lost) entitled *A Brief Relation Touching the Free School lately erected at Kirkham*; and R. Cunliffe Shaw, *Kirkham in Amounderness* (1949), 469ff.

Abergavenny (c. 1626), Blackburn (till 1641), Bury St. Edmunds (c. 1636), Carperly, Yorks (1631), Catterick (1633), Dalton-le-Dale, Co. Durham (1642), Derby (Stanley Grange, 1621–45), East Witton, Yorks (1625), Eye, Suffolk (c. 1626), Fareham, Hants (till 1635), Felixkirk, Yorks (1633), Garstang (before 1625), Hangwest, Yorks (1625), Healey, Yorks (1627), Holywell, Flint (1627), Hutton Rudby (1642), Kirkby Ravensworth, Yorks (1636), Kirkham (c. 1621–42), Leake (1627), London (Old Bailey, 1623 on), Malton, Yorks (1630), Masham, Yorks (1623 on), Nottingham (1623–c. 1638), Ratallock, Cornwall (1630–40), Richmond, Yorks (1630 on), St. Chalher, Cornwall (1625), St. Michael's-on-Wyre, Lancs (1641), Scarisbrick (intermittently), Sowerby, Yorks (1636), Thirsk (1632), Willenhall, Staffs. (till 1635), York (Holy Trinity parish, 1636).

All these were schools for boys. So far as can be discovered, there was provision for girls on home soil in only two places as yet. When Mary Ward's Institute was suppressed by Rome in 1631, one house was left open in England. But the suppression had a serious effect in cutting off the supply of women *catechists* in England which her nuns would have been able to create. And of catechists in England there was a dearth.

Fr. Gennings, the provincial of the Franciscans, sent over to Nieuport for nuns. This is the sole example of nuns actually teaching in England, apart from the tentative efforts of Mary Ward. It began in January 1639, when Fr. Gennings brought to England three sisters from the English Franciscan Convent at Nieuport, to set up a seminary 'for the help of the said convent'. Nothing is known of it beyond the possibility that it lasted till just before 1660.[1]

5. THE COMMONWEALTH AND 'CONTINUITY'

While the recusancy documents for the years of James I are prolific in new schools, and those of Charles I prolific in suppressions, the records for the Commonwealth period bring to light the earliest known cases (except Scarisbrick) where a continuity is probable from thence till today.

Long spells of undisturbed schooling had not been rare in the past. We have seen several in the time of Elizabeth; Scarisbrick had begun about 1618; Stanley Grange had been running for fourteen years when broken up in 1635, and went on again for another ten; at Kirkham

[1] Guilday, 304.

there was continuity of Catholic *ethos* for some twenty years, at Nottingham fifteen: to say nothing of centres where, despite the absence of written evidence, it is morally very likely that education was kept going continuously—the Blundells of Crosby in Lancashire, the Arundells of Wardour in Wiltshire,[1] the Welds of Chideock in Dorset, the Petres in Essex and others of the 'old Catholic families'.

The Commonwealth period itself can furnish one of the most prophetic of these two-decade schools, in Northumberland: though the precise location is not known. It was a 'select academy' started in 1649 by a Jesuit, Christopher Simpson, who had just come from the Continent. When this missioner died in 1674 his provincial (Fr. George Gray) wrote to the Father General in Rome that his 'known probity and candour *drew many of the leading men among the heretics to him*, in so much that they did not hesitate to entrust their sons to be educated by him'. In this the school anticipated the policy of the Jesuit schools later set up all over England under James II—a mixed Catholic-Protestant roll, with contracting-out of the religious instruction by the Protestant boys: a prodigy in modern education, far ahead of its time.[2]

That 'probity and candour' can endear, may be the explanation of a tombstone inscription to a Catholic priest, in an Anglican church, during the same period. The church is Somerton, Oxfordshire. The priest was Richard Todkill, ordained at Douay in 1632 and in England from 1641 until he died at Somerton in 1657. The inscription commemorates him as 'quondam hujus scholae sedulus et praeceptor egregius'. It must of course refer to his pre-Douay days. But coming from the England of Cromwell it is pleasing.[3]

The places that can claim continuity since the Commonwealth are three. They come from the most densely Catholic parts of the country, Lancashire and the hinterland of Winchester. And two of the three

[1] Cf. Oliver, *Collections*, 83.

[2] *Stonyhurst MSS.*, Anglia V, No. 88 (March 1674); Foley, iii. 116, 124; vi. 309; vii. 660; Oliver, *Collections, S.J.*, 191. In Abberwick, Northumberland, a boy of nine in the village school ran home when the Protestant ministers arrived to catechize in 1654, and when he was flogged for truancy the following day his parents withdrew him from the school.

[3] See Blomfield, *Hist. of Deanery of Bicester*, 153; Kitson, *Hist. of Manor of Haylesbury*, 206, 208, 223–4; and *S.P. Dom.* 14 Feb. 1641–2 for Todkill as one of four refusing to sign a 'Protest against Popery'. The school at Yarnton, Oxfordshire, sometimes said to have been a Catholic school under John Goad in 1646, was not so. Goad (later master of Merchant Taylors') did not become a Catholic until (acc. to Anthony à Wood) December 1660.

come from the very end of the period, when the fierce days of the 'automatic test' (the Oath of Abjuration) were disintegrating, and the hopes to be raised by Charles's Declaration of Breda were just round the corner. The places are Formby and Fernyhalgh, both in Lancashire, and Silksteed-Twyford.

At FORMBY the inhabitants appealed to the Lord Mayor of Lancaster in 1659 for leave to build a school on some wasteland. The permission was given, trustees were created, including a Blundell and a Formby, and a nominal rent of a shilling agreed. Nothing in detail is known of this school, beyond the fact of its existence, until after the end of the century, when Richard Marsh, a London Merchant Taylor who had been educated there, left a legacy in 1705 for the masters' salary. The school later fell into disrepair, and for a time into disuse, until it was rebuilt in 1750 in Pigeon House Hay, close to Formby Hall, whence it was removed ten years later to the corner still known as Old School Corner. Here it was functioning without interruption down to 1858. Its school population was never completely Catholic, but the educational roots of the Formby Catholics of today stretch back through this school.[1] The modern Catholic mission itself goes back to 1610.

The school at SILKSTEED near Winchester, erroneously supposed to have been established in the reign of James II, has been held in special reverence by those writers who have mentioned it, because it schooled Alexander Pope, and its descendant today can look back to it with practically unbroken certainty of tradition across nearly three hundred years. St. Edmund's College School at Ware 'is' Silksteed.

The traditional account, unanimous though meagre, derives mainly from the dating given by the historian John Kirk, whose collections of materials on Catholic life in England in the late seventeenth and eighteenth centuries have determined so much of later writing. According to Kirk, a Catholic school for boys was set up in a secluded spot in Silksteed in the year 1686, during the short heyday of James II. On 12 August 1688 the Vicar Apostolic of the London District, Bishop Leyburne, is found urging that Thomas Wetherby or Thomas Browne (*alias* Day), from Douay, might go to this school as assistant.

[1] Blundell, iii. 139–40, citing Formby *Bazaar Book* of 1904. There is a detailed history of this Township School, and the Marsh Trust, in *Formby Catholic Magazine*, iv. No. 49 (Apr. 1896). 'The interests of the Roman Catholics were carefully guarded from the beginning, so that they should derive their full benefit from this charity, which, being undenominational, was intended for all alike. . . .' The modern Catholic Schools in Formby date from 1872.

Its master at that time was a Herefordshire man, Augustine Taylor, educated at St. Omer and at the English College in Rome. He had come on the mission in 1670. The archives of the Brotherhood of the Secular Clergy list him as 'having taken great pains both in the school at Silksteed and in the Mission'. He retired in 1692 through ill-health (he was only fifty) and died in Winchester two years later. Taylor's successor was a Yorkshireman, William Husband (*alias* Bernard), who had been on the mission already for about a dozen years. Husband reigned at the school for only four years, till 1696, though he lived on till 29 December 1725.

The traditional account would have it that Husband's retirement in 1696 occurred simultaneously with the removal of the school to Twyford, not far away, where it came under the mastership of the most redoubtable head it ever had, Edward Taverner (*alias* Banister, *alias* John Davis), recently arrived from his ordination at the English College at Valladolid, and till now Husband's assistant. Taverner was a convinced methodologist in grammar teaching. He ruled the school for thirty years. Among his more distinguished pupils were Alexander Pope and probably Nathaniel Hooke. During his long spell as headmaster he must have been in the prime of life, for after retiring in 1726 he lived another twenty years, long enough to know of the temporary shipwreck of his work as a result of the outcry upon the 'Forty-five'.

Johnson's *Lives of the Poets* describes how, when Alexander Pope was about eight years old (c. 1696) he

> was placed in Hampshire under Taverner, a Romish priest, who, by a method very rarely practised, taught him the Greek and Latin rudiments together. He was now first regularly initiated in poetry by the perusal of Ogylby's *Homer* and Sandys's *Ovid*. . . From the care of Taverner, under whom his proficiency was considerable, he was removed to a school at Twyford, near Winchester, and again to another school about Hyde Park Corner. . . . At the last two schools he used to represent himself as having lost part of what Taverner had taught him, and on his master at Twyford he had already exercised his poetry in a lampoon. Yet under these masters he translated more than a fourth part of the *Metamorphoses*. If he kept the same proportion in his other exercises it cannot be thought that his loss was great. . . .[1]

This account and the traditional chronology of Silksteed and Twyford manifestly conflict. According to Johnson, young Pope on removal to Twyford no longer had Taverner as his master. According

[1] World's Classics edition, ii. 234.

to the Kirk tradition, not only did Taverner remain headmaster of Twyford down to 1725, but the removal of the school occurred in the very year Pope *began* his career under these successive men, and Taverner was then *at* Twyford.

There is a very different light on Silksteed's origins in the history of the present Anglican grammar school at Twyford, founded in 1793. There is a tradition in this school that its Catholic predecessor existed as early as 1696 in 'Segar's Buildings', and that the Segar boys, even earlier still, cheered *Charles II* on his way from Southampton to his new palace at Winchester.[1]

From these three accounts two problems emerge. Did the Silksteed school begin in 1686 (for which date the Kirk tradition adduces no evidence)? And did it move to Twyford in 1696? Contemporary documents enable us to answer both these questions negatively. Silksteed was much older than James II, and it was still *in situ* at least as late as 1700.

It emerges from the documents that, in this hinterland of Winchester, we are concerned with one of those pockets of Catholicism that maintained themselves largely unscathed throughout penal times. At Winchester the Catholics were buried, by collusion, in a Catholic cemetery. As early as the beginning of the Civil War they were receiving the sacraments from a priest, Thomas Woodward. The mainstays of the faith, in the surrounding countryside, were John Bilson of Silksteed, Lady Elizabeth Stewkeley, Mrs. K. Tichborne, and their vast family ramifications.[2] These families laid the foundations on which the modern Catholicism of Winchester was to be built in the next century by Bishop John Milner.

The tantalizing legend in the present-day grammar school at Twyford, whereby the Catholic schoolboys there in Segar's Buildings cheered Charles II on his way to Winchester, would date the Silksteed school from earlier still. Indeed, there is firm evidence for 1667, when one Mrs. Gage wrote to her daughter Clare, wife of John Bilson, at 'Mr. Taylor's House, Silsted', to inquire what was owing to Mr. Taylor for Henry Gage, and to suggest she also send 'Little dick' to school. Mr. Philip Taylor, himself, made his will during this same

[1] C. J. Wickham, *Story of Twyford School* (1909), pp. 3, 6–7. This account mentions Alexander Pope, and lists the Catholic masters of Twyford down to its dissolution in 1745. There was then no school on the site until the Anglican foundation in 1793.

[2] *Milton MSS.* The documents cited from here on are from transcripts in the possession of Mgr. J. H. King, Bishop of Portsmouth.

year 1667. The inventory of his goods dated 3 September 1684 discloses an item of twenty-six beds.[1]

We get light on earlier years still from an 'Account of ye Popish Schole at Silkstead, near Winchester', dated 1695/6, preserved in Lambeth Palace Library:

Silkstead house is in ye parish of Compton near Winchester conveniently situated for ye design of a Popish seminary: first attempted there by Mr. Philip Taylor master of a little school by ye College of Winchester; who after the return of King Chas. ye 2d (1660) declared himself a Papist; and removed to this house where he *still* advanced in his undertaking tho' ye school has been frequently presented by ye Grand Jury at ye Assizes, and Mr. Taylor himself has been proceeded agst in ye Ecclesiastical Court for not frequenting ye Ch. and ye Sacrament, and for teaching School without licence. . . . With very good reason 'tis presum'd that from his first attempt of forming a school there, he continued it to his death.

Since wn ye Churchwardens of Compton have been often, and yt very lately called upon to present ye school: but have pretended yt the House stands in an obscure place somewhat remote from ye rest of ye parish, and they could nt venture to present anything of that nature upon their Oaths, tho' the school is undoubtedly continued: tis said by one Mr. Barrett, formerly usher to Mr. Taylor, who was first succeeded in his ushership by one Mr. Matthews, at this time supplied by his Kinsman. The affairs of ye House are managed by one Mrs. Perkins: ye number of ye Scholars amounts almost to *fourscore*.[2]

Thus far one of the problems, the date of Silksteed school. Far from beginning in 1686, it existed before Philip Taylor removed it to Silksteed in 1660. And if the usher's name, Barrett (which occurs in no other local documents of the period) be explainable as a mistake for Barnard or Bernard (the *alias* of William Husband, later headmaster of it in 1692), we have a continuity of teamwork that may well account for the place flourishing to the extent of eighty boys after thirty years.

The other problem, of the connection between Silksteed and Twyford, is clarified by the same document of 1696, which runs straight on as follows:

Within two miles of this place there is another school, settled in ye midst of a country village called Twyford, wch is filld only with younger children and proves a Nursery to Silksted: consisting at present of about thirty children, who are instructed by ye son of Mrs. Wait, who is ye owner of ye

[1] The will (dated 25 Feb. 1677) is in Winchester Probate Court. It was proved on 14 Oct. 1684. See J. S. Drew in *The Edmundian*, xix. 74–8 (1938).

[2] *Lambeth Palace Library MSS.* 933, f. 44, Jan. 1696. My italics.

house, and ye present Housekeeper. He is assisted by one Mr. John Grove as an usher.

Silksteed and Twyford, then, coexisted, the latter a pre-preparatory school for the former. And there was another school as well. For the document goes on:

> There has lately been appointed a Third School, not far from these, under ye care and management of one Mr. Barlow [cf. the witness to Philip Taylor's will in 1677], who has provided an Auntient Gentleman supposed to be a priest of the Ch. of Rome, for ye instruction both of lesser and greater Boys. The house he has hired is called Longwood House, wch stands at some distance from any Town, but upon ye skirts of Ouslebury Parish near Twyford.

Thus there were clearly three linked schools: Silksteed, founded at Winchester by Philip Taylor before 1660; Twyford, established at some date yet unknown, as a school preparatory to it; and Longwood, started in 1695–6 by John Barlow. On this ground it might be plausible to agree that Silksteed 'removed to Twyford' in 1696 in the sense of drafting its younger boys to Twyford and its older boys to the ancient gentleman at Longwood: especially indeed as Silksteed was at last descended upon by the authorities in that very year.

On 7 March 1695/6 the Privy Council ordered the Duke of Bolton, lord lieutenant of the County of Southampton, 'that the Schoolmaster and other men and Boyes of the Popish School at Silksteed near the City of Winchester [be] seized and committed to the County Gaol in order to be prosecuted according to law, but that the Boyes be discharged and permitted to go to their respective homes'. Three weeks later, evidently to clinch matters, the Duke was told to 'give directions that the Boyes of the said school be permitted to remain there for fifteen days, except that they shall be taken from thence by their parents in that time, and afterwards to cause such of the said Boyes as shall remain there to be sent to their next of kin being Protestants respectively'.[1]

But Silksteed did not in fact disappear then, nor merge into Twyford. It carried on where it was. At the end of the century William III was again informed 'that a Popish school is kept at Silsted near Winchester'. Sir John St. Barbe was accordingly instructed, as one of the justices, to 'enquire upon oath as to the persons who keep the school, whether they are legally qualified for it. You will send up the

[1] P.R.O., *Privy Council Register*, 2/76, ff. 317, 354.

informations, which are to be handed to the Attorney-General to prosecute the offenders.' When in due course he sent the affidavits he was reminded that 'you do not say whether the school be discontinued, which I desire to know'. But manifestly it was not, for two months later (Feb. 1700) the mayor of Winchester was ordered to 'inquire and suppress it'.[1]

The contemporary documents down to 1700 thus do not clear up everything. Since Samuel Johnson's sources could hardly be at fault on the major point of Pope's having had his time wasted in passing on from Taverner, only one reasonable explanation seems available that can harmonize all the accounts. This is, that the trouble with the Privy Council in 1695/6 must have involved a brief *interruption* of the school, and that some of the boys were sent as an emergency to Twyford, Pope among them. By the time Silksteed was running normally again, which was the beginning of 1699 at the earliest, Pope had gone on to Thomas Deane at Hyde Park Corner.

The first removal of Silksteed to Twyford—changing the character and grade of the latter school thereby—may have occurred as a result of the trouble with the lord lieutenant in 1700. But on this there is no further evidence.

What the documents do prove is that Silksteed began at least twenty-five years earlier than has hitherto been supposed; that it was precisely the same kind of Catholic school, in curriculum, as those elsewhere in England training boys for the colleges abroad; that it was still at Silksteed as late as 1700, thereby surviving the Revolution; and—uniquely—that it had (at Twyford) its own pre-preparatory school. Silksteed-Twyford produced both the Bishops Talbot, their brother the Earl of Shrewsbury, the Earl of Fingal and many others of the Catholic nobility.[2]

[1] *Cal. S.P. Dom.* 1699/1700, pp. 294 (Nov. 16), 299 (Nov. 27), 372 (6 Feb.).

[2] *Masters of Silksteed School*

1660 (and before)	Philip Taylor
1684	Augustine Taylor; 1688 Thomas Browne (usher)
1692	William Husband (*alias* Bernard) (previously usher)
1696	Edward Taverner (*alias* Banister and John Davis) (previously usher)

Master of Longwood School

1695/6	John Barlow

Masters of Twyford School

1696 (and before)	—Wait
,, ,, ,,	John Grove (usher)
,, ,,	Edward Taverner (*alias* Banister and John Davis)
1726	Francis (*alias* John Walter) Fleetwood

The hamlet of FERNYHALGH, whence comes the third and last of these Commonwealth period schools, lies at the centre of another of those manifold Catholic *enclaves*. It is in the neighbourhood of Grimsargh, near Preston. Today its presbytery of St. Mary still boasts a pre-Reformation chalice.

The earliest documentation of the place dates from 8 January 1348/9, when it was licensed by the Archbishop of York for services, till the chantry was abolished in 1547. From the Reformation onwards there was no official chapel till the time of James II, when the site of the old church was cleared (1685) for the building of a new one, the land being leased by one Hugh Charnley, of Durton, yeoman, whose family are listed as Nonjurors in 1717. The church was erected on lines now long familiar in the English Catholic history of later penal times, with the priest's rooms on the ground floor and the chapel above.

But the school was by then (1685) already a generation old. It certainly dates from as early as 1650, when the priest in charge of the clandestine mission was Richard Sherburne (of the Stonyhurst family), who had returned to England from Douay as far back as 1625, having studied there under the *alias* of Tunstall.[1] Many of the books of Fr. Sherburne, still in the 'library' in a loft when the historian Joseph Gillow visited Fernyhalgh in 1883, bore the scribblings of the schoolboys. The earliest of their names were dated 1651 and 1652—Samuel Hart, Christopher Horne and Raufe Tyldesley. Gillow listed a large number of these early schoolbooks, some with the legend on the flyleaf: *In Usum Scholae Sta. Mariae ad Fontem* (the School of St. Mary at the Fountain—the School at 'Lady Well'—from the spring adjoining). When I myself visited the Fernyhalgh presbytery in 1949 the earliest of these inscribed books were not traceable. But there were still among the collection a dozen or so pedagogical books that had been used by the master. The earliest was *Education, Especially of Young Gentlemen*, published at Oxford in 1677 (319 pages). The

Masters of Twyford School—cont.

1732	Joseph Gildon
1736	John Betts
1745	Dissolved

The school, closed during the 'Forty-five, was succeeded by Standon Lordship School, Herts., in 1749. Continuity from then on is complete, but the 'gap' cannot be closed by documentary proof.

[1] Thomas Hothersall, who entered the *Venerabile* at the age of twenty-three in 1665 and gave the place of his fully-Catholic schooling as 'Grimsargh, Lancs.', must have been one of its earliest boys. Later in the century he was sending boys to St. Omer from America (Jesuit school in Maryland). *C.R.S.* lv. 607–8; Hughes, ii. 136–7.

second earliest was the *Essay of a Practical Grammar*, by the Master of Tonbridge Free School in Kent, Christopher Wase, published in 1692 (66 pages). They were respectively the third impression and the tenth edition.

Towards the end of the reign of Charles II, Fr. Sherburne was succeeded by Fr. Peter Gooden, who himself had been running a school near Lancaster, at Aldcliffe Hall, the seat of the Dalton family. At the time when Catholics were being rounded up after the 1715 Rebellion, the informer Hitchmough refers back to this school, at 'Ockly', as 'a sort of academy or little seminary' for popish youths destined for abroad.[1] Peter Gooden seems to have incorporated his Aldcliffe school into the one at Fernyhalgh. He was certainly there in 1685, as he witnessed the conveyance of the land at Lady Well for the new church, from Hugh Charnley to four trustees. The date of his arrival was in all probability 1685 exactly, for the superintendent of the Lady Well school in 1684 was Fr. Charles Penketh (*alias* Rivers, *alias* John Birkett).[2]

Fourteen years later the mission and school fell to the least forgotten of all their pastors, Fr. Christopher Tootell, brother of the malignant Church historian Charles Dodd (*vere* Hugh Tootell), who was with him as assistant for a time. Christopher had been educated at the English College in Lisbon under the *alias* of Blacoe. The moment he arrived on the English mission, in 1686, he had been placed at the new chapel opened at Lime Street, in London, under the protection of James II. But he and his fellows had soon been ousted from there, on questionable charges of Jansenism, and Jesuits installed in their place. Hence he went to Lancashire, and to Fernyhalgh in particular in 1699, as successor to Fr. Penketh.

In the reign of Queen Anne Christopher Tootell suffered much at the hands of the Anglican Vicar of Preston, Samuel Peplow, who after fourteen years of vendetta had him indicted at Preston assizes and convicted of recusancy (April 1714). This was the beginning of a long spell of alternate hiding and safety, till he died in peace at Ladywell in March 1727. A correspondence in his own hand, preserved at Fernyhalgh, speaks volumes for the strength of character of this little man. As vicar-general for the North he was frequently appealed to by Catholics anxious to relax the Lenten and other fasts in time of strain (as after 1715). Like many another pastor before and since,

[1] Gillow, ii. 526; Payne, *Eng. Cath. Nonjurors*, 356.

[2] Gillow, iii. 14, and *C.R.S.* iv. 431f.

he took the line that the treatment for adversity was not less self-mortification but more. And this at a time when his own church was twice raided (1715 and 1718) and his own people—of whom Bishop Leyburne had confirmed the surprising total of 1,099 in September 1687—were going in fear for their lives.

In 1708 he took as his assistant Edward Melling, his own nephew, who had probably himself been educated in the school. Certainly John Melling was: in 1703, as is commemorated in a book he left behind him when he went on to Douay five years later. But by then the school had come under the supervision of a matriarchal figure who is still remembered all over the Lancashire Fylde (though her story cannot be told here): Dame Alice Harrison.[1]

6. RESTORATION SCHOOLS

Apart from developments along general lines already traditional—tutoring, schooling, the traffic of boys to the Continent, the begging tours of the English 'agents' of the colleges abroad, and the mounting of the penal code—the twenty-five years of Charles II are noteworthy for the revival of Mary Ward's Institute in England and the concentration of preparatory schools in the North.

[1] *Superintendents at Fernyhalgh*

1650 (?)	Rev. Richard Sherburne (*alias* Tunstall)
1684	Rev. Charles Penketh (*alias* Rivers)
1699	Rev. Christopher Tootell (d. 18 Nov. 1727)
*1708	Rev. Edward Melling (as assistant)
*1727	Rev. Edward Melling
*1733	Rev. Henry Kendall (d. 1752)
17	Rev. John Cowban
17	Rev. John Chadwick
*17	Rev. Robert Bannister
*17	Rev. Anthony Lund
	Rev. Robert Blacoe
1823	Rev. Richard Gillow

Heads of the School

17	Dame Alice Harrison (till about 1760)
*1780	Peter Newby (from Great Eccleston) (till 1799)
1842	Miss Anne Dorothy Browne (afterwards Green)

Sources for Fernyhalgh School: Gillow, *Dict.* i. 123, 351, 565; ii. 14, 474, 526, 534; iii. 145–8, 486; iv. 4, 6, 10, 351; v. 594; *C.R.S.* xxiii. 90 note, 130–1 and notes; *V.C.H. Lancs.* iii. 124; Daniel O'Hare, *An Old Lancashire Mission . . . Fernyhalgh*, reprinted 1892 from *Ushaw Magazine*, ii. 245–57; Christopher Tootell, *Traditional Account of Our Lady's Well and Chapel in Fernyhalgh*, 1723 (MSS.—at Fernyhalgh). For the later period under Dame Alice (after 1700) see J. Kirk, *Biogs. of 18th Cent. Catholics* (ed. J. H. Pollen and E. H. Burton 1909), and his 'Dame Alice and Ladywell' (in *Cath. Mag.* iii. 30–4) (1832).

* Educated in the school.

Mary Ward had come to London again in the summer of 1639, as soon as her Institute of the Blessed Virgin had been re-approved in Rome, and had re-fitted her house there with the help of Frances Bedingfield, to serve as headquarters from which to organize schools for the London poor.[1] Her plans had then been disrupted by the Civil War. But now, on the instigation of Sir Thomas Gascoigne, the superioress Mary Poyntz was persuaded in 1667 to permit Frances Bedingfield to set up an English branch of the order. Sir Thomas offered an endowment, to be used for three houses, one in London and two in Yorkshire. Frances Bedingfield came to England, changed her name to Lang (Bedingfield was one of the most widely known Catholic names), and in 1669 perpetuated the Mary Ward beginnings by opening her Convent School at Hammersmith, adjoining the Portuguese embassy at Cupola House. Its first spiritual director was a Jesuit, Fr. Pracid; but two Carmelites followed him, and then a long line of secular priests.[2]

Frances Bedingfield was in trouble before long. The Jesuit *Annual Letters* for 1674 record her as 'a lady of good family, ripe years, prudence and piety', fined £180 for recusancy. Six years later the school was again entered by the authorities, during the Oates Plot. It was searched 'as a reputed nunnery', but upon flat denials that the house was in fact 'harbouring' priests and Jesuits it was left in peace.

This is all the more surprising in that the London of Titus Oates was highly dangerous for anyone at all whom the 'Salamanca Doctor' could plausibly denounce as teaching popery. A bishop's licence saved more than one London schoolmaster from him. Oates 'swore' three schoolmasters and two booksellers into the plot, and had them brought to the Bar of the House of Lords in 1678, testifying of Denis Glisson, schoolmaster of Warwick Street, that he 'did instill ill Principles into Children, and that he said there is no learning in Cambridge, and nothing but debauchery in Oxford'. Glisson stoutly denied the charges, proclaimed himself a Protestant, produced his schoolmaster's licence from the Bishop of London, and was discharged. William Smith, however, the schoolmaster of Islington, no more a Catholic

[1] Guilday, 211; Chambers, *York Convent*, 5–6.

[2] Many of the records of the Hammersmith school are at the Benedictine Convent at Teignmouth. A *Register* of the girls down to 1763, but of which only the first four letters survive, contains 38 under A, 138 B, 106 C and 53 D. From this it was clearly a large school. Fr. Austin Shepherd's MS. *History* of the School (? 1740) is unreliable. See also *York Convent*, 139ff.; Gillow, i. 166; *C.R.S.* xxvi. 59; and *Westminster Arch.*, Giffard Papers, xxxix, No. 134.

than Glisson but 'sworn' into the plot because he had refused to implicate others, went to gaol.[1]

The school of the Hammersmith nuns was extremely fortunate, then, to get off with no more than a search. And from that moment it prospered. Three years later the queen, Catherine of Braganza, gave the nuns a house in Whitefriars Street, whereby (at all events till the Revolution) the roll of girls is said to have risen to three hundred.[2] From now on London had its 'Pope's Corner' at Hammersmith as well as its Catholic nucleus by Lincoln's Inn Fields. Catholic schooling at Hammersmith is continuous from this time.

The Mary Ward nuns also acted on Sir Thomas Gascoigne's offer in the North. They set up at Dolebank, near Fountain's Abbey, in 1677. This was not the first centre they had sought in Yorkshire, for they had contemplated Haworth, near York, the residence of the Thewing family, and Broughton Hall (Craven), the house of Lady Tempest. Gascoigne had suggested 'Ausmotherley'. Nor did Dolebank itself become their permanent home in the shire. During the reign of James II they moved into the city of York, to the Bar Convent, where they and their school still remain today. But 1677 marks the beginning, at Dolebank, of their continuous work in the North of England. 'Mrs.' Lascelles was appointed lady abbess, and John Cornwallis became the nuns' chaplain.[3]

It is not difficult to divine why Sir Thomas Gascoigne had appointed Osmotherley, near Northallerton, as a base for these nuns. The whole of Yorkshire had recently been combed anew for recusants,[4] and they would have as neighbours the Osmotherley Franciscans, who had been there quietly amid the Hambledon Hills since 1665.

Mons Gratiae, the Franciscan missionary residence, was the gift of Mrs. Juliana Walmsley. Fr. William Shepheard took charge of it in 1666. From then till the end of the century there were only three superiors (Praeses): Fr. Francis Osbaldeston (1671–5), Fr. Marianus Napier (to 1677) and Fr. Bernardine Longworth (to 1701).

[1] *Lords Journal*, xiii. 331–2, 312; *Hist. MSS. Comm.*, Lords MSS. 1678–88, p. 53.

[2] *Domestic Intelligence*, 13 Jan. 1680; *C.R.S.* xxvi. 60; Chambers, *Mary Ward*, 515f.

[3] *York Castle Depositions*, Examination of Christine Cornwallis (Anderton), 14 Dec. 1678; Foley, v. 751f.; B. Ward, *Dawn of Cath. Revival*, i. 37. One other community of English nuns—the Blue Nuns of Paris—made attempts to establish a school in England at this time. But all the efforts were abortive. See the Diary of the Blue Nuns (*C.R.S.* viii).

[4] 1663. See *C.R.S.* iv. 266. But the York Diocesan presentments in the *Court Books* of 1662 and 1667 (R. VI. A. 26, 28) list only two recusant unlicensed schools: Gerard Hewthwaite at Stokesley, Cleveland, and Susannah Taylor at Beverley, Harthill.

The school they established at Osmotherley became very well known. John Wesley in the next century confided a paragraph about it to his *Journal*.[1] But though it had a long life, the school cannot be said to have started in the year hitherto sometimes suggested, 1672. Certainly the first Chapter, in 1665, proposed a school, but nothing was done

for some years, though a [further] resolution was passed in 1686 to open a school at Putney under the presidency of Dr. Slaughter. A real start, however, was made six years later [1692] when a school was opened at Osmotherley . . . largely through the exertions of Fr. Bernardine Longworth. Here, with varying vicissitudes, the school continued to exist for about fifty years.[2]

As to the purpose of the school, we have a pathetic revelation in the manuscript notebook of Fr. Anthony Parkinson, written during the troublous year 1714.

This school was designed to be a nursery for our Noviceship, but is only an ABC petty school for little boys to be fitted for their rudiments or for grammar to go to the monks (whose school property it is) or St. Omers; but of our Order (I know it by examining the boys themselves) they seem to have heard less than any other.[3]

Not far away was another preparatory school for St. Omer, founded earlier than Osmotherley by a Douay priest, Anthony Metham, who seems to have maintained it till 1692, when he resigned it to Fr. William Addison (*alias* Hildreth).[4]

It is probably the scale on which boys were being sent over from Yorkshire, even before the advent of either of these schools, that accounts for the charges of treason preferred against five families in June 1681—the last occasion on which such proceedings were actually carried through. The families were Coates of Morpeth, Clavering of Callaly, Widdington of Felton, Thornton of Witton and Netherwitton, and Riddell of Fenham.[5]

One other only of the Yorkshire preparatory schools for the Continent after the Restoration deserves special notice, from its whimsical name and the fact that it had a long run. It was a boarding-school,

[1] 1745. (Everyman ed., i. 522.)

[2] Dominic Devas, in Franciscan *Centenary Pamphlets* (1924), ii. 14.

[3] *Parkinson MSS.*, in Franciscan Archives at Forest Gate, London. The other main sources for the Osmotherley School are: *Acta Capitulorum, 1629–1746*, also in *Arch. Francisc*; *Register* of the Franciscan Mission at Birmingham, transl. and publ. by Phillimore. See also *The Tablet*, 29 Oct. 1904, p. 697.

[4] Gillow, iv. 570; Kirk, 163.

[5] *York Castle Depositions*, Surtees Soc. xl. 248; Foley, v. 701.

dating from about 1670, founded by Fr. Thomas Thweng, who had been a 'courier' for boys between England and Douay during the Commonwealth. He ended his days ten years later as one of the Oates martyrs. In 1684 the school passed to Robert Ward, just arrived on the mission from Valladolid. 'In his first year he taught some boyes at Quousque, then lived a year or two on what he could get at York.' It then fell to another missioner from Valladolid, John Simpson, till at least 1693, but little of its subsequent history survives.

The school is known in the records, cryptically and fleetingly, as *Quosqu*. The historian Kirk ascribed it to Conteland, the estate of the Erringtons. His latest editors corrected Conteland to Ponteland. But Ponteland is in Northumberland. 'The school at Quousque' was in fact near Carlton, in the ancient parish of Snaith, on the river Aire. The building is today a farmhouse; and the local people call it *Kuska*. The seventeenth-century Catholic school with its enigmatic Latin name is thus kept alive in local dialect.

There might well be speculation as to the reason for such a name. Was it the wistful optimism of its founder-priest, in contributing his mite to the conversion of England and wondering *quousque*? (how long?). Was it the word *quousque* issuing from the lion's mouth on the Royalist Prince Rupert's standard at Marston Moor? Was it on the contrary the realism of the priest, in wondering how long the school would last before discovery? Or had he a scholar's recollection of the formula that had reprieved some of the schools during the cataclysm of 1547 under the Chantries Act—*continuat schola quousque*? But none of these whimsies can have any substance, for the name did not originate in the fact of the school. The name itself occurs as early as 1602, in the 'Villa Quousqu' deocesis Eboracensis' whence Richard Gayle (*alias* Baynes) that year entered Valladolid and tells us of Quosque in his *Interrogatory*.[1]

One school, however, the Government did run to earth and disband with much noise. It was in the Marches of Wales, and it came to light during the Oates plot trial of the Jesuit David Lewis (son of the Morgan Lewis whom we have met as master of Abergavenny Royal Grammar School). A broadsheet after his arrest called him 'the pretended Bishop of Llandaff', and though this was proved not so he was still executed. This Jesuit affair was very much a new 'Clerkenwell' scare, for the *Journal* of the House of Lords had already discovered

[1] See Raymond Stanfield in *C.R.S.* ix. 109; Harwood Brierly in *Yorkshire Weekly Post*, 20 Nov. 1909; and *C.R.S.* xxx (Valladolid *Register*), 75.

in March 1679 a Jesuit College at Holbeck in Nottinghamshire equipped with a library worth a thousand pounds.

The college, 'at a place called the Combe, in the County of Hereford', was the Jesuit house of residence for the South Wales area, at Cwm. It consisted of 'two roomy houses hidden in a wooded combe'. Some of the books seized there, by the Bishop of Hereford (Dr. Croft), are now in Hereford Cathedral Library.[1] The excitement caused by the discovery was sufficient to warrant a Bill in Parliament for the deportation of the more prominent Catholics of South Wales and Monmouthshire to Protestant areas. The Carmelite school near Hereford, founded as far back as about 1655, disappeared.[2]

For the reign of Charles II the attested schools total twenty-one: Beverley (Harthill), Yorks (1667), Broughton, Lancs (1671), Buckinghamshire (?Carmelites, 1679), Carlton, Yorks (Quosqu, c. 1670), Claughton (Garstang, to 1671), Cwm, Herefordshire (1679), Dolebank, Yorks (1677–86), Fernyhalgh, Lancs (from c. 1650), Formby, Lancs (from c. 1659), Hereford (?Carmelites, 1655–79), London (Hammersmith, 1669 on), London (Jermyn Street, c. 1665–71), London (Westminster, 1678), London (Duke Street, 1678), Market Weighton, Yorks (Everingham Park, 1662), Northumberland (c. 1650–74), Aldcliffe, Lancs ('Ockley', c. 1680 on), Scarisbrick (continuing from c. 1618), Silksteed, Hants (since before 1660), Stokesley (Cleveland), Yorks (1662), Thorpe (near Cliffe), Yorks (c. 1680 on).

[1] Gillow, iv. 208; Foley, v. 917–29 and 468 note.

[2] The Franciscans, however, opened a residence in Hereford itself in 1684, followed by two others at Monmouth and Abergavenny in 1687. See J. G. Lynch, *Catholic Revival in S. Wales*, Univ. Wales unpubl. thesis (1942), 61ff.; and cf. *C.R.S.* xxvii. 101 note.

XI

THE FALSE DAWN UNDER JAMES II

1. JAMES II AND HIS GOVERNMENT

WHEN James II was crowned in Westminster Abbey in March 1685, with forty King's Scholars of Westminster School placed in the gallery as choristers, the final death of the Bill that would have excluded him from the throne as a Catholic was less than five years in the past.

From the earlier misfortunes of his family's policy there was much that he might have learnt. But James had little of the political realism that had enabled his brother to save the throne for him. His personal integrity was complete, but his sense of expediency rudimentary. Psychologically, he had been commander of the Royal Navy for so long that he saw his throne as a quarter-deck, and his advisers as subordinate officers. 'If James', it has been said, 'had listened to the wise counsels of Pope Innocent XI . . . the penal laws then in force would, almost certainly, have been repealed, and the statutes imposing civil incapacities have been suspended.'[1]

> Many deprecated any alteration [wrote Lingard] which might afterwards provoke a reaction. They deemed it imprudent to risk the tranquillity which they enjoyed, for the pursuit of a greater but uncertain benefit, and were content to submit to the privations imposed by the laws, provided they might be relieved from the penal and sanguinary statutes prohibiting the private exercise of their worship.[2]

Certainly the headlong career of the king brought down in ruin, along with much else, the first foundations of what could have been a missionary and educational enterprise of enormous promise.

The educational contribution was not his, though that reflects on him no more than was common to all the monarchs since Henry VIII. None of them had an educational policy as such: only as a function of their ecclesiastical policy, in the question of Church and State. James contributed little to education, even of money and patronage. He also interfered with schools surprisingly little, by contrast with his battles

[1] Surtees Soc. cxxxi, p. xv.

[2] *History*, 2nd ed., xiv. 82–3, citing Barillon.

against the two universities. But the interference began early—in the very spring of 1685, at the King Edward VI School at Birmingham; and it was symptomatic, of what he was to do over the whole field of his prerogative.

In that first spring he told the judges to discourage prosecutions and discharge all persons confined for refusing the oaths of allegiance and supremacy. Thousands of Catholics, and later some 1,500 Quakers, were set at liberty as a result.[1] When the Lords met on 19 May, the new Lord Chief Justice, Jeffreys, was present for the first time. When the Commons met three days later the king secured the rejection of a motion to put into immediate execution the laws against Dissenters. On 6 August the pope appointed a vicar apostolic of England, bringing to an end the long interregnum that had lasted since the death in exile of Bishop Richard Smith thirty years before. The new bishop, John Leyburne, a Westmorland man, was president of Douay College, and a philosopher-friend of Descartes and Hobbes. When he arrived in London in October the king housed him in Whitehall.[2] By 9 November, when the new session of Parliament opened, members were chafing at the infiltration of Catholic officers into the Army after Monmouth's Rebellion, and asked the king to curtail it. James prorogued them ten days later, for three months.[3] The pattern of all the Stuarts was repeating itself.

By the end of that first year the religious orders were returning, Catholic chapels and schools were being projected in many parts of the country (though the first shots in the battle with the universities had not yet been fired), and a dignified pamphlet war had begun.

The pamphlet war brought to the fore a remarkable body of talent on both sides. There led for the Protestants Tillotson, Stillingfleet, Tenison and Wake; for the Catholics Godden, Gooden, John Sargent and John Gother. The disputations reached their climax in 1687, when Andrew Poulton came forth from the school which the Jesuits had opened in the Savoy itself, and did battle with Dr. Thomas Tenison. A second Jesuit, Edward Meredith, published a full story of the encounter from the notes he took at it. Poulton had been so long abroad that he protested his exile had caused him to forget his English. An anonymous brochure, *The Advice*, in a gibe at Poulton's halting

[1] P.R.O., *Privy Council Records*, II, f. 413. The order in favour of '*any* Dissenter whatsoever' was late, but William Penn's gratitude involved him in charges that he had been educated at St. Omer!

[2] Brady, iii. 140 f.

[3] Clarke, *James II*, ii. 48–57; F. C. Turner, *James II*, 253–97.

English as contrasted with his fluent Latin, lampooned him in a couplet:

> Send Poulton to be lashed at Busby's school,
> That he in print no longer play the fool.

Busby's school was Westminster. Not long afterwards there were rumours that Poulton was to become its headmaster.[1]

The pamphlet war was certainly educational and religious in a real sense. James himself told the Catholics to restrict their writings to an *exposition* of doctrine. The most salient of the books issued by his own printer, Henry Hills, were of that kind: Bellarmine's *Short Christian Doctrine*, an *Abstract of the Douay Catechism*, and Bossuet's *Exposition of Catholic Doctrine*. But the most famous publication of the period is John Gother's *Papist Misrepresented and Represented*, which tabulated the deviations of Protestantism from Catholicism, in weekly parts. The literary side of the revival included also a Catholic annual: the *Kalendarium Catholicum*, which began in 1686, the first of its kind since an abortive *Almanack* of 1661, and issued by Henry Hills, late printer to Lord Protector Cromwell and Charles II.[2]

How far this 'apostolate of the press' in all its forms was ineffective, however, outside London, is well reflected in a report sent from James's secret agent for the southern and western counties towards the end of 1687, when the initiative had passed to his enemies.[3]

James's major political enterprise, the achievement of full religious toleration for Catholics by public authority, was attempted first in Scotland, by means of a Bill in Parliament in June 1686, modestly providing for 'the exercise of their religion in their private houses (all public worship being hereby excluded)'.[4] Though it came to nothing, the king went ahead in directions not liable to Parliamentary sabotage. He prepared the Chapel Royal in Holyrood House for Catholic worship; he blessed plans for a Holyrood school; and he gave an annual grant from his privy purse to the Highlands mission and to the Scots Colleges at Douay, Paris and Rome.[5]

To frustrate opposition to his plans in England he revived the High

[1] *Verney Memoirs*, ii. 456.

[2] Payne, *Old Eng. Cath. Missions*, 104, xiv.

[3] Quoted in Sir Geo. Duckett, *Penal Laws and Test Act* (1882), 223. For the pamphlet war see Gillow, iii. 584, ii. 539, iv. 565, v. 351; *Annual Letters S.J.*, 1687; Thomas Jones, *Catalogue of Collection of Tracts for and against Popery, published under James II*, Chetham Society, xlviii (1859) and lxiv (1865).

[4] *Hist. MSS. Comm.*, Laing MSS., Edinburgh, i. 446–7 (1915).

[5] Bellesheim, iv. 135.

Commission Court of the Tudors, which the Long Parliament had abolished in 1641. His commission was issued to the Archbishop of Canterbury and six others. It is of all James's actions the one which historians have found it most difficult to justify on legal grounds. In the same month that its disciplinary course began (July 1686), James followed up his Army appointments by dispensing from the Test Act four Catholic peers, so that they could be sworn of the Privy Council: Lords Powis, Arundell, Belasyse and Dover. In due course the Jesuit Father Edward Petre was also sworn, and the king sent to Rome to solicit for him a cardinal's hat. The pope, far from complying, besought the king to be less precipitate in his handling of the English situation. The attitude of Rome was later paraphrased as tantamount to saying: 'Your King should be excommunicated for thus attempting to overturn the small remains of popery in England.' And if the tartness of these words is no surprise, from the 'anticlerical' priest who wrote them, the calamitous results visible in his day may likewise attest their substance.[1] The Catholic masses were to pay for their Catholic king's Roman holiday.

He met Parliament again a year after it had expected: in February 1687.

> His Majesty [wrote a Jesuit at Liège] is resolved to ask three things: First, that by a general Act *all* Catholic peers shall be admitted to sit in the Upper House; secondly, that the Test [of 1673] may be abolished; and thirdly, which is the chief point, that all penal laws against Catholics be abrogated. And that he may the better obtain these things, he designs to let them all know: *That he is resolved to turn out all those who will not heartily act for the obtaining of them*; *and likewise dissolve the Parliament.*[2]

That was how the curtain rose on the fateful Declaration of Indulgence.

The Declaration was published first in Scotland, on 18 February, extended to England on 18 March, and published there on 4 April.[3] The proclamation protected the Church of England, but expressed the king's wish that all his subjects were Catholics, and dispensed all the penalties in force against Catholics and all other Nonconformists.

[1] Joseph Berington, *State and Behaviour of the English Catholics* (1781), p. 73, echoing a sentiment expressed by Voltaire. The Jesuit Fr. Petre has become a scapegoat for the years 1685–8. As he left no papers, no assessment of him can be reliable. It seems that his appointment was due to James's over-reliance on the advice of Sunderland. Certainly there was no chance of any preferment for Petre from the anti-Jesuit Innocent XI. Petre's actual influence on King James has yet to be discovered. See the views of Belloc (p. 206), M. V. Hay (pp. 158, 164) and F. C. Turner (pp. 304–5 and 418–22).

[2] 2 Feb. 1687. Quoted in Foley, v. 159. Italics in the original.

[3] Clarke, ii. 108–9, 112.

It was from this point onwards that James should have found how fast he was shedding his supporters. The several lists extant, of the voting strength of the House of Lords that year, are not identical, but they add up to a unanimous story. On the question of repealing the penal laws, the Lords stood 35 at the most in favour, abstainers anything from 10 to 20, and at least 86 against.[1] With the same single-minded determination as that with which he was already handling the two universities, James dissolved the Parliament early in July.

Legislative opposition thus frustrated, he turned and boldly challenged the country's executive organs In order to assess the opinion of local leaders, with a view to the elections that would produce his next Parliament, he sent out instructions to agents all over the country (25 October) to canvass the gentry. The lords lieutenant were to put to their deputy lieutenants and magistrates three questions: If he were chosen knight of the shire, or burgess of a town, would he vote for repeal? Would he in any case help to secure the election of men so minded? Would he support the Declaration of Liberty of Conscience?

The results were a palpable warning to the king. There were many defaulters, many equivocations; and altogether over half the lords lieutenant were unwilling. But James was on his quarter-deck. They were his own officers. The *London Gazette* announced on 11 December that the lists of J.Ps. and deputy lieutenants would be revised, and in the New Year 1688 half the lords lieutenant were removed.[2]

The Second Declaration of Indulgence, 27 April 1688, was thus, so far as legislature and executive and judiciary were each concerned, almost the last straw. With both sides determined on no concessions, the climax was inevitable from the moment when James ordered that on two following Sundays the bishops should have the declaration read in all churches. The seven bishops petitioned him against it on 18 May; he stood firm, and fixed their indictment for 15 June. Five days before this there came the last straw itself, the birth of a son to the queen: the prospect of an indefinite future on King James II's own

[1] *B.M. Add. MSS.* 34, 526, ff. 48 and seq. The French Archives list, and Lord Willoughby's and an anonymous list in the Portland MSS. give respectively the following totals: for repeal, 33, 33, 35; against, 86, 87, 92; doubtful, 20, 19, 10. Those agreeable to repeal included the Bishops of Durham, Chester, Oxford, St. David's and perhaps Rochester.

[2] Duckett, 194–9, 29, 172, 54, 207: from *Rawlinson MSS.* in the Bodleian. M. V. Hay, who rightly points out that Duckett's book 'emphasizes every point which can be made to tell against the King' (*Enigma of James II*, pp. 114–15), himself omits to mention the dismissals which followed the inquiry.

imperious lines. The acquittal of the bishops, and the fall of the king, were foregone conclusions. What he had suffered to build itself during the three years, in the way of a Catholic educational framework, began to be pulled down by provincial mobs for weeks even before James himself lost hope. His co-religionists whom he had gone his unwise way to serve were the first to feel the wrath.

2. SCHOOLS AND THE UNIVERSITIES

As has been said, King James had no educational policy properly so called. Education was still, in royal eyes, a function of religion and politics. His interventions in scholastic matters fall accordingly into two main categories, the dismissals and reappointments, in grammar schools and university colleges. His innovations were confined to licences-to-teach issued to Catholics under the dispensing power.

Of these latter, bearing in mind the legend that has grown up of wholesale appointments in Army and Navy and the law, there were very few.

In May 1686 he licensed Edward Sclater, the incumbent of St. Mary's Church at Putney, 'to keep schools and instruct youth and receive boarders'. Sclater had been a parson of Putney since September 1663; at first a High Churchman, and now since 1685 a Catholic. The terms of this 'Licence, Dispensation and Pardon' served in part as a model for those that followed. It empowered him to keep one or more schools, to be absent accordingly from his cure at Putney (Canterbury arch-diocese) and Esher (Winchester diocese), to employ curates in each place, to forbear all the Anglican services specified in all the statutes since the Reformation Parliament of 1529, to enjoy nevertheless the rights and emoluments and advantages of the cures of Putney and Esher, and to be indemnified from any punishment for breach of the aforesaid Acts. Edward Sclater published in the following year a quarto *apologia*, entitled *Consensus Veterum*, and advertised it in that year's *Catholic Almanack*. Upon the Revolution he joined the company of Vicars of Bray and resumed his Anglican orthodoxy.[1]

The particular gravity of the Sclater dispensation is that, in allowing him to keep his emoluments, it alienated money that properly belonged

[1] His signature is appended to all the minutes in Putney Vestry Book from 13 Sept. 1663 to 17 Apr. 1688, when that of Nathaniel Rosbury supersedes (*Vestry Minutes*, i. 331, 534). The text of the dispensation is in John Gutch, *Collectanea Curiosa* (Oxford, 1781), i. 290–3; cited from Somers MSS. (in Bodleian), ccccix. 104.

to the Anglican Establishment. It was thus as much an 'attack' on the Establishment as James's course of action at Magdalen College, Oxford, so soon to begin.

In the following February (1687) James issued dispensations to seven more schoolmasters. Of five of these nothing is known: Mordant Webster, John Duffs, Thomas Carew, Francis Nelson and Fitzraufe Chamberlain (though Nelson and Carew must have been scions of the Catholic county families of those names). The sixth man, Edward Goodall, came from Lancashire. He was an M.A. of King's College, Cambridge, Vicar of Preston, and a recent convert. Quite clearly he had solicited this licence to teach upon relinquishing his Anglican benefice. The seventh and last of the batch was John Bromley, a Shropshire man, curate of St. Giles-in-the-Fields in London till his recent conversion. His 'boarding school for young gentlemen', which was 'patronized by some of the best Catholic families', continued after the Revolution. It was to this school that the poet Alexander Pope came, in Devonshire Street, after having learnt his rudiments at Silksteed, near Winchester (under Edward Taverner), and from Thomas Deane at Hyde Park Corner. John Bromley subsequently travelled about Europe as a tutor after his wife's death.

Only five other persons are known by name to have been dispensed by James II in these terms: Henry Hills (March 1686), John Gibbs (March 1687), Obadiah Walker of University College, Oxford (May 1686), Mrs. Latham of Aintree (1686) and Edward Jolly (November 1687). Two of these—Hills and Walker—were licensed to print rather than to teach. The official record notes 'several others', but without names. We can therefore put the total of James II's licences to Catholic schoolmasters at roughly a dozen.[1]

John Evelyn the diarist was concerned in some of these licence transactions. He records how, on 12 March 1686, he refused to sign the licence-docket of Hill the printer. On 5 May, when Obadiah Walker and four other Oxford men (including Sclater of Putney) came up for consideration, licence under the Great Seal was refused, and it had to be 'done by immediate warrant, signed by Mr. Solicitor'.

James's recorded interferences with the Anglican grammar schools were likewise few. Most of them matured late in the reign.

The first was at King Edward VI School Birmingham, where early in 1685 the school charter was surrendered and a new one granted by

[1] The list is in *Hist. MSS. Comm. XII*, Lords' Library MSS., pt. vi, p. 301. See also *Lords Journal*, xiv. 394, and, for Mrs. Latham, p. 255 below.

the new king. This differentiated the school into three parts, with masters all classically trained but specialists respectively in geography, chronology and orthography. The board of governors was now packed with Tories; by September the master, Brokesby, was dismissed in favour of John Hickes of Magdalen; and the usher Joseph Webster was replaced by William Wollaston from Runcorn School (7 April 1686) and then one Solomon Whatley (September 1688). It is not certain that the new headmaster John Hickes, the king's nominee under the charter, was a Catholic. He certainly continued to hold his fellowship at Magdalen till 1702. But at the Revolution, of course, he was dispossessed of his mastership at Birmingham. The old charter of the school was restored in 1692.[1]

The second dispute, which began in the summer of 1686, was at Shrewsbury School, where the headmaster, Andrew Taylor, fell ill and thereby inspired the Catholics of Shrewsbury to try to secure the succession for a 'papist'. They chose as candidate a Jesuit, Fr. Sebrand. But when they had secured his admittance as a burgess of Shrewsbury the matter hung fire. It did not come to a head until after the king had visited the school to apply pressure, during his tour of the Midland counties (25 August 1687); then they thwarted him by a subterfuge. The headmaster, Taylor, resigned in secret in October so that the electors, St. John's College at Cambridge, could appoint one Richard Lloyd, and with the approval of the Bishop of Lichfield Lloyd was forthwith installed. (It had been a near shave, for Andrew Taylor died soon after Christmas). Lloyd remained headmaster of Shrewsbury for thirty-six years.[2]

On this tour through the centre of the country in the summer of 1687 the king took in Warwick School also,[3] to make another partisan appointment. His nominee, William Eades, cannot long have been a Catholic, for James had made him Vicar of Warwick in only the previous February. He was now appointed headmaster (13 August) by letters patent, in succession to William Martin, who was ill and died a few weeks later. This affronted both school and town. Witnesses later declared furthermore that Eades had been present at the founding of the new popish chapel in Warwick, and that he had entertained the Catholic Bishop Giffard there (September). The corporation therefore

[1] Cf. A. F. Leach, in *V.C.H.* Warwickshire, ii. 352.

[2] Cf. G. W. Fisher, *Hist. of Shrewsbury School*, 200–1.

[3] The itinerary that summer, from Windsor and back to Oxford, is in *Hist. MSS. Comm.*, R. R. Hastings MSS., ii. 182 (1930).

opposed Eades—and the king dissolved the corporation (by Order in Council in 1688). After the Revolution the dispute was resumed. The restored corporation offered Eades his arrears of salary, together with £65 yearly as 'vicar and schoolmaster', and forty shillings a year for 'repairs'. But they were adamant that he should not teach the school in person. Ultimately he agreed to all this, and Warwick School continued under deputy-masters.[1]

The final case was a reinstatement. Richard Reeve, who had had to resign the mastership of Magdalen College School in 1673 rather than conform, had gone to Douay and become a Benedictine two years later, and to teach humanities at St. Gregory's. He was now back in England. In 1688 James II reinstated him at Magdalen College School. But this he declined, and went to teach instead at the Bluecoat School, Gloucester, and subsequently at Bourton-in-the-Water. During the Revolution he was arrested (December) but released in August 1689. He died in London three years later. It has been said of him that he educated sixty Protestant clergy and forty Catholic priests.[2]

The case of Blackburn Grammar School, where the Catholic Roger Lacey was elected on to the governing body in 1688,[3] does not fall into the same category. It is an example of something temporarily licit; for under the Declaration of Indulgence Catholics could become governors of grammar schools.

These four—Birmingham, Shrewsbury, Warwick and Magdalen—are the only well-attested examples of any policy by James of infiltrating Catholics into the old established grammar schools by overt pressure. Their fewness is on a par with the king's modest outlay from the privy purse in support of Catholic education. He gave £900 to the Jesuit Savoy School in London, £350 to the Fenchurch St. School, £200 each to the Jesuit and Benedictine missions, and £100 each to the Scots Colleges in Rome and Douay and Paris, the English College at Douay and a monastery at Ratisbon.[4]

But of all his scholastic extravagances the battle with the universities has won him most odium, centring on the Magdalen and the Cambridge episodes of 1687.

They were not his first challenges to the two ancient universities, for he appointed a Catholic convert, John Massey of Merton, to the

[1] A. F. Leach, *Hist. of Warwick School*, 140 ff.; and *V.C.H.* Warwickshire, ii. 310–11.

[2] Gillow, v. 403; Foley, v. 958 and note; Wood, *Athenae Oxon.* ii. 905; Dodd, iii. 491; H. N. Birt, *Obit. Book of Benedictines*, 61.

[3] Gillow, iv. 85.

[4] *Cal. S.P. Dom. 1689–90*, p. 383.

Deanery of Christ Church in 1686, and dispensed the master and some of the fellows of University College, Oxford, from attending the Anglican service. But these were mere forays. It gave personal affront to tender consciences, but no more, that the Master of University, Obadiah Walker, declared himself a Catholic and had Mass said in his lodgings (April 1686). More ominous was his opening a public Catholic chapel in the college (August). More ominous still, his attempt to get control of the Oxford University Press. Massey, also, had an oratory at The House by March 1687.[1]

James was not lacking in advisers to spur him on. In Ireland the lord lieutenant, Tyrconnel, was himself striving to get a fellowship at Trinity College, Dublin, and even the provostship, into Catholic hands, despite the warnings of his friends that it would 'startle the Protestants'. He persuaded several of the Irish bishops to press the king on the matter.[2] The Bishop of Oxford (Dr. Samuel Parker) was even prepared to see a Catholic College established in England, at Oxford, 'that they might not be forced to study beyond sea at such great expense'.[3]

On the other hand, the very men the king was trying to advance were dubious of his tactics. The greatest of them, Bishop Leyburne, was to berate him soundly for it at the time. It was immediately after the Declaration of Indulgence that both disputes—with Cambridge and Oxford—began.

The issue at Cambridge centred on a Benedictine priest, Alban Placid Francis, who had been in Cambridgeshire since he arrived on the mission from the Abbey of Lambspring abroad. King James instructed the Vice-Chancellor of Cambridge (Dr. John Peachell) to induct Dom Francis as Master of Arts. The vice-chancellor forbore to do so. On 21 April (1687) a deputation from the university senate waited upon the High Commission Court in Whitehall. Peachell and Sir Isaac Newton led it, and Lord Chancellor Jeffreys browbeat them both on behalf of the king. They were given a week to reply to his Majesty's question of why Francis had not been admitted.

On the resumption of the proceedings the deputation politely challenged the authority of the Court of High Commission in the

[1] J. R. Bloxam, *Magdalen College and James II*, p. viii; Mallet, *Univ. Oxford*, ii. 450 f.

[2] James 'refused, either as unreasonable or else persuaded the Jesuits would be fitter for that function' than Jordan and Moor, whom Tyrconnel wanted. (*Hist. MSS. Comm.*, Stuart Papers, vi. 26–7). Spring of 1687.

[3] Letter from a Liège Jesuit, 2 Feb. 1687; in Foley, v. 158; and a pamphlet of c. 1690, quoted in Hay, 122.

matter of university appointments at all. Peachell pleaded the wording of his vice-chancellor's oath as his vindication. When in his agitation he bungled it in quoting, Dr. Cook of Jesus College who prompted him was shouted down to silence by Jeffreys. In this atmosphere the proceedings were adjourned for a month. Dr. Peachell was, however, summarily dismissed by the king from the vice-chancellorship (7 May). But James, by now embroiled at Oxford on a far graver issue than the introduction of an M.A., quietly dropped his patronage of the Benedictine Fr. Francis.[1]

The Oxford dispute was on no less a matter than the appointment of a college head: the President of Magdalen. It is this episode that has become a *cause célèbre*, since it reveals the full panoply of Stuart divine right and royal prerogative in action, and the personal tenacity of James in backing his own nerve against all comers.

In March 1687, when the President of Magdalen died, the king nominated to succeed him Anthony Farmer. The reasons which induced him to do so can hardly have outweighed the disadvantages; for Farmer was not an Oxford but a Cambridge man, he was not a fellow of Magdalen, he was not personally popular, and he was said to have taught in a Nonconformist school. On such a basis did the king fight for nine full months and repeople an entire college in the process.

On 31 March the vice-president, Dr. Aldworth, notified the fellows to hold the election of the new president a fortnight later. Before a week had passed the king issued his *mandamus* for the election of Farmer. The fellows appealed to him against this, but getting no reply by the day appointed for the election they elected John Hough. When the college visitor, the Bishop of Winchester, solemnly inducted Hough three days later, and Convocation conferred a doctorate upon him, it was patent that the king was up against a solid and unanimous front.

A deputation from the college, led by the Vice-President Aldworth and Dr. Fairfax, came before the High Commission Court in London on 6 June. As in the case of their colleagues at Cambridge, they asked for legal advice before replying to the king's demand to know why they had disobeyed him. Jeffreys gave them till the following Monday. Their reply, in writing, cited college statutes as making it legally

[1] For this dispute see the sources in Lingard (2nd ed.), xiv. 147–9; also the *Medulla Hist. Angl.*, by T. N. (4th ed. 1694), 478 f.; Gillow, ii. 33, iii. 585 f.; Clarke, ii. 127; H. M. Hyde, *Jeffreys*, 268 f.; Turner, 335. For Dom Francis see Birt, *Benedictine Obits*, 75.

impossible for them to act on the king's recommendation. Dr. Fairfax ventured to question the jurisdiction of the court.

Upon the resumption therefore (22 June) matters came to a head. The court was treated to some revelations as to the character of the royal nominee. They gave, so the Bishop of Chester confided to his diary afterwards, 'the blackest character of Mr. Farmer . . . that any modest man would blush to hear, and any on this side Hell to be guilty of it'. But the king would not be gainsaid. Aldworth was dismissed from the vice-presidency and Fairfax from his fellowship. The office of president—since in the light of the revelations James could hardly persevere with the cause of Farmer, whom even Jeffreys had now wryly admitted to be 'a very bad man'—was to stand vacant for the time being.

James now gave orders to the fellows direct. When they refused to acknowledge them he had a messenger affix them in writing to the gates of the college. When this failed, he brought the fellows before the High Commission Court for contempt. Then on 14 August he issued a new writ *mandamus* for the election of a president. The new nominee was the Bishop of Oxford, already known to be favourable to allotting one college in the university to Catholics. But this candidate (Dr. Samuel Parker) was no less ineligible than Farmer. The fellows informed his Majesty that in any case the presidency was already filled—by the John Hough they had elected in April.

At this the king decided to settle the matter in person, on the spot. He arrived in Oxford on 3 September, following his visits of castigation to the grammar schools of Shrewsbury and Warwick. The following morning he interviewed the fellows—on their knees at his express order. From this encounter he got such scant satisfaction that a month later he sent three commissioners to Oxford, to enforce his demands on Magdalen by means of a visitation, with three troops of horse to protect them. The crowds were so great that at Magdalen the proctors had to be sent for as well, to keep the peace, during the five days of the visitation (21–5 October).

In reply to the visitor (the Bishop of Winchester) Dr. Hough said as president that any decisions made by these commissioners would be null and void: for his lordship the bishop was himself the visitor, and the king could be only an 'extraordinary' visitor, and only doubtfully that. He declined to hand over the keys. The commissioners thereupon declared the president's place 'null and void'.

The fellows were then asked why, if they could not 'elect' the Bishop of Oxford, they would not 'admit' him, which was all that the king's letter asked them to do. It was at this point that the *de facto* president, Dr. Hough, returned, protesting at his deprivation and removal and appealing to the courts of justice: 'upon which the rabble hummed'. The commissioners for their part bound him over (in bond of £1,000 and two sureties of £250), and disallowed his appeal on the ground that the visitation was by commission under the Great Seal.

On the last day of the visitation the commissioners officially installed the Bishop of Oxford as president of the college. They had to do it by proxy. Called upon to submit to him, the fellows asked for time. The president's lodgings, which Hough had locked, were opened by a locksmith on the commissioners' orders. All the other keys were found inside, and the proxy (Mr. Wickens) 'was left in quiet possession, and so adjourned'.

Only two of the fellows, Charnock and Thomas Smith, accepted the Bishop of Oxford as president. On 12 December, twenty-five fellows were expelled, by casting-vote of Jeffreys in a now evenly-balanced Court of High Commission. Early in the new year Anthony à Wood noted that there was not one commoner nor nobleman left at Magdalen, whilst at Christ Church they had fallen from forty to two. A State Paper of that January (1688) listed the fellows of Magdalen as two. And then the new president died.

There are those who will have said that the death of the Bishop of Oxford at this juncture could have been utilized to save the king's position: that it was providential. But James had set his hand to the plough. He nominated a successor on 31 March. It was no less a person than one of the four ecclesiastical heads of the Catholic Church in England, appointed as vicars apostolic by the pope in this very January: Bishop Bonaventure Giffard, Vicar Apostolic of the Midland District.

Dr. Giffard was a scholar of eminence and a saintly man of forty-six. He had been educated at Douay College and the Sorbonne. A few days after his nomination at Magdalen he was consecrated in Whitehall as Bishop of Madoura. On 15 June he took possession of the president's lodgings, in a Magdalen College by now overwhelmingly Catholic through the deprivations and reallotment of fellowships. Mass began to be said daily in the chapel. A student, Henry Fleming, wrote in July that 'Dr. Giffard . . . confirmed a great many last week in the College chapel, where they have Mass daily and sermons on Sundays.

The report of the breaking of the brass eagle in that chapel is false. That College is pretty full, and all papists but two or three.' Protestant fellows who refused the president were expelled by order of the king on 7 August.

James seems to have had no appreciation of how far his headlong judgment was ruining the aspirations of his lofty motives. For him, the preferment was an act of gratitude for spiritual comfort which Dr. Giffard had given him in the bad days before his accession. But even to his leading advisers it was, by now, madness. Bishop John Leyburne, the senior of the four vicars apostolic, 'boldly told his Majesty that the fellows and students were wronged by the appointment of Dr. Giffard to the presidency, and that restitution ought to be made to them on religious as well as political grounds'. Bishop Leyburne also let it be known that he himself was 'of opinion that it had been a spoliation, and that the possession, in which the Roman Catholics now found themselves, was one of violence, and illegal'.

James went ahead. The turning-point came in July (1688) when the chancellor of the whole university (the Duke of Ormonde) died. The king at once sent a mandate to the vice-chancellor nominating as successor the Lord Chancellor Jeffreys. But the university had been learning tactics from its energetic royal master himself; and by July 1688 there were divers façades of the royal power already cracking. Convocation met in great haste, elected Ormonde's son as chancellor and apologized with profusion to Jeffreys. From then on, for the king, it was retreat.

In all this there is no call to impugn the king's motives. James II's personal integrity of character has indeed been almost regarded, by his less really critical detractors, as complete to the point of mulishness. But nothing more sharpens the tragedy of his mishandling of the universities than the fact that, pathetically enough, in those final weeks of 1688, before William of Orange landed, the flower of English Catholic scholarship was on its way home from exile in Flanders, to contribute to those seats of learning an added lustre so long denied them through exile. As late as 21 September a first colony of scholars left Douay to take up posts in Magdalen under Bonaventure Giffard. They were led by Edward Hawarden, designate professor of divinity. A second (and last) colony left on 5 October, comprising theologians and scholastics, some to teach, some to complete their studies in the halls their own grandfathers had once known. By mid-November those of them who had escaped capture in the days following the king's flight were back at Douay again.[1] Another century had yet to pass, before the ultimate 'return' of the exiled colleges during the French Revolution.

3. THE CATHOLIC REVIVAL IN ENGLAND

Below the political stage, and interested in the battles of public men only from the standpoint of peaceful citizens anxious to preserve their several vocations free from penalty, the Catholic rank-and-file at the accession of James II gloried in one fact above all. From the moment of the Declaration of Indulgence onwards, they could practise openly the religion of their fathers and bring up their children in their own faith as fast as teachers could be made forthcoming. It was no longer necessary to take frightful risks when a priest was needed for baptizing, marrying and giving the last rites of the Church. In London and perhaps twenty large centres throughout the country Mass could be heard openly.[2] There had not been, in living memory, such a freedom from suspense, nor so hysterical a realization of it. All the more reason, then, why his Catholic subjects prayed that King James would move with circumspection. The Declaration of Indulgence gave them infinitely more than they had hoped for, certainly all they wanted. The suspending power inhibited the penalties on Catholic religious observance. The dispensing power could furnish them passports into professions and livelihoods so long closed to them—and among these, that of teacher of youth.

It is no matter for surprise that in these circumstances less was done in Catholic reconstruction than the opportunity would have suggested. The opportunity was so short. Foundations had to be relaid. The achievements of the three years are in fact considerable.

[1] The Magdalen College episode is dealt with fully in J. R. Bloxam, *Magdalen College and James II* (Oxford Hist. Soc. vi), 1886. See also Lingard (2nd ed.), xiv. 150–5, 193–4 and sources; Mallet, *Univ. Oxford*, ii. 451 ff.; H. M. Hyde, *Jeffreys*, 271 ff., 288 ff.; *Diary of John Cartwright, Bishop of Chester* (Camden Soc.), xxii. 62–3, 84 note, 86–93; P.R.O., *S.P. Dom. Jas. II*, Bundle 5, No. 7: Foley, v. 823; Gillow, iii. 590, iv. 235–6, iii. 169–70, v. 374; *Hist. MSS. Comm.*, xii. pt. 7, S. H. le Fleming MSS., 212 (1890); B. Hemphill, in *Clergy Review*, Feb. 1948, 91ff.; F. C. Turner, *James II*, 335–44, 417–19, etc. Major Hay (p. 121) insists that the fellows had accepted royal dispensations from their own statutes (as to celibacy, saying Mass, etc.) when it suited them. But the gravity of James's policy resides in its inroads upon Anglican preserves. E. L. Taunton's theory of a Jesuit plot in the Oxford affair (*Jesuits in England*, 458) rebuts itself by its own narrative.

[2] In *Arch. West.* (xxxiv, No. 271) there is a list of some sixty priests in London in 1685.

Of supreme importance from one standpoint was the reconstruction of the visible organization of the Catholic Church, for the ten per cent of the population who professed allegiance to it. The old hierarchy had died out a century before; the three archpriests a generation later; and the second of the two bishops (Richard Smith) who succeeded them resigned his charge in 1631, though he did not die until 1655. For more than thirty years the Catholics of England had been without a spiritual head nearer than Rome. Hence the importance of the appointment of the president of Douay College, Dr. John Leyburne, to be vicar apostolic, in August 1685. He was a visible head, and from his quarters in Whitehall he could perambulate the country for confirmations, visitations of parishes, the consecrating of priests and the settlement of quarrels among the laity, the secular clergy and the regulars.

The ecclesiastical edifice was completed, in skeleton form, during the last summer of the reign, when three other vicariates were created. Henceforth Bishop Leyburne ruled the London District, till on his death in 1702 he was succeeded by Bishop Bonaventure Giffard from the Midland District. The Northern District was entrusted to Bishop James Smith, and the Western (including Wales) to Bishop Philip Ellis. Scotland preserved its separate ecclesiastical existence, as it does to this day.[1] Confirmations on a large scale began all over the country. Bishop Leyburne on his tour confirmed 1,153 Catholics in the new chapel at Preston in 1687, and altogether over 20,000 persons in some fifty-six northern centres.[2] The four vicars apostolic together issued a joint pastoral letter to their people.[3]

Within this framework, parochial life revived. Existing chapels were few. Even in so Catholic a part of Lancashire as Preston there was no regular chapel for the town as yet; Mass had been said intermittently since as far back as 1605; but only now was a tenement secured (at the end of Friargate), and it was to serve as chapel henceforth till 1761.[4] At Lancaster in 1687 Mass was said 'in the schoolhouse', with one of the judges of assize present.[5] At Chester the

[1] Brady, iii. 140 f.; Hemphill, *Early Vicars Apostolic*, ch. i–ii.

[2] See details in *Catholicon*, iv. 86–7 (1817). Leyburne's Confirmation Lists, place by place, dated, are in *Arch. West.* xxxv, Nos. 5–60. Their chief interest lies in the extent to which they fill a gap between the last Recusant Rolls and the earliest Baptismal Registers. See T. B. Trappes-Lomax, 'Bishop Leyburn's Visitation in 1687', summarized in *Newsletter for Students of Recusant Hist.*, IV, 1962, pp. 16–21.

[3] Printed by Henry Hills, 1688: reprinted in London in 1747.

[4] Foley, v. 395; and Gillow, ii. 144–5 for a history of the Preston Mission.

[5] Blundell, iii. 6–7.

Anglican bishop told the Recorder 'to find out a convenient place, by his Majesty's command, in the Castle or elsewhere, for the Roman Catholics' devotions'.[1] Other chapels were erected by local secular priests serving the mission, at three places in Derbyshire: Chesterfield, Newbold and Hathersage; and one was projected at Reading.[2] An alert Protestant book, published at the time to record the progress of the revival, had detected nine papist chapels by the end of 1687.[3] A body of 'Rules' agreed upon, in James's very first year, by the Catholic clergy operating in Staffordshire, shows how great the opportunity was seen to be: '21: That we endeavour for Youths of our own County to be sent to Colledges, that a succession may follow us in the Mission. 22: To the End we may have a Public Library or two in the County, 'Tis agreed to that every Brother at his Death shall leave Part of his Books to be placed in these Libraries.'[4] But while the work of the secular clergy could not be planned and co-ordinated till the framework of Church government had been fully restored (that is, till 1688), nor the shortage of priests remedied, the religious orders had their full provincial organization and could act quickly, though with limited numbers. By the end of James's first year the regulars were nearly all established in London, whence they put out branches.

The Benedictines came first, in 1685, with a community installed in St. James's Palace. Early in 1687 there came also to St. John's, at Clerkenwell, Dom James Carker, who had been condemned to death during the Oates Plot, for his priesthood, and had languished in Newgate till James's accession. At Clerkenwell he built a 'mighty pretty convent'. The king had also written to the English Benedictine nuns at Ghent, inviting the Abbess Mary Knatchbull to transfer their house to England. James himself had been converted while at Ghent. But this project was still in preparation when the Revolution came. It was in the Benedictine chapel at St. James's that Bishop Philip Ellis was consecrated in May 1688, and the Old Pretender baptized on 25 October.[5]

Early in 1686 the Franciscans, who had been at Osmotherly in Yorkshire for twenty years, opened a friary in the little Catholic seed-plot at Lincoln's Inn Fields, 'near the arches', with Paul Atkinson as

[1] *Diary*, 31 Aug. 1687 (Camden Soc. xxii. 76).

[2] Foley, v. 488. A draft circular about the Reading chapel is in *Arch. West.* xxxiv, No. 263.

[3] *Medulla Hist. Angl.*, 477.

[4] *Arch. West.* xxxiv, No. 280.

[5] Pink, *Clerkenwell*; Guilday, 249; Gillow, iv. 65; Birt, *Benedictine Obits*, 76; Weldon *Chronicle*, 231.

prefect and catechist of a community totalling nineteen friars and novices. A second Franciscan venture, on the south bank of the Thames at the Surrey end of the Fulham ferry, was a school at Putney. 'Shall there be a school of Humanities under Dr. Slaughter *in oppido Putney*?' ask the minutes of the Second Definatory (held on 15 July), and the answer was 'affirmative'. The minutes of the following 18 October decided that this 'gymnasium de Putney' should be continued. The wording is significant—it was not a novice-house but a school. The third Franciscan house established during the reign was at Baddesley, near Birmingham: an area which from now on was continuously a Franciscan mission. The king gave £180 in timber. The church built at Baddesley, by Father Leo Randolph, was blessed by Bishop Giffard only two months before it was destroyed in the Revolution.[1]

Only one Dominican friary was opened—alongside the Franciscans in Great Lincoln's Inn, February 1687; and only one house of Discalced Carmelites—in Barge Yard, Bucklersbury, in the City of London, at the end of July 1687.[2] One other centre in the City had as stormy a beginning from internal discord as it was to have a stormy end from the mob.

This was the chapel in Lime Street, by the Bavarian Embassy, on the site of the present-day Fishmongers' Hall. Its sponsors were among the leading Catholic missionaries of the day: John Gother the apologist; Andrew Giffard, brother of the vicar apostolic; James Dymock, later prior of St. Arnoud near Chartres: and Christopher Tootell, later vicar-general in Lancashire and a pillar of the school at Fernyhalgh. The trouble was that these men became embroiled in disputes with their brethren, were branded by them as 'Blackloists', and superseded in the chapel, within six months of its opening, by Jesuits.[3]

The work of the English Jesuits, indeed, during James's three years eclipsed that of all the rest. They opened no fewer than twelve schools, spread among the territorial 'Colleges' into which England and Wales had been progressively divided since the erection of the province nearly seventy years before. The efficiency of Jesuit organization, with

[1] Franciscan Archives, *Acta Capitulorum*, 1629–1746, 188–9, 194; Franciscan Centenary Pamphlets, ii. 6, 13; Oliver, *Collections*, 559; Thaddeus, *Franciscans in England*, 161.

[2] Taunton, i. 175 note; Zimmerman, *Carmel in England*, 301–2.

[3] Gillow, ii. 149, 452–3; Gregory Macdonald, 'The Lime Street Chapel', in *Dublin Review*, Nos. 361–2 (1927); and S.J. *Letters and Notices*, liv. 59–67 (1939).

a century and a half of world-wide experience behind it, was now to be shown at its elastic best.

Of the twelve schools, two were in London. Of these more anon. They were revolutionary in their up-to-dateness. The others were at Bury St. Edmunds, Durham, Lincoln, Newcastle, Norwich, Pontefract-York, Stapehill (Wimborne), Welshpool, Wigan and Wolverhampton. The extent of these schools, as centres, is at once obvious. Some of them show great adaptability to the circumstances of time and place.

The pioneer at York was Henry Hamerton, who transferred the headquarters of the York district from Pontefract to the city itself, and opened 'a flourishing school of sixty scholars'. As he had to visit the missions all over the district, he could not be always present. Accordingly, say the *Annual Letters*, 'he employed a schoolmaster, a secular, who had been educated in our schools. His pay he got from the scholars, and in addition the Father allowed him about 66 *scudi* [£20] a year.' Besides this, Father Hamerton supplied books to the poor, and catechisms, and other things necessary for instruction. All this cost nothing to the province; it was accomplished solely by means of the alms he collected. Many Protestants entrusted their sons to him to be instructed in Catholic doctrine. Public examinations of the scholars in the school, and other literary exercises, showed the great progress they made. At his visit to this York school in July 1687 Dr. Leyburne confirmed some 230 in the chapel. Father Hamerton was seized at the Revolution and taken to Wakefield and to York Castle, where he was fined and bailed. He died at Ghent in 1718. His York school is the first recorded Catholic school of penal days to run a lending-library for the neighbourhood.[1]

The Peter Hamerton, S.J., who began the school at Lincoln may have been his brother. This school was at first small, but the number of scholars flocking to it became so great that it was proposed to purchase larger premises. An agreement was almost completed for buying one of the principal houses in the city, when the rumoured approach of William of Orange put an end to all such thoughts. The school-house, in which Bishop Leyburne had confirmed 150 persons, was sacked by the mob. A bonfire was made of the furniture and books, and Father Hamerton was hunted from the neighbourhood.[2]

[1] *Annual Letters, S.J.*, 1689, in *Stonyhurst MSS.*, Anglia IV, 13. ii (Cardwell transcripts), 229 ff.; Foley, v. 727; Oliver, *Collections S.J.*, 111; Gillow, iii. 107.

[2] *Annual Letters*; Foley, v. 621; Oliver, *Collections, S.J.*, 111.

At Durham, Father Thomas Pearson called his school a *gymnasium publicum*. At Wigan there were over a hundred scholars, and under the patronage of the mayor a new church was begun, and pensioners' quarters attached to the school. Here in the heart of Lancashire Leyburne confirmed over thirteen hundred people. The priest-schoolmaster was Father James Conell, S.J.[1]

The Bury St. Edmunds school was spoken of as a school; 'the *sacellum publicum* was very celebrated indeed, and the *schola* sufficiently patronized'. About eighteen young gentlemen were regular pensioners in the house, and some of the adult townsfolk attended the school classes. It was thus a boarding and day school, with an adult extramural side. Foley quotes a laconic entry of forty years later: 'to Bury, to inquire about books and other effects left there ever since the demolition of that school, £1–3–6.'[2]

At Gateshead, Newcastle-on-Tyne, the 'well frequented classical school' had a resident priest, Philip Leigh (*alias* Layton). Here Leyburne confirmed 300 and more. One of Leigh's sermons (preached as chaplain to James II) was printed by Henry Hills. After the Revolution the author migrated, under his other *alias* of Metcalf, to the Powis family.[3]

Of the other schools of the Jesuits outside London it is worth notice that at Wolverhampton there were about fifty day-boys and twelve boarders; that at Welshpool also, where the school was under the patronage of the Duke of Powis, there were *convictors* (boarders); and that the school at Stapehill in Dorset seems to have survived till discovered and broken up as late as 1724.[4]

We come finally, in the Jesuit innovations, to the two highly remarkable schools in London: the Savoy, and Fenchurch Street. These showed an interdenominational policy unique in English history till very much later on.

The famous school in the Savoy is heralded in a letter sent by a Jesuit in Liège in February 1687: 'Many houses are bought for the college in the Savoy (as they call it) nigh Somerset House, London, the palace of the queen-dowager, to the value of about 18,000 florins, in making of which after the form of a college they labour very hard,

[1] *Annual Letters*; Foley, v. 319; Oliver, *Coll. S.J.*, 186 note; Blundell, ii. 70.

[2] *Ann. Letters*; Foley, v. 526, 538; Oliver, *Coll. S.J.*, 206 note.

[3] Gillow, *Church in Gateshead*, 45; Foley, v. 660, vi. 418.

[4] For these see Foley, v. 943; *Exeter Post Master or Loyal Mercury*, 2 Oct. 1724; *Ann. Letters*.

that the school may be opened before Easter.'[1] It was actually opened on Whit Sunday (24 May).

The provincial (Fr. John Keynes) had wanted not only public chapels in the metropolis but a centre where the Society could live in community and no longer in billets. The General in Rome (Charles de Noyalle) had approved the project prior to his death the previous December. The site secured was on the Thames bank, in the Savoy, facing the open fields on the south bank. As soon as some troops who were occupying it had been removed, and a minimum of alterations carried out, Jesuit life in the building began: and the school.

At the opening there were already 250 boys. A prospectus had been spread broadcast, designating the school as open *gratis*, for the teaching of Greek and Latin, to any boys irrespective of their denomination or condition. There were two classes to begin with, under two masters, Andrew Poulton and Edward Hall. Soon they had to send for a third master, Thomas Parker from Belgium, as the daily intake rose so rapidly. When the school reopened in September a fourth master had been added, Richard Plowden, brought specially from the college at St. Omer. The classes were held in separate rooms: Grammar, Syntax, Poetry. Before long the school was challenging the London grammar schools to public 'scholastic contests'. James II himself gave some £900 towards extensions and improvements, following the occasion of his visit to the school in October 1687, when three boys delivered addresses to him in Greek, Latin and English. 'The King went by water to the Savoy, and was met on the steps [of the Water Gate] by the Provincial . . . who conducted him to the Chapel and School. He was so pleased with the Greek, Latin and English speeches that he gave them gowns and [said] they should be called his scholars.'

In this house, till the Fenchurch Street School was gained later, the provincial himself took up residence, with Charles Palmer as first rector, Thomas Green as minister, William Mumford as *socius*, Edward Tidder (the procurator of the province) and John Persall (King's Preacher). The masters—Poulton, Hall, Parker, Plowden—soon found themselves teaching more than 400 children, over half of them Protestants.[2]

[1] *Somers Tracts*, ed. Scott, ix. 76–8, and quoted in E. L. Taunton, *Jesuits in England*, 455.

[2] For the site, see S.J. *Letters and Notices*, liv. 52–9 (1939); for the Prospectus, Foley, v. 263ff.; for the Staff, Foley v. 265, and Gillow, iv. 32, v. 272, 351; for the king's visit, *Hist. MSS. Comm.*, Downshire MSS. 272–3 (also quoted in *Letters and Notices*). See also Strype, *Stowe's Survey* (ed. 1720), ii. bk. 4, 107–8.

The Fenchurch Street School came into existence (25 March 1688) to relieve this pressure. It was administered from the Jesuit chapel that had been functioning in the City already for two years, adjoining the Bavarian Embassy and protected by the Lord Mayor from any danger of mob-hostility. James II made the school an annual grant of £350. It was a smaller school than the Savoy, since its numbers could be taught as one class, by Father Charles Petre, brother of the king's Jesuit Privy Councillor.

We can see the revolutionary character of these London Jesuit innovations nowhere better than in the *Rules* of this Fenchurch Street school. The three salient regulations are worth quotation in full:

III: And although youths of different professions, whether Catholics or Protestants, come to these Schools; yet in teaching all, there shall be no distinction made, but all shall be taught with equal diligence and care, and every one shall be promoted according to his deserts.

IV: There shall not be, either by masters or scholars, any tampering or meddling to persuade anyone from the profession of his own religion; but there shall be all freedom for every one to practise that religion he shall please, and none shall be less esteemed for being of a different religion from others.

V: None shall upbraid or reproach any one on the account of religion; and when any exercise of religion shall be practised, as hearing Mass, catechising or preaching, or any other, it shall be lawful for any Protestant, without any molestation or trouble, to absent himself from such exercise if he please.

The order of the day at the Savoy school was the same, the Protestants being 'in no way restrained in their religion or required to assist at Mass or any [of the Catholic] public devotions'.[1]

Given the manifest innovation embodied in this interdenominational policy, several points of commentary suggest themselves. First, those who believe (with Major M. V. Hay) that James II meant what he said in extending freedom of conscience to *all* Dissenters, and that the Declarations of Indulgence were but implementing a determination he had expressed as early as 1674 (when he had ordered the Governor of New York to 'leave *everyone* in peace and quiet on the subject of religion)',[2] will see in the Jesuit schools set up in London under his

[1] Full text of Fenchurch St. *Rules* in the Bodleian: Asmole F. 1 (4). Printed in *The Month*, cxxviii. 264ff. (1916). Cf. Clarke, *James II*, ii. 79, from 'King James, Loose Sheets, p. 18'. See also *Venetian Newsletter*, 3 Oct. 1687, and Terriesi's *Dispatches*, xvii. 82.

[2] Hay, 77; T. Hughes, *Jesuits in N. America*, ii. 143.

patronage an enlightened policy in religious education hardly visible anywhere else in Europe at the time. Secondly, those who reflect how far in advance of Catholic opinion this Jesuit policy indeed was, may detect caution rather than modesty behind the Jesuits' own humble account of the schools in their *Annual Letters*. Thirdly, the fear of 'Jesuitry' still prevalent in England, and the political unwisdom of the king in nevertheless appointing Edward Petre to his Privy Council, made it easy enough for honest Protestants to impugn the schools' prospectus altogether and regard their practice as mere biding-the-time: especially since, as the figures show, the sheer educational quality of the schools attracted a flock of Protestant parents, and thereby gave anxiety to the Establishment.

Ironically enough, therefore, these Jesuit schools were a collateral cause of that Protestant charity school movement which was to dominate the eighteenth century. This is not to say that without Poulton and Petre there would have been no charity school movement. Nor that it would have otherwise tarried for a generation. The problem of schooling the urban masses in London was already in men's minds. But the Protestant movement to cope with this began when it did, because of the example, and the success, and the feared consequences, of the English Jesuits.

'The scholars bred up under Poulton the Jesuit at the Savoy', warned Luttrell, 'are to be elected King's Scholars [at Cambridge] and sent to Maudlin College in Oxford.' The Bishop of Ely (Symon Patrick) explained that 'the Romish priests were then so busy that they set up a school to teach youths for nothing, which we thought might draw many into their snare, and therefore we agreed to do the same . . .'.

They did it by setting up a school in the churchyard of St. Martin-in-the-Fields, under the care of 'an excellent master Mr. Postlethwaite' (later master of St. Paul's School). This enterprise did not outlast the reign of James II, for at the Revolution they 'thought the money might be better employed to the relief of poor Vicars'. Nor was it the first of its kind, for as early as 1685 a Protestant draper, William Blake, had used the term 'charity school' for his own venture at Highgate. In June 1687 four Anglican bishops designed to erect a 'free school' in Lincoln's Inn Fields, and 'the project is afoot in divers other places, the Protestants being resolved not to be outdone in charity by any of a different persuasion'.

It is remarkable how, long after the charity school movement was well established, its supporters were still reminded in charity sermons of its anti-popish origins. 'Every Charity School', said Dr. Kennett in 1706, 'is as it were a fortress and a frontier-garrison against Popery . . . and a Grace and defender of our Reformation.' The school at St. Margaret's, Westminster, set up in 1688, had been started, said Hendley, 'to countermine the policy of the Jesuits, who at that time had erected a Charity Grammar School in the Savoy, to corrupt and poison the minds of the poorer sort of youth'. And the momentum lived on.[1]

The London of 1688 (centenary year of the Armada) must indeed have alarmed anyone haunted by 'popery and wooden shoes'. The Jesuits were in Fenchurch Street and the Savoy; the Benedictines in St. James's and at Clerkenwell; the Franciscans and Dominicans in Lincoln's Inn Fields; the Carmelites in Bucklersbury. Of 'fashionable' Catholic schools for boys there were at least two of very recent origin. One, on the fringe of the suburbs at Hyde Park Corner, was run by a layman, Thomas Deane. It was to this school that the young Alexander Pope came after his period of 'rudiments' under Edward Taverner at Silksteed near Winchester. Deane, we are told, had stood in the pillory for his principles, and it was probably on that account that the Catholic gentry sent their sons to him; for he was 'an incapable teacher'. Certainly he seems to have untaught Pope much of the grounding he had had at Silksteed. Pope passed on from him to the second fashionable Catholic academy, that of John Bromley (licensed by James II in February 1687) in Devonshire Street, Bloomsbury.[2]

Out at Hammersmith, too, the Mary Ward convent school of 'Mrs. Long' (Frances Bedingfield) still flourished, and its sister-school at the Bar Convent in York was well under way. Hammersmith had now taken in the nuns from St. Martin's Lane (1685). By the end of 1686 Frances Bedingfield had gone north to start the Bar Convent school, leaving Cicely Cornwallis in charge. From then onwards the two schools were under separate headmistresses. Towards the end of 1689, we are told, the queen opened 'a school for maidens under four women in the habit of nuns. No religious distinction will be made; poor and

[1] Luttrell, *Brief Relation*, i. 437; *Hist. MSS. Comm.*, Downshire MSS., 1A, p. 246; *Venetian Newsletter*, 20 June 1687; Kennett's Sermon of 16 May 1706 (publ. 1729); W. Hendley, *Defence of Charity Schools* (1725), p. 1. See also M. E. Jones, *Charity School Movement* (1938), 110; J. W. Adamson, *Short Hist. of Education* (1919), 197. A not untypical Protestant verdict is that of Macpherson (*Hist. of Gt. Britain*, 571)—'His erecting popish schools to seduce the children of his subjects from Protestantism were instances of insults to his people as well as a folly in himself.'

[2] Cf. George Paston, *Mr. Pope*, i. 5.

rich to enjoy the benefit, provided they come in clean and decent habits.'[1]

Elsewhere the revival was gathering strength. Not only were there the other ten Jesuit schools opened throughout the rest of the country, and the Franciscans at Osmotherley, and the schools continuing from earlier Stuart times at Scarisbrick and Fernyhalgh and Formby and Silksteed; but public chapels were functioning at York (under the Benedictine Francis Lawson),[2] Gloucester, Cambridge, Exeter, Hatfield (under the patronage of the Earl of Salisbury),[3] and Formby, and there are at least two other schools in the provinces which are worthy of special note.

The first of these was at Stafford, and intended expressly for the poorer children of the neighbourhood. It was founded by a secular priest, Daniel Fitter (? Fisher), whose family came from the Catholic *enclave* of Wolverhampton. He had been trained in the English College at Lisbon. At the Revolution the school was swept away.

The other school, at Aintree near Liverpool, was run jointly by a surgeon and his wife, Richard and Mrs. Latham. From this fact we may infer that it was a boys' boarding-school. The Lathams were prosecuted for teaching without licence, but the king intervened and licensed them in 1686. When the royal dispensation was flouted by the town authorities, James characteristically dismissed the mayor and senior aldermen.

In Wales, where the reign shows no new schools, beyond that of the Jesuits at Welshpool, the salient event of the three years was the issue of a catechism in Welsh, published in London in 1688, the work of Hugh Owen, S J., who was at Holywell, where there was a Jesuit and also a secular mission.[4]

The existence of one more school is known: at Lancaster; for Mass was said there in 1687 'in the schoolhouse'. But we have no details.[5]

4. THE DESTRUCTION, 1688–9

The Catholic king had thus brought it about that his co-religionists were free to worship in public, wherever they could build or rent a

[1] See Harting, *Cath. London Missions*, 185 ff.; *York Convent*, 77; *Hist. MSS. Comm.*, Downshire MSS., 282.

[2] *Hist. MSS. Comm.*, Rydal Hill MSS., 208; Birt, *Benedictine Obits*, 74.

[3] Taunton, *Benedictines*, i. 175.

[4] Gillow, v. 223; Oliver, *Coll. S.J.*, 153.

[5] Blundell, iii. 6–7.

chapel or a schoolhouse. They were temporarily as free from the penal laws as the Declaration of Indulgence and a crop of dispensations, backed by the sanction of dismissal against fractious local officials, could make them. The ecclesiastical structure of the Catholic Church, as a tolerated minority body, had been restored. Catholics held public positions out of all proportion to what a mere 'general toleration', without patronage, could have secured them. Six members of the Privy Council were Catholics; two Commissioners of the Treasury; half the lords lieutenant and deputy-lieutenants and sheriffs and justices of the peace. Three Oxford colleges had Catholic heads and more than a sprinkling of Catholic fellows. There were some ten new houses of the religious orders. There were some twenty new schools established since the opening of the reign: twelve of them Jesuit, the others by laymen, and secular or regular clergy. The total of Catholic schools functioning in England and Wales at the height of the revival under James II must have been many more than these that can be documented.

Apart from the Catholic courtiers, this revival had been the work of apostles rather than politicians: laity who had (from experience, and from the memories of their own families) everything to lose and nothing to gain from political insinuation; clergy who, though a few acted otherwise, had been barred from political matters since the foundation of Allen's college in exile at Douay in 1568. As the king proceeded on his way, this rank-and-file knew what appalling risks their pastoral work was entailing. Should he go down, they would go down again with him. Better never to have risen.

The aged Lord Belasyse dated their ruin from James's second address to his first Parliament, in 1685; he made the prophecy the same night. And although it is policy rather than prattle that makes revolutions, the prattle of the day, too, had its part in the final collapse. There is a world of background significance in the report of a newsletter in March 1688 that 'of a corpse whose fragments were found in divers quarters of the city, the homicide and murderess has been discovered in the person of its wife, and thus all suspicion and discourse computing the crime to the Jesuit Fathers, and the Catholics, ceases'.[1] In such a climate there was danger in the very fact of open Catholicism; in the very sight of the friar's habit in the street, and the little Protestant boys turning in at the gates of the Catholic schools.

[1] Quoted in Hay, 62.

There was, moreover, an outward manifestation of Catholic piety that both exasperated the Protestant populace and alienated intellectual circles: the exploiting of alleged miracles, which may have been true miracles or may not, but brought the whole connotation of 'miraculous' into disrepute and tended to bear out, in undiscriminating eyes, the words of the Elizabethan reformers on the idolatry of Catholics. Such may well have been also, for those with access to the records, the discrepancy between King James's £2,150 given to schools and colleges, and the £4,000 he expended on healing-medals when he went round touching for the King's Evil.[1]

The storm began to break only a fortnight after James had begun in a hurry to try to repair his long chain of blunders. He had admitted three Protestant Dissenters to the Privy Council in the summer (1688)—an action that can hardly have reassured the Anglicans. On 21 September he had disclaimed any notion of undermining the Establishment, and had promised to call a Parliament for November. A week later a special Forty Hours' Prayer began in the Chapel Royal, and he issued a proclamation refusing foreign help against the now certain invasion by William of Orange. He would rely, he said, on English loyalty.

When the bishops met him on 3 October they proffered him Ten Heads of Advice, reminiscent of the Grand Remonstrance which Parliament had addressed to his father forty-seven years earlier. Some of these—the restoration of Oxford and Cambridge universities, the abolition of the Ecclesiastical Court, the restoration of the corporations—he had already promised. Others of the points were educational: he must employ only persons legally qualified, he must remove the four vicars apostolic, and he must withdraw teaching licences from Catholics and 'forbid them to teach schools'. These he did not act on at all; they touched the faith by touching the spreading of the faith; and to the end of his days, unlike his brother, he would not do that at any cost whatever.[2]

At Oxford he restored Dr. Hough and the extruded fellows on 11 October. Charnock, a fellow who had become a Catholic, was dispossessed. The Bishop of Winchester did not actually carry out the mandate of restoration till the 25th, on account of news reaching him which seemed to make it likely that the king would stiffen his attitude

[1] See p. 239 above, and *Cal. Treasury Book*, xii.

[2] For the Ten Heads see Turner, 419, and Lingard, xiv. 227 and note.

in the foreign political crisis and want to countermand the order. The delay was costly to James in revived mistrust.[1]

At Cambridge, Sidney Sussex College was restored on 12 October. Dom Alban Francis, whose degree had been the start of the trouble, had to flee. The crowd sacked the chapel in which he had been wont to say Mass, looted the vestments and plate, and went on to 'Bennett's College', where they forced a priest Scott to hide from them 'in a bogg house'. They made one priest 'dance naked in a ditch till he promised to change his religion'.[2]

Simultaneously the destruction in London began. The school of the Jesuits in Fenchurch Street was razed to the ground by the mob on 11 October. The Savoy school was broken up. A newsletter of that same day reported it as 'shut up, one of the masters having taken with him twenty scholars for Dover, in order to go beyond sea [to St. Omer]. On Sunday Mr. Peters preached again in Lime Street nevertheless, reflecting on our English Bible, which occasioned a great disturbance. . . .' The actual building in the Savoy was not destroyed, 'for fear of the neighbouring barracks'. Six years later an astrologer divined some treasure there, hidden and left by the Jesuits, and many people went to dig, with a guard set over them, 'but it is thought will signify nothing'.[3]

Soon after William of Orange landed at Torbay on Guy Fawkes Day (on the tide of what is surely a high-watermark of betrayals), the outbreaks were resumed. The Benedictine house at St. John's, Clerkenwell, was destroyed despite the calling in of soldiery to repel the mob.[4] The London house of the Mary Ward nuns was destroyed and they moved out to the convent at Hammersmith.[5] The Jesuit centre and school at Wolverhampton were overthrown: 'The greater portion of our Library, which was well stocked, was burnt in the marketplace. The schools were demolished (the houses which we rented from the Earl of Plymouth were through fear left untouched); the benches, reading-desk, chairs, the ornamental woodwork, framed after the model of our continental schools, also the entire household furniture

[1] *Hist. MSS. Comm.*, Le Fleming MSS., 226; Lingard, xiv. 227; Mallet, ii. 457; Bloxam, 252–3.

[2] Le Fleming MSS., *ut supra*, p. 226. The panic of 1688, due largely to the machinations of Hugh Speke, and recalling the panic of 1641, is analysed by Brian Magee in *The Month*, clxxvii. 334–44 (1941).

[3] *Annual Letters*, at Stonyhurst; Foley, v. 271; Le Fleming MSS., 213; S.J. *Letters and Notices*, Ap. 1926; *Hist. MSS. Comm.*, J.R.P. Coffin MSS., 386a.

[4] Pink, *Clerkenwell*, 310; Taunton, ii. 179.

[5] Guilday, 212.

—all was either plundered by the mob, or appropriated by the Commissioners who were sent. . . . Some hope is entertained, I trust not in vain, of a restoration.'[1] In York, upon a rumour that the Catholics were about to murder their Protestant neighbours, after Danby had seized the city on behalf of William of Orange and arrested its governor Sir John Reresby, the Catholic chapel was pulled down by a mob; and the seminary established by Henry Lawson in the Manor of York only a few months earlier came to an end.[2] At Lincoln 'the rabble . . . burned popish school and chapel . . . which endangered sundry houses'.[3] Henry Hills, the king's Catholic printer, had his offices ruined; and the London and other chapels, closed by the king's order since 9 October for greater safety, were burned down.[4] James's issue of writs, on 27 November, for the calling of a Parliament for 15 January, was a finger in the dyke after the dyke had burst.

On 11 December he left London for France. On Christmas Day, after the episode of his return and second flight, and much to the relief of William, he landed there. The new year was to reverse the engines of English history: or such Catholic engines as the mob had left still working.

James II's latest and most dispassionate biographer (F. C. Turner) is ready to acclaim his integrity of character, and not to quarrel with a Catholic king's determination to relieve his co-religionists of the penal laws and make Great Britain Catholic. But his methods, in an age of dissembling raised to a fine art by his brother Charles and all his own advisers, were the methods of a man too honest to dissemble. In such an age, bearing in mind the national dread of the Catholicism he stood for, such methods were inevitably fatal.

'God grant that such a great prosperity', a Scotsman, Jameson, had written soon after James's accession, 'be not a forerunner to some adversity, and such a sudden calm be before a tempest.'[5] For a wind favourable to Catholic influence was truly dreaded. Not by the nation as a whole, but by the vested interests of Protestantism and property. If it was inconsistent of them to condemn Louis XIV's persecution of Protestants in France and yet condemn Protestant dissenters at home

[1] *Annual Letters*; Foley, v. 420, 450.

[2] W. E. Tate, *Some School References in the Memoirs of Sir John Reresby, 1634–89* (1959).

[3] *Hist. MSS. Comm.*, D. of Sutherland MSS., 198a.

[4] Lingard, xiv. 271 f. For the destruction of the chapel at Exeter, which William entered on 9 Nov., see Oliver, 14, 25, 366.

[5] March 1685; Blairs Archives; quoted Hay, 216.

such as William Penn for joining with English Catholics against a parallel persecution, it is equally true that logic could have no effective part in public affairs as then agitated. The fear was that repeal of the penal laws would lead 'many to turn papist that now dare not', and to Catholic predominance.

The likelihood of any such result, even by the subtlest methods of expediency and dishonesty had James been ready to stoop to either, was in fact negligible. 'Everything corporate in England (University, Bar, Borough)' was against it. Hilaire Belloc's estimate of one-seventh to one-eighth of England actively Catholic may be too high; but even he put the number prepared to sacrifice all for the faith at one in twenty.

For English Catholic history the tragedy lies in what the king brought down with him into shame and execration. When he came to the throne, the Catholic minority were already moving into that frame of mind so characteristic of them in the next century (and so self-inhibiting to them in the freedom of the nineteenth), of wanting to be left alone, in their exclusion and obscurity, to contrive what comfort they could from a company of immigrant priests, a few Mass centres and a handful of schools. The impact of James II on their fortunes was to mean that this new trend now pursued its course with a significant difference: that what might have been (but for Jacobitism and further harsh repression) a steady ten per cent of the population, diminished so much that Bishop Challoner, visiting the South of England Catholics in the mid-eighteenth century, could find no more than 25,000. A dwindling remnant. In 1688, Jacobite movements in the future notwithstanding, the English Catholics 'realized that the Church had lost the English people, and in the discouragement of this knowledge they fell into a sort of lethargy'.[1]

For it was soon only too clear how the official wind had changed. The year 1689, the first of William and Mary, is the year of the Convention Parliament. It is a year in which, at first, many complaisant Protestants who had done King James's bidding stood suspended between hope and dread, and others who had done King William's bidding, before he was King William, looked now for spoils.[2] But very soon the situation became clear. The ports were watched again for papists coming and going; and the old English saga begins again with Alexander Gordon, last heard of teaching as a Catholic in his own

[1] E. H. Burton, *Challoner*, i. 12.
[2] Cf. *Cal. S.P. Dom. 1689–90*, p. 378.

school in London in 1665–70, now caught coming from Ireland on his way presumably to France.[1] Inquiries went out as to gifts of land for Catholic purposes during the late reign, so that they could be annulled under the Acts against 'superstitious uses'.[2] A (spurious) Third Declaration of King William himself heralded a renewed pamphlet war against the papists, typified in *A Short and Easy Method proposed for the Extirpation of Popery in the Space of a Few Years*, which would have banished every papist found in the British Dominions.[3] The middle of June 1689 saw a Bill in Parliament on 'the presentations and advowsons of Papists to the two Universities'.[4] It passed. And it was followed by Acts to disarm all papists and reputed papists, prohibit them from owning any horse worth more than £5, and re-impose the new oaths on all ecclesiastical and civil office-holders.[5]

The coping-stone of the Revolutionary Settlement of 1689, the Toleration Act, was not strictly a measure of toleration at all. It did not repeal the penal laws. It merely granted exemption from them to such persons as should fulfil certain prescribed conditions; and its seventeenth clause excepted from its benefits 'any papist or popish recusant whatsoever'.[6]

There was no pogrom of the kind seen at hysterical points in the past. But the penal code was stepped up. By 1691, the oath was to be tendered to every suspect, with seizure of his goods if he refused. By 1699, papist lands were to be taxed according to the amount of 'horse and foot' they should provide.

And in the closing year of the century, 1700, not only was the reward for informers against anyone saying Mass fixed at £100, but any heir who should not have become an Anglican by the age of eighteen was to be completely disinherited, the fine for sending children to the colleges abroad was set at £100, and henceforth the penalty on any Catholic found keeping a school was raised to imprisonment for life.[7]

[1] Ibid., 1700–2, p. 540.

[2] Cf. *C.R.S.* ii. 299 f., for the bequests made to the Jesuit College at Combe (Cwm), Herefordshire.

[3] For the pamphlet offensive see Cecil Robinson, *Religious Toleration under William III*, Univ. Leeds unpublished Thesis (1933), 30, 59 ff.

[4] *Hist. MSS. Comm.*, Beaulieu MSS., p. 201.

[5] 1 Will. & Mary, cc. 26, 15, 8, 9.

[6] 1 Will. & Mary, c. 18; text in C. Grant Robertson, *Select Statutes . . .*, p. 70, and cf. J. N. Figgis, in *Cambr. Mod. Hist.* iii. 740.

[7] 11 & 12 Will. III, c. 4.

Small wonder that the coming eighteenth century, under the penal laws, was to witness almost the extinction of English Catholicism. 'Converts were few and apostates were numerous. . . . It were well if the little flock could escape destruction from without and desertion from within. Therefore it lived in obscurity, and needed all its energies even to keep its life within it.'[1]

[1] Burton, *Challoner*, i. 69.

EPILOGUE

Round about the time that Dr. Barret was lobbying the burghers of St. Omer for leave to bring into their town his handful of English *parvuli* from Eu, and Fr. Robert Persons was on the brink of news from London that would send him hot-foot to Madrid to coax from King Philip a corner for the teaching English Jesuits in that very city, the stonemasons were at work in a remote part of Lancashire, upon a mansion going up for the obdurate recusant family of the Shirburns, their new hall in their park at Stonyhurst.

Exactly two hundred years later the exile school, driven from among the foreign people who had nurtured it, sought refuge in the land where all its generations of scholars had been born, and the descendants of the families that had made the school found a home in the hall that had begun while they were beginning.

The school, St. Omer, is the historic symbol of the Catholic Englishman of penal times, who went abroad in youth, at lively risk to all his family by proclamation and distraint, to return anon as priest or layman and fill the ranks depleted in his absence. And Shirburn Hall is the historic symbol of those who made him possible, the 'old Catholic families' who gave in quite immense proportions their substance to the cause and their sons and daughters to the Church.

That the school and the hall began together is the sheerest of coincidences. Nor is it any less chance that the Oxford college of William Allen, who in the sixteenth century saved English Catholic education from extinction, is the college of John Henry Newman, who in the nineteenth crowned it. Historical study may never abide coincidence. But of meditation it can be the very essence.

From the broad standpoint of English education at large, the Catholic resistance to the Establishment made no appreciable impact after the first shock, when a centuries-old and alarmingly vigorous institution had had to be simultaneously rooted out and replaced. In the seventeenth century the pulpits and the masters' desks had all been re-staffed. Licence and patronage, under a new management firmly entrenched, controlled school and university, teacher and book, and the shocks from the Elizabethan departures and dismissals had been taken in depth.

In the seventeenth century the grammar school masters ejected were few. There were fewer left to eject. But some of the few were in key-schools where, by outwardly conforming, they were able to be some solace to Catholic parents who used the grammar schools for the sake of their sons' careers. Of this company are James Shirley of St. Alban's School; John Goad of Tonbridge School and Merchant Taylors'; Richard Reeve, of Magdalen College School and the Gloucester Bluecoat School; Morgan Lewis of Abergavenny; John Hickes of the King Edward School at Birmingham; Richard Bradley, the usher of Blackburn; Simon Dormer of Eye in Suffolk; Richard Fletcher of St. Michael's-on-Wyre in Lancashire.

The hole-and-corner schools that men like these nurtured in their outlawry, a few of them fabulous in continuity, some of them in a bizarre sense travelling-schools, as one watches the quarter sessions records chase a man from village to village over the years, and none of them licensed by either the Establishment that hunted them or the Catholic Church that depended on them, must have amounted to hundreds.

Without any doubt, the 'bumper' decade, twenty-eight popish schools in the annals of one shire around the time of the Powder Plot, was not exceptional. It is only that for other decades there is nothing to draw on comparable to Peacock's *Yorkshire Catholics of 1604*.

All the schools traceable in seventeenth-century England were for boys except four (Hammersmith Convent 1669, York Convent 1686, the Blue Nuns under James II and the Ghent Benedictines), and the 'all' is a hundred and thirty that are surely far from the true total, which can probably never be known.

The documented masters at work in the country from James I to James II number about 170, over a hundred of them lay men and women. The many more, working as tutors in the guise of servitor or secretary to the family and its estates and neighbourhood, cannot even be guessed.

That there were many other Catholic schools besides the ones that have got into archives is proved from the Roman *Responsa* of youths who had presumably or explicitly had a Catholic upbringing. Lancastrians among them, for instance, had been so reared in Preston, Euxton, Eccleston, Cockerham, Singleton, Woodplumpton—apart from the centres where schools can be definitely proved from other sources. Others cite Hexham, Southolt in Suffolk, Garway in Herefordshire and numerous locations less precise. And so on round the colleges.

On the other hand, ironically enough, every young Catholic who went oversea to become a priest with his education from an English public grammar school was relieving his exile college, academically, by releasing a 'humanities' place for someone less classically prepared. The *Venerabile* in the seventeenth century welcomed three Old Westminsters, two Old Etonians, one Merchant Taylor. Not all the boys named their grammar school. Those who did make a rich spread —Abergavenny, Boston (Lincs), Brewood (Staffs), Bury St. Edmunds, Carmarthen, Clitheroe, Cowbridge, Cripplegate (under Farnaby), Giggleswick, Kirkham, Leominster, Ottery St. Mary, Salisbury, Shrewsbury, Upsall (Yorks), Wantage and Worcester, all of them noble schools. But the university men are much fewer than in the time of Elizabeth. To Rome in the century there went only eleven from Cambridge, six from Oxford, three from the Inns of Court, two from Leyden and one each from St. Andrews and Trinity College, Dublin.

It can safely be inferred that a majority of the secret schools, known and unknown, were training pupils for the colleges abroad: as regards the orders, all their schools. This is not only a natural inference, but is borne out by the few pointers that have survived to give any inkling of the curriculum—as at Scarisbrick and Fernyhalgh, and by the *Responsa* of the boys on arriving overseas.

Six of these seventeenth-century schools can show a very long continuity, some of them till the present day: Scarisbrick (from about 1618), Fernyhalgh (from about 1650), Silksteed-Twyford (from about 1660), Formby (from 1659) and the girls' schools at Hammersmith and York.

In all probability there were many more 'two-decade' and even longer-lived Catholic schools than those discovered. The layman William Allen at the Nottingham Sessions in 1623 and again fifteen years later may well be not only a case but a type. Nor is it likely that the school which Fr. Daniel Fitter 'opened' at Stafford after the accession of James II was really started then—he had been in the district thirty-two years. Nor did all those who found a vocation go abroad at once: John Ball in the 'thirties taught for eight years after his conversion before departing for the Venerable English College.

The unpublished researches of the first man to look into the printed evidence at all systematically, W. F. Hastings, C.M., in 1923, led him to general conclusions which manuscript sources studied since have considerably modified so far as quantity is concerned. And this will continue to happen more and more definitively as recusant-researches multiply. But his qualitative conclusion cannot today be advanced very much further than where he left it:

Up and down the country a small number of schools were kept up. They were scattered here and there in remote places, their existence was always timorous, and their continuance always precarious. Their pupils were few as a rule, and their entire history is very obscure for want of records. We hear of them at all more by accident, and indirectly, than otherwise. It is truer then to speak of educational work than of schools. . . . The schools represented individual efforts. . .[1]

We now know, above all from the *Interrogatories* and *Responsa* from the Continent, that many of the schools represented much more than individual efforts, that they were a policy, and an attempt at a network. No one at the time knew better than the superiors of the exiled colleges, from the autobiographies they required all their entrants from all over England to provide, what the educational situation at home was, and what its needs and their own. Hence one reason, significant all along, for the large proportion (about a third) of clergy among the attested schoolmasters at work in the 'English Vineyard'.

Today we can calculate, from the cumulative evidence of this minority demographic group who became priests, that in this seventeenth century not merely a third had been 'always Catholic', as in the later years of Elizabeth, but nearer three-quarters. At the same time, the other quarter were no longer 'lapsed' Catholics who had been subsequently reconciled, as in Elizabethan days, but mostly Protestants who had been converted. These converts show how the climate of the country had changed, an inescapable conclusion which the high proportion of 'born Catholics' does not modify. For the 'always Catholic' are evidence not that the chance of a Catholic education in Stuart England was better, but that the ranks of the Catholic minority had closed. The one-third 'always Catholic' of them in 1603, only one long generation after the Elizabethan settlement, can tenably have meant a one-in-three chance of a Catholic schooling (cf. page 86 above). But the higher proportion later is from a smaller global total of Catholics. The closing of the ranks is demonstrated, moreover, by the fact that those ordinands from the 'Catholic' areas, Lancashire and

[1] W. F. Hastings, *The Education of English Catholics . . . to 1800*, (Univ. London thesis, 1923), 341.

Yorkshire and London, in the seventeenth century are one-third of all. In Elizabeth's day they had been a quarter, with relatively fewer from the landed families.

For the humble folk of the period, the children of the yeoman and the labourer, no safe generalizations can be made. We know that for some of them there was a Catholic village school, or a master operating in his own house or lodgings, and that the family tutor in the grange or manor or hall could be available for them no less than for the children of the retainers. But on what scale this happened is guesswork, beyond the obvious conclusion that it was most likely in the Catholic 'pockets' and least likely in the towns.

That the English Catholics had an educational policy, even while bereft of an English bishop from the resignation of William Bishop in 1631 to the appointment of John Leyburne as vicar apostolic under James II in 1685, is beyond dispute. Beneath the policy lay one constant and inflexible principle: to keep the faith alive through priest and schoolmaster. For the rest, it was a matter of improvising, each time the supply of either was threatened by Act or proclamation or capture or poverty or recusant-hunt. The first improvisation was the exodus to Louvain after 1558, to keep Catholic Oxford and Cambridge alive. From it came the whole College Movement. The last improvisation was James II's constitutional shifts to secure a Catholic college in Oxford. From this came final disaster.

In between are the small host of schoolmasters and mistresses, and catechists and tutors, practising unlicensed a sacred craft for which in times of security the Catholic Church, no less than the Anglicans, required not only a licence but training and formation. The modern lay Catholic master in the Catholic school of today would duly have emerged, but the historical circumstances in which he actually did emerge were those of penal England, when there was no challenge to him because without him there would so often have been nothing. He was a prodigy. Certainly the Council of Trent had not had him in mind. And he was the salt of the earth: from the nine of him who are among the English Catholic schoolmaster martyrs, to men like Eugene Macalister in Glengarry, who declined two-fifths of the pittance available so that another teacher could be had with the remainder.

Of all the defenders of English Catholicism none met the challenge more 'organically' than the Jesuits, through the 'mixed' St. Omer school of 1593 and the outline-organization of the English province in 1620, whereby when the dawn seemed to appear with James II the Jesuits were all ready to fill in the outline forthwith.

Together, regulars and seculars, lay grammar schoolmasters who had kept their posts, and private schoolmasters and tutors who had lost them, they contrived that although the Catholic population of England had fallen catastrophically between the death of Elizabeth and the accession of William III, no longer a-third-to-a-half but the beginning of Bishop Challoner's dwindling remnant, the chance of a Catholic schooling in England was not worse at the end of the century, for the contemporary Catholic minority, than it had been at the start, unless one impugn the *Responsa* of the seventeenth century as too frail a sample.

In the few regions where there was continuity over long periods, we can say it was the schools kept the Catholic faith alive. Elsewhere, that is the monument of the mission priests on their travels, the men whose presence, in the dark century of dwindling to come, would be made known across a valley by white linen 'spread to dry' on the bushes, so that villagers long without the Sacraments could be happy again for a time.

Without the schools the faith could still have lived. But not without the clergy. Every Christian in every age has known this. It is the profoundest element in the whole history of the penal days. And that is why, under Providence, the supreme saviour of English Catholic 'education under penalty' is the Oxford don who, knowing it, was first and greatest to act on it: William Cardinal Allen.

APPENDIX

1. Scotland

The reorganization of Scottish education on Protestant lines began in 1560. See Strong, *History of Secondary Education in Scotland* (Oxford, 1909), 21, for the Catholic contribution down to then, 57–61 for John Knox's scheme. Many priests had fled to England in 1563 to avoid the persecution. By the middle of the reign of James VI all but one of the peers had taken the oath, though only about twenty clergy (Bellesheim, *History of the Catholic Church in Scotland*, transl. Hunter Blair, Edinburgh, 1889, iii. 74, 422). Further reforms, including the universities, were carried out after the abdication of Mary Stuart in 1568 (ibid., 204).

There was a Scottish College already at Paris, dating from 1326. For the Scots College at Douay, see p. 116 above. The Jesuit College in Paris, founded in February 1580 by Bishop John Leslie on the model of Douay, was closed for lack of funds ten years later, reopened at Douay in 1593 on the return there of the English College from Rheims, moved to Louvain in 1595, and finally back to Douay in 1608. See Hubert Chadwick, S.J., in *Eng. Hist. Review*, lvi. 570–85 (1940), which corrects the biography of the college given by Bellesheim and others. Scotland was important also as a possible refuge for English Catholics should James VI favour them. See L. J. Hicks, S.J., in *C.R.S.* xxxix. p. xli ff.; and Bellesheim, iii. 252. But in 1600 he sought the advice of the English bishops on the best means of securing the conformity of his own dissident schoolmasters (Bellesheim, iii. 358).

For the penal legislation in Scotland under Elizabeth, see *Acts of the General Assembly* for the crucial years 1563, 1565, 1578, 1587 (pp. 33–4, 60, 693, 213–4, 431, 433–5, 437, 715–6); and *Acts of the Parliament of Scotland*, i. 124, iii. 347, iii. 701–4, iii. 712. Also J. Durkan, 'Education in the Century of the Reformation', in *Innes Review*, spring 1959, 67–90.

The Commonwealth period gave Scotland the Parochial Schools Act of 1646, re-enacted fifty years later, a bulwark of modern Scottish education. Towards the end of his Protectorate Cromwell further decreed £1,200, out of money from rents which had gone 'in the time of popery' for the upkeep of church-officers, to furnish schools in the Highlands. The Congregation of Propaganda, in Rome, decreed 500 crowns a year to make possible ten mission-priests in those same Highlands, since Fr. Ballantyne there had as yet only five (Strong, 89; *Cal. S.P. Dom.*, 1658, p. 4; Bellesheim, iv. 44, 49, 63, 71).

There was no Catholic school in the Lowlands in the time of Charles II, and only two in the Highlands, under the protection of the Macdonalds—in Glengarry and on the island of Barra. The Glengarry schoolmaster, M. Eugene Macalister, appears to have begun teaching as early as 1662. The procurator of the mission pleaded in 1664 that he be given a salary, and retrospectively at that; and Propaganda agreed, voting him fifty *scudi* a year. Since, however, he was happy to accept thirty, there were twenty *scudi* available for a second Schoolmaster on the Scottish mainland if only one could be found (*Arch. Soc. Cong. Prop. Fide*, Rome: in *Innes Review*, V. i (1954)). It looked for a time as if one could, for in 1665 George Hay, an alumnus of the Scots College in Rome, was urged not to join the Benedictines as he wished, but to go home and open a school in the Highlands. Nothing came of the suggestion, even though Propaganda allowed that the masters' incomes be augmented by fees from the parents of their pupils. To Rome all this was a blow, since one motive in the Propaganda initiative had been to remedy, by educational activity in the Highlands and the Isles, the reluctance of the Scots to send out recruits for the Scottish colleges overseas, which the solitary priest in Scotland was bewailing. Far from being ready as a recruiting-ground, the Scots Catholics were beseeching Rome for priests, schools, schoolmasters, books, catechisms, chalices, vestments, and were meanwhile continuing to send their children (exclusion from the sacraments notwithstanding) to a non-Catholic teacher in the Highlands.

The danger of apostasy implicit in this practice was obvious. So was the danger accruing from the deliberate policy of the Privy Council, in trying to eradicate the faith by enforced proselytism. For the seizures of Catholic children in Scotland in the seventeenth century, see *Acts of the Privy Council of Scotland*, series ii, part 1, pp. 245–50, 363; part 3, pp. 45, 69, 88–9, 156, 220. For the period after 1660, ibid., i. 65–6; iii. 94; ii. 370–1; iii. 449, 452, 474; iv. 122, 309; v. 95–6; xi. 317. Also *Records of the General Assemblies' Commissioners*, ii. 106, 124, 227, 234–5, 347, 353, 369, and xxv. 201, 350, 416. The cases of the earls of Huntly and Angus are given (p. 208 note) above. In 1672 there were three: the Countess of Traquhair, Lord Semple and the Wauchope family. Fr. Winster's report to Propaganda in 1668 shows why indeed this device was not 'like some others temporarily suspended but is continually being put in execution'. Douglas, Errol, Winton, Sutherland and Caithness apostatized as a result of it, and drew off others. In March 1681 Propaganda decided to continue supporting the Highland schools. Alexander Leslie's strictures that same year on the education being given in the colleges abroad are noticed on p. 156 above.

2. Ireland

In Ireland, educationally, the dissolution of the monasteries in 1537 virtually destroyed the existing educational system, and Henry VIII's Act for creating parish schools came to little. This Act, however, became the basis of English educational policy in Ireland from then till the establishment of the Free State in 1922. It was revived by Elizabeth in 1569 (J. J. Auchmuty, *Irish Education: a Historical Survey*, London, 1937, 40–2, 44). The Irish colleges founded abroad in imitation of the English Catholic practice are dealt with in W. P. Treacy, *Irish Scholars of the Penal Days* (New York, 1887), ch. 3 and 7–14. The most recent account of the whole problem of Catholic education in Ireland since the Reformation is that of Sister A. M. Gallagher, O.S.F., *Education in Ireland* (Washington, 1948). The early Irish colleges were: St. Geneviève's, Paris, 1578; Salamanca, 1582; 1595, Lisbon (by Cardinal Ximenes); 1596, Douay (largely through Christopher Cusack); 1628, Rome (St. Isidore's, by Luke Wadding); see Treacy, 74ff.

The reign of James I brought not only a fresh plantation of Ulster and a Privy Council decree setting up a Protestant free school in every county (the origin of the Royal Schools), and not only an adoption of most of the English penal code, but the suppression of the last surviving school that would not conform (that of Lynch in Galway): wherefore the Irish too had only one alternative to the illegal colleges abroad—the future hedge schools at home. (J. J. Auchmuty, *Irish Education*, 46 ff.; *Tudor and Stuart Proclamations*, ii. 19, 24; *Cal. S.P. Dom. Ireland*, 1612, p. 289. Similarly the royal attempt at a national system of parish schools for Scotland dates from this reign: 1616—see J. Strong, *Secondary Education in Scotland*, 106.)

The assault on the Catholic family in Ireland was more formidable than in England or Scotland. 'Transportation into England, as well as removal from their parents if left in Ireland, was to be organized for the perversion *en masse* of the children of the Irish people. Protestant apprenticeship was to be the means of changing them from their religion and even from their race', by Cromwell's decrees. These Irish decrees alleged as justification that the lack of schooling made the children thieves and worse, that there was a shortage of labour in England, and that Protestant education would improve the children. They were taken from their parents at ten years of age (T. Corcoran, *Catholic Lay Teachers and their Illegal Schools* . . . (Dublin, 1932), 14. And cf. the Acts of 1709, 1711 and 1733).

For Catholic Ireland the Commonwealth meant, literally, hedge schools: for a proclamation against papist schoolmasters in Ireland went out in May 1654, with commissioners to enforce it, and next year Cromwell ordered his Commissioners for Transplantation to send to the Barbados all such whom they found (*Tudor and Stuart Proclamations*, ii. 65). The hedge schools were rooted in the people and taught by outlawed men hewn from peasant stock. 'The poorest and humblest of [those] schools gave instruction in reading, writing and arithmetic; Latin and Greek, mathematics and other subjects were taught in a great number of schools; and in many cases [till after 1800] the work was done entirely through the medium of the Irish language.' They throve, 'outnumbering all other schools, and so profoundly national as to hasten the introduction of a State system of education in 1831' (P. J. Dowling, *Hedge Schools of Ireland* (1935), 20 f.; Auchmuty, 13 f.).

3. The Penal Laws affecting Education

1559 1 Eliz. Cap. 1
Act of Uniformity.

1563 5 Eliz. Cap. 1
Oath for Schoolmasters.

1570 13 Eliz. Cap. 1
Forfeiture of all fortune and property for anyone leaving the country unlicensed and not returning within six months of warning.

1581 23 Eliz. Cap. 1
Fine for keeping a non-churchgoing, or unlicensed, schoolmaster: £10 per month.

1585 27 Eliz. Cap. 2
Penalty of high treason for priests, deacons, religious or ecclesiastical persons coming into the realm. Harbourers of these to suffer death and forfeiture as felons. Any others in the seminaries abroad to return within six months and conform, on pain of high treason. Fine for sending children or others overseas without licence of the queen or four Privy Councillors: £100 for each offence.

1593 35 Eliz. Cap. 2
The 'Places of Abode' Act; restrictions.

1604 1 Jac. I Cap. 4
Fine for sending anyone or any child, or going, to a seminary or college abroad: £100 for each offence. Person or child going or being sent forfeits all estates. No woman or child to leave the country without licence of the king or six Privy Councillors. Penalty for keeping a schoolmaster, or being an unlicensed schoolmaster, after next Michaelmas, 40s. per day; half the fine to the king, half to the informer.

1606 3 Jac. I Cap. 5
Licences to travel outside the five-mile limit of 1593 now to be from the king or three or more Privy Councillors or four justices of the peace. Recusants to be considered as excommunicated persons. Recusant children to be baptized by the lawful minister within one month, on pain of fine of £100, one-third to the king, one-third to the informer, one-third to the poor of the parish. No child sent overseas for education to enjoy any of his fortune until, at eighteen, he takes the oath of allegiance; the fortune to be enjoyed meanwhile by his next of kin not a

recusant. Non-recusant next of kin to enjoy the fortune of all at present being educated overseas who do not return within six months and (if over eighteen) take the oath.

1627 3 Car. I Cap. 2

Anyone going, or being sent, beyond seas for education in any priory, abbey, nunnery, popish university or school, to be disabled from suing, or holding any legacy, and to forfeit all goods and chattels.

1662 13 & 14 Car. II Cap. 4

Penalty for being, or keeping, unlicensed schoolmaster in private house: three months' imprisonment for first offence, three months' imprisonment and fine of £5 for each subsequent offence.

1665 17 Car. II Cap. 2

Recusants teaching school to be fined £40 for each offence.

1673 25 Car. II Cap. 2

The Test Act.

1700 11 & 12 Gul. III Cap. 4

Fine for sending a child abroad for a Romish education: £100, all of it to the informer. Lord Chancellor to make an order in cases where popish parent refuses to maintain his or her Protestant child. Penalty for recusant teaching school unlicensed: raised to imprisonment for life.

4. The Colleges and Schools for Boys, founded abroad during Penal Times

1568 English College, Douay (Allen)
1576 Scots Jesuit College, Tournai
1578 Irish College (St. Geneviève's), Paris
1579 English College, Rome: the *Venerabile* (Allen)
1580 Scots College, Douay
1582 English School at Eu (Persons)
1582 Irish College, Salamanca (bought by Spain, 1962)
1589 English College, Valladolid (Persons)
1592 English College, Seville (Persons)
1593 English College (School), St. Omer (Persons) (Stonyhurst, 1794)
1595 Irish College, Lisbon
1596 Irish (Secular) College, Douay
1600 Scots College, Rome
1600 Irish College, Antwerp
1605 English Benedictines, St. Gregory's, Douay (Downside, 1814)
1606 English Benedictines, St. Laurence's, Dieulouard, Lorraine
1607 English Jesuit Novitiate, Louvain (1614 to Liège, 1622 to Watten)
1611 English Benedictines at St. Malo

1611 English Benedictines at Chelles, near Paris
1612 English College, Madrid
1614? English Franciscans at Gravelines
1615 English Benedictines, St. Edmond's, Paris
1617 English Franciscans, St. Bonaventure's, Paris
1621 English Benedictines, St. Vedast, Douay
1625 Irish College, Rome
1628 English College, Lisbon
1631 Irish College, Prague
1633 Scots College, Madrid
1657 English Dominican Novitiate, Bornhem
1660 English Dominican School, Bornhem
1660 Irish College, Toulouse
1667 English College, St. Gregory, Paris
1667 Irish College, Paris
1667 Irish Dominican College, Madrid
1669? English Benedictine School, St. Laurence's, Dieulouard (Ampleforth, 1802)

NOTE: The corresponding foundations for girls are in W. J. Battersby, *Educational Work of the English Religious Orders of Women.*

BIBLIOGRAPHY

I: UNPUBLISHED SOURCES

BRITISH MUSEUM, London

Harleian MSS.: 288, No. 48—conveyance of English boys to France, 1584; 295 and 296—letters from Valladolid; 4147f; 6803f.

Lansdowne MSS.: 50—Catholic books found at Oxford, 1596; 84—to Burghley, about a 'barrel of books', 1597; 96—letters from Rectors of the English Colleges abroad, 1586 on; 97—English refugees in Spain; 846—Jesuit College at Cwm, Monmouthshire, 1678.

Sloane MSS.: 1456—Letters and Papers of Dr. Joseph Webbe (c. 1622–3).

Additional MSS.: 9354, St. Omer College Composition Lists, 1622–70; 20739, Names of Convicted Recusants, by Counties, 1671; 21203, Papers relating to English Jesuits, 16th and 17th cent.; 22656, List of Lancashire Recusants, c. 1655; 28092, f. 47, Proposals for Extirpating Popish Seminaries beyond Seas, 1680; 30092, f. 138–9, Letters to Burghley on Recusants, 1592; 31824, Papers relating to English Catholics, 16 and 17 cent.; 32092, Advice of the Privy Council on the Growth of Recusants, c. 1613 (f. 218); 34242, Return of Sequestered Recusants, 1656; 34526, Lords' Division Lists on Repeal of Penal Laws, 1687 (f. 48).

BODLEIAN LIBRARY, Oxford

MSS., Engl. Hist., c. 148—Richard Bentley, 'On the Introduction of Popery into the Universities (under James II)'—42 pp., with appended pamphlet 'Review of Cambridge under James II', 1717.

Rawlinson MSS: State Papers of James II.

PUBLIC RECORD OFFICE, London

Flanders Correspondence.

Privy Council Register.

Roman Transcripts.

State Papers Domestic: the originals of a few documents (where '*Cal.*' is omitted from footnote references): Elizabeth to Charles II.

State Papers Domestic, James II (not yet printed).

WESTMINSTER ARCHIVES

(At Archbishop's House, Westminster. There is a description of them, dated 1876, in Hist. MSS. Comm. Fifth Report, pp. 463ff., and by E. H. Burton in *The Tablet*, 1925, cxiv. 6, 110, 174.)

Vol. 1: Pamphlets, 1610–1823.

Vol. 2: Oates Plot.

Vol. 3: Pamphlets, 1651–1828.

Vol. 4: Protestant Tracts, 1674–1771.

Vols. 9–11: Miscellaneous Pamphlets.

Vol. 12: Catholic Tracts, 1607–88.

Vol. 15: On the Repeal of the Test Act (James II).

Vol. 19: Colleges of Douay, St. Omer, etc.

Vol. 30: Constitution of the English College, Douay, 1690.

Vol. 34: Third Douay Diary—original (printed *C.R.S.* 10–11).

Vol. 35: Fourth and Fifth Douay Diaries—originals (pr. *C.R.S.* 10–11).

Vol. 36: Seventh Douay Diary—original (pr. *C.R.S.* 28).

Vol. 37: Spanish Correspondence, 1596–1607.

Vol. 45: Stuart Papers.

Vol. 49: List of Douay Clergy.

Vol. 52: MS. History of Douay College, 1622.

Vol. 57: Paris Seminary Register, 1668–1784.

Vol. 58: Dom Basil's Life of Mary Ward.

Vol. 78: Douay College Visitations, 1612 and 1626.

ST. EDMUND'S COLLEGE (OLD HALL GREEN, WARE) ARCHIVES

English College, Douay, *Rule Book* of 1642.

USHAW COLLEGE (DURHAM) ARCHIVES

Douay Papers, Nos. 16–17 (on the College Oath).

There is an analysis of the Ushaw archives in M. V. Sweeney (*see* below, under University Theses).

FRANCISCAN ARCHIVES (at the Friary, Forest Gate)

Acta Capitulorum, 1629–1746: *Registrum Fratrum Minorum S. Provinciae Angliae.*

Fr. Anthony Parkinson's *Notebook*, 163 pp. MS., indexed.

DOMINICAN ARCHIVES (at St. Dominic's Priory, London)

Anglia Dominicana: Hist. Records (MSS., ed. C. F. Raymond Palmer, O.P.), 9 vols.

JESUIT ARCHIVES

Arch. S.J., Rome England / Flanders / Germany — transcripts, to early seventeenth century, at Farm Street, London, and in *Stonyhurst MSS.*—see below.

Stonyhurst MSS. (at Stonyhurst College)
Anglia 'A':

Vol. 2: 12a—Narrative of Persecution in North of England, (?1595); 24—Persons to Holt, 15 Mar. 1597, on state of the English Colleges in Spain, Flanders and Italy; 67—St. Omer College Constitution of 1600.

Vol. 3: 53—Persons to Winslade re. Catholic emigration to N. America, 18 Mar. 1605; 99—Fr. John Price's Account of the Foundation of the Engl. Coll. Seville (1 Mar. 1610).

Vol. 4: 4—State of the Engl. Coll. Rome, and list of *alumni*, 1613; 9—Fr. Henry Silisdon to Owen, on the removal to Liège, 5 July 1614; 86—Fr. Geo. Wright on Emperor Ferdinand's intention to found a College at Osnabrück on lines of St. Omer, 16 Sept. 1630; 95—Fr. Blount to Fr. General, on Lord Petre's plan for an S.J. College at Chelmsford, 27 Aug. 1632; 96—layman's opinion of the Venerabile Oath of *alumni*.

Vol. 5: 13—Fr. Edward Courtenay's Report to the General on St. Omer, 13 Dec. 1641; 77—Fr. Geo. Gray to the General, on d. of Fr. Christopher Simpson, 3 Mar. 1674; 111—Fr. John Clare to Fr. General on the house in the Savoy, 9 Apr. 1691; 112/118—letters to Fr. General on change in the scholars' dress.

Vol. 7: 50—On the foundation of the English College at Rheims in 1579; 51—Question of changing the Oath of *alumni* at the Engl. Coll. Rome; 96—'Short Account of the Founding of the English College, Rome', attached to text of Visitation Decree of 1739.

Vol. 9: Catalogue of Recusants in Diocese of Durham, 1611.

Collectanea 'B': (i.e. of Fr. Christopher Greene, d. 1697)
Verstegan's 'Advices from London', March 1592 to Nov. 1593; Nos. 43, 45, 57, 69, 71, 75, 77, 79, 81, 83, 95, 97, 107, 109, 117, 123, 127, 143, 145. (There are transcripts of these at Farm St., London; and the collection is printed in *C.R.S.* 52 (1959).)

Collectanea 'C': Fr. Gerard documents on Gunpowder Plot period.

Collectanea 'N': Fr. Greene's own First Notebooks.

Collectanea 'M': Fr. Greene's own transcripts.

Collectanea 'P': Persons and Garnet transcripts.

Litterae Annuae of St. Omer College:
Transcripts of the originals in Brussels Archives; by Cardwell; 4 vols. (There are copies of some of these at Farm Street.)

Pollen, J. H., S.J. Unpublished MS. *Continuation* of his *English Catholics under Elizabeth*, at Farm St.

St. Omer College *Custom Book*, 1620 (C.II.19).

St. Omer College *Composition Lists*, 1622–70 (transcript of *B.M. Add. MSS.* 9354) (C.II.5).

St. Omer Municipal Archives: Magistracy's Deliberations, late sixteenth century: transcripts by John Morris, S.J. (Copies also at Farm St.)

UNPUBLISHED UNIVERSITY THESES

BISHOP, E. W. *Education in the Commonwealth: 1640–60* (Univ. London, 1942).

BRADDOCK, A. F. *The Influence of Catholics in the Matter of Education in England* (Univ. London, 1917).

HASTINGS, WM. F. *The Education of English Catholics, 1559–1800* (Univ. London, 1923).

KITCHING, J. *Catholic Education in the N. & E. Ridings of Yorkshire, 1571–1870* (Univ. Durham, 1956).

LOOMIE, A. J. *Spain and the English Catholic Exiles, 1580–1604* (Univ. London, 1957).

MOORE, L. S. *The Position of Roman Catholics in England, 1685–8* (Univ. Cambridge, 1956).

O'DWYER, M. *Catholic Recusants in Essex, 1580–1600* (Univ. London, 1960).

ROBINSON, CECIL. *The Toleration of Roman Catholics under William III* (Univ. Leeds, 1933).

SWAN, C. M. J. F. *The Introduction of the Elizabethan Settlement into the Universities of Oxford and Cambridge . . .* (Univ. Cambridge, 1956).

SWEENEY, MORGAN V. *English Catholic Education in the North from the Reformation to Catholic Emancipation: 1580–1829* (Univ. Leeds, 1946).

WILLIAMS, J. A. *Catholic Recusancy in Wiltshire, 1660–1791* (Univ. Bristol, 1961).

YOUNG, L. G. *State Intervention in Education in England under the Early Stuarts* (Univ. London, 1938).

II : PUBLISHED SOURCES

PUBLIC RECORDS

Acts of the Privy Council, to 1689.

Calendar of State Papers Domestic, Elizabeth to Charles II.

House of Commons *Journal*.

House of Lords *Journal*.

Spanish Calendar.

Statutes of the Realm.

Acts of the Parliament of Scotland.

Acts of the General Assembly of the Church of Scotland.

ENGLISH PROVINCE, S.J., *Letters and Notices*

(Privately printed; files at Heythrop College and at Farm St.) ii. 257ff. (1869), Scottish Mission, 1610–1716; v. 50 (1868), Wigan Schools; vi. 250ff. (1869), Holywell Mission; xi. 116ff. (1875), Worthington Family; xxxvii and xxxviii (1922), The St. Omer Press.

CATHOLIC RECORD SOCIETY (1904–63; 55 volumes)

Vol. 1: Sander's 1561 Report to Card. Moroni; Lists of Prisoners, 1562–80; Obituary of Dom John Huddleston.

Vol. 2: Memoirs of Robert Persons, S.J., ed. J. H. Pollen, S.J.; Lists of Catholic Prisoners under Elizabeth; Records of S. Wales Catholicism in seventeenth and eighteenth centuries.

Vol. 3: Tower Bills, 1575–89; Recusants of Masham, Yorks, 1589–1628.

Vol. 4: Memoirs of Robert Persons, continued; Tower Bills, 1595–1681; Nuns of the Institute of Mary at York, 1677 on; Fr. John Birkett, 1679–80.

Vol. 5: Unpublished Documents relating to the English Martyrs, ed. J. H. Pollen, S.J.

Vol. 6: List of Convicted Recusants under Charles II.

Vol. 8: Diary of the Blue Nuns, 1658 on.

Vol. 9: Allen Correspondence, 1579–85, ed. J. H. Pollen, S.J. Priests in England and Wales in 1692.

Vols. 10 and 11: Third, Fourth and Fifth Douay Diaries (1598–1654), ed. E. H. Burton and T. L. Williams.

Vol. 14: Robert Persons' 'Annals of the English College at Seville', and correspondence 1589–94, ed. J. H. Pollen, S.J.

Vol. 18: Recusant Roll No. 1 (1592–3).

Vol. 22: Diocesan Returns of Recusants in England and Wales, 1577. Recusants and Priests in England and Wales, and Priests beyond Seas, March 1588; Prisoners in the Fleet, 1577–80; The Archpriest Controversy; Michael Tirrye, schoolmaster.

Vol. 25: Dominicana: Letters of Cardinal Philip Howard; English Dominican Papers, 1619 on; English Dominican Books and Papers, 1624 on.

Vol. 26: Letters and Papers of Nicholas Sander, 1562–80.

Vol. 28: Seventh Douay Diary (1715–78), ed. E. H. Burton and E. Nolan.

Vol. 29: Records of the English College, Madrid, from 1611, ed. E. Henson.

Vol. 30: Registers of the English College, Valladolid, from 1589, ed. E. Henson.

Vol. 33: English Benedictine Papers, of Fr. Leander and Fr. Baker, including reports on the State of the Engl. Ben. Congregation in 1613, 1633 and 1637.

Vol. 34: London Sessions Records, 1605–85, ed. Dom Hugh Bowler.

Vols. 37 and 40: *Liber Ruber* of the English College, Rome—*Nomina Alumnorum*, 1579–1630–1783.

Vol. 39: Letters and Memorials of Robert Persons, S.J., to 1588, ed. L. J. Hicks, S.J.

Vol. 41: Letters of Thomas Fitzherbert, 1608–10, ed. L. J. Hicks, S.J.

Vol. 52: Letters of Richard Verstegan, 1590–1617, ed. A. G. Petti.

Vol. 54: Records of the English Coll., Rome: *Responsa*, Pt. I, ed. Anthony Kenny; and Vol. 55 (Pt. II).

ROYAL COMMISSION ON HISTORICAL MANUSCRIPTS

Beaulieu MSS.; J. R. P. Coffin MSS.; Downshire MSS.; De Lisle and Dudley MSS.; Miss C. Griffith MSS.; Hereford Corporation MSS.; House of Lords Library MSS.; R. R. Hastings MSS.; Laing MSS.; Leybourne-Popham MSS.; S. H. Le Fleming MSS.; Mar and Kelly MSS.; Poll-Gall MSS.; Rydall Hall MSS.; Salisbury MSS.; H. D. Skrine MSS.; Stuart MSS.; Duke of Sutherland MSS.; Westminster Diocesan Archives (summary—5th Report, 1876); Talbot MSS.; Francis Whitegrave MSS.; Wilts. Quarter-Sessions Papers.

CONTEMPORARY WRITINGS AND DOCUMENTS

ALLEN, WILLIAM. *An Apologie for the Two English Colleges*. 1581. *See* also Knox, T. F.

BATESON, MARY (Ed.). *A Collection of Original Letters from the Bishops to the Privy Council, 1564*. 1893. (Camden Society, vol. 9.)

CARAMAN, P. (Ed.). *Autobiography of John Gerard*. 1952.

CARDWELL, E. *Documentary Annals of the Reformed Church of England: 1546–1717* (2 vols.). 1839.

—. *Articles of Religion . . . Canterbury: 1547–1717*. 1842.

CARTWRIGHT, JOHN (Bp. of Chester). *Diary*. (Camden Soc., vol. 22.)

CATHOLIC RECORD SOCIETY. (See page 279 above.)

CECIL, WM. (Lord Burghley). *Advice to the Queen in Matters of Religion and State*, 1583. (Somers Tracts, IV, i. 101–8.)

CHALLONER, R. *Memoirs of Missionary Priests* (1741). Ed. J. H. Pollen. 1924.

CROSSLEY, J. (Ed.). *Diary and Correspondence of Dr. J. Worthington.* (Chetham Society, 1874–6.)

D'EWES, SIR SIMONDS. *Journals of All the Parliaments during the Reign of Queen Elizabeth.* (Ed. Paul Bowes, 1682.)

FIRTH, C. H. and R. S. RAIT (Eds.). *Acts and Ordinances of the Interregnum, 1642–60* (2 vols.). 1911.

FITZHERBERT, N. *De Antiquitate et continuatione Catholicae religionis in Anglia et de Alani Card. vita libellus.* 1608.

FRERE, W. H. (Ed.). *Visitation Articles and Injunctions of the Period of the Reformation.* 1910.

FULLER, THOMAS. *Church History* (to 1648). (Ed. J. S. Brewer). 1845.

GEE, JOHN. *The Foot Out of the Snare* (3rd ed.). 1624.

GERARD, JOHN. *See* Caraman, P.

HEYWOOD, JAMES (Ed.). *Oxford University Commissions.* 1853.

—. and T. WRIGHT. *Cambridge University Transactions.* 1854.

KNOX, T. F. (Ed.). *The [First and Second] Douay Diaries.* 1878.

—. *Letters and Memorials of William Cardinal Allen.* 1882.

LOYOLA, ST. IGNATIUS. *The Spiritual Exercises.* (Editions in English by W. H. Longridge, 1919, and T. H. Moore, S.J., 1949.)

MORE, H. *Historia Missionis Anglicanae Societatis Jesu.* 1660.

NICHOLAS, E. *See* Tyrwhitt, T.

OWEN, LEWIS. *The Running Register....* 1626.

PACHTLER, G. *Ratio Studiorum et institutiones scholasticae Societatis Jesu per Germaniam olim vigentes.* (4 vols.) 1887–94.

PEACOCK, EDWARD. *A List of Roman Catholics in the County of York in 1604.* (Transcribed from Rawlinson MSS., B. 452, in the Bodleian.) 1872.

PERSONS, ROBERT, S. J. *Letters and Memorials:* vol. 1, to 1598 (Ed. L. J. Hicks, S.J.; *C.R.S.* 39.) 1946.

PUGH, R. *Blacklow's Cabal.* 1680.

RAINE, JAMES (Ed). *Depositions from the Castle of York, relating to Offences committed in the Northern Counties in the 17th Century* (Surtees Society, vol. 40). 1861.

ROBERTSON, SIR C. G. *Select Statutes, Cases and Documents....* 4th ed. 1923.

RUSHWORTH, JOHN. *Historical Collections ... 1618–29.* 1659.

SANDER, NICHOLAS. *Rise and Growth of the Anglican Schism.* 1585. (Ed. David Lewis, 1877.)

—. *De Visibili Monarchia.* 1571.

SCHROEDER, H. J. (Ed.). *The Disciplinary Decrees of the General Councils* (i.e. to 5 Lateran, 1512–17). 1937.

SCOBELL, HENRY (Ed.). *Acts and Ordinances, 1640*. 1658.

—. *Acts of Parliament, 1648–51*. 1651.

State Trials (Ed. W. Cobbett), vols. 7–10. 1809–26.

STEEL, R. (Ed.). *Tudor and Stuart Proclamations*. 1910.

TURNER, G. L. *Original Records of Early Nonconformity under Persecution and Indulgence*. (2 vols.) 1911.

TYRWHITT, T. (Ed.). *The Journal of Sir Edward Nicholas*. 1766.

VAUX, LAWRENCE. *A Catechism of Christian Doctrine, necessarie for Children and the Ignorant People*. (Ed. T. Law, 1885.) 1567.

VERNEY, F. P., and M. M. (Eds.). *Verney Memoirs*. (2 vols.; 3rd ed.) 1892.

WADSWORTH, JAMES. *The English Spanish Pilgrim*. 1630.

WATERWORTH, J. (Ed.). *The Canons and Decrees of the Council of Trent*. 1848 and 1881.

WILKINS, DAVID. *Concilia Magnae Britanniae et Hiberniae*. 1737.

WINWOOD, SIR RALPH. *The Winwood Papers*. (*Hist. MSS. Comm.*)

WORTHINGTON, J. *See* Crossley, J.

YEPES, DIEGO DE. *Historia particular de le Persecución de Inglaterra*. 1599.

PERIODICALS (detailed references in footnotes)

Albanian (organ of the Eng. Coll. Valladolid); *American Catholic Historical Review*; *American Historical Review*; *Ampleforth Journal*; *Catholic Almanack*, 1661–3, and *Kalendarium Catholicum*, 1686; *Clergy Review*; *Douai Magazine* (organ of Douay Abbey, Woolhampton); *Downside Review*; *Dublin Review* (1836 to date); *Edmundian* (organ of St. Edmund's College) (1883 to date); *English Historical Review*; *Innes Review* (organ of Scottish Cath. Hist. Cttee.) (1950 to date); *Letters and Notices, S.J.* (see page 279 above); *Lisbonian* (organ of the Eng. Coll. Lisbon) (1909 to date); *Month* (ed. by the English Jesuits) (1860 to date); *Oscotian* (organ of Oscott College, Staffs.); *Royal Historical Society Transactions*; *Stonyhurst Magazine* (1881 to date); *Ushaw Magazine*; *Venerabile* (organ of the Ven. Eng. Coll. Rome) (1921 to date).

BIOGRAPHIES

Collective

BEALES, A. C. F. *A Biographical Catalogue of Catholic Schoolmasters at work in England, from 1558 to 1700, with an Index of Places* (Catholic Record Society, *Recusant History*, vol. vii, no. 6, 1964).

BIRT, H. N. *Obit Book of the English Benedictines*. 1913.

BURTON, E. H., and J. H. POLLEN. *Lives of the English Martyrs*. (2 vols.) 1914.

CHALLONER, (Bp.) RICHARD. *Memoirs of Missionary Priests, 1577–1684.* (Ed. J. H. Pollen.) 1924.

CLEARY, J. M. *A Checklist of Welsh Students in the Seminaries, 1568–1603.* 1958.

FOLEY, H. *Records of the English Province of the Society of Jesus.* (8 vols.) 1877–83.

GASQUET, A., CARDINAL. *Obit Book of the Venerable English College, Rome.* 1929.

GILLOW, JOSEPH. *Bibliographical Dictionary of the English Catholics, from the Breach with Rome in 1534, to the Present Time.* (5 vols.) 1885–98.

KIRK, JOHN. *Biographies of Eighteenth-Century Catholics.* (Ed. J. H. Pollen and E. H. Burton.) 1909.

LAW, T. G. *A Calendar of the English Martyrs.* 1876.

OLIVER, GEO. *Collections towards Illustrating the Biography of the Scotch, English and Irish Members of the Society of Jesus.* 1845.

PALMER, C. F. R. *Obituary Notices of the . . . Dominicans of the English Province since 1650.* 1884.

WARD, (Bp.) BERNARD. *Menology of St. Edmund's College.* 1909.

Individual (alphabetically by *subject*)

Allen, William, Cardinal, by A. BELLESHEIM, 1885; BEDE CAMM, 1908; M. HAILE, 1914; T. F. KNOX, 1882; B. WARD, 1913.

Campion, Edmund, by R. SIMPSON, 1867 and 1896; EVELYN WAUGH, 1935.

Gardiner, Stephen, by J. A. MULLER, 1926.

Garlick, Nicholas, by EDWARD KING, S.J., 1904.

Jeffreys, (Baron) Geo., by H. M. HYDE, 1940.

Mary Tudor, by J. M. STONE, 1901; B. M. I. WHITE, 1935.

Mathew, Sir Tobie, by DAVID MATHEW, 1950.

Oates, Titus, by JANE LANE, 1949.

Pole, Reginald, Cardinal, by W. SCHENCK, 1950.

Sander, Nicholas, by J. H. POLLEN, S.J., 1891.

St. Angela Merici, by MARY REIDY, 1962.

Walsingham, Sir Francis, by CONYERS READ, 1925.

Ward, Mary, by M. C. E. CHAMBERS, 1885; MARY OLIVER, 1960.

STUDIES OF SCHOOLS AND COLLEGES

English College, Douay

DODD, CHARLES (i.e. Hugh Tootell). *History of the English College at Doway.* 1713.

WARD, BERNARD. *History of St. Edmund's College*. 1893.

Engish College, Rome (Venerabile)

GASQUET, A., CARDINAL. *A History of the Venerable English College, Rome*. 1920.

TOWERS, EDWARD. *The Opening Years of the Venerable English College, Rome*. (In *Ushaw Magazine*, No. 58.) 1910.

'The English Hospice in Rome': VI Centenary Issue of the *Venerabile*, vol. xxi, May 1962.

Engish Colleges in the Peninsula

BLACKFAN, JOHN. *Annals of the English College at Valladolid, 1598–1616*. (See *C.R.S.* xxxx, and *Month*, xcii.)

CROFT, W., and J. GILLOW. *Historical Account of Lisbon College*. 1902.

St. Omer College

BLED, O. 'Les Jésuites Anglais à Saint-Omer', in *Bull. Hist. Soc. Antiq. Morinie*, viii. 1896.

CHADWICK, HUBERT, S.J. *St. Omers to Stonyhurst*. 1962.

DESCHAMPS DE PAS. *Histoire de Saint-Omer* (to 1870). 1870.

GERARD, JOHN, S.J. *Memorials of Stonyhurst College*. 1881.

—. *Stonyhurst College*. 1894.

GRUGGEN, G., and J. KEATING. *Stonyhurst: Its Past History*. . . . 1901.

HICKS, L. J. 'The Foundation of the College of St. Omers', in *Arch. Hist. Soc. Jesu.*, xix. 1950.

PIERS, H. 'Notice historique sur le collège anglais de Saint-Omer', in *Arch. . . . Nord de France*, ii. 1885.

WILLAERT, L., S.J. 'An English College in the Netherlands', in *American Cath. Qtrly. Review*, xxx. 1905.

—. 'Le Collège anglais de Saint-Omer: les Débuts', in Cath. Univ. of Louvain, *Recueil des Travaux*, xl–xli. 1914.

Benedictine Colleges

ALMOND, CUTHBERT. *History of Ampleforth Abbey*. 1903.

AVELING, H. 'Pensioners at the English College at Dieulouard, 1619–1756', in *Recusant History* (*C.R.S.*), V. i (1960).

BIRT, H. N. *History of Downside School*. 1902.

CODY, J. S. 'The Benedictine Convents in England', in *Ampleforth Journal*, ii–iii. 1881.

CONNOLLY, HUGH. *Some Dates and Documents for the Early History of Our House* (i.e. Downside). 1930.

WELDON, BENNET. *Chronicle of the English Benedictines* (1709). (Checked by Edmund Bishop in *Downside Review*, xvi., 1895.)

Dominican Colleges

PALMER, CHARLES F. R. *Bygone Colleges: Bornhem and Carshalton.* 1889.

Bar Convent School

COLERIDGE, H. J. (Ed.). *St. Mary's Convent, Micklegate Bar, York.* 1887.

Scottish Colleges

BAXTER, J. H. 'The Scots College at Douay', in *Scottish Hist. Review*, xxiv. 1926.

BROWN, WM. E., and others. *The Scots College, Rome.* 1930.

CHADWICK, HUBERT, S.J. 'The Scots College at Douay, 1580–1613', in *Eng. Hist. Review*, lvi. 1941.

GOLDRICK, WM. 'The Scots College, Madrid', in *Innes Review*, iv. 92–109. 1953.

NEW SPALDING CLUB. *Records of the Scots Colleges.* 1906.

Irish Colleges

BOYLE, P. *The Irish College in Paris, 1578–1901.* 1901.

BRADY, J. 'Irish Colleges in Europe and the Counter Reformation', in *Proc. Irish Cath. Hist. Cttee.* 1957.

TREACY, WM. P. *Irish Scholars of Penal Days.* 1887.

TUNNEY, C. 'The Irish Colleges Abroad', in *Tablet*, 24 July 1954.

General

DANCOISNE, L. *Mémoires sur les Etablissements religieux . . . qui ont existé à Douai.* 1868–79.

—. *Histoire des Etablissements religieux britanniques fondés à Douai avant la Révolution Française.* 1880.

JONES, LEANDER, O.S.B. *Apost. Missionis status in Anglia.* (In Clarendon State Papers 1767, i. 199f.) 1634.

MANN, T. A. 'A Short Chronological Account of the Religious Establishments made by English Catholics on the Continent', in Soc. Antiq. London, *Archaeologia*, xiii. 1800.

PETRE, HON. E. *Notices of the English Colleges and Convents established on the Continent.* 1849.

STEINHUBER, A., CARDINAL. *Geschichte des Kollegium Germanikum Hungarikum in Rom.* 1906.

Universities and Public Schools in England

CURTIS, M. H. *Oxford and Cambridge in Transition*, 1558–1642. 1959.

CUST, L. *Eton College.* 1899.

DRAPER, F. W. M. *Four Centuries of Merchant Taylors' School, 1561–1961.* 1962.

FISHER, G. W. *Annals of Shrewsbury School.* 1899.

FORRESTER, E. G. *History of Magdalen College School.* 1950.

LEACH, A. F. *The Schools of Medieval England.* 1915.

—. *Educational Charters.* 1911.

—. *English Schools at the Reformation.* 1896.

—. *History of Winchester College.* 1899.

MALLET, C. E. *History of the University of Oxford.* (3 vols.) 1924.

MULLINGER, J. B. *History of the University of Cambridge.* (3 vols.) 1873.

RASHDALL, HASTINGS. *The Universities of Europe in the Middle Ages.* (Ed. Powicke and Emden; 3 vols.) 1936.

SAMPSON, W. A. *History of Bristol Grammar School.* 1912.

SARGEAUNT, J. *History of Westminster School.* 1898.

STOKES, C. W. *Queen Mary's Grammar School, Clitheroe.* 1934.

STOWE, A. R. M. *English Grammar Schools in the Reign of Elizabeth.* 1908.

VENN, J. A. *Alumni Cantabrigiensis . . . . to 1571.* (4 vols.) 1922.

WATSON, FOSTER. *The English Grammar Schools to 1660.* 1908.

WICKHAM, C. T. *The Story of Twyford School.* 1909.

À WOOD, ANTHONY. *Athenae Oxoniensis.* (Ed. Bliss; 4 vols.) 1816.

OTHER MODERN WORKS

ALBION, GORDON. *Charles I and the Court of Rome.* 1935.

ALLISON, A. F. and D. M. ROGERS. *Catalogue of Catholic Books in English . . . 1558–1640*, in 'Biog. Studies' (*C.R.S.*), 1956.

ANSON, PETER F. *The Catholic Church in Modern Scotland.* 1937.

ANSTRUTHER, G. *Vaux of Harrowden.* 1953.

ATTWATER, DONALD. *The Catholic Church in Modern Wales.* 1935.

AUCHMUTY, J. J. *Irish Education: A Historical Survey.* 1937.

BACKER, ALOYS. DE (S.J.). *Bibliothèque des Ecrivains S.J.* (7 vols.) 1853–61.

BATE, FRANK. *The Declaration of Indulgence.* 1908.

BATTERSBY, W. J. *De La Salle: A Pioneer of Modern Education.* 1949.

—. *De La Salle: Saint and Spiritual Writer.* 1950.

BEALES, A. C. F. 'Education under Mary Tudor', in *The Month*, June 1955.

—. 'Popish Schools under James I', in *The Month*, April 1952.

—. 'Popish Schools under Charles I', in *The Month*, July 1953.

—. 'The Catholic Educational Revival under James II', in *The Month*, August 1951.

BELLESHEIM, A. *A History of the Catholic Church in Scotland.* (4 vols.) Transl. D. O. Hunter Blair. 1887–90.

BIRRELL, T. A. *A Newsletter for Students of Recusant History.* (From 19 van Nispenstraat, Nijmegen: periodically.) 1958 on.

BIRT, H. N. *The Elizabethan Religious Settlement.* 1907.

—. 'English Refugees in the Low Countries', in *Downside Review*, 1915–16.

BLOXAM, J. R. *Magdalen College and James II.* (Oxford Hist. Soc., vi.) 1886.

BLUNDELL, F. O. *Old Catholic Lancashire.* (3 vols.) 1925.

—. *Ancient Catholic Houses of Scotland.* 1907.

—. *The Catholic Highlands of Scotland.* 1907.

BRADY, W. MAZIERE. *Annals of the Catholic Hierarchy in England and Scotland: 1585–1876.* (3 vols.) 1887–93.

—. *The Episcopal Succession in England, Scotland and Ireland: 1400–1875.* (3 vols.) 1876–7.

BROWN, BALDWIN. *An Historical Account of the Laws enacted against the Catholics, both in England and Ireland.* 1813.

BURKE, THOMAS. *Catholic History of Liverpool.* 1910.

BURTON, EDWIN H. *London Streets and Catholic Memories.* 1925.

BUTLER, CHARLES. *Historical Memoirs of English, Irish and Scottish Catholics.* (4 vols.) 1819–21.

BUTLER, E. C. *Notes on the . . . Restored Congregation of the English Benedictines.* 1887.

CAMM, BEDE. *In the Brave Days of Old.* 1899.

CAPECALATO, ALFONSO. *St. Joseph Calasanctius, Founder of the Pious Schools.* 1850.

CARLETON, J. G. *The Part of Rheims in the Making of the English Bible.* 1902.

CASSIDY, P. F. *Catholic College Foundations . . . in the U.S.A., 1677–1850.* 1924.

CONSTABLE, J., S.J. *A Specimen of Amendments* to Dodd's *Church History.* 1741.

CORCORAN, T. *Studies in the History of Classical Teaching.* 1911.

—. *State Policy in Irish Education, 1536–1816.* 1916.

—. *Some Lists of Catholic Lay Teachers and their Illegal Schools in Ireland in the Later Penal Times.* 1932.

COTTON, HENRY. *Rhemes and Doway: an Attempt to Show what has been done by Roman Catholics for the Diffusion of the Holy Scriptures in English.* 1855.

COURZON, COMTESSE R. DE. *The Condition of English Catholics under Charles II.* 1899.

COOKE, W. H. D. 'The National English Institutions in Rome in the 14th Century', in *Dublin Review*, cxxxiv. 1904.

DEPLACE, LOUIS, S.J. *L'Angleterre et la Compagnie de Jésus, 1540–81.* 1890.

DESTOMBES, C. J. *La Persécution Religieuse en Angleterre sous les Successeurs d'Elizabeth.* 1864.

DEVAS, DOMINIC. *Franciscan Centenary Pamphlets: No. 2, The Second Province, 1618–1838.* 1924.

DINGLE, A. T. *History of Osmotherley.* 1950.

DODD, CHARLES (i.e. Hugh Tootell). *The Church History of England 1500–1688.* (3 vols.) 1737.

—. *The Secret Policy of the English Society of Jesus.* 1715.

DOWLING, P. J. *The Hedge Schools of Ireland.* 1935.

DRANE, A. T. *Christian Schools and Scholars.* (2 vols.) 1867.

DUCKETT, SIR GEO. *Penal Laws and Test Act.* 1882.

DURKAN, J., and others. *The University of Glasgow and the Catholic Church: 1450–1950.* 1950.

ELLIS, T. P. *The Catholic Martyrs of Wales.* 1933.

EVENNETT, H. O. *The Cardinal of Lorraine and the Council of Trent.* 1930.

FARRELL, A. P., S.J. *The Jesuit Code of Liberal Education.* 1938.

FITZPATRICK, E. A. *St. Ignatius and the Ratio Studiorum.* 1933.

FOLEY, HENRY, S.J. *Records of the English Province of the Society of Jesus.* (8 vols.) 1877–83.

FORBES-LEITH, WM., S.J. *Memoirs of Scottish Catholics during the 16th and 17th Centuries.* 1909.

GALLAGHER, (Sr.) A. M. *History and Administration of Education in Ireland.* 1948.

GARDINER, S. R. *The Parliamentary Debates of 1610.* (Camden Society, vol. 81.) 1862.

—. *Commons Debates of 1625.* 1873.

—. *Lords Debates of 1621–6.* 1870–9.

GEE, HENRY. *The Elizabethan Clergy and the Settlement of Religion, 1558–64.* 1898.

GOODIER, ALBAN. 'The Society of Jesus and Education', in *The Month.* 1906–7.

GORDON, J. F. *The Catholic Church in Scotland.*

GREEN, T. L. *The Secular Clergy Fund of the Late Midland District: commonly called Johnson's Fund.* 1853.

HANS, NICHOLAS. 'The Roman Catholic Tradition in Education', in *Year Book of Education*, 1938.

HAVRAN, M. J. *The Catholics in Caroline England.* 1962.

HARTING, JOANNA H. *Catholic London Missions, from the Reformation to 1850.* 1903.

—. *History of the Sardinian Chapel, Lincoln's Inn Fields.* 1905.

HAY, M. V. *The Jesuits and the Popish Plot.* 1934.

HEMPHILL, B., O.S.B. *The Early Vicars Apostolic of England: 1685–1750.* 1954.

HUGHES, PHILIP. *The Reformation in England.* (3 vols.) 1950–5.

HUGHES, T. J., S.J. *Loyola and the Educational System of the Jesuits.* 1906.

—. *History of the Society of Jesus in North America.* (2 vols.) 1917.

HURSTFIELD, J. *The Queen's Wards.* 1959.

—. 'The Succession Struggle in late Elizabethan England', in *Elizabethan Government and Society.* 1961.

JACOBSEN, J. V., S.J. *Educational Foundations of the Jesuits in 16th Century New Spain.* 1938.

JARRETT, BEDE, O. P. *The English Dominicans.* 1921.

JONES, M. G. *The Charity School Movement in the Eighteenth Century.* 1938.

JONES, THOMAS *Catalogue of Collection of Tracts for and against Popery published under James II.* (Chetham Society, vols. 48, 64.) 1859 and 1865.

KELLY, BERNARD W. *Historical Notes on English Catholic Missions.* 1907.

KENNEDY, W. P. M. *Parish Life under Queen Elizabeth.* 1914.

KNOWLES, D. M. *The Religious Orders in England.* (3 vols.) 1950–9.

LAW, T. G. *The Archpriest Controversy.* (Camden Society.) 1898.

—. *Jesuits and Seculars in the Reign of Elizabeth.* 1889.

LEATHERBARROW, J. S. *Lancashire Elizabethan Recusants.* (Chetham Society, vol. 110.) 1947.

LECHAT, ROBERT, S.J. *Les Refugiés Anglais dans les Pays-Bas Espagnols, 1558–1603.* 1914.

LEYS, M. D. R. *Catholics in England, 1559–1829.* 1961.

LILLIE, H. W. R., S.J. 'The English Martyrs and the English Criminal Law', in *Clergy Review*, Oct. 1936.

LINGARD, JOHN. *History of England.* (2nd ed.; 14 vols.) 1823.

MACDONALD, GREGORY. 'The Lime Street Chapel', in *Dublin Review.* 1927.

MCGUCKEN, WM. J., S.J. *The Jesuits and Education.* 1932.

MACKINLEY, J. B., O.S.B. 'The City of Our Martyrs [Douay]', in *Dublin Review*, vol. 35. 1884.

MACLEAN, D. *The Counter-Reformation in Scotland: 1560–1930*. 1931.

MADDEN, R. R. *A History of the Penal Laws enacted against Roman Catholics*. 1847.

MAGEE, BRIAN. *The English Recusants*. 1938.

MATHEW, (Archbp.) DAVID. *Catholicism in England, 1535–1935*. 1936.

MAYER, M. H. *The Philosophy of Teaching of St. Thomas Aquinas*. 1929.

MAYNARD, THEODORE. *A History of the Catholic Church in America*. 1948.

MEYER, A. O. *England und die Katholische Kirche unter Elisabeth*. 1911.

—. *England and the Catholic Church under Queen Elizabeth*, trans. J. R. McKee. 1916.

—. 'Der Toleranzgedanke im England der Stuarts', in *Historischen Zeitschrift*, vol. 108. 1912.

MONTMORENCY, J. E. G. DE. *State Intervention in English Education*. 1902.

MORRIS, JOHN, S.J. *The Troubles of Our Catholic Forefathers*. (3 vols.) 1872–7.

MULLAN, ELDER, S.J. *The Sodality of Our Lady*. Engl. ed. 1912.

NEALE, J. E. *Elizabethan House of Commons*. 1949.

—. *Elizabeth and her Parliaments*. 1953–7.

NOTESTEIN, WALLACE. *The Commons Debates of 1629*. 1921.

—. *The Commons Debates of 1621*. (6 vols.) 1935.

O'HARE, DANIEL. *An Old Lancashire Mission . . . Fernyhalgh*. 1892.

OLIVER, GEORGE. *Collections Illustrating the History of the Catholic Religion in the Counties of Cornwall, Devon, Dorset, Somerset, Wilts. and Gloucester*. 1857.

O'REILLY, BERNARD. *St. Angela Merici and the Ursulines*. 1880.

PARRY, A. W. *Education in England in the Middle Ages*. 1920.

PAYNE, J. O. *Old English Catholic Missions*. 1889.

POLLEN, J. H., S.J. *The English Catholics in the Reign of Elizabeth*. 1920.

POLLOCK, SIR JOHN. *The Popish Plot*. 1904.

SCHWICKERATH, J. *Jesuit Education*. 1903.

SEATON, A. A. *The Theory of Toleration under the Later Stuarts*. 1911.

SHAW, WM. A. *A History of the English Church, 1640–60*. (2 vols.) 1900.

SMITH, H. F. RUSSELL. *The Theory of Religious Toleration in the Reigns of Charles II and James II*. 1911.

SMITH, W. VINCENT. *Catholic Tyneside, 1534–1850*. 1931.

SOUTHERN, A. C. *Elizabethan Recusant Prose*. 1950.

SPILLMAN, JOSEPH. *Geschichte der Katholiken Verfolgung in England, 1535–1654*. 1900–5.

STAPLETON, MRS. BRYAN. *History of the Post-Reformation Catholic Missions in Oxfordshire: 1603–1905*. 1906.

STONOR, R. J. *Stoner*. 1952.

STRONG, JOHN. *History of Secondary Education in Scotland*. 1909.

TAUNTON, E. L. *The English Black Monks of St. Benedict*. (2 vols.) 1897.

—. *The Jesuits in England, 1580–1773*. 1901.

THADDEUS, FR., O.F.M. *The Franciscans in England, 1600–1850*. 1898.

TIERNEY, M. A. *Dodd's Church History of England . . . to the Revolution of 1688*. (But only to 1629.) (5 vols.) 1839–43.

TURNBULL, G. H. *Hartlib, Dury and Comenius*. 1947.

VINCENT, W. A. L. *The State and School Education in England and Wales, 1640–60*. 1950.

WILLIAMS, W. LL. *The Making of Modern Wales*. 1919.

WOOD, NORMAN. *The Reformation and English Education*. 1931.

ZANFAGNA, (SR.) MARY L. *Educational The oriesand Principles of Cardinal Silvio Antoniano*. 1940.

ZIMMERMANN, G. R. *Carmel in England*. 1899.

Also the volumes of the *Victoria County History*

INDEX

NOTE: For schools and schoolmasters *see under:* Schools, Catholic; Schools, Grammar; Schoolmasters, Catholic.